THE HIDDEN HIPPOPOTAMUS

AFRICAN STUDIES SERIES 28

The African Studies Series is a collection of monographs and general studies
which reflect the interdisciplinary interests of the African Studies Centre at
Cambridge. Volumes to date have combined historical, anthropological,
economic, political and other perspectives. Each contribution has assumed
that such broad approaches can contribute much to our understanding of
Africa, and that this may in turn be of advantage to specific disciplines.

BOOKS IN THIS SERIES

THE HIDDEN HIPPOPOTAMUS

Reappraisal in African history:
the early colonial experience
in western Zambia

GWYN PRINS

Fellow of Emmanuel College, Cambridge
College Lecturer and
Director of Studies in History

CAMBRIDGE UNIVERSITY PRESS

CAMBRIDGE
LONDON   NEW YORK   NEW ROCHELLE
MELBOURNE   SYDNEY

Published by the Press Syndicate of the University of Cambridge
The Pitt Building, Trumpington Street, Cambridge CB2 1RP
32 East 57th Street, New York, NY 10022, USA
296 Beaconsfield Parade, Middle Park, Melbourne 3206, Australia

First published 1980

Phototypeset in V.I.P. Times by
Western Printing Services Ltd, Bristol
Printed and bound in Great Britain
at The Pitman Press, Bath

British Library Cataloguing in Publication Data
Prins, Gwyn
The hidden hippopotamus – (African studies series;
28 ISSN 0065–406X).
1. Lozi (African people)
2. Acculturation – Zambia – Western Province
I. Title   II. Series
301.2′41′096894   DT963.42   79–41658

ISBN 0 521 22915 4

086153

iv

Mbu. . .wa fulanga meyi matungu,
musheke ni mu k'onga.

The hippopotamus. . .swirls the deepest waters [in the river],
the white sands of the shallows betray him.

(Version of a still well known Luyana proverb as it
was recorded in about 1895; Jacottet, *Études*, vol. III,
p. 188, No. 2)

kwa Sichaba
ni kwa lubasi lwa ka
buka ye i fiwa
ka lilato

Contents

Figures

Tables

Preface

The historian of an African society most closely resembles that circus acrobat who balances at the apex of a human pyramid. Whatever he can do there and whatever he can see from his vantage point he owes in large measure to those who support him. The making of this book has been a long and expensive process and the pyramid is commensurately large.

The research upon which this work is based was conducted in two stints. The first, from October 1972 to October 1976, was financed by a Hayter award from the Department of Education and Science, a University of Cambridge Allen scholarship, grants from the Jan Smuts Memorial Fund and an interest-free loan from Emmanuel College. From March 1973 to May 1975 I lived in Bulozi. The second stint, from October 1976, was made possible by a Research Fellowship at Emmanuel College. From January to September 1977 I returned to Bulozi to continue my field research, a trip facilitated by an SSRC Research Project grant and a further interest-free capital loan from Emmanuel College which enabled me to purchase a new and specially equipped Land Rover that was shipped to Africa for my use. Throughout the work, the College has stepped in to help where others could not and by ensuring that, particularly on my second field trip, I had the tools for the job, this concern has significantly improved the type and quantity of work that I could do. My gratitude to the Fellowship is profound.

During my first stay in Zambia I was affiliated to the Institute for African Studies of the University of Zambia. The Director of the day, J. van Velsen, loaned me an Institute Land Rover and my thanks go to him and to the international team of six mechanics who taught me to take it to pieces and to renovate it, component after component as each failed, so that it finally worked reliably. On the second field trip the Director of the Livingstone Museum, the late K. Mubitana, the acting Director M. Chellah and their staff gave us a most hospitable *pied à terre* and a lot of practical help. The tragic early death of Kaf Mubitana in a motor accident in June 1978 is a bitter blow to all who seek to understand Zambia's history.

But in Zambia, home for three years was Sefula. I am deeply indebted to the Rev. Musialela and the Western Presbytery of the United Church of Zambia who permitted us to use a house on the Mission Station during our first trip and to M. Thompson, headmaster of Sefula secondary school, who loaned us a leave house in 1977. But home is more than a house. The Rev. and Mrs E. Berger helped us to learn the Lozi language and to learn about the people whom they loved and served for nearly half a century until the Rev. Berger's death in 1978.

From officers at every level of the Zambian Government I received interest and much help. My thanks go to successive Permanent Secretaries for Western Province with whom I had dealings, to the Provincial Administration staff in Mongu, to District Governors, District Secretaries, their staffs at the Bomas and the members of the Messenger Service in all the Districts of Bulozi. Of the specialist departments, the Mechanical Services Branch, Mongu, came to know my Institute Land Rover rather well in 1973–5. In other departments, I thank D. Vernon of the Agricultural Research Station, Mongu and his staff; M. Cessford, R. Billington, B. Mushewa and M. Soepboer of Government and Aid agricultural extension services respectively; S. Revell, Veterinary Research Officer, District Veterinary Officers R. Nelson and J. Jørgensen and their staffs; Drs Blom, de Vente and van Rhijn of Senanga hospital simultaneously and successively and their staffs; the doctors and staffs of the Mission hospitals at Yuka (Kalabo District), Luampa (Kaoma District), and Mwandi (Sesheke District) and D. K. Sitali, Clerk of the High Court at Mongu.

The work would not have been possible in the form which it took without the interest and help of the late *Litunga* Mbikusita Lewanika, the *Litunga* Ilute Yeta, *Ngambela* G. Mukande and the members of the Lealui Kuta. Similarly, at Nalolo I am deeply grateful to the *Mulena Mukwae* Makwibi Mwanawina and the *Ishee Kwandu*, to the *Sambi*, B. Muhongo and the *Natamoyo, Mwanamulena* M. Yeta, both of whom travelled with me at different times in search of certain types of informant, and to the members of the Nalolo Kuta. I owe special debts to my friends *Mutompehi* S. Situmbeko, who taught me much and helped me a great deal when I was still floundering and uncertain, and *Mutompehi* Y. W. Mupatu, one of Bulozi's foremost historians with whom I had the privilege of working closely over many months in 1977. Arthur Siyunyii and I had a lot of fun in the course of doing a lot of work together and in 1977 Christopher Wamulume laboured long hours transcribing tapes of formal traditions. Many school teachers and local court staff helped their

xii

neighbours to record their village and personal histories for me and my deep thanks go to them and to the hundreds of people all over Bulozi who allowed me to learn from them.

Friends elsewhere in Zambia made essential and much appreciated contributions, especially the Lorenzes who made their home our home in Lusaka. Erhard Lorenz read early drafts of the work and made acute and important criticisms; for this and much more my wife and I are grateful. Peter Hutchinson of the Zambia Meteorological Service, J. G. M. Simpson, and Mrs M. Plesner helped in different and valuable ways. S. Branum and pilots of the Government Flight enabled me to make photo reconnaissance over the floodplain.

I received help from the staffs of the National Archives of Zambia, Lusaka; the Air Photograph Library, Mulungushi House, Lusaka; the National Archives of Zimbabwe, Salisbury, and, while I was there, Dr I. Phimister guided me in their use. In Europe I was assisted at the Public Record Office, London, at Rhodes House, Oxford and by the archivist of SOAS Library, London. Mlle J-M. Léonard of the Bibliothèque du DEFAP, Paris went to great pains to help me find material during a visit made possible by a generous grant from the University of Cambridge Political Science Fund. In Switzerland I am much indebted to the Bolanzes, to Mlle M. Borle and to the Rev. J-P. Burger. The Rev. Burger gave to me freely from his deep knowledge and extensive and precious sources about Bulozi. He read this book in manuscript with a meticulous detail from which I profited enormously. Sadly, he died whilst it was in press. In England, M. Armor, G. C. R. Clay, Miss D. Mallion and E. Wulfson helped through diverse and important contributions. My typist, Patricia Reay, created miraculous order from a ramshackle draft.

My academic debts are few but deep. David Phillipson talked to me about Zambian archaeology; Jock Galloway has pondered my air photographs; many of the basic ideas were argued out with Richard Waller, John Waliggo and my students between 1976 and 1978. I owe much to John Iliffe who has been a meticulous and invaluable critic at all stages of the work, not least during the writing of this book. I am also grateful to several of the participants in the 1976 Bologna conference of anthropology and history for comments on an early paper about problems of interpreting oral data.

Many friends and colleagues within and without the academic world have read part or all of the completed manuscript. Since it would be invidious to have to name some and not all, I shall name none. But I am very deeply indebted to them all for valuable comments which of course does not mean that they necessarily agreed with all they read. Responsibility for the final analysis is mine alone.

Preface

My last debts are really prior to all the others. They are to my parents, who saw to it that I had the right skills and encouraged me to go to Africa first in 1969 when the seeds of the present work were sown, and to Miriam. She has been part of the whole process: the excitement of fieldwork, the discoveries of new materials, the flux of ideas, innumerable drafts of each sentence; but also the other things: the physical hardships, the illnesses, the worry, the frustration. She survived and therefore so did I and so the work has been finished. What more can I say? Oh yes, our dog, Mister Bear, who hunted mambas, cobras and scorpions and so ensured that Miriam survived deserves the last word, for in a sense it all depended on his sharp nose.

Emmanuel College   Gwyn Prins
Cambridge
October 1979

Glossary of commonly used Lozi terms

A note about plural forms. Lozi nouns form their plurals by taking *prefixes*. There are at least nine classes of noun, classified by their prefix forms. (I write 'at least' because a recent dissertation upon the structure of Silozi proposes that we should entertain substantially more categories!) As a rule, there is a special plural prefix corresponding to each singular prefix. Below, I give the plural forms which are used in the text in parentheses after the singular, and also provide cross-references.

balimu	see *mulimu*	*mazulu*	see *lizulu*
baloi	see *muloi*	*mbuwa* (*Luyana*)	the king, as in *likomu za mbuwa*, royal cattle
bonamukau	see *namukau*		
buhobe	porridge		
buloi	witchcraft	*mishiku*	see *mushiku*
busunso	relish	*mukulo*	floodplain/ bush margin
coliso	installation		
Kuta	court	*Mulanziane*	senior chief in the Sesheke (southernmost) district
lapa (*malapa*)	courtyard		
likolo (*makolo*)	'regiment' or labour unit		
		Mulena Mukwae	chieftainess of the south
likute	politeness, respect		
lilalo	see *silalo*	*muleneñ*	capital town
lindaleti	see *ndaleti*	*muliani*	medicine
lindumeleti	see *ndumeleti*	*mulimu* (*balimu*)	spirit
liñaka	see *ñaka*	*muloi* (*baloi*)	witch
liñomboti	see *ñomboti*	*Muluilonga*	'the Noble Age' (also *mulongalui*)
litino	see *sitino*		
Litunga	'the Earth': the king	*muñ'a munzi*	'owner of the village'; village headman
lizulu (*mazulu*)	raised mound in the plain	*mushiku* (*mishiku*)	descent group
		mushitu	the bush, forest
mafulo	floodtime encampment, travelling camp	*Nalikwanda*	royal barge
		namukau (*bonamukau*)	state garden
makolo	see *likolo*	*Natamoyo*	'Minister of Justice'
malapa	see *lapa*	*ndaleti* (*lindaleti*)	guardian of *namukau*
maoma	royal drums		

ndumeleti (*lindumeleti*)	roving emissary; tribute collecting chief	*ñomboti* (*liñomboti*)	priest-guardian
Ngambela	'speak for me': 'Prime Minister'	*ku omboka*	'to get out of the water': to transhume
ngomalume	Dance of the Men	*silalo* (*lilalo*)	territorial unit
Nyambe	the High God	*sishanjo*	rich peat soil
ñaka (*liñaka*)	healer, practitioner	*sitino* (*litino*)	royal grave
ñamba	tribute		

1

Introduction

1.1 A BROAD JUSTIFICATION OF THE SUBJECT

In this work I tread again one of the best blazed paths in the historiography of central Africa. This may appear to be perverse at first sight because there might seem to be many areas less studied and therefore more deserving of attention than Bulozi. Certainly my choice demands justification.

Some years ago I, like many others at that time, decided to examine the response of migrant labourers to their work experiences within the southern African economic sphere. To do this to best advantage, I felt that an area had to be found which had already attracted a wide literature, to serve as a pedestal upon which a work of social history could be erected. I chose Bulozi. It was an obvious candidate, possessing a weighty anthropology by the late Professor Max Gluckman, a pre-colonial history by Dr Mainga, a modern political history by Dr Caplan and a history of the reign of King Lewanika by Mr Clay.[1] The historical works all overlapped in the 1880s and 1890s and therefore offered an unusually varied and detailed examination of those crucial years of primary European contact and the establishment of colonial rule. There was also a generous sprinkling of incidental literature.[2]

From the table of contents it will be evident that this pedestal proved to be flawed. This work is not about migrant labourers; instead it is an attempt to build anew that pedestal upon which this and other social analysis will later stand. The underlying logic is simple: a satisfactory (reliable, credible) account of the Lozi experience of the colonial era cannot be written unless the events of that era can be situated within their full local context (meaning not a model of social structure but an understanding of historical process. I do not believe that it is possible to create a satisfactory static model of a social structure). Any other course makes more assumptions about Lozi society than can be safely risked, particu-

1

larly in view of my awareness of the mutability in the data and the fallibility in the research techniques, which permeates this work. So, for various reasons of methodological and theoretical deficiency which have resulted in a lack of appropriate and properly controlled data, it has not been possible to write this satisfactory account before. Since the received analyses fail my tests for reliability, I place no weight upon them in my investigations.

At the outset, it must be said that white power never attained a high intensity in Bulozi. There was nothing like the onslaught faced by peoples to the south in the 1890s, largely because Cecil Rhodes dreamed of gold under Lobengula's land, not Lewanika's.[3] But there were also other simple differences – of place and timing. Bulozi was north of Matabeleland, across the Zambezi, so the Lozi elite, who were more remarkable for their basic unanimity than their divisions in the late nineteenth century, were in a position to see what happened to the Ndebele when they fell before Rhodes' soldiers. Thus when the time came, shortly after the 1896–7 war to the south, they fought the British South Africa Company with guile, not guns. But it would not be correct to see this object lesson, powerful as it was, as fundamentally causative. It only reinforced tactics whose roots lay nearly twenty years back when, as this work will show, the Lozi elite took a series of decisions about how they would handle European intrusion, regardless of the external motivation of Rhodes and his band, decisions which were diametrically opposite to those taken by Lobengula.[4] So complex local variables make it exceedingly difficult to erect a paradigm of colonial encroachment or even, as Dr Lonsdale remarked, of the differences between situations.[5] But historians hanker after explanatory models and one, in more – or less – refined form, is still frequently used to describe situations like these; it has been heavily in evidence in the literature on Bulozi. It is a bi-polar axis of resistance and collaboration.

Finding this model inadequate, in order to periodise the qualities of the conquest of segmentary lineage-based societies in Nyanza in western Kenya, Dr Lonsdale adapted a spectrum of definitions first applied to Ugandan kingdoms, a generically different sort of society. He was able to show how, when the British in western Kenya became increasingly unable or unwilling to negotiate peaceful resolutions of disputes between groups, their position changed from one of 'coexistence' (power *in* Nyanza) through 'ascendancy' and 'domination' to 'control' (power *over* Nyanza).[6] No single case can offer a universal paradigm, but since it appears that paradigms are a currency in which one cannot help but deal, this spectrum of the intensity of power looks sturdier than others addressed to the externally described impact of Europeans, not least

2

because it has been found to work in rather different African societies. By thinking in terms of this spectrum of definitions, we can thus add precision to our statement that, in Bulozi, whites possessed neither the will nor the force to dispose of a high intensity of power. But under the circumstances, without the distractions of war, we are able to study in fine detail a delicate and rather different process taking place.

In this book we shall see the Lozi elite drawing upon concealed resources of power in order to extract from the late-nineteenth-century colonial encounter tactical advantages which their European protagonists never understood (and therefore never recorded in consecutive prose). This is the point made allegorically by the Lozi proverb from which the book's title comes. For these advantages, the Lozi elite paid the price of the surrender of certain superficial types of power, but in the longer term, a price was incurred which the Lozi in their turn never understood, and which was eventually paid in full at the end of the colonial era. The very success of the elite in the late-nineteenth-century encounter made it possible for Lozi from all segments of society, not just the elite, to believe the illusion that their society was less changed by that encounter than hindsight and analysis reveal that it actually was. The history of how reality and illusion simultaneously interacted to create the colonial *modus vivendi* whilst both actually drifted apart, how the illusion was sustained whilst the actual fabric of Lozi society altered, and what happened when the underpinnings of the illusion were torn away, will be the subjects of subsequent work.

One obvious implication of an analysis such as Lonsdale's is to cast doubt upon the value of the resistance/collaboration axis which was employed to give shape to earlier treatments of Lozi history. This axis is an anachronistic use of terminology because it confounds too many local variables which, when given weight, crumple the clear outline of the assumed definitions. More importantly, it assumes that the dynamic of initiative is more or less similar to what occurred on the ground: the arrival of uninvited, intrusive Europeans in a land of superficially passive or visibly violent Africans whose role in either case was to react to external stimuli. It will be clear from the approach and assumptions which I adopt in this work that the axis oversimplifies and unnecessarily restricts our view of this, and probably any, situation.

But although it is more supple and therefore more workable for the basically 'external' approach, the spectrum of the intensities of power can only embrace awkwardly the problem of the differential perception of a relationship. It does not have enough dimensions to cope. Therefore, since that problem lies close to a central concern of this book, I think that for the moment it is best to look after the data and hope that the paradigms will look after themselves later. I shall return to the question briefly at the beginning of Part IV.

1.2 A STATEMENT OF GOAL, METHOD AND SCOPE

The defining goal of this work is to present a demonstrably reliable narrative history of the period between 1876 and 1896 in Bulozi. To attain this goal, we have to plot a course through treacherous waters. In particular, two circumstances threaten us with shipwreck. On the one hand there are dangers lurking in our most accessible sources. If we rely primarily upon the judgment of those European observers, even the most expert, whose writings are the largest corpus of detailed evidence which we possess, we are defenceless against their conscious or unconscious bias due to personality or circumstance. Historians who recognise this danger seek to compensate for such bias. In part, and in my opinion in small part only, this may be done internally by astute and rigorous use of the archival data. But there is a healthy feeling that for best results such compensating judgments should be based upon knowledge external to the written sources, knowledge of the other side – the African side – of the situation under scrutiny.

The sentiment is quite plainly well founded, but the risks of acting upon it are if anything greater than those attendant on the use of archival data, for the historian must now sail past uncharted perils and few have possessed a sound enough ship or the requisite skill to make the passage. A little bit of cosmetic fieldwork is worse than none at all, because it gives a false sense of security to the researcher and a false aura of roundedness to the research. Field data cannot be used to control written data unless they can themselves be controlled. I am increasingly struck by the importance and complexity of conscious and concealed invention as a historical phenomenon in my field data, and it causes me to see how these two aspects of controlling sources are fundamentally symbiotic. I shall shortly explain how this observation informs the methods I use in my work.

Some historians have understood well enough the dangers of attempting to gather field data without the time or the linguistic skills to do it properly and have therefore turned to the works of anthropologists, seeking there the knowledge that will enable them to control their written sources. A subsidiary aspect of this book is to show some of the dangers which may result from placing reliance upon work of that type. As I have said, I see practical and theoretical objections to attempting static structural analysis of any society.

The six chapters which follow are my attempt to provide a comprehensive and reliable account of Lozi society between 1876 and 1896 in a form which is comprehensibly organised without doing violence to the internal logic of the data. The last two chapters of the book relate the narrative of those years in a form which preserves the momentum of the flow of events. At the same time they show how, why and with what effect our understanding of other levels of dynamic in the situation enable us to deploy fully the superficially easily accessible written data.

The book is constructed of four logically cumulative parts, each containing two chapters. The first part identifies the relevant contextual dimensions of time and space, and then describes the different scales of social organisation. We see how, once aware of the constraints upon the data, we should visualise Lozi society in the late nineteenth century as possessing simultaneously qualities of great fluidity and the potential for quite specific precision. I show how the dynamics of all scales of society depended upon this superficial paradox. The second part then describes the material components of Lozi society, first examining the level of production and the social relationships defined there, and then examining the level of distribution and exchange and the wider-scale social relationships defined there. These chapters and Part III are organised in the light of two considerations.

The first is of definition, where we encounter an inescapable Procrustean choice: if the data are approached with too rigid a theoretical preconception, we may produce an elegant logic of analysis but we risk crushing the unique qualities of our data. But at the other extreme, with insufficient analytical containment, the data may indeed dictate their own patterns, but they will be incomprehensible.[7] Therefore each situation demands its own compromise. While I impose a framework upon the analysis here by separating activities of production from those of distribution and exchange, I refuse to permit myself further scope in supplying definition to the shape of the work. Instead, each chapter is given its substantive form by the relevant Lozi concept: the one about production is organised by the image of proper diet; the one about distribution and exchange by the image of proper behaviour. These are 'core concepts', and the identification and consequent mobilisation of 'core concepts' are fundamental to Parts II and III. This leads us to the second consideration, which is methodological.

A synchronic structural analysis of any social situation is predicated upon three assumptions: that if the researcher is sufficiently skilled, he will theoretically be able to gather tolerably bias-free data; that such data will by definition be tolerably reliable and representative of the society under scrutiny; and that if the researcher collects enough of it, the resulting logical construct placed upon those data will explain most of the most important aspects of that society. I find none of these assumptions tenable. A lot of work now points to the unattainability of the first.[8] Awareness of the historical phenomenon of invention in field data suggests that it is unlikely that the second assumption will be upheld by the study of one historical moment and, as a consequence of these two doubts, the third assumption falls. But the last assumption is unhelpful for another reason. The first two assumptions underpin the third which is about the scope of the analysis. In the form in which this assumption is given, the way it presents its account of that scope is analogous to an architect's drawings of a building. Remove the first two assumptions and our confidence in the detail in those drawings collapses. We then understand that we know much less than we once thought. Therefore, in order to discover what we do know reliably, it becomes vitally important to know what we do not, or cannot, know. It requires a conceptually converse approach which is, in contrast, analogous to an artist's drawings of the space between buildings. This is what I am mainly concerned with in Part III.

If the material component of Lozi society is the warp of the fabric of its history, then the intellectual component is the weft. They are inseparable but distinct. However, the problems of availability and interpretation of data are at their most acute when we turn to African intellectual history. Only in a handful of cases do we know anything about it. But I think that it is essential that we should seek such knowledge if we are to feel any confidence in analyses of other aspects of society. In cases built upon ignorance of this ignorance, I feel no confidence. I am reassured where I read an assessment of relative ignorance.[9] In Bulozi we are unusually well provided with contemporaneous written material of sufficiently high quality which, when it is correctly treated, can yield datable information about Lozi cosmology on a useful scale.

The ahistoric image of Lozi cosmology which is projected by Professor Gluckman's work is of a unitary order in natural equilibrium; its characteristic paradigm is that of the 'Reasonable Man'. He suggested that this paradigm was fundamental to Lozi legal thinking, hence to the most important areas of social values where the quick of economy and culture were to be found. But here I show that Lozi cosmology projected a fundamentally dualist perception of existence. Although internally dichotomous, overall this dualist perception formed a common thread linking together the royal and the public rituals which expressed it. The form of beliefs associated with the dualist perception created forms of ritual expresssion, which by their nature have left us more observations than is usual of artifacts, places and actions. But the two chapters where I present the data on cosmology are relatively short; in comparison with information about concrete phenomena, of which more observations

6

could be made, we possess but little information. Therefore again I employ a knowledge of 'core concepts' to organise what we do have and also to indicate what we do not have. Then we can examine the pattern of exposure and hiddenness over time and wonder why it is like that. In the colonial encounter, 'core areas' tended to be concealed and 'core concepts', which appear within them, tended to display remarkable stability (which is not to be confused with changelessness).

I must justify and amplify the preceding sentence. It is founded upon three converging assumptions which I think can be made and defended; they underpin the methodology used in this book. For clarity, the three assumptions may be stated baldly thus:

(1) People place a higher priority upon feeling that they understand and control a given situation than upon actually doing so. Sometimes the two goals coincide, but not always. This assumption has a behavioural consequence which is useful to historians: people tend to favour familiar idioms over unfamiliar ones to express things which they consider to be very important.

(2) Occam's razor should be applied to historical explanations and, in the context of all the relevant data, the simplest explanation is to be preferred.

(3) 'Core areas' do not necessarily behave or appear the same in societies which are dominated by a scientific way of thinking and those which are not.

These assumptions rise from different sources. (1) is an observation about human nature; (2) is a methodological premise; (3) is conceptual and axiomatic: the ways in which we can employ (1) and (2) really hang upon what we take (3) to mean.

1.3 A MAINLY PRACTICAL DEFENCE

The first two assumptions combine to support a hypothesis which may be investigated entirely without recourse to theory: that 'core concepts' tend to persist and tend to retain their form. The difficulty with such a hypothesis is that it can be accused of circularity (core concepts persist; what persist are core concepts) and of perpetuating 'faith in a static Africa' or 'the myth of Primitive Africa'.[10]

Since there is no reliable way of knowing where core concepts may pop up – indeed, being so pervasive and therefore so vulnerable, part of their defence may be their unpredictable location – we need a guide. For the historian of an African society, the best guide is a thorough working knowledge of the present-day form of the society. But since we cannot make reliable synchronic observations, it follows that our only probe and

7

our only defence against invented traditions – our sword and buckler – is simultaneously to concentrate upon the detail of historical process. In fact I have found that my studies of past and present Bulozi, of which this book forms the first part, are entwined in an inescapable dialectic (some further detail about this matter is given in the Appendix). Our task may be expressed differently: it is to grasp in the most precise forms possible the relationship over time between historical realities and psychological realities.[11] How can this be done? We must study all the time-scales of change.

'Historical realities' are most vividly seen in the rapid flux of events which is described in what Fernand Braudel called 'event history' (*l'histoire événementielle*). 'Psychological realities' are to be grasped in the study of trends (*conjonctures*) which have a tendency, on the logic of assumption (1), towards considerable periods of stability; deeper still in the cosmological resources of a culture, there are long-term considerations (*la longue durée*) which alter even more gradually. Core concepts belong to these deeper levels.[12]

It is observation of the interplay of these levels of variably changing time-scales which give us the essential ability to defend ourselves against invented traditions: we can locate them *through time* and thus see when and why they appear and disappear. This is our buckler. In turn it enables us to examine intelligently the performer's relative ranking of concern with different concepts over time from which we can ascertain with more confidence and probability which are peripheral, which are perceived as central, and thus, incidentally, to rebut the criticism of circularity. This is our sword. Furthermore, once we have obtained this sort of knowledge, we can use it in a reciprocal role to test our data, employing our knowledge of the location of core areas as an index of reliability; but this requires great care because the danger of circularity is less easily combated here.

Both Part II and Part III, addressing respectively the material and intellectual components of Lozi culture, contain diachronic narrative passages which display the relevant concepts in motion through our period. Thus they perform simple historical tests upon the analyses offered. Furthermore, the main areas where tradition has been invented are circumscribed so that confidence may be felt in defending against the charge of circularity the identification of core areas and the description of core concepts proposed in these chapters. The key is that by studying how phenomena on the different levels of time-scale engage, we may make rankings and evaluations in the contemporaneous materials using criteria beyond the perceptual horizons of their authors, but with defensible claims to relevance in Bulozi. I shall deal with possible criticism of this view at the end of the chapter.

8

The conclusion of this book is not very startling. Areas of Lozi society and culture are shown to have changed easily, often dramatically, others to have remained (on assumptions (1) and (2)) the same; I propose that much of what changed would not have done so as easily if much of what remained stable had not been so unmoved. Unlike many historians of Africa, I do not see the demonstration of responsiveness and change in African societies faced with the colonial experience to be a sufficient or even a particularly elucidating objective. The best way to knock over the cardboard figures erected by those who would claim that Africans have no history worthy of the name, that it is merely the sterile gyrations of barbarous tribes, is not to put up more tired ranks of cardboard figures – resisters, collaborators, modernisers, traditionalists, etc. The best way is to be as interested in stability as in change, even more interested in their interplay and to write in a thoroughly old-fashioned way. Old-fashioned ethnography and old-fashioned narrative history set within and informed by a robust and simple process model of differential change in historical time-scales may make it possible for rounded people to be portrayed.

Women tending their cooking pots under a smoke-blackened shelter or wielding their hoes under an enervating October sun; old women cradling their grandchildren; men patiently watching over their cattle grazing in the silent vastness of the Zambezi floodplain; old men gravely debating in the public square of the capital; fever-racked traders and exhausted hunters; isolated and hungry missionaries: these are the people of a past generation in Africa whom I seek to rescue from the desiccative condescension of posterity. Their need today is as great as was that of the early English working class nearly twenty years ago.[13]

Core concepts in Lozi society as I shall describe them may be conveniently grasped through an analogy. They were like an overarching, unconscious and unwritten Lozi constitution. The central tenets of this constitution were concerned with the relationship of the individual to his society. The individual had rights to subsistence and duties to ensure that those rights were enjoyed by all who were deemed to be within the society. (The definition of 'society' is examined in the next two chapters.) 'Subsistence' was a concept with resonance in all the spheres of a man's existence. It was physiological (food, shelter), social (right order and reciprocity in one's dealings with others) and even, in times of extreme stress, cosmological (right order and reciprocity in one's dealings with the unseen forces). This definition is predicated upon my view of the third assumption which I set down earlier. Therefore while the substance of this book defends my view empirically, here I outline the theoretical supports.

1.4 A MAINLY INTELLECTUAL DEFENCE

Consciously or by default all studies of this type adopt a stance on the question of how scientific thought and its material manifestations relate to their own and other modes of thought. For example, it might be argued that my third assumption is incorrect; that there is no major difference between modes of thought. Professor Goody has argued powerfully that it is when men master the art of writing, and alphabetic literacy in particular, that they can then escape from the tyranny of dynamic and sequential performance in the oral transmission of information. This is fundamentally a *technical* achievement with huge intellectual consequences. The literate man can study a static 'text'; its semi-permanent form overcomes the otherwise insuperable problem posed by the limited capacity to store information in the human memory alone. Men can view information in a different way when it is preserved in a 'text'. Rationality and scepticism in thinking are favoured. The accumulation of knowledge on the scale made possible by the mechanical act of writing makes certain sorts of knowledge – abstract knowledge – more accessible. In this way, Goody suggested, arises the questionable dichotomy between scientific and other modes of thought.[14] I do not entirely agree. This important argument is certainly a most necessary element in explaining the emergence of scientific thought and it is too often ignored. But I suggest it is not sufficient in itself.

Dr Horton has offered a view of the difference between modes of thought which has been influential. It provides two central insights. The first helps to explain the tenacity of core values even under considerable stress, as during a colonial experience, as well as the organised incoherence of thought patterns. Horton distinguished low and high intensity situations in life and pointed out that we use common sense, a logic that is not consciously spelt out, in 'low intensity' situations, and only mobilise theory when the stress mounts. Then, in a non-scientific (or as he labelled it, 'traditional') culture, if negative evidence appears which could falsify important core beliefs, its action is blocked and the belief system is thus protected; whereas in a scientifically oriented culture, the result of such a challenge would be the formulation of a new hypothesis. Even if only the observation is correct, it underlines the importance of looking at persisting idioms in the data. But why does negative evidence become blocked, particularly when it is clear that in 'low intensity' situations non-scientific medical practitioners, for example, experiment all the time?[15]

Horton's now famous answer is his second insight:

> that in traditional cultures there is no developed awareness of alternatives to the established body of theoretical tenets; whereas in

scientifically oriented cultures, such an awareness is highly developed. It is this difference we refer to when we say that traditional cultures are 'closed' and scientifically oriented cultures 'open'.[16]

However, from one side, case studies like Janzen's *The quest for therapy in lower Zaire* show precisely that people within non-scientific cultures can and do display awareness of alternatives and employ those alternatives without slipping through the looking glass into a scientific world view. They do so freely when required in 'low intensity' situations and when shielded by selective blocks to falsifiability in 'high intensity' situations. From the other side, work like Kuhn's *The structure of scientific revolutions* suggests that scientifically oriented cultures may not be as 'open' as it once seemed.[17]

I think that we may go beyond Horton's second insight to a more fertile interpretation of the difference between modes of thought. It was implied in the definition of subsistence which I gave above: whereas in scientifically oriented cultures, the concentric physiological, social and cosmological spheres of existence are sharply drawn and discrete so that activity in one need have no implication in others, in non-scientific cultures the spheres are acutely interactive. This difference is not unlike that between 'status' and 'contract' as described by Sir Henry Maine when considering the history of legal theory. Gluckman used Maine's terms to situate Lozi law mainly on the 'status' side of the divide where, in our image, the spheres are interactive. Professor Gellner has explained this vital contrast between the spheres and their separation in scientific culture as sign and effect respectively of the enthronement of truth as the primary judge of evidence. He then organised some of the qualities to be discerned in non-scientific cultures and we may profitably employ his distinctions. He proposed four.[18]

One quality has already been noticed. It is that a concept will have a role to play in many spheres. The scientific world view distinguishes between what is testable and what is not, but the non-scientific world view does not recognise this boundary between the empirical and the transcendent. There is, in Gellner's phrase, a 'low cognative division of labour' and a proliferation of roles.

A second quality is bound up with this. Because of the interaction of the spheres, non-scientific cultures possess a wider and more insistent definition of 'normality'. It differs from the relatively less important and antiseptic position of this notion in a scientific world view, where 'normality' might mean simply those commonest mechanisms which do not have to be explained from first principles every time but may be taken for

11

granted. The difference is that the 'normality' of a non-scientific culture is both cognative, in that by definition it requires *no* discussion (unlike in the scientific world view where *some*, perhaps different, sort of discussion is entailed), and also moral, in that it defines a social as well as a natural order. I see this socially charged 'normality' as effectively the same as the 'moral economy of the poor' as it has appeared in other historical contexts; it in turn is the equivalent of those Lozi core concepts which I likened to an unwritten constitution.[19]

Thus the third quality which deserves emphasis is that, when the different spheres of a culture interact, it is possible that many more aspects of that culture are involved in supporting the accepted image of understanding and control in its particular environment than in a scientific culture. So core concepts, or 'entrenched clauses' as Gellner called them, are more pervasive and, because an action or concept may reverberate in other spheres than its own, the converse of core concepts' technically greater vulnerability is their greater importance for social definition than in a scientifically oriented society. Put another way, more of the fabric of life benefits from reinforcement from entrenched convictions. This strikes me as a good explanation for Dr Horton's observation of the persistence of idioms in non-scientific cultures. It underscores again the importance of our concern with perceiving core areas. However, one implication of the morally defined 'normality' within which core concepts are found is that explicit information from the inside of a core area may not be accessible to us. So we must be prepared to be sometimes content with defined areas of ignorance. These are the 'black holes' of our subject.

Already I have stressed that, for practical reasons, it is essential to distinguish invented traditions from those which were really pivotal if we are to rebut the criticism of circularity. But there is a more urgent justification for that task; it lies in the fourth quality of a non-scientific world view which Gellner proposed. When the boundary between the empirical and the transcendent is not recognised, then truth is not the sole arbiter of knowledge. Knowledge has, in Gellner's felicitous phrase, no 'diplomatic immunity'.[20] In other words, the autonomy of fact exists in roughly inverse proportion to the pervasiveness of core areas. So this is the short explanation of how large-scale manipulation and invention of evidence happens and why it is entirely to be expected. It confirms the correctness of our tactics in being especially concerned with such phenomena. But is it sufficient reason for those tactics?

While my explanation may be allowed within its own terms, it could be argued that it is simply beside the point. However coherent their internal justification, the techniques which I advocate will perhaps never lead me

12

to that demonstrably reliable history which I said was my defining goal because, to put it bluntly, I hold too naive a view of how the world works. I do seem to see that all human situations have an objective reality, which may be perceived and described by employing certain well tried techniques of historical analysis, but which is often distinct from what the mass of exploited within a given situation may think is the nature of their condition. Sometimes the masses do conceive of their situation in terms which are congruent with its deduced, objective reality; but frequently they are in error, bemused through the agency of social myths, religious doctrines and the other expressions of the ideological hegemony of the ruling class. They are said to be in a state of 'false consciousness'.

My problem is therefore both simple and serious. The techniques which I have considered fail to make clear distinction between the views and feelings of the actors and the objective reality within which they lived. Thus I commit the category mistake of equating their false consciousness with reality. In this way I mystify myself and my readers needlessly. I do not devote adequate space or energy to discerning the exact articulation of the modes of production and exploitation or the patterns of class conflict in Lozi society. I have spurned the advantages offered by the power and privilege of abstraction, and by the common stock of well tested and finely honed *a priori* concepts with which I could have sliced through the obfuscating layers of false consciousness to expose the real relations within Lozi society that alone provide a secure foundation for the task which I have undertaken. Worse still, instead of helping to make Lozi history plain, I have merely provided support for the enslaving myths of a defunct indigenous ruling class.

The form and direction of this criticism both spring from a thoroughly reductionist – or as Professor Rader calls it, 'fundamentalist' – Marxism.[21] By this is meant an uncomplicated interpretation of the relationship between material 'base' and cultural 'superstructure', wherein this relationship is considered to be both central to Marx's theory of history and unidirectional: causal force flows upwards. This 'fundamentalist' position views as straightforward the famous distillation of Marx's theory given in the Preface to *A contribution to the critique of political economy*. The sentence 'The mode of production of material life *determines* [my emphasis] the general character of the social, political and spiritual processes of life',[22] is taken to mean just what this translation says.

Such fundamentalist Marxism is not uncommon, and it appears to be the inspiration from which is drawn much recent interpretation of the behaviour of Africans in southern Africa since the colonial impact of the late nineteenth century. Therefore it constitutes an intellectual force in its own right and as such it is, in my opinion, an impoverished hypothesis;

13

nor is it clear that Marx himself shared it. Professor Rader mentions Marx's quip that 'all I know is that I am not a Marxist'[23] and he argues in his book that Marx's work, including the Preface translation (mistranslated as given here, he suggests),[24] supports an interpretation which relegates the 'base/superstructure' model to a lesser – expository – role, merely proposing a general hierarchy of phenomena within a more subtle and interactive model of social reality seen as an organic totality. But Rader's case for a consistent and humanist Marx is not our concern here; I mention it simply in order to give cogency to the label 'Marxist', which I prefer to equate with the 'fundamentalist' interpretation. What is interesting is the consequence of adhering to a strictly constructed materialist ethic. In the present case, the logic of analysis in terms of externally explained 'exploitation' cannot, by definition, take seriously the possibility that the actor's 'problem' of false consciousness arises not from misperception, but from his own durable and different standards of equity and exploitation, defined with reference to *his* core values: to his 'moral economy'. But the reply would be that these values are a false consciousness too; as King Lear told Cordelia, 'Nothing will come of nothing, speak again.' So we enter an elegant circle where we may canter around *ad infinitum*, like genteel horsemen in Rotten Row.

When we start with a set of ground rules which already disqualify ideas as serious candidates in our search for the potential motive forces of material change, then it becomes permissible and helpful to clear thinking to prescribe the application of words like 'real' and 'objective' to parts only of the human context. But it is all real, always, everywhere. So there are no comfortingly precise and generally applicable concepts, like one of 'exploitation', accumulating increasing predictive power, sloughing off their burden of value judgments, waiting to be picked up and used to dissect any given situation in the way that a surgeon can use the same instrument for the same task on any patient. The aura of scientific detachment is spurious.

The theory of false consciousness is in fact easily explained within the terms that I proposed. It is a block to falsifiability, protecting the entrenched core concepts which are beyond debate by the obvious expedient of declaring to be illegitimate any negative evidence which could arise from taking people's world views seriously. By contemplating its awesome arrogance, we see again the vital need for a converse approach which is initially inductive, not deductive, set within a conceptual framework broad enough that we may find sufficient common language to enable us to communicate intelligibly what we discover without being penned in to an unacceptable degree by the preconceptions of that language. Yet as I noted earlier, this is a Procrustean choice and there are

14

no entirely painless or perfect answers. We have to make the best we can of that.[25]

This being so, we are ultimately thrown back upon the more simple minded tests which we may make by examining the interplay of different levels of historical time-scale. I have now defended the importance of looking for core areas and core concepts both on practical and theoretical grounds; I have outlined and defended the technique that I shall use to undertake the search; I have also suggested that a close examination of narrative history may give us a medium different from that within which we prosecuted our primary search and where we may assess the qualities of those core values and their specific cultural expressions which we have identified. Therefore the biggest test of the various arguments put forward by this book is in fact the relationship between Part IV – the narrative part of the work – and what has gone before.

We embark upon the last two chapters equipped with our cultural chart of core areas, some core values and the forms of their expression. I show how in consequence we are able to reinterpret apparently familiar and obvious events in a quite different way, one which can tolerate examination at the highest magnification possible in the data. I show that far from it being the case that royal power was forcibly diminished in direct and inverse proportion to the increase of European power, as some historians who used the 'resistance/collaboration' bi-polar axis as their model have thought, or that Lozi social fabric crumbled, or that King Lewanika won a temporary but rapidly eroded advantage over some of the early white arrivals in his country, as others have suggested, almost the reverse took place. The Lozi emerged from their early colonial experience with considerable political success, their state and self image intact, having made great strategic use of their white protagonists' inability to remove the blinkers fashioned out of their own cultural view of the world. When I consider this period of Lozi history as a whole, I am inclined to share the opinion of the playwright Wole Soyinka when he wrote about the groping encounter of a colonial presence with a Nigerian culture: 'The Colonial Factor was an incident, a *catalytic incident* merely.'[26] But, as my emphasis suggests, it was not an incident to be underrated, for it left nothing unaffected. But the nature of change was not simple in fact or simple to perceive, nor was it necessarily the most important or likely product of catalysis.

While most of the events of this period of Lozi history are familiar from other books about Bulozi, the primary sources which I use to examine them are not, because this work is fashioned overwhelmingly out of those sources closest to the point of transmission. I work at the smallest remove possible in order to minimise the danger of further accumulated bias which increases with each step away from the original. The original private journals, notebooks and correspondence of all the major European actors are used whenever possible in preference to published and edited editions of their work; published edition references are given where it has been possible to check against the original letters, because the books are more accessible. However, some of the most valuable of these materials have either not been fully utilised before, or not used at all because I have only recently rediscovered them.

16

Part 1

2

Contexts

2.1 GEOGRAPHICAL

In its upper reaches, the Zambezi winds southwards through a diamond-shaped floodplain about one hundred miles long.[1] The floodplain is the most striking feature of the geography of western Zambia. For the Luyi who considered themselves to be the 'true' Lozi, who dominated it politically and in important aspects culturally also, it was the centre of the world.

When places are important to people they often show it by giving them many names: the British have several for their islands. In Luyana, the old language, the Lozi call their floodplain Ngulu, Liondo and Mbunga, and in Lozi, the *lingua franca* of all the ethnic subgroups of the area, Bulozi. Used thus, the association is direct: the floodplain is the land of the Lozi par excellence.

In Lozi mythology, the river was the home of three beasts whose different attributes reflected the close intertwining of a recognition of the might of this complex and changeable environment with the human response to that power expressed primarily through the institution of Lozi kingship. First was the monstrous water-snake Lingongole. Mere mention of it struck fear into paddlers in the 1880s. Known as the confidant of chiefs it embodied the awesomeness, the irresistible force and the inscrutability of the Zambezi river. The white cow Liombekalala, metempsychotic form of Mbuywamwambwa, mother of the first chief, was known as the maker of kings, conferring power from a different source than visible ritual. Also in the river lived Ñondwatuya, a buck whose sharp hooves incessantly scrabbled at the bank, changing the river's course.[2]

The river was an unquestioned, familiar and yet little comprehended fact of life: 'Billowy, wavy river! Nobody knows whence it comes or whither it goes', sang Livingstone's paddlers. 'Never friendly', laconically observed the missionary Adolphe Jalla forty years later.[3]

19

Below the floodplain, the Zambezi runs through a valley where thick bush crowds down sloping banks to the water's edge, and then enters a passage of rapids in the midst of which are the Ngonye Falls at Sioma. The falls are the stopper in the bottle of the floodplain; the constriction which they create, after the rains in the headwater catchment area have swollen the torrent of the river, is the reason why the upper Zambezi floods every year and has thus created the floodplain.

From the river at Sioma, dry and sandy bush, largely uninhabited, stretches unbroken to the west to the separate catchment basin of the Mashi river and beyond into Angola. To the east, dissected by many rivers and streams, it extends to the forest and tsetse belt of the Kafue watershed. But upstream, just south of the present Senanga township, the horizons expand; the forest is no longer dominant, for here the floodplain begins.

The bush which surrounds the floodplain is similarly sandy and infertile, but rivers flow through it on both sides towards the Zambezi and their valleys thrust like fertile fingers into scrub forest which is relieved otherwise only by pans and brooks, most of which are small apologetic intrusions into the forest cover where the shallow water-table touches the surface.

The floodplain is virtually treeless, and therefore is one of the largest unbroken expanses of lush grazing free from tsetse fly in central Africa. Transhumance has been possible because the surrounding bush is also tsetse free. The floodplain is like an ocean, and not only when the flood is at its height in March – Liatamanyi 'the month of much water'. As the traveller enters the plain and the ragged edge of the forest tree-line recedes, the *mazulu* – conspicuous and sometimes huge mounds – scattered over it, with what according to tradition are the oldest Luyi villages perched upon them, appear like galleons frozen in motion. The trees which shade each village are sails, dark and leafy against the bright, grassy sea of the plain.

The ecology of Bulozi is dependent on rainfall both locally and in the wetter northern regions of the Zambezi headwaters. Local rainfall is important for the cultivation of staple cereal crops, but external rainfall sustains the soil patterns of Bulozi. Local rain is controlled by the movements of the Intertropical Convergence Zone which governs the oscillation of the central African rainbelt. Different parts of Bulozi are therefore unequally vulnerable to vagaries of climate. The 'planting' rains come from the thunderstorms of October and November and are followed after an Indian summer by the main rains, which usually fall between late October and March. Failure of the planting rains or abnormality of the main rains can have severe agricultural repercussions, except in the generally wetter north.[4]

The northern catchment area rains are important because most local rainfall is lost in evaporation or transpiration and it is the floodwaters which are mainly responsible for the recharge of the aquifers that run underneath the shield of Kalahari sands surrounding the floodplain. These aquifers supply the root systems of the bush. They discharge along the edges of the river valleys and, supremely, of the Zambezi floodplain, thus providing in the seepage zones the constant moisture needed to maintain the catena of soil types at the margin of floodplain and bush. This belt of soils is of vital importance to the pattern of human settlement in Bulozi.[5]

The floodplain itself is a mosaic of soils. The Zambezi runs in a sand-lined bed that lies on viscous clay in a shallow depression in the centre of the floodplain. In archaic usage, this area is Mbunga, and when a speaker in the floodplain refers to Bulozi, it is of this area that he is thinking. Away from the floodplain, Bulozi refers to its entirety, whilst outside the region, the name embraces the whole area of floodplain and bush.

To either side of the river, a traveller may pass over patches of sand, of heavy clay or of loam, all within a few hundred yards. However, the mounds (*mazulu*) upon which the old Luyi villages are built are not all of natural origin. Some, called *liuba*, were of wholly artificial construction but most *mazulu* probably began as ant or termite hills to which men then added their labours.[6]

Reaching the edge of the floodplain, the traveller enters the *mukulo*, that belt of varied soils where plain-dwellers built temporary villages to which they migrated, literally 'to get out of the water' (*ku omboka*) when the flood was high. It is where most of the population, no longer trans-humant, lives permanently today. *Sishanjo*, peat soils that need to be drained to be agriculturally usable, slope upwards and become the sandier *matongo*, wetter towards the floodplain, dryer and with a decreasing humus content towards the *mushitu* (bush). Most villages stand in the *matongo*. Climbing further, the sand becomes purer yet until the traveller stands among the scrub trees of the *mushitu*. Fig. 1 shows graphically the varied nature of this environment.[7]

2.2 ETHNIC

King Lewanika ruled Bulozi from 1878 to 1916, a reign briefly interrupted by an ultimately unsuccessful *coup d'état* in 1884–5. During his reign, the floodplain and its immediate periphery were inhabited by several distinct groups, and the further hinterland by a galaxy of satellite peoples. It is difficult to use contemporaneous evidence directly to state

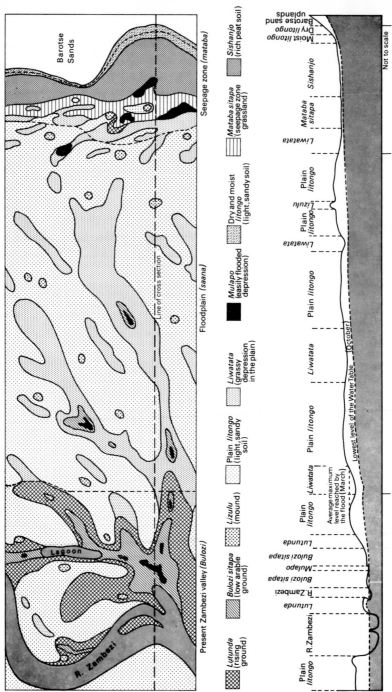

Fig. 1 The varied face of the floodplain.

22

with any confidence which of these peoples were part of Lewanika's kingdom, because the judgment of who was within and who was without the Lozi kingdom varied from observer to observer. Language differences have been used most frequently as the major criterion. While I believe that this was a sensible choice and I shall do the same thing myself in Chapter 3, Section 1, nineteenth-century observers were concerned only to classify, which they did with varying degrees of ability, and not to judge the cultural qualities implied in a given relationship of languages, and therefore their judgments varied enormously. For example, Livingstone made a single distinction between the Kololo rulers and the indigenous people. He wrote in his journal that the 'languages of the black race which inhabits the river seem to be all dialects of one tongue. . .They bear the same relationship to Sichuana as the Latin does to French or English.'[8] In this he was mistaken.[9] At the other extreme, Emil Holub listed eighty-five distinct tribes within what he called the joint Lozi/ Mbunda kingdom whose heartland he never visited. Of these, seven were singled out as especially important: Lozi, Mbunda, Tonga, Kalaka, Nkoya, Mbowe and Nanza. The list in itself revealed Holub's ignorance, mingling indiscriminately as it did peoples with different kinds of affiliation to the state and omitting several arguably more important tribes.[10]

All the peoples of Bulozi (except an insignificant number of Bushman hunters) spoke Bantu languages. The ancient language of the rulers was Luyana, although by 1876 Kololo, a new language formed out of the Sotho brought to Bulozi by Kololo invaders from the south in the early nineteenth century, was the dominant *lingua franca*, retained and used after the Kololo who had originally brought it were ejected from power in 1864. The peoples of the geographical heartland of Bulozi spoke predominantly Luyana-related languages, but not exclusively so, and the fact of a language being closely related to Luyana was not an automatic index of political relationship. Take for example the Mbunda speakers who followed two Mbunda chiefs entering Bulozi about the turn of the eighteenth century. Mbunda is a quite different sort of language, but the followers of Mweneciengele and Mwenekandala were fully integrated in the geographical and political centre of Bulozi. Bulozi was an integrative kingdom. The peoples of the heartland were primarily those who called themselves Luyi, or those closely related to them: Kwangwa and Kwandi to the east of the floodplain, the people of Mulonga, the Simaa, Imilangu, Mwenyi, Nyengo, Makoma and Mbowe to the west and the Mbunda of Mwenekandala and Mweneciengele.

The peoples of the proximate hinterland who rendered regular tribute to the Lozi king and had done so for a long time by Lewanika's reign also spoke languages of various origins. Some spoke Luyana-related lan-

23

guages like the people of the Mashi river; others spoke Tonga languages, the Totela, Toka and Subiya. The Nkoya to the east are a good example of the difficulty encountered in distinguishing between the old established category and that of distant peoples only recently brought under Lozi hegemony in the late nineteenth century: although the Nkoya share important rituals and ritual objects of ruling with the Lozi, and although their formal tradition connects together the founders of the Nkoya and Luyi dynasties, modern informants, especially young men, claim that the Nkoya were only made tributaries to the Luyi in Lewanika's time. Other tributaries to Lewanika who more certainly fell into the category of the recently affiliated were some Kaonde and fewer Lunda who owed allegiance to Chief Msiri in the modern Shaba Province of Zaire during Lewanika's reign. Lewanika staged military campaigns to reinforce his overlordship of the Luvale and the Ila (Mashukulumbwe) in the 1880s and 1890s. He strengthened his grip over the Subiya primarily by deploying patronage. The locations of these various peoples are shown in Fig. 2.

Most of the satellite peoples were originally matrilineal in descent and frequently uxorilocal in residence. The 'true' Lozi (Luyi) were bilateral in descent and usually patrilineal in residence. Tellers of the formal royal tradition relate the switch from a female to a male chieftaincy close to the beginning of most recitals. The story revolves around the question of exerting authority effectively over a number of groups. The men who lived in the village of the female chief Mbuywamwambwa felt that women could not do this. The point was brought home to them when several of Mbuywamwambwa's sons returned from a hunting trip to the west of the floodplain. At Mutungi pan they had met a man, Isimwaa, who took a fish from each of the fishermen there and gave the princes a gift. It showed them the principle of collection of tribute and the relationship of power it expressed. The men then plotted a *coup d'état* but were overheard and reported to Mbuywamwambwa. She pre-empted the men's action by proposing a change to a male chieftaincy with her son Mboo as chief (and herself as *eminence grise*, which has since been the recognised role of the royal women).[11]

There is no direct evidence for Lewanika's time, but the twentieth century has seen a steady adoption of bilateral descent and patrilocal residence by formerly matrilineal peoples. The change has been both fostered and recorded by legislation, since it made the administrator's life easier.[12]

Circumstantial evidence that will be displayed below indicates that during the 1890s ethnic groupings in Bulozi showed definite variation in residential patterning and accompanying styles of building whilst existing within an encompassing political culture which included broad, stable and varied stylistic regimes. The only detailed study of artifacts from the early

24

colonial period is Christol's illustrated account of Lozi art, made in the early 1900s. Carved stools, canoe design, knife and scabbard, wooden cooking spoons, basketry of grass and of roots (*mukenge*), a hand piano (*kañombyo*), all show great similarity in shape and in applied design when compared with what modern Lozi craftsmen describe as the 'best' modern work.[13]

Jalla and Coillard, the pioneers of the Zambezi Mission, recorded another indicator of distinctness that has since become rare. They observed that 'true' Lozi filed their teeth and tattooed their faces in a specific pattern.[14] Other peoples did this also, notably the Lunda, Nkoya and Ila, but below I suggest that cultural distinctness and Lozi hegemony were not mutually exclusive. In Chapter 3, Section 1, I shall explain the different types of affiliation to the Lozi state which I have now mentioned and located.

2.3 THE LONG PERSPECTIVE: ARCHAEOLOGICAL EVIDENCE

The distant origins of these diverse peoples still remain obscure because the history of Bulozi from the archaeological record is only now beginning to be written. The task has been hampered because, while oral tradition has not been fully utilised for historical analysis, problems have arisen from too literal an interpretation of the mainline formal traditions.[15] Although Bulozi is archaeologically one of the least explored areas of Zambia and although there are environmental factors which militate against the physical survival of viable sites, a pattern has emerged in outline at least.[16]

Five Stone Age sites in southern Bulozi show settlement of that area by Wilton culture people.[17] Overlay showed that the Wilton and Early Iron Age peoples coexisted for some time early in the Christian era,[18] and that like present-day populations they sought sites beside dambos and river valleys.[19] However, the earlier suggestion of a homogeneous Early Iron Age culture, site typed 'situmpa', with possible connections to the Dimple-ware culture of East Africa, has now been discounted[20] and instead Dr Phillipson has proposed a two-stream Early Iron Age. One major and two minor sites in Bulozi at present support the hypothesis of a Lungwebungu tradition which flourished around AD 750 to 1000, covering the Northwestern Province and Bulozi as far south as Senanga and the Matabele Plain. This archaeological tradition was quite different from the Dambwa and related Kalomo cultures to the south and east which, from the Kalomo evidence, appear to have been moving from a hunting to a domesticated economy at about the same time.[21]

The edges of this 'interface' are now coming into sharper focus. Recent work in the Machili area and a survey in southern Bulozi suggest that the divide between Phillipson's streams lies somewhere between Sioma and Katima Mulilo. Early Iron Age materials which have been identified in these areas show clear differences and soon it is hoped that excavations above and below the hypothesised divide will clarify them further. The Machili findings indicate firm links to the Copperbelt through copper artifacts but, equally, stylistic connections to the south. This fits the two-stream theory.[22]

For reasons that are as yet unknown, a sharp break in pottery traditions occurred towards the end of the first millennium throughout central Africa, affecting the eastern stream. Swiftly, Later Iron Age cultures superimposed on the existing ones, but there is no archaeological evidence to suggest either large-scale movements of people or an origin external to the region for these new cultures.[23] The western 'Lungwebungu' stream showed much greater continuity between Early and Later Iron Age traditions than was seen to the east; indeed, it remained stable until the intrusion of the 'Linyanti' tradition with the Kololo in the early nineteenth century.

This type of evidence has important implications for the oral traditions of migration which many Zambian peoples possess. Dr Roberts has observed of the Bemba that their migration legend cannot be taken as evidence of any large-scale movement, but rather that it should be envisaged as serving 'to give the Bemba imperial tradition the stamp of high antiquity', a point which he believes has wider significance.[24] Such a view may well be peculiarly appropriate for Bulozi because although no stratified Iron Age sites have been discovered which would yield a firmer terminal date for the Early Iron Age,[25] as I have observed, the local Lubusi variant of the 'Lungwebungu' tradition shows greater continuity than is seen to the east.[26]

Dr Roberts has observed that in western Zambia the two distinct yet linked Luyana and 'Wiko' (western border satellite people) language groups, variants within Guthrie's 'K' group of languages, roughly correspond in their compass to that of the 'Lungwebungu' pottery tradition. Further, he notes that the linguistically separate Kaonde area to the northeast of Bulozi corresponds to a gap between the 'Lungwebungu' and 'Luangwa' pottery traditions. He proposes that these linguistic/ archaeological congruences and the linguistic differences both point towards a similar hypothesis of long stability and relative isolation from the rest of Zambia for the cultures of this region. This complements the sparse archaeological data which exist.[27]

The best hope for further precision lies in the systematic excavation of a floodplain habitation site. In the meantime, it is possible that attempts to date iron slag recovered in the village of Lubindatanga, the first iron-worker in the formal tradition, may be revealing. But a village site promises the best sequential set of dates.

So, to summarise, our present scant archaeological data suggest that there were three phases. In the first, Wilton culture Stone Age people alone were in evidence; in the second there was a long period of coexistence with Early Iron Age immigrants, one stream entering the north and central part of Bulozi, creating a 'Lungwebungan' culture of notable durability, another stream entering the south of the country and showing signs of greater contact with the peoples to their east. In the third phase, for as yet unknown reasons, the transition to the Later Iron Age was relatively rapid although the *degree* of change was different in each stream. However, the evidence is sufficient to suggest that the Luyana migration myths are not necessarily to be read as an explanation of these events. Therefore a considerable lacuna still exists between archaeology and oral tradition and the loose ends of dates drawn from the former cannot be knotted across areas devoid of evidence to speculative dates derived from the latter.

2.4 THE LONG PERSPECTIVE: ORAL TRADITION

In trying to date the creation of political organisation, no great weight can be placed on either the reliability or the absolute significance of a date drawn from speculation about the succession list. Only the trite observation that the Lozi list is relatively long can be made. Such speculation assumes that time has a single quality alone, akin to technological man's preoccupation with precise measurement.

In fact we can distinguish three sorts of time definitions in the Lozi material. There is the realm of what Evans-Pritchard called 'pure myth' where events lie in an undifferentiated time perspective. In this, the most prestigious period of time, are the myths of genesis and the foundation of the kingship. Then follows the time of 'tradition' where time is sequenced but relates to structural concerns and does not mirror actual chronological distances. Here are the deeds of kings. It is *Muluilonga*, a wistful word which carries the suggestion of noble and bygone days. Finally we reach historical time which is placed by contemporary oral sources during the reign of King Sipopa (1864–76) for matters of political tradition, presumably because this was the end of Kololo rule. In the 1890s it was placed commensurately earlier, towards the end of the reign of Mulambwa. These distinctions are valuable because they class oral data by their significance to the performer. It is not helpful to judge materials of one category by criteria appropriate to another.

The Lozi king-list begins in the time of myth and extends to historical time. Viewed with the eye of recent time as it passes through 'traditional' time, the list becomes telescoped, for king-lists perform other functions there than those of mere dating. They may be implicit statements about social priorities, emphasising the career of a chief or king whose attributes are relevant to problems prominent at the moment of the performance. They may also be statements about the structure of social groups – 'codes' whereby different groups explain to themselves their relationship to their neighbours through real or fictitious genealogies.[28] I suspect telescoping in the Lozi case when I compare an individual commoner genealogy, which is not loaded with the extra burdens of kingliness, with the royal list. In the commoner case, where I consider that rough chronological speculation is less risky, a wide disparity with the received chronological interpretation of the king-list is to be observed.[29]

Another dimension may be distorted in the opposite direction in too literal a reading of *Litaba za Sichaba sa Malozi* (History of the Lozi nation), the 'official' version of Lozi royal history. This book was sanctioned by Lewanika after his visit to England for Edward VII's coronation in 1902; the material in it was approved by king and court and related to the missionary Adolphe Jalla by Chiefs Kalonga and Nalubutu sometime between April 1903 and late 1908.[30] In the *Litaba za Sichaba*, the gradual expansion of the kingdom is a strong theme, pursued in later academic writings. Yet the first written reference to Bulozi in 1795 is in a paragraph which accords adjectives of power and size to other neighbouring peoples but gives none such to the Lozi, and in 1893 Lewanika admitted to the missionary Arthur Baldwin that formerly Bulozi was not large.[31]

I suggest that the explanation is that in 1893 Lewanika had not yet entirely grasped what things most impressed Europeans in general and colonial officials in particular. These things were age, systematic organisation and size, precisely the qualities projected through the *Litaba za Sichaba*. However, we can see evidence of Lewanika's education in these matters. Early in his dealings with Coillard, the first missionary of note, he bombarded him with questions, asking how he compared to other African rulers. Six years later he wanted to know more precisely how the Lozi 'constitution' compared to those of the Tswana and the Ndebele.[32] But it was after the arrival of the first Resident in 1897 and his visit to England in 1902 that he learned very quickly indeed.

Elsewhere in Africa, during the manoeuvring for advantage which followed initial contact, royal genealogies were lengthened, elided, created and forgotten as required. Often, the discovery of antiquity may be seen as a response to loss of sovereignty.[33] Yet the manipulation of

28

tradition offered wider possibilitites than this and in the Lozi case I suggest that emphasis upon antiquity resulted from a challenge to sovereignty. The most important result of Lewanika sanctioning an official version of Lozi history was to strengthen the shutters behind which lay much of the propulsive force of Lozi society, for the *Litaba za Sichaba* set limits upon what the Lozi elite were prepared to allow whites to be interested in through its very subject matter. By confining attention in these areas, enquiry could be deflected from other 'hidden' parts of Lozi culture; thus considerable flexibility of action as well as ideological integrity were preserved.

The tensions arising from this struggle to maintain flexibility as well as ideological integrity, often invisible to an uninformed reading of the archival record, form a prominent strand in the analysis I propose below. An awareness of the biases thus inscribed in the observed contemporaneous data has a controlling role in my selection and blending of the whole spectrum of available material.

But to return to the formal tradition specifically, I see little benefit in detailing a composite version of the materials within the first two categories of time here; it has been done often enough before.[34] Furthermore to do so is confusing because it blurs awareness of the 'watersheds' within the data. Here, the watershed between traditional and historical time which distinguishes material with definite narrative intention from that where this function is subordinate or absent is prominent. My concern now is with a period on the modern side of that divide. The chronological limits of this book arise from a desire to keep this distinction crisp and therefore references to the earlier stages, when they occur, are not set in full context for which I do not apologise.

So I shall now narrow the focus. The last context to be set is political and historical, to give an outline of events leading to the eventually firm seating of Lewanika upon the throne in late 1885.

2.5 THE SHORT PERSPECTIVE: HIGH POLITICS

The earliest reliable date in modern Lozi history is about 1840 when Bulozi was invaded by the Kololo, one of the groups which travelled north as a result of the *Mfecane*, 'the crushing' – that series of profound disturbances in the interior of southern Africa related to the tempestuous fortunes of the Zulu empire. The reasons why they conquered and successfully ruled Bulozi are not clear, nor is there a wholly convincing explanation of the nature and circumstances of their expulsion in 1864.[35]

Soon after this event, it is said that Toka and Totela in southern Bulozi rebelled against Luyi control, but that King Sipopa reasserted his rule and came to rely upon these groups for support against the Luyi 'traditionalists' led first by the *Ngambela* (Prime Minister), Njekwa, and after Njekwa's death by his successor Mamili.

In all his writings, the Czech traveller Holub gave an opinion of Sipopa's rule as relatively weak and vicious. From his visits to Sesheke he concluded that the north was of sufficiently new incorporation to deserve a hyphen 'Marutse-Mambunda' in his description of the country.[36] But Holub leaned heavily on secondary reports from informants visiting Sipopa's capital for many of his judgments, which should therefore be treated with caution. The position with regard to the relation between north and far south was more likely the reverse. Both a descendant of Sipopa's and another unrelated modern informant agreed that by leaving the northern capital, Lealui, and going to Mulimambango (the present Sesheke) to hunt elephants (Holub thought it was to be near traders), Sipopa sacrificed some support: 'Sipopa was blamed because he never remained in one place; he moved too much. How can the Government be stable if the Chief wanders?'[37] Later it will be made clear how by moving his capital out of the floodplain Sipopa distanced himself from sites with ritual significance, which may explain the 'traditionalist' reaction. In contrast, Lewanika refused to make the same mistake when urged by Coillard to transfer his sister Matauka from Nalolo to Sesheke.[38]

Mamili eventually engineered Sipopa's overthrow in 1876; Sipopa fled, was wounded and died. The site of his death was described by Christina Coillard two years later: at 'Ali Ka Soga Bonki' she watched members of her party 'beating their chests and knocking their heads on the ground (as signs of mourning) which filled us with melancholy to witness'.[39] Those intervening two years had been a time of confusion.

Mamili had a youth, Mwanawina, installed as *Litunga*, but the puppet turned on the puppeteer and Mamili himself was toppled. In the mainstream formal tradition this is attributed to a hunger for power beyond his due; Mamili died shortly thereafter. But perhaps because of lack of skill or unfairness in his handling of patronage, Mwanawina aroused resentment and a broad coalition of chiefs overthrew him in turn in 1878. After a dramatic race to seize the royal drums (*maoma*), essential symbols of power, Luboshi, the son of minor chief Litia, but raised at Sipopa's court under the system of *lifunga* (described below), was proclaimed ruler with the support of Silumbu, brother of the late *Ngambela* Njekwa, who became Luboshi's *Ngambela*.

Luboshi was an uneasy king faced with the threat of the deposed Mwanawina and the demands of rival factions upon his power of patronage. His name, meaning 'the man with the powerful grip', became ironically appropriate.[40] Mwanawina attempted a counter-coup in 1879, but

30

Luboshi defeated him in battle at the Lumbe river. However, he was less successful in his attempts to satisfy the appetites of his other rivals. Mataa, leader of one faction, fomented discontent especially in the south and in 1884 staged a palace rebellion which temporarily expelled Luboshi from his capital, Lealui. A puppet of Mataa's, Tatila Akufuna, was installed; his sister Maibiba replaced Luboshi's sister Matauka as *Litunga-la-Mboela*[41] at Nalolo, the southern capital[42] (see Figs. 20 and 21).

Luboshi retired to the Mashi valley to recruit support and he returned late in 1885, ousting the rebels in a pitched battle between Lealui and Mongu hill early in October when Mataa was killed and the Sikufele family, who had supported him, scattered.[43] Although it was applied to him before his restoration, by that action Luboshi confirmed his praise-name *Liwanika la matunga* (one who gathers together), which is usually corrupted as Lewanika, the name which I shall use henceforth for the sake of clarity.[44]

31

3

Boundaries

This chapter will both refine and synthesise the general contextual statements of Chapter 2. It will argue that we should conceive of Lozi society in our period as much more fluid, with much less formalised bureaucratic structure than has hitherto been thought. I believe that this more flexible pattern has persisted for a long time although it is not possible to be precise about how long. The superficial contrast between flexibility and durability is akin to the superficial paradox of simultaneous vagueness and precision in social definitions which is a recurrent theme of this chapter.

Gluckman's image of a well ordered, highly centralised, hierarchical state apparatus, has survived unchallenged this long because historians have not studied and understood the context of the creation of their source materials – in this instance early-twentieth-century archival data. The problem was introduced along with an indication of my solution of it in Chapter 2, Section 4, above. The problem is not unique to Bulozi although so far it has not received the attention it deserves. Dr Twaddle has shown convincingly how an image of Ganda society which projected order and clear organisational form was invented to meet a specific set of political needs and, as I shall show here and further in Chapter 5, the same thing happened in Bulozi.

Aware of this and therefore able to control our data with some claim to reliability for the first time in the study of Bulozi, I remove the patina of interpretations previously proposed and reveal very different evaluations of social institutions at all levels. I begin at the largest scale by exploring further the nature of political and cultural affiliations in Bulozi and then progressively intensify our focus until it rests upon the physical nature of the village. From here we are then able to proceed to an analysis of social relationships within these material and spatial frameworks in the next two chapters.

32

In Professor Vansina's categorisation, Bulozi was an 'Incorporative Kingdom'. He used comparative data to suggest the type of interaction between heartland and periphery that might be expected in such a situation and made clear that 'incorporation' did not automatically imply homogeneity.[1] Our direct evidence supports this, for Lewanika's actions showed that he recognised a clear distinction between the heartland and peripheral tributary regions. But how can the differences between these areas be reliably drawn? The western boundaries first indicated by Major Goold Adams and finally embodied in the British submission to the King of Italy's boundary arbitration of 1905 as well as in the northeast were, like the wilder territorial claims to be heard today, means of making political capital.[2] Initially it suited the British South Africa Company to support the maximum claims of Lozi rule. In response, Lewanika and subsequently his son Yeta pressed for areas where they could hope to gain something and in any case would lose little, whilst quietly abandoning what was beyond hope.[3] For example, three of the four *lindumeleti* (emissary chiefs) in Angola were recalled and reassigned after the border arbitration.[4]

Whilst such an approach through conventional data suits the distant areas only loosely connected to Bulozi, given the past and present political sensitivity of the subject which is a prime candidate for invented tradition another sort of criterion must be found for the regions ringing the plain.

In Chapter 2 I observed that early white sources tended to rely a great deal on language as the basis for drawing ethnic distinctions. I said that the logic was sound, for language and culture are closely intertwined. However, those observers only used one of the two qualities of insight which linguistic evidence offers. They categorised on the basis of aggregated similarities of languages; but the words people use often reveal attitudes more reliably than consciously expressed opinion does. Therefore an examination of the similarities and differences in words used offers a reliable pathway through the shifting sands of opinion. I shall now look at each type of information in turn, first reassessing the general pattern of language relationships in slightly more detail, showing how language alone is not a criterion of political and cultural affiliation, and then exploring the second quality and showing that an informative pattern can be uncovered. I tread in the field of comparative linguistics with trepidation and a clear awareness of my relative ignorance.

The first published categorisation of the languages of Bulozi based on a competent knowledge of some of them was by E. Jacottet. However, he could not draw on personal knowledge of the country and his analysis was based upon information from three Lozi, two Subiya speakers and one

Luyana speaker, who visited him in Lesotho for several weeks in 1895.[5] Whilst his work has been the most influential upon subsequent academic work, I prefer to use the unpublished categorisations made by Adolphe Jalla in Bulozi after June 1892, because Jalla was in the country and therefore had the possibility of a wider range of sources. He was, like Jacottet, also a very gifted linguist. His categories were closer than those of Jacottet to what subsequent systematic analysis reveals to be the pattern of language. Fig. 3 brings together for the record the findings of all the main studies of the languages of Bulozi using Jalla's categories (those groups marked with Roman numerals) as the matrix. I have arranged the groups schematically in their relative geographical positions so that the figure may be conveniently compared with Fig. 2. Fig. 3 shows that Jalla's categories coincide quite closely with the most modern studies, for example the conclusions reached by Professor Fortune, which also appear on the figure.[6] There are three inferences which we may draw from these two figures: first that we can see a clear pattern of language which has lasted over the last century, secondly, that the pattern does not of itself enable us to delineate the Lozi political or cultural sphere and, thirdly and incidentally, that we may have some confidence in Adolphe Jalla's expertise.

We now have a fairly good idea of the pattern of languages, but this pattern does not permit us to proceed beyond a simple statement of itself. The inferences about the quality of political and cultural relationships which early observers made on the basis of this type of data were unsound, a conclusion also suggested by their wide variance. To ask questions about these relationships, we need to obtain different and appropriate linguistic data. In order to enable us to do this, I collected wordlists of different types in four languages from different groups: Lozi, the modern *lingua franca*, related to both Kololo and Luyana; Luyana, the ancient language of the rulers, pivot of Fortune's eastern cluster; Imilangu, a Luyana-related language of Fortune's western cluster, and Mbunda, the unrelated language which has been politically and culturally the most important in Bulozi for the longest time. The different types were based on Swadesh's 200 word list of 'non-cultural' words central to any vocabulary, and a number of specialist sub-vocabularies of my own invention. Here I shall make use of the contrast between the Swadesh list and a list of words to do with ruling and authority.

Interest is in a time three and four generations ago. Dr Roberts has suggested that, with the conspicuous exception of Lozi, it is probably reasonable to think that Zambian languages have been stable for much longer than that. However, since Lozi is a newer language, created out of the fusion of Kololo and Luyana in the mid nineteenth century, it therefore has the greatest reason for historical volatility. It is valuable to chart the nature of its changes over the last century, since an understanding of them will show us whether we may have confidence in Dr Roberts' suggestion or not.[7]

Contemporary commentary on change in Lozi suggests that it is not wildly unrealistic to use recently collected wordlists for our purpose, since the main trend reported in this, the most mutable language between the 1880s and 1930s, was a steady increase in the amount of Luyana in it. In 1888 Coillard thought it scarcely worthwhile to study 'Serotse' (Luyana) since so few people understood it, but in 1913 Adolphe Jalla wrote to Coillard's niece that he was preparing a 'Sikololo' vocabulary and grammar:

> With your uncle we had hoped that Sesuto would gain and Sikololo, its patois [Lozi] would lose, but the contrary took place and if we continued to use Sesuto we would soon speak a language almost foreign. . . We have long left lots of Sesuto words and adopted Sikololo ones in conversation and also to a certain degree in preaching.

It seemed that Livingstone's hope that 'a good expressive language will spring up out of the materials now brought together'[8] was proving to be more realistic than the expectations of 'Sikololo's' eclipse by 'Sesuto' (the language of the Basuto). Twenty-two years later, Jalla introduced the first Lozi dictionary by observing that 'The name itself of "Sikololo" has almost vanished; it has been replaced by "Silozi" which twenty years ago was synonym of "Siluyana". . .'[9] Since the 1930s there has been relative stabilisation, but a shedding of obsolete words which is reflected in the newest Lozi dictionary, compiled in the late 1960s.[10] It is a curious reverse camber given that Kololo was adopted at all. I think that we may use Dr Roberts' assertion safely.

The assumption I am going to make is deliberately simple: if closely related languages have markedly different words relating to power and authority a flexible form of overrule is suggested and the converse may also hold.

Different subgroups of vocabulary within a language seem to respond differently to pressure from a superimposed language. Aware of this, but also that Table 1 reveals no consistent pattern in those word groups associated with power and ruling, I take direction and marked degree of divergence as general pointers. They may be made more precise by looking at the composition of the wordlists themselves.

The Swadesh list has been taken to represent the operational vocabulary and to indicate the degree of relationship between any two lan-

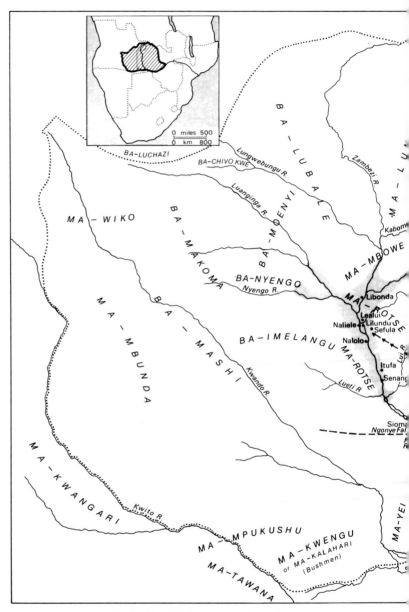

Fig. 2 Peoples of Zambezia, 1890s, as seen by Jalla.

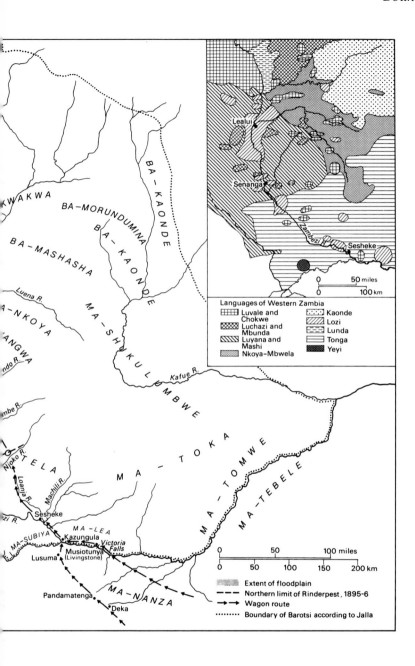

KWAKWA

BA–MORUNDUMINA

BA–MASHASHA

BA–KAONDE

BA–KAONDE

–NKOYA

MA–SHUKULUMBWE

ANGWA

Luena R.

ndo R.

mbe R.

Kafue R.

Lealui

Senanga

Zambezi R.

Sesheke

Languages of Western Zambia

Luvale and Chokwe
Luchazi and Mbunda
Luyana and Mashi
Nkoya–Mbwela
Kaonde
Lozi
Lunda
Tonga
Yeyi

0   50 miles
0   100 km

MA–TOKA

MA–TOMWE

MA–TEBELE

TELA

Njoko R.

Loanja R.

Machili R.

zi R.

Sesheke

MA–LEA

MA–SUBIYA

Kazungula

Victoria Falls

Lusuma

Musiotunya
(Livingstone)

Pandamatenga

MA–NANZA

Deka

0   50   100 miles
0   50   100   150   200 km

Extent of floodplain
Northern limit of Rinderpest, 1895-6
Wagon route
Boundary of Barotsi according to Jalla

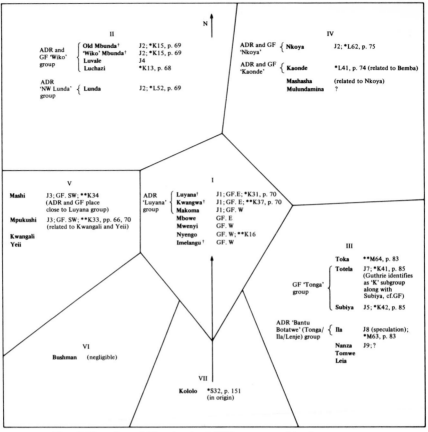

Fig. 3 Peoples of Zambezia, 1890s, grouped by language.

I–VII   Jalla's categories

J1–J9   Jacottet's nine groups (*Études sur les langues du Haut Zambèze*, vol. I, pp. viii–xi).

ADR   A. D. Roberts, *A history of Zambia* (London, 1976), pp. 68–70 (based on an unpublished study by M. Kashoki and M. Mann; see further, S. Ohannessian and M. Kashoki (eds.) *Language in Zambia* (Oxford, 1978)).

GF   G. Fortune, 'The languages of the Western Province of Zambia'.
   GF. E: eastern Luyana cluster
   GF. SW: southwestern Luyana cluster
   GF.W: western Luyana cluster

*, **   Precedes references to the revised Guthrie classification (M. A. Bryan (ed.), *The Bantu languages of Africa* (Oxford, 1959)). A single asterisk indicates that Guthrie possessed first-hand data on the language, double asterisk that he did not.

†   Indicates that I collected first-hand data on the language.

38

guages. In the first column of each pair in Table 1 is given the ratio of superficially similar to dissimilar roots in the Swadesh lists for each pair of languages. In the second column of each pair is given the ratio for the special subgroup of words relating to power and authority.[11]

TABLE 1. *Relationships between four languages*

	Luyana		Imilangu		Mbunda	
Lozi	1:3.2	1:1.2	1:6	1:1.5	1:13.7	Nil
Luyana			1:0.82	1:2	1:3	1:36
Imilangu					1:3.5	Nil

Viewed from the standpoint of Luyana, Mbunda and Imilangu display less relationship in their ruling words than in their basic vocabulary; this is especially marked for Mbunda. Imilangu and Mbunda are radically different languages but since they are intertwined in their geographical incidence, they inevitably exhibit a certain degree of relationship although they share no common ruling words. Given the social integration of people of old Mbunda stock[12] and the fact that, despite their close relationship, Imilangu has fewer ruling words in common with Luyana than other words, I would argue that these languages reflect a political culture in which the distinct identities of peripheral groups were not crushed, since were this so one might expect the widespread use of alien words for alien institutions.

The relationship between Luyana and Kololo which together made Lozi permits this theme to be followed further but offers a different slant and some idea about the different degrees of permeability in subgroups. Here the major language was peripheral to what was, after 1864, a continuing Luyi state. Christina Coillard was surprised that the Luyi adopted their ex-conquerors' language, as was Jacottet, and the conventional wisdom to be found in Jalla's introduction to the first dictionary and in elite oral sources is that this was due to the influence of Kololo women married by Lozi after the expulsion of the Kololo rulers.[13] This would fit with the changing composition of Lozi already mentioned, for as the generation of Kololo women died, so would the language be repopulated with Luyana, like dandelions reappearing in a garden path, whilst the high proportion of Luyana ruling words was less likely to change than other cultural word groups, for the institutions persisted.

To judge whether this is a viable explanation, we may find a helpful analogy in the theory which Phillipson proposed to explain how completely another facet of Kololo culture, the 'Linyanti' pottery tradition,

39

overlaid what was already there. The Kololo potters were women but Phillipson suggests that in the pre-existing society the potters were men; whilst male potters in both the pre-existing and the invading cultures can lead to a merging of traditions, when the invader culture has women potters it replaces that of the pre-existing culture.[14]

The basic operational vocabulary and grammar which the child learns, he learns from women; words describing the specific nature of his society, of which ruling words are among the more specialised, are learned later and more under the influence of men. Below it will be seen how these learning processes may fall on either side of a dramatic division in Lozi childhood. Our adaption of the theory would therefore be that the influence of the Kololo women during the first process, whether due to weight of numbers, prestige or for some other unknown reason, overlaid Luyana. In this the contribution of that other commonly suggested influence, the schools of the Zambezi Mission, the first of which began to teach in Sotho at Sefula on 4 April 1887, should not be ignored, but must perhaps be relegated from a formative to a reinforcing role. The other vocabularies, more under male control, fused.[15]

The relationship of Lozi to Imilangu illustrated in Table 1 shows another sort of pattern. Lozi, and that means its Kololo component, contributed more ruling words than there were common words in the basic vocabulary. Does this reflect domination? The relationship of these two languages on the Swadesh list is largely mediated through the common ground of Luyana and so Imilangu shares almost nothing with Kololo, yet it has Kololo ruling words. Kwangwa, an eastern cluster language spoken in the eastern hinterland of the plain and also, like Imilangu, close to Luyana in its operational vocabulary, displays the same phenomenon. The following suggested explanation is valid for both.

The answer lies in the nature of the words. 'Royal establishment', 'public courtyard', 'councillor', 'minor chief', are the words of static rule in the floodplain. Compare with 'Prime Minister' (*Ngambela*), 'spear' (*mbinji*), 'tribute' (*ñamba*), 'gong' (symbol of office – *ngongi*), 'wardrum' (*lioma*), 'politeness' (*likute*). These are the elements of the more fluid pre-Kololo Luyi state and are Luyana's contribution to Imilangu and Kwangwa's stock of ruling words. Kololo contributed to Imilangu, Kwangwa and Lozi the words connected to the more fixed style of rule which followed Sipopa's foundation of and Lewanika's continued use of Lealui as a capital.

An aspect of this conclusion is to provide support for the earlier suggestion that too literal a reading of the theme of the expansion of the state apparatus in the official version of formal tradition might extend the time-scale of the creation of that apparatus further back than is probably justified.

The nature of rule as it is viewed through these data contrasts interestingly with the impression given in formal royal traditions, but it harmonises with commoner accounts of the growth of the state and with the new data and reinterpretation of state organisation given below (Chapter 5, Section 3).

Most recitals of the royal tradition have to the fore episodes that are grandiose and outward looking. There is the strife between the first male chief Mboo and his brother which culminated in Mwanambinyi's dramatic and magical exodus to the south of the floodplain with his people and herds; the capture of the first royal drums of the south from satellite people near Katima Mulilo by Ngombala's daughter, Notulu, first *Litunga-la-Mboela* (chieftainess of the south); the battles of Mange, chief of the breakaway and then reintegrated Kwangwa; the incorporation of the Mbunda peoples of Mwenekandala and of Mweneciengele to whom Mulambwa granted the right to retain his royal drum. All are described through bold deeds and colourful tumult.

Histories of commoner families give a more pacific impression of the extension of hegemony, and here it is seen as a less dramatic and less unified process. In the periphery, the Totela, who lived around the Lumbe, Kakenge and Njoko rivers in eastern Senanga district, were incorporated by chiefs who came to hunt and stayed to rule. It was the same on the upper Lui and at Lui Wanyau.[16]

Other areas were populated by special groups. Lepers and those with disfiguring diseases were sent to Kalabo district since their presence east of the Zambezi was thought to endanger the ritual purity with which the *Litunga* should be surrounded. Madmen were sent to the remote bush of Shekela, an area first colonised by hunters coming south from Kalabo and herders of royal cattle sent to graze them there during the time of flood.[17] The sequence of hunters followed by herders was also reported at Sibukali and in the Siloana Plains.[18]

Settlement accounts in heartland communities revealed how interwoven with the periphery relations might become. In their family traditions, the dominant kin of individual villages related that they moved long distances, often outside their 'original' home areas, to their present sites, although they then remained there for generations without movement. The given locations of origin are the cypher to crack the code because, I suggest, these names are claims to identity as well as geographical statements. Illustrated on Fig. 4 and in Table 2 are the claimed movements of the dominant kin of some villages founded before 1885 in three locations, two near or in the floodplain and one in a bush river valley.[19]

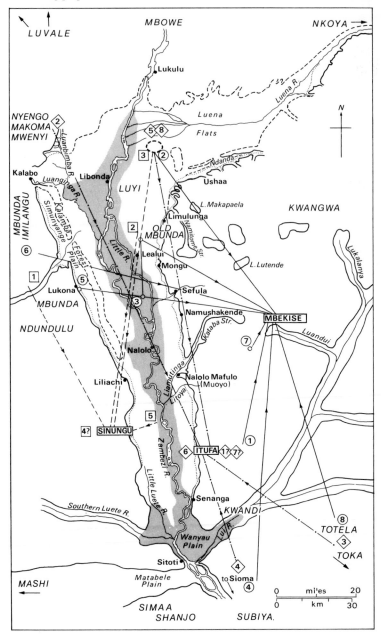

Fig. 4 Some claims of origin (see Table 2). Names of peoples are shown in large letters. Arrows indicate claimed movement from place of origin to the three areas studied. The centre of the floodplain is shaded.

TABLE 2. *Tribe names claimed by dominant kin in villages from three areas*

Mbekise		Sinungu		Itufa	
①	Kwangwa	☐1	Kwandi	◇1	Kwangwa
②	Kwangwa	☐2	Kwandi	◇2	Kwandi
③	mixed	☐3	Mbowe	◇3	Toka
④	Subiya	☐4	Mbowe	◇4	Ngalanga
⑤	Toka	☐5	Kwandi	◇5	Kwandi
⑥	Kwangwa			◇6	Kwandi
⑦	Luyi			◇7	Luyi
⑧	Totela			◇8	Kwandi

Numbers within symbols refer to Fig. 4.

These claimed movements from fairly random villages were of two types. Both related to the question of ethnic identity and both point towards the same sort of interpretation. The first are those which specify an origin external to the floodplain. On the basis of genealogies which I have investigated and where I think that I was told the truth, Jalla's assessment may be accepted as a fair generalisation: few people in Bulozi could claim much genetic exclusivity. Intermarriage with Toka, Tonga and other eastern peoples occurred from the royal family downwards.[20] For example, the guardians of Ikatulamwa, village of the first chief, are of Tonga extraction from Chief Monze's family as reflected in the proverb 'The Litunga also belongs to Tonga and Totela. These Tonga did not come to be slaves but to judge in the Kingdom.'[21] Another example would be the social assimilation of the 'old' Mbunda of Mweneciengele and Mwenekandala.[22] So some of these claims – the most distant – are likely to be factual; yet they coexist with protestations of 'pure' Loziness. Fig. 5 illustrates this.

After hotly attacking Dr Mainga's *Bulozi under the Luyana kings* for denying the 'Loziness' of many 'real' Lozi, the informant of Fig. 5 defended his own claim via his paternal grandmother by observing simply that if one was fortunate enough to have some superior blood in one's veins, one 'clung to it'. He uses his grandmother's familial name and identifies himself through her *mushiku* (descent group).[23]

The second type of claimed movement on the map are references to the 'original homes' of specific *mishiku*. They may be interpreted in the same

43

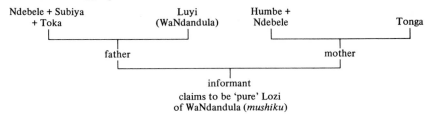

Fig. 5 A family tree to illustrate the prestige of Luyi ancestry.

way as the informant above viewed his genealogy: for example, several villages in this sample and many others elsewhere claim origin from Mutindi, a village north of Lealui in the floodplain, which is in reality a claim of age and status within the heartland.

It is a commonplace that people are 'situationally selective' in their identities. People in Bulozi had a rich choice, one geographical, one social, for each scale: 'region' and 'tribe' were for coarse tuning out of the country; 'district' and '*likolo*' ('regiment'/political sector) for strangers in Bulozi, and 'village' and '*mushiku*' for fine tuning at home. *Ku shikula* (to greet someone by his *mushiku* name) is to express a detailed knowledge of a person.

The ethnographic data contain no reliable information from which we might describe the exact patterns of permitted and prohibited marital and sexual behaviour among kin in Lewanika's time. Because of ambiguities in Lozi kin vocabulary, I cannot subject genealogies to such scrutiny. Certain general statements, such as against incest between brother and sister and against close cross-cousin marriage, are recoverable from oral evidence, but the dynamics of kin must be sought elsewhere. The pattern of relationships within a village is revealed in the spatial organisation of huts and courtyards, discussed below, and in a non-territorial form of social organisation. But in 1940 and subsequently, Professor Gluckman argued that kin words were calibrated through literal reference to specific mounds (*mazulu*).[24] For several reasons I dispute this emphasis. Indeed, were it so, the last twenty years should have seen extreme social disorientation as the plain has been abandoned. I would suggest that the role of the *mishiku* has been underestimated.[25]

As the earlier example illustrated, *mishiku* offered a means of identification at the same time precise and vague. The paradox was essential both for maximising inclusiveness and for minimising tension between scales of identity. *Mishiku* could be inobtrusive or forceful as the situation required: could this be why the early ethnographers missed seeing them? The institutions which they described – those of the middle scale – are less easily recalled than *mishiku* except by certain specialist informants.

44

Some *mishiku* originated with royal individuals: WaMwambwa from the female chief Mbuywamwambwa; Inalishuwa contained many of royal blood; WaNdandula and WaNamuchoko were also of early and royal origin. But others, acknowledged as equally old, are called *za sichaba* (of the nation), for example, Noshaa, Namenda, Naluya and Nalitongo. The dividing line is hazy. 'Where do chiefs come from?' demanded a retired *Sambi* (prime minister of the chieftainess of the south) rhetorically. 'From people!'[26]

Informants distinguished two periods of clan creation. The first was at the time of the first two male chiefs, Mboo and Inyambo, and the second was during Mulambwa's reign when some *mishiku* were named after his wives. The royal establishments were not able to produce 'definitive' lists for me, I think probably because to do so would vitiate the fruitful ambiguity; however, around 1930, one named informant could list over forty.[27] But the historical depth of *mishiku* is evident. The hazy elision of royal and commoner in the account of their origins will be recalled later when we examine ritually expressed social distance. So if the stress is relaxed from the rigid way in which Gluckman applied it, there emerges a more flexible and workable model of how kin ties adapted to settlement pattern in the Lozi environment.

Returning to family traditions, several villagers, especially in the immediate hinterland of the floodplain, related how their forebears came as colonists in charge of royal cattle, as hunters of royal animals (elephant, lion, hippo, eland), to cultivate land given in return for labour in *bonamukau* (state gardens), or to render special services like operating the porterage of canoes at the Ngonye Falls.[28]

Most vividly remembered are the displacements ordered by Lewanika. Enough is known of these for us to be able to see how the king used his powers of patronage in this respect very shrewdly to reinforce the state at around the time that white contact with Bulozi was intensifying. The process is described and discussed in the next chapter, but here it serves to support the image, which emerges from these family histories, of a Lozi political culture (as distinct from a state apparatus) coherent at the grass-roots over a multi-ethnic area for quite a long time. Like the linguistic evidence adduced earlier, this 'unofficial' strand of family traditions supports the revised view of the organisation of the Lozi state which this chapter proposes.

3.2 THE SMALL COMMUNITY

The floodplain's edge was the point at which a person halted if he was unable to demonstrate his position within the Lozi nation through belonging to a recognised *mushiku* or plain village. With a few exceptions, like the old Mbunda chiefs and certain alien families rewarded for services rendered, floodplain land was not available to non-Lozi in the sense just defined. Only after much protest did the colonial authorities succeed in changing this situation on the floodplain margin in the 1950s. However, immigrants might be granted sites on bush lands at all times for these were also in the king's gift.

In Lewanika's time, the division between Lozi and non-Lozi was sharp, but it is important to realise that it referred to a principle of law, not to a rigid physical segregation, and was therefore flexible; wives, wives' kin, servants and slaves all lived in the plain. The principle referred to the primary holder wherever he or she was, provided his or her presence was socially legitimate in that particular place.

A man or woman, including slaves, had right to land so long as he or she used it. A youth was given his own land when he married or acquired dependents. Women – who married earlier, often soon after puberty – were given marriage land (*mubu wa linyalo*) by the husband. The grant of land carried a series of reciprocal obligations sensitively described by Gluckman.[29] Land was heritable, but if the person moved away for long enough to suggest that the move was permanent – and several attempts were made to fix a minimum period in years for this during the twentieth century – then title in that land reverted to the king in whom all the land of Bulozi ultimately was vested. Lewanika made considerable strategic use of his powers to grant new title, but usually in so doing the king was guided by the advice of the headmen and local chiefs who wished to keep up the numbers in their area.[30] But neither 'title lands' vested in certain state offices nor state lands (*bonamukau*) were open to occupation by users in this way.[31] The key to the system was folk memory of land allocation. There was a possibility of misleading the king in this, but to do so deliberately was actionable.[32]

The legal principle which mediated disputed title was rooted in an assumption of the existence and general acceptance of this collective memory. It linked legitimate title to previous use by demonstrable kin. The principle of *muliu* thus defined originated in the aftermath of the Kololo occupation:

> It began after the Makololo were defeated. Sipopa who succeeded as king did not stay long in the central part of the kingdom; of course Lealui was founded by him. But as he was a hunter especially of elephants he moved . . . leaving the capital in chaos. Those who came back from the places of exile began to claim lands here and there which were not theirs.[33]

The informant, formerly a very senior judge, went on to explain how dishonest claims of redemption (*muliu* from verb *ku liulula*, to redeem) proliferated again during Lewanika's exile, and so upon his return he formalised the existing principle more concretely

> to say that all those who can prove beyond all reasonable doubt that their claims are true, come forward now. Those whose cases were genuine were given back their land. To those whose cases would not hold water he said, 'No! This is the last time that *muliu* should be used. It confuses the nation. It prevents production of food.' . . . So the law was promulgated that no-one should claim *muliu. Muliu* should end.[34]

But the principle was deeply engrained and it continued to be used so that, in 1926, the colonial authorities urged Lewanika's successor Yeta to repeal it, which he did on 29 October 1927.[35] But this had little effect for it was still in use when Gluckman collected his case records in the 1940s and, on 11 October 1955, *Litunga* Mwanawina reconfirmed Yeta's proclamation, adding a £20 fine to encourage its observance. The case mentioned in note 32 comments upon the success of that measure.

The demonstration of a land claim depended upon the elasticity possible in recounting family history and kinship. Gluckman's acute perception of the link between inventing a narrative past and describing structure[36] antedated the current debate in this area by twenty years.

I have argued that a precise imprecision may be seen in forms of society which define the boundaries of society at several levels. I now suggest that a material complement was to be seen in the styles of what was built upon the land, styles which showed a tendency towards heterogeneity, and in the spatial patterns of houses, which showed differentiation. Different ethnic groups had distinct building styles specific to themselves in our period and in the material culture of everyday life there was simultaneously considerable intermingling.

We can distinguish three main styles of house. The first is the Luyi *longo* (pl. *maongo*), built in the style called *mifelo*. It was elongated and low with a small entrance in the middle of the long side. Built of saplings, it had a pounded dung floor.[37] The building technique was the same as that used for temporary huts such as can be seen today in fishermen's camps in the plain, although these are small in comparison to Sipopa's buildings at Sesheke in 1875, which were up to ten yards long and six wide. Holub thought that two thirds of the buildings in Sipopa's capital were of this style.[38]

The second style consisted of small circular huts with daubed reed walls, smeared on both sides except for slave houses which were smeared on the inside only. The name *situngu* (pl. *litungu*) derived from the method of construction. *Ku tungeka* means 'to start by making the roof of the house' which in turn is functionally related to the plural noun *tungolo* – the saplings used in this work. The conical roof was of different pitch with different peoples and was thatched with a thin water-resistant grass, *mwange (Loudetia* spp and *Aristida* spp).[39]

A third style of building, *masaela*, was introduced by the Kololo. Holub much admired these large circular houses with twin concentric walls which were used by the elite. Their construction required more concentrated manpower than ordinary people could or would wish to devote to housebuilding.[40]

Elevated granaries were of two types: *lishete*, which are most common today and are unsmeared, and *lifalani*, which I found only in the plain, which are smeared. Villages also had covered cooking areas built by the method *ku tungeka* to protect the hearths during the rain. Blackened by smoke, these shelters were and are the realm of the women. Much indirect power is located there.

These shelters were also the focus of the expenditure of much male and female energy, for in the plain fuel was scarce. Firewood had to come from the floodplain edge by canoe or by shoulder to supplement a ligneous grass, *mañele*, which grows in the plain. The importance of *mañele* in daily life may be judged from the fact that its name once graced the southern royal establishment.[41]

Because of the annual transhumance, huts used to be rebuilt or repaired in the plain and at the margin each year, hence the predominance of the simpler *maongo* and *litungu* in contemporaneous photographs, sketches and descriptions. But there has since been a trend, only recently accelerated, to build more permanent houses in the *mukulo* and virtually to abandon the plain.

In the late nineteenth century, the only more substantial structures were the square houses of Lewanika and certain other chiefs, the first of which were built by Mambari traders and others by men trained in the Paris Evangelical Mission.[42] Any attempts by commoners to build such houses led to reprisals.[43]

However, the characteristic which most clearly distinguished Lozi from other villages of a century ago was the segmentation of the village into *malapa* (courtyards) bounded by *makwakwa* (reed fences). These surrounded houses and physically defined social geography.

The layout of courtyards has ritual meaning at the royal establishments and, as will shortly be seen, the units they identified defined the economy of the small community. Types of fence denoted the status of the inhabitant: the woven design was only to be seen in the fences of the *kwandu*

Fig. 6 The design of huts and appearance of courtyards in the 1890s.

Fig. 7 The design of huts and appearance of courtyards in the 1970s.

49

(palace); sharpened stakes protruding above the level of the reeds were the prerogative of selected chiefs.[44]

Malapa are now no longer exclusive to Luyi; nor are the forms of social organisation which they contain. It is a further example of 'Lozification'. These organisational forms I shall now describe and shall suggest that we can reasonably conceive of certain essential elements being stable over the last century. So on the one hand I utilise information from European sources just used to describe the shape of settlements in our period; on the other I rely on oral evidence and field observation of the relationship between social organisation and visible village layout. Then I invoke Occam's razor and read parts of the modern material into the older upon the rationale indicated in Chapter 1.

Part II

4

Production

This chapter is organised by the Lozi core concept of the spectrum of diet. Only from this standpoint can a clear understanding of the pattern of production be obtained. The concept is explained in Section 1. In Section 2, I examine the range of crops available in Bulozi and argue its antiquity. These two phenomena have long wavelengths of time. Then I look in detail at agriculture during the 1880s and 1890s, often considered by other historians to be times of ecological disaster. I show that this was not so in Bulozi because of important and specific large-scale improvements in agriculture. The narrative of these developments has vital significance for our subsequent assessment of the colonial impact of those years and, more basically, of the king's real power. Section 3 returns to the question of labour and, in the light of our knowledge about agriculture, I show what slavery was and, equally important for such a loaded concept, what it was not in Bulozi in the late nineteenth century, thereby correcting further mistakes by other authors. The final section deals with the other part of the diet, the provision of animal produce. It centres upon the nature of cattle owning and upon the cultural and economic statuses of cattle in Bulozi, all of which have been badly misunderstood in the received description; Gluckman argued forcefully that cattle affairs were of little consequence in comparison to other aspects of the Lozi pattern of production. Our revised account, which proposes the reverse of Gluckman's position, in consequence enables us to look afresh at the political use which Lewanika made of cattle patronage in the 1880s and 1890s; our new insight reveals a judgment upon the Lozi politics of the period which converges with that found in our narrative of agricultural change.

4.1 THE DIVISION OF LABOUR

The typical Luyi village of the later nineteenth century was not large.[1] Each contained a dominant kin group, its bilateral affines and servants

53

with different degrees of freedom – royal establishments, however, were larger.[2] Many of the peripheral groups were originally matrilineal as has been mentioned, but adopted the bilateral descent system and settlement pattern as well as other features of Luyi villages. As already noted, the relationship of individuals was reflected in the pattern of the village.[3]

Each adult who was not a slave lived in his own hut built within a reed or grass fence which thus formed a courtyard. Young children lived in their mothers' huts; older children might also be there, or they might be with relatives or taken for training at a royal establishment under the system of *lifunga*. Subordinate adults might have their own huts in separate or communal courtyards. Slaves slept in an outer ring of unenclosed huts at the edge of the village near where the cattle were stake-tethered or penned in a kraal.[4]

The method by which a man rose to the position of headman was not clear cut. It was by 'flexible descent' within the resident kin, for which the image of election is too precise, for seniority and proximity to the previous headman were important although not irresistible determinants. The flexibility ensured that common sense overruled anomaly in the procedure of selection so that half-wits and people considered to be undesirable could be passed over.

The installation ceremony was very similar to that for senior chiefs when succeeding to a title in council. The whole village gathered in the evening and, even though the choice had already been made, the men sat outside the candidate's house and engaged in a lengthy and uninhibited discussion of the merits of the candidate and the duties of a headman. Finally some of them rushed in and seized the candidate, dragged him from the house and covered him with a blanket. When this was removed, he had 'inherited the name' (*ku yola libizo*) of *muñ' a munzi*, (literally: owner of the village). With the name he had inherited the concomitant power.[5] However, the wrong choice could be made and if a headman resisted other, usually witchcraft related, incentives to reform his ways, he might in the last resort be coerced by legal process.[6] The power of the headman embraced land allocation, but his most frequent and dramatic statement of influence was in the distribution of food and as mediator of the reciprocity upon which land holding, land use and consumption depended.

The spatial patterning of a village was a map containing statements of social affinity and reflecting the demands of the productive process. Each courtyard was a cell containing different types of labour which combined to create the subsistence economy. The relative proportions of that labour were expressed by the ranking of foodstuffs in the diet.

The division of labour was broadly that men provided animal protein and women and slaves vegetable protein and starch. It was reflected in the pattern of diet. All main meals should consist of two parts: *buhobe*, a cooked porridge of cereal or root staple,[7] and *busunso*, a relish which might be of animal produce – fish, *mafi* (soured milk), white or red meat[8] – or of vegetables like sweet potato (*ngulu*), Livingstone potato (*sikuswane*), ground nuts, bambara nuts, pumpkin, even *shombo* (cooked cassava leaves) in lean times.[9] But for the Lozi, 'there can be no real fête without meat'.[10] Salt and more recently cooking oil were and are regarded as essential to a satisfactory *busunso*.[11] This description of the pattern of diet, supported above with unconnected references, may be seen as a connected thought in notes made by Coillard in the 1890s:

> The woman . . . like everywhere in Africa is a beast of burden. She busies herself with house-building, cultivating the fields, preparing the meal for supper, obtaining fuel whilst her husband fulfils his labour dues to his chief, listens to discussion of affairs in the assembly [*forum*], goes hunting or fishing. . . .[12]

In the Luyi diet, a mixture of *mafi* (soured milk) and *buhobe*, often the leftovers of the previous evening, stirred to a paste-like consistency, was taken after rising. This was called *ilia* and is the specifically Luyi food.[13] The Luyana word for food is *silia*.

At midday, roasted whole cassava, a filling and thirst-quenching food, might be eaten. Being easily portable this is traditionally the food of travellers and cultivators. The main meal of *buhobe* and *busunso* was in the evening; its preparation began in mid afternoon. In 1908 the average daily intake per person of *buhobe* was reckoned to be four and a quarter pounds.[14]

If *bucwala* (millet beer) or *sipamu* (distilled soured milk) had been prepared, it was usually after the evening meal that men would drink it. Women and children were forbidden to touch alcohol unless given to them by a man. Mangoes, oranges and other fruits of relatively recent introduction were eaten at any time, with or between meals when in season.[15]

The affairs of cattle were the dominant concern of men, whether they owned or used many or few.[16] Women had no part in them. An early official recorded a belief that 'if women enter a cattle kraal, it will bring an immediate and untimely menstrual discharge'.[17] Meat and milk were highly regarded foods. Milk is an essential ingredient of *ilia*, the Luyi food. Most types of fishing – with spears (*ku waya*), with traps and fish dams (*makuko, bwalelo*) and with fish fences (*liandi*) – were men's work, but not the catching of small fry (*nakatenge*) in scoop baskets (*mashiño*). Hunting in all forms was men's work. It had a specific hunters' disease cult

55

(*Manyanga*) and curing song sequence which marked off the boundaries of occupation.

Luyi men were directly involved in the village's cultivation in three ways: the decision of when to plant was theirs and it is often reported that sowing was once men's work; hoeing, which was not considered honourable, was therefore women's work. Secondly, clearing trees in bush gardens was men's work.[18] Finally, they contributed indirectly to agriculture through their part in the construction of the network of drainage canals in the 1890s which brought many new acres into production. The history of this programme – Lewanika's most widespread and easily visible mark upon the face of the Lozi countryside – is told in the next section.

Once dug, the canals were kept open by communal labour. In Kataba valley, a small tributary of the main plain, it was described thus:

> The people organised themselves. They went to the woods to get sticks to make fences [*liandi*] and with them they blocked off half the canal to keep the water away from where they were digging. Each person dug his own section of small canals [*mingunja*], but on the big canal everyone worked.[19]

But there were sanctions for those that did not. At a meeting in 1950 when an attempt was being made to reactivate the canals, *Ngambela* asked, 'What happened if a man failed to dig under Lewanika?' 'Our cattle were taken from us by Mukwakwa [third in the Nalolo hierarchy of chiefs] who made us work', was the blunt reply.[20] The sheer scale of Lewanika's drainage projects which mobilised free and slave labour together in 'regiments' (*makolo*) suggests that there was a lot of male labour available at that time, surplus to the direct requirements of village agriculture. It looks like a further case of underproduction such as Sahlins has described for other situations.[21]

The stigma of wielding a hoe was evidently reduced for men when doing communal labour. Such labour was performed beyond the domestic scale where domestic values were suspended and such circumstances were not abnormal. Some surplus male and female labour had normally been applied to work in *bonamukau* (state gardens), although here it was not strictly divorced from the village, for it fed back, literally, to the village economy.

State gardens were scattered throughout Bulozi. It is said that the system was most fully expanded under Lewanika and indeed he used state gardens in the same way as royal herds, to cement loyalties. Furthest from the heartland, *bonamukau* were supervised by *lindumeleti* – emissary chiefs, especially concerned with collecting tribute; within the heartland

56

and its hinterland, the guardians were called *lindaleti*. These men were also game wardens, protecting nesting sites. Whenever his state garden needed attention, the *ndaleti* reported to his royal establishment and was there empowered to collect labour for the task. Because of the range of crops grown, judging from modern observations, it was less likely that a seasonal bottleneck occurred in Bulozi as a result of these labour demands than in regions with less diversified agriculture.[22]

The diversity of male occupation suggests a well tuned ecological balance in a system which displayed remarkable resilience for the next three generations. To anticipate the story briefly in order to underline that point, the 1890s saw much natural impediment to agriculture, but this was offset in the wider society by a substantial increase of acreage, shortly to be described. The first quarter of the twentieth century saw a shrinkage of acreage again because of reduced application of concentrated labour and because of the fragmentation of the village economy; possibly the effects of both were accentuated by adverse climatic conditions. However, just as 'horizontal' productivity lost ground, two major technological innovations permitted the first 'vertical' amelioration of productivity since the invention of the efficient hoe-blade. Iron three legged pots (*lipoto*) arrived in force in the 1920s and ploughs in the 1930s.

Lipoto released women from the cooking fire for other tasks; children took over the watching of pots. The risk of leaving valuable food unattended in a clay pot balanced precariously on the burning fuel (there are no stones in Bulozi and fired bricks did not become widespread until the mid century) was not acceptable. However, a child could be left safely to tend a stable self-supporting iron pot.[23] Ploughs were more radical. They enabled a small number of men to replace a great deal of female labour, but they were resisted for a long time because (not without good scientific justification) ploughs were believed to destroy the soil's ability to retain moisture.[24]

Notice that the contrast between a narrow band of techniques of production and the range of productive possibilities has a persisting importance. The contrast is essential to any discussion of slavery in Bulozi and, by extension, to a theory of the state. Awareness of this ecological tuning is also important both for understanding how the Lozi of the 1890s survived their environment and, later, in explaining the elasticity of their political and economic response to the colonial world. More immediately, it must be in view before completing the description of productive forces. Notice further that what is under examination is not trade, but the possibilities hypothetically open to the labour force of the small community. Whatever was achieved within this circumscription was

57

complemented by subsistence exchange described below in Chapter 5, Sections 1 and 4.

4.2 *BUHOBE*: THE RANGE OF AGRICULTURE

'If agriculture were a test of civilisation then these are not savages',[25] observed Livingstone of the inhabitants of Bulozi. Eclecticism and tolerance in performance were the impressions of Lozi agriculture given by early European observers. Newly arrived from arid Botswana, which may have coloured his enthusiasm but not the basic detail recorded by a meticulous observer, Livingstone described the floodplain proper when he reached it a month later as a cornucopia: 'There is not want of food in this fertile valley. . . .' 'The people are never in want of grain . . . there are so many things a man can find in it for food.'[26] 1853 was a year of moderate to low flood, and these observations were made in the lean winter months. In August 1855 descending the river he collected thirteen oxen as gifts of food, again in the lean time and despite the fact that 'this last year, the water approached nearer to an entire submergence of the whole valley, than has been known in the memory of man',[27] so these were not optimum conditions either.

The floodplain is not an undifferentiated expanse of peat soils, for as Chapter 2, Section 1 explained and Fig. 1 showed, it is a complex mosaic of many different soil types. Therefore a wide range of different crops can grow in the plain itself where dry sand and heavy clay delimit the range of soils. In 1853 Livingstone wrote of 'Caffre corn of great size and beautiful whiteness, Pumpkins, melons, beans, Maize and earth nuts, Moanja or Manioc, Sweet potato and another kind of potato called sekhutsane, sugar cane and the Banana further North.'[28] 'All the mounds and islands of the Barotsi Valley are taken advantage of for growing mealies and white *mabali* [sorghum]', wrote a mission artisan from the vantage point of Sefula, above the Valley. Cassava, he reported, was 'grown everywhere in the border of the . . . Valley'. This was in 1887, a year of low flood again and therefore similar to 1853 and of opposite disadvantage to 1855.[29]

It is a reasonable assumption that the basic agricultural system must be older than the Kololo occupation, indeed possibly much older. We can use linguistic evidence to sharpen this suggestion quite specifically, at the same time ranking the relative importance of the different food crops. Sorghum (*makonga*) was the most important cereal: it was grown in a heavy earth garden (*tite*) that might require draining (*ku tokola*) through side drains (*mingunja*) – all unadulterated Luyana words. With sorghum the truth of the assumption may be checked from different sources.

Legends spoke of sorghum as the original food grain and it was the royal food; royal title-lands in the Kataba valley which had a reputation for fertility despite its name (Kataba' means 'little marsh') carried sorghum grown for the use of the court at Nalolo. In Livingstone's opinion, 'Lekoñka [was the] corn of the Barotse.' Sorghum was seen in tribute brought to Sipopa at Sesheke and from the Totela of the Njoko River to Lewanika twenty years later. A proverb calls 'Makonga the best seed in the forest clearing.'[30]

The Kololo introduced two new varieties of sorghum (*maelepu* and *munanana*) but as Livingstone and Waddell observed, white sorghum (*lukonga/makonga*) was the most common. The millets – *mauza* (Lozi), *mangu* (Luyana) and *lukesha* (Lozi), *luku* (Luyana) – are also known as old crops grown in bush soils and wet soils respectively.

Maize had arrived in Bulozi early enough to have acquired a distinct Luyana name (*mundale; mbonyi* in Lozi) and certainly before Livingstone.[31] Sweet potato had a name which was also a Luyana name for the plain. Coillard suggested it was because, when the flood was up, the *mazulu* looked like sweet potatoes swimming in the water.[32] Cassava had been there long enough to have a name different from that used by the people who brought it and also from the Kololo (Mbunda: *lupa*; Luyana: *mwandi*; Lozi: *mwanja*).[33]

Thus in its essentials we see the same spectrum of crops that was described by Gluckman in the 1940s, almost the last moment at which it was to be seen in this form. Briefly, the most striking change of the mid and later twentieth century has been the eclipse of sorghum as the main grain crop on the best soils. It is explained frequently that this is because maize is much less susceptible to bird attack (which is true) and thus the change of crop is to be understood as another aspect of the nucleation of society, for bird scaring is only effectively organised on the village scale; nuclear and small extended families do not command the labour to do it well on their own.[34] However, the late-nineteenth-century spectrum can be confirmed from contemporaneous observations: immediately after the political turbulence of 1884–5, people at Sesheke, one of the centres of unrest, were observed replanting cassava, beans, sweet potato, sorghum and maize in drained soil and millets on the sand. They told the observer, Waddell, that he would see greater variety in the Valley. In fact, four days before, Waddell's employer had visited the site of his future Mission Station for the first time. He described the villages on the slope of the Sefula hill as 'half hidden in their gardens of maize, "mautsa" [*mauza*, millet], sugar cane, manioc, etc.'. Waddell's informants were correct.[35]

So far I have shown from observations noted by European visitors that the elements of the agricultural system were stable from the 1850s to the

59

1880s and I have suggested that, since the introduction and spread of cultivars tend to be structural changes with long wavelengths of historical time, the pattern may have been stable for longer than that. But it is rather important to study the agricultural system of Bulozi on a much shorter time-scale, indeed sometimes looking for almost weekly changes during some spells of our period because there is a hypothesis that during this time one of these structural and therefore immensely important turning points occurred.

The 1890s brought plagues of locusts, human and cattle epidemic diseases, abnormally low floods followed by abnormally high floods and unusual cold to Bulozi. All that caused Clarence-Smith to describe the 1890s as 'a decade of especial tribulations of a biblical kind'.[36] The occurrence of the events is not really in dispute, but the interpretation placed upon them and the subsequent speculations erected upon those inferences is. For example, Mainga inferred from this catalogue of misfortune that Lozi agriculture crumbled under the onslaught, leaving a 'frightened, sick and famished nation' to face the human onslaught of the British South Africa Company administration at the end of the decade. Indeed, of recent years it has become quite popular to cast Nature in the role of the artillery bombardment 'softening up' African societies before the infantry assault of colonial rule.[37] I cannot judge the hypothesis for other situations, but is it correct here? If it is, it has important implications for how we can and should consider the high politics of the colonial impact; it should incline us to accept the sort of analyses which we have already been offered. However, I shall now suggest that it is not.

In this section and Section 4 of this chapter I shall demonstrate that the 'disasters' were not fatal to an agricultural system which was in fact dramatically strengthened during the 1890s; that the major means of that strengthening, Lewanika's drainage programme, was in fact facilitated by the abnormally low floods of the early 1890s; that the smallpox and rinderpest epidemics gave Lewanika specific and considerable political advantages on the eve of colonial rule which, together with patronage powers over newly drained land and his adroit use of the social machinery available to relieve stress, especially state gardens (*bonamukau*) and royal herds (*likomu za mbuwa*), resulted in a nation more cohesive and united than it had been for several generations at least, if not ever before. But before doing this, we must discover why the other dramatic and Hobbesian images have arisen.

Coillard, founder of the Zambezi Mission, saw the improvement of African agriculture to be an agreeable but not fundamental part of his work. He lost his box of seeds when a wagon en route to Sefula to establish the first Mission Station overturned in a river, so one of his first actions on arrival was to write off for 'coffee, tea, cotton and other tropical or semi-tropical produce' including guava, pawpaw, orange, lemon and tangerine seeds.[38] The seeds and Auguste Goy, a Swiss agricultural missionary-aide, both arrived at Sefula at the beginning of the next rains. The vegetables germinated but shrivelled in the sun; Goy found his environment equally inhospitable. Coillard thought that his helper's role should be one of growing food just for the use of the missionary families; Goy thought his task should be the propagation of new techniques through the establishment of a model farm with evangelisation following in the wake of good acts. In this he was supported by the other young missionaries, Jeanmairet and Louis Jalla at Sesheke, and a frequently acrimonious debate about the basic tactics of the Mission, made the more bitter by personal animosities, split the pioneers between February 1888 and August 1889. Events proved Coillard to be right. Whilst the Mission stimulated limited market gardening nearby and Jalla subsequently made a careful list of the new species they had introduced, it did not start a chain-reaction of improving agriculture, nor could it, since the new crops, like other aspects of the Mission's work, were restricted by the king. Only

M. GOY

Fig. 8 Auguste Goy.

fruit-seeds escaped him and especially *olonji* (a visibly recent loanword) spread up and down the floodplain margin.[39]

Coillard's desire to establish some source of food under his own control is easily understood. The letters and especially the private journal of his wife are dominated by the difficulties of obtaining food and in particular the harrowing hours of haggling over price.[40] 'Our Heavenly Father is mindful of our wants and supplies them day by day. The fish arrived just in time to be cooked for dinner', she wrote. Five days later, simply, 'I am thankful, oh so thankful to have been able to buy some food today'.[41] Her very close supervision of the foodstore was one of Goy's complaints against her, but on many days the missionaries went hungry. A boycott was an easy way for Lewanika to blackmail and taunt them.[42] After a year of eating almost nothing but sweet potato, Emma Jalla could not touch them again without revulsion. Her daughter also remembered an occasion when, after having to refuse a basket of sorely needed sorghum because the seller wanted an equal weight of trading beads, her mother collapsed in uncontrollable tears.[43]

Thus it was not surprising that for polemic and personal reasons the missionaries' public reports of the general food supply written for their European readers displayed the dimmest side. However, despite all their personal disappointments and privations, Jalla confided to his notebook, below a meticulous list of indigenous crops: 'Il n'y a jamais famine (seulem. disette) au Bo-Rotse ppt. [proprement] dit' (There is never famine (only shortage) in Bulozi proper). He made the same evaluation retrospectively in his Lozi language publication.[44] This judgment is widely reflected, from Lozi elite who might be expected to see the past rosily and from slaves and members of satellite tribes under tribute to the Lozi who might not.[45]

From a group of villages in the Kataba valley emerged this account: of them one, Lipaa, was that of a guardian of a nearby state garden, two others were commoner villages of old settlement, the third, Ikuñi, was established on Lewanika's orders in the 1900s. The histories of all the villages agreed that the major arterial canals were dug communally, the side drains individually by each village on its own land during Lewanika's time. The state garden was worked communally and a state storehouse stood near the royal *mafulo* (occasional floodtime residence) under the guardian's control. In later years, *Mulena Mukwae* Matauka spoke with pride of her Kataba canal and said that her best gardens were those in the Kataba valley. An elderly informant from Nakapu village paced out with me those areas of the valley that he remembered were cultivated when he was a child. The drainage canal in the southwestern part of the drained area shown on Fig. 9 is now invisible on the ground.[46] The point of the

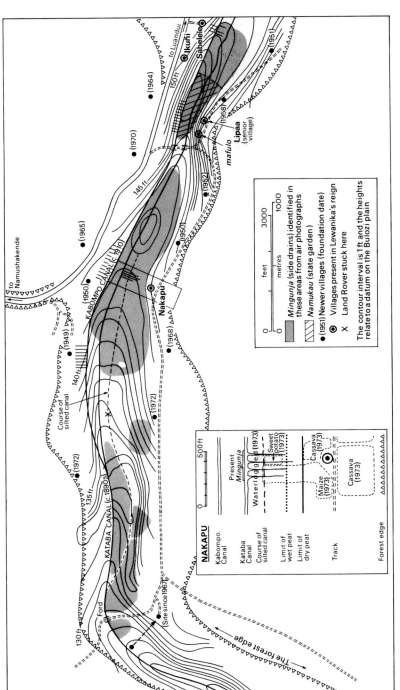

Fig. 9 Part of the Kataba valley, Senanga District.

63

example is clearest in the figure which corroborates the old men's tongues and feet: since we know that the layout and size of villages has not changed greatly, then Kataba had more cultivated land and a smaller population at the time of stress and therefore was better placed to survive it. The time of 'Mungole' (Coillard) – the 1890s – is remembered as a time of plenty which, corrected for rose tint, may mean not a time of dearth,[47] this without considering hunting, trade or the social relief system of the state.

Coillard selected Sefula as the site for his first Mission Station for many reasons – its elevation, its sorcerers' graveyard, but 'above all this river which one ascends by boat will enable us to carry the Gospel out to distant places. If we should have the means, we could canalise that river as far as the Zambezi.[48] His attitude to the canal, as the gardens, was that evangelisation came before all else and that all should be subordinated to that end.

Lewanika gave Coillard permission to recruit labour and within days of his arrival Auguste Goy had set to work to canalise the Sefula stream. Between 14 November 1887 and 10 February 1888 he supervised the construction of one and a quarter miles of canal, seven feet wide, in the Sefula valley, assisted by Mwanangombe[49] and Kamburu. He had to stop when he ran out of supplies and when his labour force went off to raid the Ila.[50]

Goy's canal does not seem to have been the first in Bulozi, for in the same month that he began work, Coillard's horse shied at 'a sort of canal. A deep and artificial stream' threequarters of the way from Sefula to the nearby village of Namboata.[51] Headman Nalumango told Rev. Burger that people had drained *sishanjo* gardens with *malomba* (furrows) before; it was the idea of a wider system using an arterial canal that was new.

On Wednesday, 4 January 1888, the Mission at Sefula welcomed a most significant visitor. 'He is intelligent, skilful with his hands, an ingenious workman, incomparable hunter and fisherman, influential councillor, eminent statesman, all that with a dignity which is not demeaning. . . He has a truly extraordinary influence over the king. Nothing is done without his consent.' This was Nalubutu, the man whom Coillard labelled in his public letters as the arch enemy of the Mission, leader of the 'Conservative Pagan' opposition to Lewanika's policy of welcoming contact.[52]

> He admired my study, the walls, the woodwork, the windows; he had to put his finger on the glass to satisfy himself that it was really there. Then he went and stood some distance away contemplating our roofs for a long time and heaving a deep sigh [he said], 'What a pity that I am old, I would learn to do all that. . .'. *But above all it was*

64

Fig. 10 Nalubutu.

> *Mr Goy's works that were marvelled at*. 'What a stream! It is a little Zambezi! And what food this land will produce! Little work [is needed] to extend the canal as far as the Zambezi. And that canal', he added, stressing each word, 'we shall make. . .'.[53]

In fact no one worked on any canals for more than a year. Goy lost his labourers in January and his patience with François Coillard's authoritarian attitudes and Christina Coillard's 'rather difficult character' before then. He left Sefula to go to Sesheke and in fact refused to return to work under Coillard personally.[54]

Lewanika was also otherwise occupied, busy raiding and then distributing Ila cattle for most of 1888 and building his huge new royal barge *Nalikwanda* early in 1889. However, canals were not forgotten. He reportedly gave Coillard ten head of cattle to help defray the expenses of the Sefula canal.[55]

On 20 May 1889, Mwanangombe began the seven and a quarter miles of canal still to be dug to reach the river, but he made slow progress for lack of spades.[56] He worked whilst Coillard was negotiating the Ware Concession for mineral rights to the southeast periphery of Bulozi, but when his employer had accompanied Ware down river, he barely made progress. He was so short of tools that after two hours negotiation he and Mme Coillard had to barter a printed cotton blanket, a loin cloth, a head-scarf and Mwanangombe's own linen jacket for one spade, 'as he *must* have the spade for his work'.[57]

By April 1890, the canal had cost Coillard £150 and was still not finished,[58] but Lewanika and Nalubutu had seen that the idea would work and very soon after the end of the Lochner negotiations (described below) the first of three winter seasons of major construction began. Coillard had earlier lent Lewanika a trench spade and blacksmiths had made a 'fare attemp immating it. But as many were required, they contented themselves by converting their primitive hoes into spades.'[59]

Lewanika's first project was strategic – a five mile communication link between Lealui and the Zambezi. The Sikalongo canal necessitated the joining up of some existing natural waterways and the tapping of a lake to increase its flow. By November 1890, 'hundreds of chiefs and thousands of people' had completed the excavations, but there was a technical hitch: the feeder lake was not providing sufficient water.[60] So the end of the construction season left Lewanika with food for thought. Coillard was not happy either. His impotence compared to the king's ability to mobilise labour reduced him to rage when he rode out to see his canal in December and found Mwanangombe and his men sitting around or sleeping at four o'clock in the afternoon.[61]

The 1891 flood was small and Lewanika moved to his floodtime camp late. Accompanied by hundreds of canoes, the two *Nalikwandas* – the old one of 1888 and Lewanika's monster of 1889 – came to a *mafulo* (camp) at Sana near Sefula. The entire mission paddled down Mwanangombe's completed canal for the first time to welcome the king.[62] However, signs of changing loyalties began to show in Mwanangombe, the canal builder. Coillard became anxious when he saw him more and more in the company of the apostate Seajika who was now Lewanika's secretary. When Lewanika complained bitterly to Coillard that the Mission was taking no new apprentices, Coillard's anxiety was compounded with irritation, because the previous July the king had summarily ordered the Mission's first trained apprentice, Kanoti Nalumango, and the other apprentices, to come and build him a palace at Lealui.[63]

Lewanika went hunting in the hinterland and returned to Lealui on 22 or 23 May after only a brief stay at the floodplain margin. Coillard visited him a few weeks later and the king told him that 'the next month' he was going to dig a canal as far as the Lui river.[64] Coillard scoffed. In fact, during the 1891 construction season, the Sikalongo canal was connected to a new trunk canal about seventeen miles long which ran northeast from Lealui to the mouth of the Namitome valley. There it merged with the Namitome stream, some miles of which were also canalised that year. When James Johnston, a visiting medical missionary, saw it in December 1891 he wrote of a waterway fifteen feet wide and six feet deep, 'navigable for large canoes and tapping one of the most thickly populated districts of the Zambezi valley'.[65] Without considering the canalisation of the Namitome stream, the new trunk canal – the Mwayowamo – of the dimensions and length which Johnston recorded had involved the excavation of over eight million cubic feet of earth in about five months.

During the 1892 season, the canalisation of the Namitome stream and its tributaries and the digging of *malomba* (secondary furrows linking side drains (*mingunja*) to the main arterial canals) in the pans thus linked to the drainage system was substantially advanced, although work continued on the system in the following two seasons.[66]

Lewanika then turned his attention to the potential of the valley margin peat (*sishanjo*) soils. In 1893–4 one of the biggest floods in living memory occurred. In May 1894 Coillard revisited Mongu hill, one of the sites offered to him on his first visit ten years before, and from there looked out over the flooded landscape. He decided to go north by canoe up the floodplain edge.

> Passing Kanyonyo I wanted to visit the large village of Mukoko. How astonished I was to find myself paddling in a wide and deep

67

canal! Lewanika had certainly spoken of it to us, but as something of slight importance. However, when it is completed – and it nearly is – it will drain all the edge of the valley from Nañoko, the temporary capital [near Limulunga], as far as Sefula, more than twenty kilometers [in fact nearer nineteen miles] and will empty its waters into our canal. What is best is the enormous quantity of arable land thus recovered by this drainage. Here then is our canal number three.[67]

During the next fifteen years, drainage works continued. Extensive pans were drained at Nangula and Ndanda in the eastern bushlands, other streams were canalised and valleys drained, notably the Litoya valley in Senanga district and, in the Lui valley, the Luandui, Kalendela and Nangalala canals fed into the Lui river system. In 1893 when there were rumours of an Ndebele invasion, Lewanika mused aloud to Coillard the idea of damming the Lui river and flooding the entire valley as a strategic barrier. All the major canals could be considered strategic; informants were of the opinion that the Sikalongo/Mwayowamo system was carried to the south of Lealui, thus making a barrier parallel to the Lui valley, for similar strategic reasons.[68]

To the west of the floodplain, the *Mulena Mukwae* Matauka had a canal built to Lukona/Musisimi, draining parts of the Simunyange plain, and Lewanika built one in the mouth of the Ndoka valley.[69] To undertake these massive projects, Lewanika and Matauka mobilised their people during the slack period of winter through the *makolo*, the same social units in which, in their military guise, in 1888 they had gone off to raid the Ila. The descriptions make it quite clear that this was not 'slave' labour as Johnston, the passing visitor, had assumed: in November 1890, Coillard wrote of 'bodies of men running from all sides in their thousands' and controlled by 'hundreds of chiefs'. Waddell was more practical and precise. 'The work was soon accomplished by thousands of men who were summonsed with their respective chief who acted as forman or managin Engenears.'[70] Indeed, it was not manpower, but 'managin Engenears' which Lewanika lacked, as he had already complained to Coillard. He 'repossessed', in Waddell's word, Andrease Mwanangombe, the builder of the Sefula canal, in January 1892 and the following month ranted at Coillard, telling him that he was worn out and that what he wanted and needed were men to train artisans.[71] Earlier writers have tended to assume that the king's request should be taken at face value, and that it shows what he considered the most important gain to be made from his contact with the missionaries. One of the aims of the rest of this book is to restore this indisputable desire of Lewanika's to its correct proportion in relation to other less easily perceived aspects of his conduct. But this is not to deny that his achievement in canal building was quite extraordinary. Fig. 11 gives an impression of what was done in these years; it is an objective indication of Lewanika's real power to be taken more seriously than Coillard's opinions.[72]

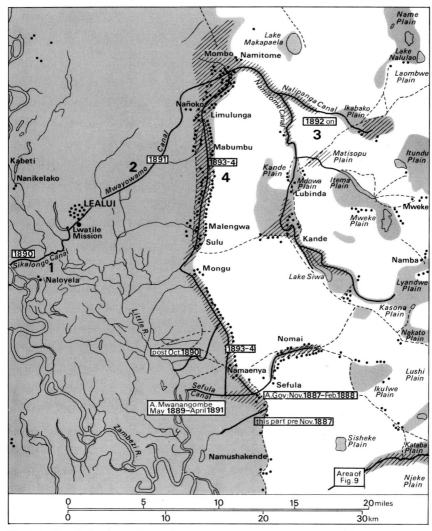

Fig. 11 Canals in central Bulozi: November 1887 to approximately 1894. Dates show when work began, and numbers 1–4 show the sequence of construction. Cross-hatching indicates areas where side drains can be confirmed from air photographs. The floodplain is shaded.

The purpose of the undertaking was expressed in the name of the Mwayowamo: 'Who does not wash there shall not be rid of dirt',[73] i.e. whoever does not benefit from the canal has only himself to blame. Lewanika followed up the construction by establishing villages of young people on the banks of the new waterways to help bring the newly drained land into production and, of course, incidentally to strengthen his patronage ties. Near Limulunga, some areas were reserved as *namukau* (state garden), some allocated as title land (*Ngambela* has sizeable holdings there), but most were granted with village sites in the usual fashion.[74]

The new acreages would have been coming into production progressively after 1892–3. It is impossible to know exact figures but from the foregoing description they must have been considerable. The Namitome arterial canal system alone is over forty miles long. Kataba and Ushaa were not isolated examples.

Therefore when we neutralise the melodramatic tendencies in published Mission sources, and pierce the ossifying effect of such periodic data as there are, when we read the evidence of our feet and of air photographs and are thus able to compensate for the rosy tinge in oral information, an interpretation of all these diverse sources points towards an ecologically resilient, long established and effective agricultural range for the later 1880s made additionally productive by the concentrated application of surplus labour at the turn of the decade. It is reasonable to visualise the produce of the newly opened and therefore highly fertile peat soils (*sishanjo*) combining with the swelling of the national herds as a result of the raids upon the Ila in 1888 and the Luvale in 1892 to cushion the impact of most aspects – the smallpox epidemic of 1892–3 excepted – of 'disaster decade'.[75]

4.3 SOME DEGREES OF FREEDOM

In my initial survey of labour, the work of women and the work of slaves were lumped together. That is correct as a generalisation of how slave labour entered the economy, but it is necessary to be more precise about the nature of the institution if it is to be positioned in all its social dimensions. Few transplanted concepts possess the resonance of 'slave' and it is possible to be misled.[76]

The Marxian sociologists Hindess and Hirst described a 'slave mode of production' as one where the labourers are separated from the means of production and alone are unable to set them in motion. Since slaves had their own gardens in Bulozi, the definition does not apply. Indeed, when the concept of this separation and especially of the slave having no part in activating the system is scrutinised with the sensitivity recently devoted to the ante bellum Southern United States, one wonders where to look for this 'mode'.[77]

Two other criteria offer a more illuminating use of the concept of slavery. Strickland called a slave one who is the legal chattel of another and may be 'sold, punished and exploited with near impunity'. Finley suggested that as well as this powerlessness, weight should be given to the extent of 'deracination' of the slave within the society where he worked.[78] These are the benchmarks in the choices of nomenclature made here.

The first task is to define terms. 'Slavery' is commonly used to translate three Lozi words describing two different concepts: *butanga,* and *buzike* or *bukoba*. Jalla described slavery in Bulozi in detail and since his evidence has subsequently been most influential, it is worth examining it carefully. 'No-one is free in bo-Rotse. The King is by right the master of all, chiefs like others. He takes into his service whoever he wishes, making the sons of the highest chiefs his personal servants. But he is not free himself, autocrat that he is. He also fears the Ma-Rotse.' Jalla then went on to list by number four categories of slavery: 'domestic slavery', 'slaves brought as tribute', 'slaves captured on raids' and 'slaves in compensation or settlement of debt'.[79]

In these descriptions it was not difficult for both missionaries and administrators to observe that perhaps ninety per cent of the population were ex-slaves; that 'on sait qu'au Bo-Rotse proprement dit les esclaves forment la majorité'.[80] But in so doing they were permitting themselves an admittedly convenient congregation of several discrete Lozi institutions under a banner which their respective audiences expected to see.

On closer examination, Jalla's description embraced:

(1) *Lifunga*: a system under which children of chiefly families were brought up in the royal courtyard where they were pages and domestic servants. Subsequently they were placed as chiefs or judges themselves or given in strategic marriages. Luboshi (Lewanika) was brought up in this way at the court of Sipopa.[81]

(2) *Butanga*: everyone, including the king, was a *mutanga*; he was *mutanga wa sichaba* (servant of the nation). Jalla correctly mentioned the reciprocity entailed and the point is essential. It was central to the relationship of king and nation as the next chapter shows. It was the dominant theme in commoner praise-sayings (*maloko*) addressing the king, and in the songs of the royal band and the jokes of the jester at the time of the installation (*coliso*). *Mutanga* is best translated as 'the common man' with an implication of social responsibility.[82]

71

(3) Slaves in settlement of debt were more correctly bondsmen. There was no prohibition against such bonding in legal settlement and no excluded class not at risk: 'If there is no foreigner, a Lozi may enslave someone he knows well.'[83] Luyana has no precise word for 'freedom'; in Lozi, the Kololo *tukuluho* is used. But the debate must not be tinted all one hue. The task, as Finley described it, is to locate where on the spectrum between equally notional rightlessness and absolute freedom was the 'bundle of rights' which each person possessed.[84]

(4) 'Slaves brought as tribute' were *liketiso* in the strict sense which is revealed in the derivation of the word: it is from the verb *ku keta* (to choose) and thus has the meaning 'that which is set apart' with the implication of special decision. In this it carries a different weight from the other word used for tribute, *ñamba*. But such slaves were like those in the last category:

(5) 'Slaves captured on raids', for both were called *ba buzike* or *makoba*; but *buzike* really covers both categories. *Buzike* is a Toka-Leya loanword. These captives were in particular the spoil of raids in Lewanika's reign upon the Ila to the west and especially upon the Toka-Leya to the south. The linguistic and social connections are therefore unsurprising. These people tended to be concentrated near royal establishments.

Let the history of one couple of *ba buzike* serve to illustrate their life. The husband was captured in Lewanika's last raid on the Ila in 1888 at which time he was a small baby. He was raised at Lealui, but permitted his roots, for he was socialised as an Ila. Ila was his first language and some of his teeth were removed in the Ila pattern. He was attached to a minor chief's household where he was a cattle herd and was trained in handcrafts. His first wife was a Lozi and he was placed with her on royal land at Namboata. They divorced and he married his second wife in about 1927. She was a Toka and was brought as *liketiso*. From the age of puberty she laboured in the fields of the *Mulena Mukwae* Matauka at Nalolo. In 1922, the Native Commissioner insisted that these women be paid and in consequence she was permitted to leave. Prior to that time, her life was like that of a slave in the ante bellum South. She and her companions toiled under threat of the *pafa* (hippo-hide whip), although its actual use was infrequent. She was fed and housed in a village set apart from others. But in 1922, when offered the choice of pay or departure, a substantial number elected to remain, although she did not.[85]

In the opinion of this old couple, people under *buzike* were never more than a small proportion of the population. The general incidence will never be known, but there is consistency in oral sources which include the Lozi elite, satellite tribes and missionaries resident in the 1930s that people under *buzike* were about a quarter to a third of the population in Lewanika's time. Since the positions of slave houses in floodplain villages can still be roughly identified, a further check is possible. The ratio between the inner core of villages and the outer perimeter of unenclosed (slave) houses is about three to one.[86]

Those held *ka buzike* in villages retained their roots and often their language; there was no religious distinction between them and their masters as there was between Nigerian Hausa farm-slaves and theirs.[87] The institution did not have long geographical stability – their masters had only a short time before been under alien rule – and all the evidence points towards frequent movement in status.

Ex-slaves relate that they were treated like other villagers in all respects except two. They could hold land and be married into the family, they addressed the headman as 'Father', took his name, and could be rewarded or chastised at his discretion. But they had no right of movement away from the village, nor control over their own time. This was expressed by a Luyana proverb with baleful succinctness: 'A slave is like [dry] bark which softens when placed in water.'[88] It is because of this aspect of powerlessness, and by this criterion alone among those proffered, that *buzike* is correctly translated as slavery. In practice, the village headman exercised the same sort of control over all his people, but the slave, like the child, had more difficulty and faced more immediate danger in defying it.

The categories of slave and free were not mutually exclusive. Jalla recorded that a Lozi could be deprived of rights and work off debts in bondage. Equally, a slave could by marriage or act of his master's will shed his old status.[89] The best illustrations are of Coillard's people. His first convert Andrease Mwanangombe ('Nguana Ngombe' in Coillard's texts) was a slave, son of an Ila father and a Toka mother, given to Coillard to be his servant. Similarly the first Lozi evangelist Philip Nyondo was in origin an Ila slave. Andrease became apostate in January 1892 and went back to work for Lewanika who made him emissary (*ndumeleti*) at the strategic border settlement of Imusho (on the present Caprivi Strip border). Nyondo remained an evangelist, was made a *sikombwa* (steward) and given land by the king.[90]

Birth was no absolute determinant of position in either direction. The relationship was encapsulated in the saying, *Si ku nuinine ku si tundo*, 'Although I am your chief, I know where you come from', i.e. although

73

you are under my power, I know that in origin you are my relative. Such awareness of interrelatedness and mutual dependence reflected, on the one hand, the restricted possibilities for materially expressed differentiation of status in a society of limited technology; on the other – and contingently – the concept of ownership in such a society.

Recall that it was only during the next generation that technology offered widespread help at the level of the individual cultivator standing in his individual garden. Given the limited ways in which productivity could be enhanced vertically in the fifteen years following Lewanika's return from exile (late 1885), the only strategy, and also the wisest in a temperamental environment, was to expand horizontally. The concentrated and similar labour of bondsmen, slave and free within the *makolo* (explained in Chapter 5, Section 3) created Lewanika's network of canals, at once agricultural and strategic, which was complemented by the king's placement of new villages to exploit the drained land and by the policing of the communal work of old villages. But secondly, without a concept of individual property in land, but instead one which projected *relationship*, such fluidity in social status was logically entailed. That the state of *buzike* was both undesirable and reversible and in either case a fate of men regarded as men, not as chattels, was implied through its other name, *makoba*; in a telling dictionary entry, Jalla gave a 'slaveowner' as *mulen'a makoba* which has two levels of translation: 'master of slaves', but also 'master of spells that are effective at long range'.[91] *Buzike* was a threat to the individual on a par with evil magic (*buloi*).

If *butanga* is thought to have been no firm social delineator and if even *buzike* was enmeshed in a flexible web of social possibilities, is it helpful to talk of classes, and in particular to seek for evidence of class conflict in this situation? The answer is a qualified yes to the former, no to the latter. First the qualifications.

What you see depends upon the place from where you look. From the standpoint of the relationship of individuals to the material means of production, Bulozi might fit closely to Worthington's ratio of one to nine 'clean handed' to 'dirty handed'.[92] That ratio reflects the narrow band of technical possibility; it does not explain the available evidence describing Lozi society. In order to do that the simultaneous, equally influential and intangible needs of men must be considered. Then it is possible to give explanatory force to the actors' own descriptions and behaviour. Oral testimony and an examination of social institutions in its light reveal that social differentiation was labelled by reference to kin and to the *redistributive* process. The only people who identified themselves vis-à-vis their neighbours through reference to a process of production at all were those once under *buzike*.

Then here can be seen a conspicuous and self-conscious minority. Do these people evince class struggle, open or repressed? The test lies in the events surrounding the Emancipation Decree of 1906. I will discuss these events elsewhere, but being so emotionally charged, they percolate through all contemporaneous European comments, which offer benignity or horror, to taste.[93] Most researchers have also chosen in these terms, but since there are no data to confirm these opinions (which is all they are) either way, a more oblique approach is indicated which tries to fit the events into what else is known about the history of Lozi slavery, especially for the years following the decree.

Matauka's fieldhands are a conspicuous example, of value because their fate was extreme and therefore noticed. They were observed and written about in 1902; they were reported again in 1920 and their condition had not changed. Worthington wrote more truthfully in private than it was expedient to admit in public when he explained to the High Commissioner after the Proclamation of Emancipation that 'the status of slavery (tho' not yet of course the habit in the minds of the people) has been abolished by law'.[94]

The bracketed portion of that observation loomed large in the evidence of a murdered woman's husband twenty years after the Proclamation.

> I have known the accused for many years and have lived with him for many years since I was a piccanin . . . The accused went after Nyantumba and said to her, 'What right have you to go where you like, here and there, you are only a slave, without asking my permission . . .' 'I am going to kill you because you will not obey me.' The accused did not address Nyantumba by her name, he addressed her as 'my slave. . .'. He told me to take Nyantumba's baby. This I did. . . The accused tied her around the ankles and her arms behind her back. He then tied her around the neck. . . He ordered me to go a little way away. I went fifty paces and remained kneeling. . . Nyantumba was lying on her stomach after being tied. The accused then pulled very tight the rope round her neck. He used both hands and also used his foot against her shoulders. I came closer and found Nyantumba dead but still twitching. . . I saw my wife being killed but I could not interfere because I was afraid. . . I thought that the accused would kill me too.

When the body was discovered:

> The accused replied that he had murdered her and asked me to untie him and that he would pay compensation with cattle.[95]

These two pieces of evidence exist because of Native Commissioner

Simey's outrage and a Lozi native court's desire to get the accused, Kapata, executed. So although they cannot be regarded as typical, each illustrates an important point. The first is the social effect of constraints within the agricultural process.

It will be recalled that the women fieldhands did not all seethe out of the cauldron of their condition when the lid was raised. If working for the Princess Chieftainess was hard it was also hard, although less conspicuous to the blinkered gaze of Native Commissioners, to be a woman at home. If you were to be paid, it was arguably better to work for the Chieftainess. That this was their logic may be inferred from the fact that when they were not paid, they too left.[96]

The murder case revealed how soft the bark could become, in the terms of the proverb. It could be read as an example of violence suppressing reaction, but its main significance was that it appeared at all in the records of the colonial courts. Generally cases of this kind only appeared if the Lozi so desired.[97] Because it transcended the boundaries of acceptable behaviour, Kapata's case pointed back to that boundary. It reinforces the impression that the version of social reciprocity practised towards slaves, whilst rendered more paternalistic by the degree of power in play, was nonetheless not divorced from the concepts governing behaviour on other rungs in this stratified society.[98]

This same impression is made by the absence of 'combination' among *batu ba buzike*. It cannot be wished into the data by assumption, neither can an image of repressed potential be comfortably entertained. The Lozi state did not possess the technology or institutionalisation of violence to achieve that. There is no good evidence that the 'regiments' (*makolo*) ever served this purpose, as has been suggested.[99] Yet it would be equally insensitive to read the absence of a Lozi Spartacus as evidence of craven passivity.

Writing of Languedoc village society after the end of the Albigensian crusade, Le Roy Ladurie conducted his study with the same logic and pattern that I employ here, permitting the indigenously defined units of society to give form to the work. In the Lozi case, it was the *lapa* (courtyard), in Languedoc it was the *domus* (household) that was central to face-to-face society. Working outwards from this viewpoint we may observe the behaviour just described in both southern France and central Africa. Just as a slave member of a Lozi village regarded the village headman less as an oppressor, more as a source of potential advantage, so did the shepherd-servant Pierre Maury regard the heads of the households where he worked; just as village headmen regarded the powers above them less as a force of homogenous oppression, more as resources of influence to be mobilised to their local advantage – the very grist of a relationship of patronage – so did the rural cliques and rival households of Montaillou regard the seigneurie.[100] People like the Namboata couple could be swept up into the wider Lozi identity and the presence and practice of these possibilities might carry more weight – and hope – in slaves' minds than other courses of action. The high degree of incorporation to be seen in the genealogies and geography of contemporary villages is witness to this. But for most male slaves the reality of manumission was the transfer of their main labour from the coerced production of starch staple crops in the fields to the catching or herding of the providers of relish.

4.4 *BUSUNSO*: FISH, GAME AND CATTLE

A relish of cassava leaf was a sign of poverty and lean times. The best *busunso* was of animal proteins and fats: fish and milk were the commonest, meat was a treat and fat meat was the food of kings.

I shall argue that fish and game formed one category, cattle another. The categories may be distinguished on practical and cultural grounds, for whilst the use of fish and game animals posed mainly technical problems, cattle, although providing a less common relish through their meat, were more intimately part of the social fabric, more valued and more thought about. As Evans-Pritchard wrote of the cattle keepers and farmers of a south Sudanese floodplain, '*cherchez la vache* is the best advice that can be given to those who desire to understand Nuer behaviour'. It is not a bad guide to Bulozi either, as this section will show.[101] Here I am concerned to produce conspicuous evidence relating to rituals, imagery, cattle vocabularies, the role of cattle in the domestic economy and systems of ownership. Later, aware of the deep commitments which this evidence has illustrated, we shall be able to use this knowledge in judging aspects of the colonial contact. But first to fish.

The river system of the upper Zambezi supported three main types of food fish: varieties of bream (*papati, mu, njinji, seo, mbufu*), varieties of barbel (*ndombe (minga* when small), *silutupwi*) and tiger-fish (*ngweshi*). They have been there for as long as concerns us; all these names are Luyana (*ngweshi* is spelt *ngwesi*, the only alteration). Livingstone described tiger-fish and 'perch' in 1853; Coillard recorded the names and described the species in 1885. 'A fisherman' in Luyana is '*aluyi*'.[102] As Gluckman rightly observed, 'Fish are Lozi relish.'[103] Bream, tiger-fish and crocodiles form an ecological balance, as was discovered in the late 1950s: when the crocodiles were massacred, the tiger-fish population exploded and the bream populations consequently fell.[104] But the balance was intact in the 1880s when the arriving missionaries found crocodiles to be very numerous and aggressive and fish to be remarkably plentiful.[105]

So fish (and most types of game) were like a crop which men harvested in the same way that women harvested sorghum or maize. Fishing was not a ritually specialised occupation although certain types of net and areas of water were restricted to certain people at certain times. But it was always the techniques, not the act of fishing which was controlled. The various types of nets and fish dams used at different stages of the flood were the focus of attention and dispute – not the fish. Fish dams (*bwalelo*) and proprietary fishing rights were therefore an aspect of land law, and were inherited, transferred, disputed and adjudicated in the same way as land.[106]

Fish are conveniently small pieces of protein and could be obtained directly, through fishing, or indirectly, through exchange, in many different ways. They were common relish and culturally neutral. Fish do not figure in any of the important life rituals of the small or wider community. Fish were the commodity collected by Isimwaa to make up his tribute to the first male chief in a common version of that tradition, but they feature as objects, not as animals. Similarly, fish were predators or prey, no more, in a fisherman's song of the 1890s.[107] I know of only one common proverb and no praise-saying about fish alone, as distinct from fishing.[108]

The eating of fish is regulated by only rather prosaic taboos. For example, a girl before puberty (*mwalyanjo*) should not eat fish gills lest they make her labia become hard like them. Fish are plentiful, a point made eloquently by the convention that the *Litunga*, or anyone wishing to show his importance, should not turn over his fish to eat the other side. Perhaps plenty breeds contempt, for along with millet beer fish have been the medium through which poison was administered, at least since Lewanika's time. *Ku ca litapi* – to eat fish – is still an understood euphemism for 'to be poisoned'. Fish are Lozi poison, too.

Small game – duiker, buck, etc. – were really only larger and rarer pieces of protein, also a crop to be harvested, but hunted and distributed under stricter rules. A communal hunt in which antelopes trapped on islands by the rising flood were slaughtered for the annual provision of skins and dried meat, just as fish were communally speared when trapped in pools by the falling flood, was organised by chiefs and sometimes the *Litunga* oversaw it, as in 1887. Large game was even more closely controlled. All game was owned by the *Litunga*, but he released this property from his absolute control in the last of his initiation rites – a hunt in an area of high plain called Sanya, just south of Limulunga.[109] But cattle were entirely different: *Nakawa lu kula mubonda* ([The gift of] a cow erases all faults).

During the last half of the nineteenth century, the Lozi herds contained cattle of two distinct types. Livingstone described them closely in 1853:

> They have two breeds of cattle among them. One called the Batoka, because captured from that tribe, is of diminutive size, but very beautiful; and closely resembles the shorthorns of our own country. . . The other, or Barotse ox, is much larger, and comes from the fertile Barotse valley. They stand high on their legs, often nearly six feet at the withers; and they have large horns.[110]

Both were strains of Sanga stock, that is, Zebu based crossbreeds. The 'Batoka' cattle were Ila/Tonga shorthorn Sanga; the 'Barotse' breed, a cross between Longhorn humpless and cervico-thoracic humpless Zebu. The 'Barotse' were very similar to the Ngami cattle to the south in Bechuanaland, which the traveller and trader James Chapman described in 1862 as 'large, lank cattle with very long and ponderous horns'.[111] In 1882 and again in 1888, the Lozi raided many more shorthorn Sanga from the Ila people, and so in Coillard's photograph of cattle at Kazungula in 1885 and in other, literary, sources of the 1890s, the types of cattle may be distinguished as easily as was possible for Livingstone.[112]

It has long been thought that Sanga cattle entered central Africa from the north. That view is refined in a recent theory suggesting that their diffusion was closely linked to the cultivation of land which thereby created ecological 'interzones' hostile to tsetse fly. Through these zones the cattle could pass down the forest/savanna border into the Zambezi valley and thence to the fly-free floodplain.[113]

Throughout our period, Bulozi had a cattle reputation. In 1853 Chapman noted the passage of a man 'sent by Dr Livingstone for a further supply of provisions, as he intended going to Barotseland, the land of cattle'.[114] When he reached it the next month, Chapman's rival, Livingstone, wrote that 'The great valley is not put to a tithe of the use it might be. It is covered with coarse succulent grasses, which afford ample pasturage for large herds of cattle; these thrive wonderfully and give milk copiously to their owners.' Livingstone saw these herds to be the main determinant of social geography, 'The mounds on which the towns and villages are built being all small, and the people require to live apart on account of their cattle.'[115] Serpa Pinto echoed this opinion twenty-five years later: 'The Luianas are no great tillers of the land, but they are great rearers of cattle. Their herds constitute their chief wealth.'[116] Four years later, the missionary Arnot saw large herds of cattle beside the river between Nalolo and Lealui; he thought that the Lozi were 'all, more or less, breeders of cattle'. On his first visit to Lealui, Coillard saw the 'king's herds' grazing, whilst the early impression of the Methodist missionary,

Arthur Baldwin, was that 'most of their humaneness is showered on their cattle. . . They never kill any of their stock unless some chief is passing and wants food.'[117]

The following year, a passing observer saw, presumably, some of the raided Ila cattle near Lealui: 'The grassy plains on either side of us abounded with cattle of small size, but in splendid condition', while in 1895, another traveller found 'small muscular cattle with smooth hair and short horns' and also 'far more powerful' Barotse cattle proper at the Njoko river, near the northern limit of the rinderpest epidemic probably active at that time. In the same year, the missionary Auguste Goy, now married and stationed at Sesheke, described the very numerous herds of cattle which enlivened the monotonous plain near Nalolo.[118]

The exception to this consensus was a subsequently influential passage where Coillard described the Lozi as 'not at all a pastoral people. . . The Makololo initiated them a little into the pastoral life. . . They kill and eat like greedy children beginning with the best. When the herd has vanished, each man looks at his neighbour and raises the cry, "To the Mashukulumboe [i.e. the Ila]".'[119]

Thus Coillard sets the tone for a chapter condemning the last great cattle raid. Seeking the worst vilification of it that he could imagine, Coillard called it 'The [Paris] Commune [of 1871] in an uncivilised [*sauvage*] land'; his editors removed the epithet, presumably because of the unlikely possibility, given the solid bourgeois readership of such publications, that someone might be offended. Unlike the contents of most of Coillard's public letters, the passage was not drawn from a basis in the private journal. It was added to embellish the letter whose primary concern was to interpret behaviour: 'Who can foretell the moral – rather let us say *immoral* and political – consequences of these five or six months of national licentiousness, the letting loose of the passions of all these savage tribes. . .' It is unsupported in other primary written or oral sources (including Coillard's observations in his journal) and has, in my opinion, been taken incorrectly.[120]

At the time that Gluckman wrote, his ideas were cast within the restrictive framework of Herskovits' 'cattle complex'.[121] This typology has been superseded by a more viable economically defined 'spectrum' image, ranging from notional 'pure' pastoralists to agriculturalists.[122] On it, the Lozi would sit well towards the latter, but they are on the spectrum, for whilst I shall shortly show how cattle were integral to different scales of the political economy of late-nineteenth-century Bulozi, they were also integral to different scales of the moral economy, because cattle possessed powerful cultural significance.[123] A legacy of the 'cattle complex' is that this last phrase might be assumed to mean a mystical, irrational devotion to cattle, often seen in an overriding desire to accumulate animals for 'prestige'. This is part of the history of anthropological theories, not of the Lozi, who used their cattle with culture-specific rationality. The commonly employed criterion of rationality has been taken as willingness to sell stock for cash or barter. In Bulozi changing circumstances might or might not favour sale. Particularly in the early years of the twentieth century circumstances fluctuated greatly and both responses may be seen.[124] Therefore this is not a very useful distinction. We must look elsewhere for culture-specific rationality.

Below it will be shown that the kingship expressed and guarded the core values of society with the greatest visible intensity. Therefore the involvement of cattle and of cattle imagery in important moments of royal *rites de passage* suggest the area where we might begin our search and the type of explanation which we might use.

The association of cattle and kingship begins beyond the horizon of tradition in unstructured time. There the praise-saying *ngomb'a Mbuyu* in its name and its opening lines associates cattle with Mbuywamwambwa, 'mother' of the nation: 'Cow of Mbuyu! Famous member of the royal family renowned for generosity! Do not praise the cow if it feeds you and your children, but praise the king for daring to give it to a poor man!'[125] The connection between Mbuywamwambwa and cattle is echoed in two other traditions: the one, that Mbuywamwambwa gave birth alternately to a calf and to a child with horns of flesh which were removed with medicines, is well known, appearing in the *Litaba za Sichaba*.[126] It relates to the praise-saying. The other is less well known: that the *Liombekalala*, the white water cow, is in fact Mbuywamwambwa, and it relates to the rituals of kingship. One analogy used for the installation rites of the *Litunga* is that the candidate is licked on the night of his installation by *Liombekalala*.[127]

The cattle associations continue. In a version of the quarrel between Mbuywamwambwa's sons, Mboo and Mwanambinyi, given to Coillard in the 1890s, their test of strength was through a contest between their favourite bulls which Mwanambinyi's lost.[128] A praise-name of the *Litunga* is *ngochana* (small calf). Completely white and completely black cattle were frequently used in the rituals of the royal graves, where milk was the usual medium through which the spirit of the deceased king was consulted.[129] On the occasions of national emergency when *sombo* (ritual sacrifice) was made at Nakaywe, the priest-guardian Ilinangana threw all types of seeds and plants on a piece of bare ground and then slaughtered oxen and bullocks over it.[130] Similar sacrifice of cattle was made at a *Litunga*'s funeral. A 'beast of mourning' was the correct gift to show sympathy with the bereaved, as Lewanika did to Coillard when Mme Coillard died.[131]

Lozi of all ranks were ideally welcomed at birth with a calf named for the child, and boys were educated in the cattle camps. Cattle were infrequently used as bride-price in Lewanika's time for, as will be seen, other methods of controlling ownership existed. But a wedding feast ox (*sichabuhobe*) presented by the groom and not part of the dowry (*sionda*) might be eaten. Divorce could be obtained on payment of an ox as fine to the previous husband.[132] People were compensated at law, mourned and buried with cattle.

Intimate involvement with cattle, behaviour and images is evident in detailed vocabularies for cattle diseases and cures and cattle management which I have heard used but of which I have only an inadequate knowledge. It is also to be seen in the specialised cattle nouns; I know of eighteen covering the age span of cattle. The nouns give coarse definition, but colour adjectives give fine focus upon each individual within a herd. Thus it is easily understood that complex permutations are possible. Then there is a vocabulary of verbs of cattle behaviour which offers further precision.

Two points need to be made about adjectives. Lozi, like many Bantu languages, is poorly supplied with these parts of speech; its subtlety and gradation comes from manipulation of verb prefixes and suffixes. So when there are adjectives, it is worth looking at them with care. Therefore it is significant that of all Lozi colour adjectives, those relating to cattle hues are by far the most refined. Table 3, showing the non-cattle colour adjectives, illustrates this. Compare the cattle colour and marking adjectives in Table 4.

Why this concern? In terms of the 'cattle complex' this demonstration of its existence is sufficient explanation; but the moral and political economies are inseparable. The link was clear in the praise-saying *ngomb'a Mbuyu* which later on eulogises cattle as 'a basket: when you go to them you come away with milk and with cattle dung'.

TABLE 3. *Basic colour adjectives in Lozi*

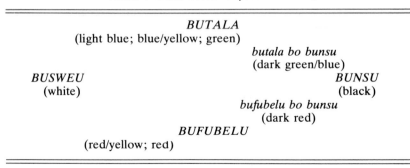

BUTALA
(light blue; blue/yellow; green)

butala bo bunsu
(dark green/blue)

BUSWEU   *BUNSU*
(white)   (black)

bufubelu bo bunsu
(dark red)

BUFUBELU
(red/yellow; red)

82

TABLE 4. *Adjectives of cattle colour and markings*[a]

Plain colours

White
Sweu
Swanyana

Grey
Puzwa
Puluzwana

Dark brown
Soto
Sotwana

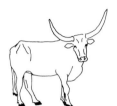

Black
Nsu
Swana[b]

Grey-blue buff
Seta
Setana

Red brown[c]
Kunoñu
Kunwana[b]

Patterns

Black and white *nkone*[d]
Kozwa
Kozwana

Black and white
spots or patches
of flecks
Tululi
Tuluzana

Red and white (often
nkone pattern)
Silu
Silwana

Black and white with a
stripe over the back and
around the chest
Sasa
Sasana

Brown and white
spotted
Paswa
Paswana

White muzzle (any body
colour)
Sumu
Sunyana

---

a The upper adjective of each pair is masculine, the lower feminine.
b These adjectives are also used to describe the skin of women.
c Interbreeding with Ila/Tonga shorthorn Sanga in particular has introduced this colour.
d The pattern illustrated here (the colour occurs in the panel). It is often named thus in central and southern Africa after the Zulu and Swazi name.

Milk was a central element of the diet, providing one of the commonest *busunso*. Dung, applied systematically, enriched the fragile plain-edge soils (*litongo*) and improved the soils on the tops of *mazulu* (mounds) in the plain which are usually poorer than the undrained *sishanjo* peats, but because higher, are less at risk to flooding and offer a longer growing season. Accurate application of dung with minimum effort was achieved by stake-tethering (*ngombe fungwa*) with *lipumba* (ropes fixed to the ground).[133] Possession of cattle or access to cattle was essential for the best exploitation of the domestic economy. How this was achieved and how political and moral economies intertwined may be conveniently understood by examining the forms of ownership, descending from the largest scale.

The mythic elements in the visible connections between cattle and kingship paralleled the movement of cattle ownership from the king to the people. Cattle were primarily a public resource, like land or water or air, but their shape and mobility and the method of their utilisation imposed specific patterns of access. The increased prominence of individual ownership of beasts has been an aspect of the fragmentation of the domestic economy and of the simplifying urges of colonial administration during the twentieth century. Our period was the last during which the full range of patterns of access operated, as changes began with the coming of substantial migrant wage labour after the mid 1890s and important mutation occurred after the pleuropneumonia epidemic of 1914 to 1916.

The court ballad about the cattle of Mwandi (a well renowned rich pasturage in the northwest of the floodplain) relates how the royal herds came into being. Early in traditional time, the Lozi herd was grazed near the capital, but Luvale raided the cattle:

> They tried to move the cattle from one place to another in hiding, but the people said 'We cannot be without cattle at the capital. We need milk for the children. These people are annoying us. . .' Eventually Yeta I said, 'All right, let us move our cattle so that the Luvale may lose their way. . .' However, because they were so many, it was decided that the cattle be divided up under certain indunas. One is Inyambo, another is Namulata. 'So now', the people said, 'let us do this: each one should take up a certain number of cattle, not as a whole, but divided up. . .'[134]

Thus is explained the creation of royal herds – *likomu za mbuwa*. Rather like human organisations (*makolo*), more herds were created over time (Chapter 5, Section 3), probably reaching greatest elaboration during Lewanika's reign. The names of the herds tell of their nature and functions:[135]

84

Kabeti	Those of *Ngambela's likolo*
Mangongi	Those of the *Makolo* chiefs (to help feed visitors to court)
Ndalo	Those who wander (?)
Malwamunga	Those of the founder (?)
Malabo	?
Siliangiwa	'What is continually eaten will not multiply'
Mabetwa	Those with carved horns
Busetana	The grey-blue cows
Nalikolo	Those of Yeta I
Mufulu	Those of the royal drum (an old established herd)
Mungulo	Interpretation unclear. The last herd created by Lewanika (kept at his *sitino*, Nanikelako)
Mukota	?
Kakula	?
Mazwezi	The nursing cows (kept near Lealui to provide milk for the court)

The names indicate that the herds were specialised by function, some by appearance and some by ownership. All were supervised and inspected by the chief herdsman *Imutongo* and the chief-in-council titled *Isikeme*. From Lewanika's time, royal herds were branded with a 'W' (*nombolo*, number, meaning brand; loanword). Informants throughout the hinterland related how royal herds were used as instruments to colonise new lands, how royal cattle were given in return for tribute and how individual herdsmen might start their own herds from gift beasts and offspring.[136]

Throughout his reign Lewanika made skilful use of raided cattle in his handling of internal patronage politics. Contemporaneous sources enable us to give a shape to the widespread, repeated and unfocused oral reports. George Westbeech, the trader friend of Sipopa, Lewanika's predecessor, reckoned that the new king obtained upwards of 20,000 head in the winter raiding season of 1882.[137] Many more shorthorn Sanga were obtained from the Ila in 1888, herds described as 'uncountable' by an eye-witness who encountered the king on his way home after the raid,[138] while still more were obtained from the Luvale in 1892.[139] Earlier in this section, I gave sightings of these animals in subsequent years.

The political value of these herds was greatly enhanced for Lewanika by one of the natural 'disasters' of the 1890s. During the later years of the decade, a great epidemic of rinderpest ('cattle plague') swept southwards through tropical Africa. Rinderpest is a filter-passing virus of great virulence which affects a very broad range of wild and domestic ruminants. It can be transmitted directly or indirectly. It is a disease which spread outwards from an original focus in south central Europe, entering Africa most probably in 1887 in Indian store cattle imported into Eritrea at Massawa by Italians.[140] Leaving behind famine, accentuated by (1886–7) drought, in Ethiopia, the rinderpest moved south through Kenya, reaching the interlacustrine region and the northern Zambian plateau in 1892.[141] In 1896 it crossed the Zambezi, but it also ravaged Sesheke district, the southern gateway to Bulozi. However, this is not generally realised. Professor Gann wrote that 'Barotseland was not affected by the epidemic' and others have followed him in this opinion.[142] Therefore it is well to spell out the evidence.

The missionary stationed at Sesheke in early 1896 was the same Auguste Goy who had begun to dig the Sefula canal while he was Coillard's aide nearly ten years before. He was now married and his wife Mathilde kept a diary. In April 1896, Goy returned to Sesheke after a tour of evangelisation in what is now northern Botswana and the Caprivi Strip. Goy had a raging fever and died. Her husband's death and her own subsequent experiences stimulated his widow to publish a short account of their work.[143] Thus we have a detailed description from the centre of the infected region: 'In February 1896, the cattle plague burst upon the country. . . this disease was new to us and in truth, we did not know the remedy for it.'[144] The missionaries lost their entire herd of dairy cattle and when they learned that the epidemic had also struck in Bechuanaland (Botswana) and in Matabeleland, they realised that their communications with the south were cut off also and that they could not reprovision themselves. In April Mme Goy was able to obtain a milking cow from 'a native village where the cattle had been less decimated than where we live'.[145] But she was short of European foodstuffs and, more importantly, running low on the calico and white trading beads used to barter for local produce. She had to live – like the African population – on maize flour, sweet potatoes and 'a sort of courgette'. She decided to leave Bulozi and in September Adolphe Jalla sent her twenty head of oxen from Sefula in the heartland of the country 'where the cattle plague has not exercised its ravages'.[146] However, Mme Goy waited a further three months in Sesheke before leaving in order to be sure that the animals were healthy.

This account tells us two things about the rinderpest epidemic in Bulozi. First, it only affected the south. This was confirmed more precisely in October 1896 when the visiting Major Goold Adams reported that the epidemic had infected Ilaland and southern Bulozi as far north as Sioma, but that the rest of the country was untouched. Secondly, it suggests that the disease passed like a bush-fire: terrible in its immediate fury but leaving a sterile area behind. That is exactly what one would expect of a rinderpest epidemic in a previously uninfected region. Indeed, we may confidently suggest that the 'front' moved through the Sesheke region in February 1896 and was then gone, for we next see it reported at Palapye in Bechuanaland, to the south across the Zambezi, on 10 March.[147] Whilst Mme Goy's single milking cow of April cannot carry upon its back alone the supposition that Sesheke was already clear of the disease, we may reasonably place it upon the twenty trek oxen that she was able to bring in safely from outside in September. Coillard noted the dispatch of these oxen, using a past tense about the disease, in December, and we may safely assume that Mme Goy was his informant for that observation.[148]

Therefore if Mme Goy could bring in new stock, so could other people, which is the major point of this detailed case. 'Shortly after this [the extermination of all the cattle]', stated the Sesheke District Notebook in a report written in about 1912, 'Lewanika restocked the district by sending down cattle from Barotse [that is, the floodplain] to many of the Indunas [chiefs] and others. For some years the cattle apparently thrived. . .'[149] This is a pregnant comment, for the implication which it contains is not difficult to see and is very important: it means that Lewanika restocked the district from royal herds in the Valley, thus renewing patronage bonds throughout this strategic region in the most concrete way possible at precisely the critical moment, just before the arrival of the British South Africa Company administration in October 1897. The timetable which Mme Goy's experiences give us enables us to see that this interpretation of Lewanika's action is technically feasible.

Disease had already served Lewanika well in this region, for the smallpox epidemic of 1893–4 had in April 1893 carried off the *Mulanziane* Mwanañono Kabuku who, although he was Lewanika's nephew, had not been his creature. Thus in July 1894, after much deliberation, Lewanika was able to install his son Litia to supervise Sesheke from Kazungula, the most strategic place in a strategic area since access to Bulozi across the Zambezi was regulated from there.[150]

The line between personal and royal control of royal cattle was hard to draw. The herdsman had usufruct of milk and manure and might receive the gift of a calf or beast for good husbandry. However, ultimate disposal of cattle, which after 1900 increasingly meant sale to white traders, was reserved. All the trader materials corroborate this wide royal control of sale. The same relationship existed between any owner and any temporary herdsman under a *mafisa* arrangement whereby, during the flood, cattle owners in the plain lent their animals to people in the bush to herd until the waters fell. Frequently long-standing arrangements grew out of this, but it seems that a prior kin link was by no means necessary to the establishment of a *mafisa* relationship.[151]

At village level, the distinction between communal and personal rights in the animals, which were herded together, was clear, but movements between categories of ownership was possible. Thus some animals, which were given names, were the property of individuals. In 1886 Waddell described how 'the young animals' horns are trained into shape by the Borotse. . .[who] also cut and slit the animals' ears into various shapes as private marks'. Bertrand described 'ears artificially shaped' in 1895.[152]

Theft of cattle was therefore possible, but the definition was regulated by the status of the individuals involved. A stranger was severely punished. In 1929 a thief told a Magistrate's Court how, in the old (i.e. pre-administration) days, the punishment was to cut off the offender's ears and to force the return of the beast together with two others belonging to the thief.[153] However, a relative in need could take another relative's animal (*ku funda*) provided that he followed certain rules. He should clip the ear of the animal first, by night, to signify his need and if the owner did not respond voluntarily, then he should take the animal from the herd before the eyes of witnesses and in daylight. Early administrators found it difficult to grasp this rather subtle concept, and misunderstanding of the nature of *ku funda* lay at the heart of a near crisis between the king and the British South Africa Company in 1914.

The system was still common in the early 1920s and cases recurred with decreasing frequency thereafter. As the assertion of absolute personal ownership strengthened, so did the royal herds shrink, *ku funda* retreat and the habit of giving cattle as bride-price (*sionda*) become pre-eminent as the mechanism for distributing cattle.[154] This was because the colonial era uncovered new fruits in the 'basket' of cattle besides the milk and the manure that were essential and central in our period.

5

Distribution and exchange

The foregoing description of the method of production was developed from the social geography of the village. I return to the same standpoint in order to begin the account of the distribution of the fruits of that labour.

In comparison to the narrow spectrum of possibilities in techniques of production from the land, a much richer range was available at the level of redistribution. Here I offer a systematic account, beginning at village level. It displays the resources available for social labelling so that when that is described, it will be intelligible. It was here that people applied their intellectual energy to create their society's distinctive patterning.

It will be recalled that the individuals of each *lapa* (courtyard) had their own recognised gardens and their own grain stores in or near the *lapa*.[1] By mid afternoon, the women took grain and began to pound it into meal in their mortars (*licika*). The mortar was one of a woman's most personal possessions; she took it into and out of marriage. To reverse and sit on a woman's mortar was a form of insult and threat. The pounded meal was blended with water and salt and cooked into *buhobe*. The men would furnish fish or small game meat, but the women themselves would collect vegetable *busunso* (relish).

'When the sun eats the leaves' (*lizazi ha li ca matali*), at dusk, all the inhabitants of the village would gather at the headman's courtyard, bringing their cooked food with them. The headman would then direct the division of bowls into groups, each with *buhobe* and *busunso*. One group would be left inside his courtyard and he would eat there with the mature free men. Another would be in the cooking area of his senior wife (*musali yo muhulu*) where the women would eat. Here was the moment when sanction could be exercised against the lazy or unwanted, for they could be denied access to their rightful group. The children were fed apart, as were slaves, who would sit together outside the core of the

89

village and might eat all together, men, women and children, or might divide in the same way as their superiors. This system was called *ku ca ka silyela*.[2]

Oral sources suggest that the system began to weaken and to be replaced by a pattern of nuclear families, feeding themselves alone and eating alone, in the 1920s. A sign that this was an aspect of the fragmenting village economy is that frequently the cost of food was given as explanation. Today the old system is not common. I have only observed it in a very remote village of royal herdsmen, far to the west. However, vestiges of it survive much more widely for within the nuclear family it is formal for men and women to eat separately. This may be widely observed, and is reported by another researcher at Lui Namabunga.[3]

Silyela was complemented by a parallel procedure used for high status food. Whenever a cow died or a large game animal was killed, it was dismembered and distributed to the various courtyards to be cooked. One eye-witness reported that the pots were assembled in one place and that the women worked together. The parts were cooked in different pots and were allocated following an established system: the tripe and intestines went to the unmarried women, the heart, most of the head and the flank went to the owner or hunter, other meat to other men, the chest fat and scapula (*lisapyana*) to any person of royal blood present and so on.

This type of distribution, which was not a daily affair, appears to have become rarer before *silyela* withered. However, an Afrikaaner cattle officer witnessed it in the Siloana Plains in the 1940s. Early sources refer to gorging, of meat when it was available (and to the excellence of its preparation). This is not unusual in a climate where meat putrifies easily, but Holub saw meat being sun-dried also.[4]

Ku ca ka silyela makes two points with force. First, it showed how food changed its nature once it was cooked. Grains in a grain bin were individual property. They faced two possible futures – the field again, or the mortar. As soon as the food alternative was activated, the social claims latent in them took priority. Thus the effects of shortage could be generally shared and mitigated and those who for reasons of youth, slavery, sickness or other disqualification did not contribute much or any food could be fed.

Secondly, therefore, *silyela* reproduced the community, including the slaves who, *ipso facto*, were visibly within the community. It was a 'collective mode of appropriation'. But it was more than this, for here at this level and not at the level of production society was defined in detail. The small community used the richer expressiveness at the level of redistribution through *silyela* to restate its social hierarchy each day. One is compelled to follow the logic of the people themselves.

The importance that was attached to this total social necessity may be deduced from the fact that through this system shortage hit all, labourers and non-labourers alike. It indicates a set of extra-economic priorities at work influencing the material base of the community. These priorities constituted the *moral* economy, in contrast to the material economy which it embraced and directed. I used this term before when describing attitudes to cattle and, as I did there, here again it has to be stressed – in order to stifle at birth a common reaction to such a statement – that of course this usage should not be taken to imply that Lozi villagers were people insensible to motivations of the market economy. Simply, the creation and manipulation of surplus in the sense in which we generally take it was a lower priority than the dominant concern, which was to ensure the survival of the moral community with the minimum risk of famine. 'Safety first' behaviour like this does not, of course, carry within it an inevitable implication of changelessness, stagnation or an inability to innovate. The history of the expansion of Lozi agriculture during the 1890s is ample rebuttal of that. But such actions have what I earlier called culture-specific rationality. However, if the fabric of the participants' moral economy is dismissed as 'false consciousness' and/or ignored, then that becomes difficult to understand.[5] Yet the moral economy at work is all that the system *ku ca ka silyela* shows.

Furthermore, *silyela* showed how uneven accumulation of surplus was not feasible. What was surplus to the 'reproduction of necessary labour' was committed to the 'reproduction of the community'. Together these functions defined 'essential consumption' or 'subsistence requirement'. This was at once a physiological and a social phenomenon; even, in times of extreme hardship, potentially a cosmological one. The social component was flexible and so in consequence were the 'subsistence requirements' of the community. It is in contrast to this that the word 'surplus' is usefully defined. This concept of subsistence, to be discerned also in Gluckman's work, had ramifications which extended far into the wider society.

There is a lot of abstract debate about what exactly words like 'subsistence' and 'surplus' can and should mean; it is conducted often using the sort of terms which I have placed in inverted commas above. Because of this literature, it is doubly important to make entirely precise the origins and form of usage which I ascribe to these concepts. Since I derive my meanings from the way that Lozi people talk and act, I stress both – origin and form – by summarising the relationship of these words in a drawing of a Lozi grain bin (*sishete*). Readers who like visual reinforcement for schemes of ideas will find an illuminating drawing of the 'mode of production/social formation "articulation" ' in E. P. Thompson's book, *The poverty of theory* (Plate IV).[6] It offers a useful comparison with Fig. 12 here.

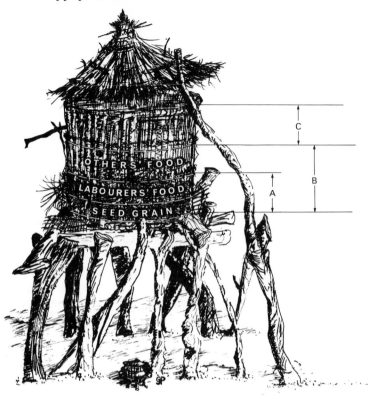

Fig. 12 A Lozi grain bin: definitions of 'subsistence' and 'surplus'. A = reproducing necessary labour. B = reproducing the community (product of surplus labour). A + B = *subsistence*: 'essential consumption'. C = *surplus*: potential available for wider social commitment.

The fundamental importance of sustaining the small community remained an integral part of the wider net of subsistence. This was most striking in the disposal of the produce of state gardens. These gardens absorbed surplus labour, but social commitment could, in necessity, embrace the whole: 'Lewanika had *bonamukau*. These were gardens which were not cultivated so that only he the king might live. No, they were to reap food for the kingdom [*mulonga*]. It was done so that people who were starving if their crops failed could be helped.'[7] *Bonamukau* were scattered throughout the land. They were not 'private estates'. Their products were dispersed in three ways: some were placed in storehouses at the village of the guardian (*ndaleti*). They could be released in time of need as described in the quotation. Regularly *lindumeleti* (roving emissary chiefs) collected produce which was taken to the capital Lealui as *ñamba* (tribute). On arrival, most went into public storehouses and a smaller amount, *nubu*, to the Newa storehouse to feed the non-labouring royal court.[8]

The attachment of an alien concept of 'private' ownership illustrates the danger of arguing by lax historical analogy and transposed terminology. Especially in relation to agricultural produce, the usage cannot be sustained for reasons explained above. The task is to grasp the internal logic of ownership in the way that Gluckman does in showing how *buñ'a* (ownership) was a function of *relationship*, not of inanimate matter. That is why I also insert vernacular words to label culture-specific concepts.

Redefinition of hierarchy within the wider horizon was most visible in the ceremonial allocation of specific parts of royal game animals, notably elephant, hippo and eland, to specific office holders. Gluckman was surely correct in seeing these ceremonies as powerful celebrations of group identity and social patterning exhibiting reciprocal obligation through the display of patronage. The power of such exchanges was seen when Gluckman's informants compared them to 'medicines'.[9]

Reciprocal obligation and social delineation emerge with force from the recollection of a son of one of Lewanika's bodyguards (*boimilema*).

> The Mission Station Lwatili is only half a mile from Lialuyi. In those days the King owned very very big wooden bowls which were heaped with chunks of fat cooked beef; others were filled with *buhobe*, still others with *ilia*, some with cooked crushed maize. These bowls were prepared in one of Liwanika's pantries and on the appointed day they were moved under the trees on the public square.
>
> The Rev Coillard or one of the teachers would tell us that all pupils had to go to the Kuta. When we got there we used to sit down and give respect shouting 'Yooshoo-o-o' three times, sitting and rising. Then we would sit cross-legged by classes and the teachers would distribute the food to us equally. After eating our fill we were taught to render proper thanks to the King. He would always come out and see us eating and before we dispersed he would admonish us, 'Work hard! The country will be in your hands! Make it prosper!'[10]

Here was the village level distribution in all its essentials echoed at the top of the hierarchy. However, as Jalla's diary indicated, what Mupatu describes was not unique to privileged schoolboys. Visitors to the capital were fed from these same storehouses, from tribute, and if the regional hunger-relief supply stored at an area's state garden was for any reason exhausted, whole villages might be summoned to the capital, there to be fed over the lean time. This was an immensely effective way of defining inclusiveness in the society, and so denial of access to this type of patronage was mentioned specifically as a reason for resentment against Lozi emissaries by one informant immediately after he had described the process of 'calling in' just mentioned.[11]

The fruitful contradictions of this testimony underline that, from a headman's courtyard to the capital's public square, this was certainly a device for feeding bodies that lived in a risky environment, but that also, through making explicit an accurate perception of social status, it reinforced that sense of understanding and of control over their environment which was also a basic need. Nor was that need specific to Bulozi although the form of its expression naturally was; it has been perceived in widely different societies.[12] These ideas are most directly accessible through the cosmology which is studied in the next chapters.

5.2 THE ENERGISING PRINCIPLE

To complete the portrait of village life in the 1880s and 1890s and before looking at forms of wider social organisation, we must explain how the components which have been dissected were energised. It was through *likute*, a nebulous concept embracing politeness, deference and cooperation in its meaning and facilitating social labelling and reciprocity through its practice.

From the time that a Lozi child was born until it reached the age of self awareness, it was regarded as being the embodiment of an ancestral spirit. During this time it was given a sort of interim name, often quite ugly – Filth, Sorrow, Nobody, for example – and protected with charms in order to make it an unappetising morsel for evil spirits. Royal children were kept closely hidden so that not even their sex might be known. It was properly named at about the age of two or three which was also about the time that it ceased to suckle. The name was bestowed by an older relation who could be of either sex but was very frequently a grandmother. If the name did not 'fit', the child could fall ill. Then it was necessary to test other family names whilst throwing a libation of salt, tobacco and meal pounded together into a powder into the corner of the hut (*ku pailela*). When the child ceased to convulse, the correct ancestral name had been found. It had become a complete person. The Lozi were not alone in taking this view of small children. The Chaga, for example, distinguished three periods of infancy with three names for babies: *mnangu* (the incomplete), *mkoku* (the little one who fills the lap) and *mwana* (infant). The behaviour described here fitted the first Chaga period which was evidently shorter.[13]

Before this transition, the small child was never disciplined. It grew 'like a wild tree' in Jalla's phrase. But then came an abrupt, possibly traumatic change. The principles of *likute* were instilled, especially with the flat of the hand: 'A child is like a small bird, he fears when he sees an adult.'[14]

For this education, the child often went to live with relatives or might be taken under *lifunga* for training at a royal establishment. In either case, children over about five or six were worked hard. Girls swept, pounded meal, drew water and in particular supervised babies. Boys were sent out to herd cattle. A missionary who was heavily involved in opening school annexes in remote areas in the 1930s summarised the obstacles tersely as 'wood, water and cattle'. These were the labour inputs lost when children went to school.[15]

Some of the most frequently encountered proverbs reflect how *likute* spanned society:

A young man who is hated by people cannot grow old – he will die before he grows a beard.

It is easy to choke an old man, but you will bring a curse on yourself.

A man who does not accept [drinking] water from friends is disliked by everyone.[16]

These proverbs also touch upon a contrast in the society between *likute* and violence. It was seen and noted before the onset of colonial rule with all the stresses and resultant social tensions which accompanied it and to which some have ascribed this phenomenon. It struck Holub and later Coillard, who pondered why 'these people used to soaking their hands in the blood of their chiefs and their brothers . . . are the most polite people in the world and I even believe that they surpass the Parisians. A master always addresses his slaves, even the youngsters, *shangwe*. One slave never speaks to another without employing the same term.'[17] Details of brutality filled pages of early Mission publications and it is unlikely that they were fabricated, although they may have been embroidered, because the meticulous Jalla kept a list of dates and events of this type, culled from the pages of his daily diary. In any case, the basic observation is corroborated more dispassionately in case records where time and again it seems that something snapped and a docile man became a killer.[18]

The basic currency of *likute* was the elaborate ritual of greeting. Because this was so, the account just given may be empirically tied to the 1880s and 1890s. Different spoken formulae, gestures and variation of hand clapping (*ku kandelela*) defined quite precisely the relationship of the participants. At the apex was the *shoelela* or homage already described by Mupatu. It was rendered to give thanks to Nyambe (the High God), at royal grave-sites and to the king, 'Nyambe's servant'.[19] Under Kololo influence, the praise-cry *'Tau Tuna!'* (Great Lion!) joined the Luyana *'Yooshoo!'*,[20] but during Lewanika's reign the Kololo epithet faded and the pure Luyana form remained alone when it was described in 1913 at a hunting camp.[21]

To *shoelela* confirmed a grant of land or of office or a legal judgment. All allegiance was symbolically renewed at the installation of a new king or chief by mass homage. The trader George Westbeech described this sensitively in August 1886:

> All the dependents of the tribes big and little subject to Shesheki and who have to take their tribute to that town have been called up to Shoellella [to the newly appointed *Mulanziane* Kabuku, who was to succumb to smallpox in 1893]. We have no English meaning for the word, but you will be pretty near the meaning by using the words: offering, thanks and praise, and asking for peace, or as they say, sleep.[22]

Its accompaniment for conversation was a hollow clap made with partly cupped palms repeated three times, each a careful crescendo and diminuendo, seated on the ground. 'No one can stand up before him [Lewanika], or say a word, or pass him a glass of water without grovelling and clapping hands.'[23]

The common clapped greeting was made differently by men and women. Least formally, for example between people carrying loads, it could be a bending of the knees and the free hand slapping the thigh. The correct form between unrelated people was 'to kneel on the ground facing each other and looking at each other out of the corner of the eye, to clap hands and together to repeat *"Shangwe"*. . .'.

Greeting between kin was different again. The participants sat on the ground, itself an important sign of familiarity, and kissed the upturned palms of each other's hands in a crossways sequence.[24] Great favour could be shown to a commoner by a senior chief or royal person by placing saliva on the commoner's tongue.[25]

I have shown how *likute* was expressed at the scales of distribution in everyday life; it was also present in the central ritual statement of the cohesion of the whole society, the great Dance of the Men, *ngomalume*, danced at the new moon. It was 'the sacred dance of the Barotses', Mukamba the future *Ngambela* explained to Coillard at the time of his apostasy, 'and no one has the right or the freedom to absent himself from it'.[26] Its true significance was carefully concealed from him, Coillard

96

thought. He suspected that it was obscene.[27] It was danced in the royal establishments, notably during the installation ceremonies and at times of national emergency, and on a smaller scale in the villages at the rebirth of the moon each month that was deemed to be propitious – that is, that was not soiled by some event of national mourning.[28] Usually meat was provided.

The form of the dance on the rare occasions that outsiders have witnessed it has changed in no significant detail since it was described in the late 1890s to Jacottet in Lesotho. Coillard's eye-witness account of 1886 is the most graphic: men of all types and descriptions girded their waists with civet-cat tails; drums were planted in the centre of the public square, and 'a great circle formed around the drums and before the king and the dance began. All took part; the old men like Taka-taka and very young boys; the most important chief like the very least . . . the old Nalubutu also was there, in such matters, as in etiquette, he is a great authority . . .' The style of dancing was specific: a 'strange trembling' of the lower part of the body whilst the upper part remained immobile. The circle moved very slowly from left to right. The style contrasted with the women's dance which Coillard had witnessed three days earlier; it was also a slowly revolving circle around the drums but the dance was athletic shaking of the shoulders. The *ngomalume* has a quite distinct drum rhythm:[29]

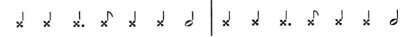

5.3 THE SHAPE OF A POLITY

By the same token that earlier the spectrum of proper diet was used to explain the range of agriculture, which was used in turn to situate the discussion of slavery that followed, here we are obliged to follow *likute*, like Ariadne's thread, into the complicated wider social organisation in order to give the subsequent description of redistribution in the state full meaning.

The institutions of the Lozi state pertaining to the royal establishments are the most described feature of the country after its topography. This concentration of attention was for obvious reasons: observers tended to assume that central political institutions were the most important and symptomatic aspects of the culture; indeed if such institutions did not exist they might be imagined into existence. Furthermore, early observers were also relatively immobile and the observations were relatively easy to make. Study of the expansion of the pre-colonial Lozi state, the form of control in its peripheries and the explanation of how this control worked, which are all by force of circumstance largely inferred, have been tinged by this imbalance.

In the 1940s, Professor Gluckman's image of the Lozi state was moulded by two observations and a hypothesis which he inferred from them. From his first paper about Bulozi onwards, Gluckman emphasised the great ecological variety of the Lozi environment which made possible the production of an unusually wide range of foodstuffs, as described in the previous chapter. He was also impressed by the sheer size, complexity and hence the expense of the Lozi state apparatus as it was to be seen in the royal establishments. He sought an explanation of the latter in terms of the former. He argued that the huge central state apparatus served as a redistributor of all the varied produce of the land which flowed physically towards the capital as tribute and back into the community as patronage. This was a functional justification for a structural fact. The social vehicles which transported this traffic were institutions of the large political scale, institutions which tied men together by virtue of personal relationship, not primarily connected to location upon or possession of land. These were called *makolo* (*likolo* in the singular). Land-based institutions of this scale did exist, called *lilalo*, but Gluckman thought that they were relatively new and unimportant.

While there has subsequently been dispute about the nature of these institutions, which we shall examine shortly, there has been no fundamental reexamination of Gluckman's notion of the kingship as crucial redistributor of essential foodstuffs. There are two preconditions before that task may be attacked. First, an alternative general theory to that of structural functionalism is needed; secondly, we must have new and different types of information.

Professor Gluckman was inescapably constrained by the physical difficulties of having to travel by foot or canoe with carriers. This simple fact of material life imposed a pattern upon his movements, upon what he saw, upon how he was seen, how he obtruded into the society, upon the choices which he could make in dividing up his available time in the field and, consequently, upon what he both chose and was able to write about. He was only a little more mobile than had been the early observers of the late nineteenth century. These circumstances were as much beyond his control as theirs, for in fact it was only the military requirements of the Second World War which changed the situation.

In the aftermath of the war, large numbers of army-surplus Jeeps and Chevrolet trucks found their way into tropical Africa, rather as obsolete European infantry guns had done when European armies had been reequipped in earlier centuries. These American machines were the first four-wheel-drive vehicles to appear in Bulozi and therefore to offer a new prospect of mobility through the soft Kalahari sands of the country. But it was really only when the Land Rover, a radical improvement on the war-time Jeep, arrived in the 1950s that it became logistically feasible to obtain descriptive data more widely than Gluckman was able to do, yet still within a reasonable span of time.

Therefore a more responsive theoretical framework combined with very many thousands of Land Rover miles together fulfil our preconditions. I have used the new data gathered in this way, coupled with hindsight, to address two linked questions which arise from the received interpretation: why did the relationship of centre to periphery come to be explained as it was there? Does evidence exist to offer a more satisfactory resolution of the underlying question? This second question continues the main thrust of the analysis, but I cannot ignore the first without leaving puzzlement.

Oral testimony about institutions of the Lozi state gathered from members of the elite represent a formal tradition different from those of foundation myth or royal sequence. Like them, it is formal in the sense that Professor Finley has described the construction of Homeric epic poetry by rhapsodists: the 'stitching together' of pieces of oral material. Unlike them, the pieces of material are bulkier and easier to discern;[30] they will be described shortly. Each related to an aspect of the 'Traditional Lozi Polity', which is capitalised to distinguish an assumed fixity, convenient to the concepts and purposes of European observers and administrators, from a reality which the earlier discussion of boundaries has already indicated was a more fluid network of relationships. This fluidity was noticed in other central concepts during our dissection of village society. Here its implication is that the possibility existed for the pieces to be stitched and restitched into patterns reflecting the personality, purpose and point of time of the informant. Therefore it is especially important to distinguish the types of data within the received account and to accord appropriate treatment to each.

There has been a general consensus about the forms and purposes of the central institutions of rule in the capitals – the physical centres of the kingdom – where they were observed at first hand and at length. Within days of his first arrival at Lealui, Coillard made incidental notes of certain offices of state which were present under Tatila Akufuna. Unsurprisingly, he wrote most about the powers of the two state officers most immediately visible and with whom he would have had direct dealings: *Ngambela*, the 'Prime Minister' – spokesman for the people to the king – and *Natamoyo*, the second ranking chief, whose person and courtyard offered sanctuary to any accused person. This role impressed Coillard

99

who wished to represent himself as a *Natamoyo*.[31] But Jalla's notes offer the best description of the offices and procedures of the capital because he tied these carefully to the symbolic layout of buildings, locations and courtyards within Lealui: empirical evidence which has persisted through time.[32] The importance of this pattern may be judged from the fact that whenever the king travelled, the spatial relationship between the shelters of office-holders, groups and ritual objects was preserved in the camp (*mafulo*). The pattern of courts of the Royal Council associated with this layout – *Siikalo, Saa* and the 'kitchen cabinet', *Situmbu sa Mulonga*, which had freer access to the king's audience chamber (*kashandi*) – was observed from Sipopa's time onwards.[33] Also seen was the spatial separation between *makwambuyu* (councillors of the right-hand mat) and *likombwa* (stewards who sat to the left and were in charge of the *kwandu* (palace), the enclosures of the king's wives, the public and the royal storehouses).[34]

The title histories of each of the most important offices, as distinct from their arrangement into councils, march back in time with the formal tradition of the dynasty.[35] The *makolo* (military/service units) possess a similar depth of tradition. These were institutions of a large scale. The sequence of their foundation and the names of those chiefs associated with each were also recorded in detail by Jalla. Descriptions of the use of the *makolo* in war, to hunt, to dig canals as boon labour and to undertake repairs in the royal enclosure are present in the archival sources.[36] However, information about the constitution of the *makolo* is largely inferred; thus it is a fertile ground for invention.

The same is true for the land district (*silalo*). Holub wrote impressively of 'Governors of Provinces' of whom he had heard in 1876, but there is a curious contrast in later material. Generally the missionaries wrote about *makolo* and the administrators emphasised 'selaale'. In 1906 Worthington listed all the areas of Lealui District, with their chiefs, as part of the organisation of hut tax.[37] Yet it seems likely that the nested Chinese boxes of village (*munzi*), *silalanda* (a group of closely related villages), *silalo* and *sikiliti* (English loanword: district) did not stack so neatly until that moment. But it would be equally incorrect to suggest, as Gluckman has done, that prior to colonial times there was negligible territorially defined administration.

At issue are those areas of Bulozi distant from the royal establishments (*mileneñi*) but not so far as to be clear tributaries like the Ila, Luvale and parts of the Tonga. These tributary areas were more often visited by travellers in the 1880s and 1890s,[38] since the main concern in the early phase of the scramble for Barotseland was to settle boundaries.

The account of state structure in the twilight areas, which were most of the heartland and periphery away from the rivers and wagon trails, was restitched twice, in the 1900s and in the 1940s, at times when the historical justification of a certain patchwork was an aspect of hot contemporary politics.

During the second phase of colonial contact, the British South Africa Company urgently needed to attach its administration to existing indigenous forms. Once Lewanika grasped this, appropriate forms in the shape of the nest of Chinese boxes became visible. The high exposure of the *lilalo* which resulted left the *makolo* in the shade and this was used to advantage when the next restitching took place.

From early in 1939 the *Litunga* Yeta, Lewanika's son and successor, lay paralysed and speechless. From January 1941 his *Ngambela* was Kalonga Wina. He, the *Moyo* Imwambo (Yeta's senior wife), and the group of councillors associated with them, sought to create a legitimacy in European eyes for the unusual power they exercised.[39] A part of this, which created embarrassment by implying that the colonial authorities had fundamentally misunderstood the Lozi political system, flowed from their assertion that the 'regiments' (*makolo*), not the territorial units (*lilalo*), were the indigenous units of government. One of that group of councillors, the late Francis Suu, put to me his view that 'The silalo did not exist until the colonial government came.'[40] Such views achieved wide circulation and impact in ethnographic publications where Professor Gluckman asserted that due to this fundamental blindness, 'the result has been utter confusion'.[41]

Wina was driven from the Ngambelaship for, at the very least, failing to give a satisfactory account of the circumstances surrounding the sudden death of King Imwiko in 1948.[42] However, the terms within which Lozi administration was henceforth examined were set. Whilst Gluckman took the line already portrayed Mainga argued diametrically against it. She thought that territorial units were basic and that *makolo* and *lilalo* tended to be geographically conterminous. (Gluckman had thought that they were not, although he admitted that in daily operation there was a good degree of overlap.)[43] In this way the debate entered a cul-de-sac; but an understanding of why it happened is of importance in resuming the quest for explanation, aware of the pressures upon and tolerances in the data. This point deserves full amplification.

In translating *likolo* I have used the word 'regiment', always in inverted commas, or the clumsy formula 'military/service unit'. The translation 'regiment' has been common and the military implication has been pronounced in the literature, but it needs to be used with care; hence the inverted commas. In order to explain why and also to disarm the beguiling precision of the received accounts, the debate about *makolo* and *lilalo*

101

(personal and land-based social institutions) in Bulozi may be instructively compared – in type, if not exactly in substance – with the yet more colourful history of the way in which the basic structures of the Ndebele state, south of Bulozi across the Zambezi in Zimbabwe, have been described over the last century.[44]

The conventional wisdom about the Ndebele state in the Matopos area is of a dominating royal capital, described like Lealui in Bulozi, surrounded by a relatively small number of 'regimental towns' – 'colossal strongholds' 'commanded' by a chief who was 'appointed' as a royal official. 'Regiments' (*amabutho*) were grouped into four 'divisions' under regional 'commanders'; the whole hierarchy presented an inextricable interweaving of political and military functions. The Ndebele had a 'military state'. However, the difficulty with this static image is that it gives no idea of how such a society could exist over time. For example, what happened when the 'regiments' aged? Dr Cobbing has reexamined this description from a historian's perspective and has discovered three problems with the account. Two are analytical, one is methodological; the former flow from the latter and together they illuminate our discussion of state structures in Bulozi.

The basic error which Cobbing has documented was an excessively uncritical belief in the scientific status of one's predecessors' writings which was reduplicated in successive generations of authors. We can now see that in Bulozi accounts of state structure were types of traditions invented – the patchwork restitched – for particular purposes at particular times. In the same way, Cobbing has been able to show that in Matabeleland two major analytical problems were the result of this same single methodological error.

The first of these analytical faults was that Ndebele society was consistently and inflexibly viewed on too large a scale to permit the indigenous units of society to be understood. The European notion of 'division/province' was an early import; but there was no siNdebele word for it, although attempts were made to manufacture one! The same preoccupation with the scale of 'provinces' has been seen above in descriptions of the Lozi state, where the result was that, just as *ibutho* was stretched to cover an imported concept in Matabeleland, *lilalo* and *makolo* were manipulated whilst institutions of the middle scale, like the descent groups (*mishiku*), were underrated or missed.

Secondly and most strikingly, Cobbing showed how the 'province' became a 'division', the senior chief a military figure. The piece of writing which set this warrior cast upon all subsequent Ndebele studies was produced by a visiting British army officer (who might therefore be expected to see the world in terms of the military hierarchy) who had, at the time that he wrote, known the Ndebele for about a fortnight. Cobbing offered in addition a reappraisal of Ndebele society which need not concern us here, for the point of this comparison has not been to argue any broad similarity of substance between the cases, but rather to underline the creative potential of a far more modest expectation of the elucidating capacities of the data, an assumption which thus frees the historian to use his critical faculties.

It is not enough to understand where, why and how the explanation of the Lozi state entered a cul-de-sac; we must attempt to get out of it, as Cobbing also tried to do further south. A three point turn is required. Two points have already been mentioned – a view of social differentiation in the light of the foregoing discussion of *likute* (politeness, right behaviour) and new first-hand data from the edges of the heartland. The third emerges from these – paying attention to a ritual artifact in order to locate foci of power.

Among the sketches of musical instruments which he made in Sesheke in 1876, Holub drew an iron, flange-welded, bifurcated clapperless double bell. It was of a type similar to those of the Lunda/Luba area of the southern Congo, but was more than an instrument, for the *ngongi* was a symbol of power in Bulozi as in other African kingdoms.[45]

Lingongi are best known in the rites of installation of certain very senior chiefs, notably *Ngambela* and *Natamoyo*. The heads of certain 'regiments' were invested with *lingongi* with which they 'beat out' instead of crying out the praise phrases as they led their people in homage. *Lingongi* continued the progression of the physical expression of *likute* through clapped and spoken formulae.

Fig. 13 Clapperless bell, 1880s.   Fig. 14 Clapperless bell, 1970s.

The association with *makolo* ('regiments') was to be seen in Jalla's 1936 *Dictionary* definition: 'native gong used by headman to assemble people for public works or war'.[46] Therefore I was initially surprised to find in an isolated valley a man listed by Gluckman as a 'pure' *silalo* territorial chief, who had not been a 'regimental' chief, possessing an *ngongi*. His testimony was of value not as a repressed 'truth', but because it opened the way to utilising a mass of other data. It may be summarised thus.

The original holder of an *ngongi* received it from the king in recognition of prowess. (This informant's forebear settled in that valley as a hunter.) The name *Bo-ngongi* was given to the holder of the artifact, but *ngongi* also came to mean a social entity. Initially the superior of the area tended also to be the chief of the kin. But the reputations of certain *lingongi* – social entities – attracted strangers and so in this way, as well as through marriage, people of different descent groups (*mishiku*) came to live under one *ngongi*. Yet they retained allegiance to their kin superiors and through them to the 'regiment' (*makolo*), whose foundation in kin terms was attributed to the 'brothers' and 'sisters' of Mboo (categories which included royal wives).[47] Thus it is quite possible to find both the kin/territorial congruence in Mwandi/Ukolo near Nalolo and at Namaenya near Sefula from which Dr Mainga generalised and the dispersion of *mishiku*, hence *makolo*, which impressed Gluckman. It is immediately evident that here *makolo* fuse with the origins of *mishiku*.

As with *mishiku*, and I suggest for the same reasons, it proved impossible to assemble a definitive list of *ngongi* holders. But from observation, there were three classes: the 'special service' category, containing people like the family of Lubindatanga who is credited in formal tradition with the discovery of smelting. They held *ngongi* at Nangula, as does the ironworker of the Nalolo court who lives in the Kataba valley. Certain guardians in charge of state gardens held *lingongi* as did emissaries in outlying areas. Secondly there were some territorial chiefs; thirdly there were some 'regimental' heads.[48]

Lingongi were made by a few closely controlled ironworkers like Lubindatanga and they are to be found throughout the heartland and periphery. Stylistically, the shape and size of the bell and the flange-welding were always the same in examples that I have seen. The only variation was in the manner of attaching the two bells, either by hot weld or, less commonly, with a coil of metal from the base of one bell hammered flat around the stem of the other. It all suggests dispersion from few sources of manufacture. *Lingongi* – bells and social entities – begin to look like a stage in state organisation preceding the evolved forms (*makolo* and *lilalo*) that have occupied attention in the past, a stage from which *makolo* and *lilalo* developed.

This view is supported in the evidence on the origins of territorial units (*lilalo*) from elite informants not involved in the Wina affair and from illiterate authorities on Lozi history renowned in their own communities.[49] A consensus was heard that indeed Suu had been correct; the word *silalo* was not in general currency until the colonial government began. However, the institution to which it was applied was older. Territorial power in small groups of villages (*silalanda*) was expressed through *lingongi* before the Kololo came. In areas close to the royal establishments the extent of this territorial authority grew. Chiefs of Salondo, Siwito, Tungi, Sinumuyambi, Liala and Muyema held *lingongi* near Lealui and a similar picture existed in areas near Nalolo.[50]

Thus, the resources were available from which a wide variety of responses could be fashioned when the need arose. A further implication is that the shading between heartland and hinterland in Vansina's notion of the 'Incorporative State' was subtle, at least as far as the edge of the immediate periphery. Beyond, roughly, Sikongo to the west, Lukulu to the north, the Lui river to the east and Mwandi to the south, it would be correct to think of roving, tribute collecting officials (*lindumeleti*) at any time as emissaries among people who were not their own.

5.4 PATTERNS OF THE LARGER SCALE

Here I examine the exchange of objects with use value. The long-distance trade in ivory, guns and later items of conspicuous consumption is logically located in an account of external trade which will be the subject of future work. This trade revolved mainly around the category of 'kingly things' which Lewanika expanded to contain the wider trade horizons of the 1890s.[51] Here the concern is with tribute (*ñamba*). In the terms defined earlier, in Fig. 12, tribute was produced from the surplus available once the subsistence needs of the small community had been met. Recall that in the account of how that was done, the spectrum of expected diet was employed to orient social organisation and social geography.

Local exchanges in the past cannot be studied directly because there can be no contemporaneous internal data. However, modern exchanges of this type are visibly organised by the same relative ranking of diet. Floodplain villages rich in fish and cattle exchange fish freely for starch staples grown in the bush to augment their own staple production, but they exchange grain for high status meat killed in the bush. This means that, if possible, people prefer to obtain meat from someone else's dead beast because live cattle are socially gratifying. Recent studies support this interpretation. The ranking of the items in the 'basket of cattle' described above persisted as recently as 1966–7 when thirty-three per cent of 188 answers from 121 Mongu District cattle owners said that milk production was the primary economic function of their cattle. Twenty-four per cent thought it was manure and nineteen per cent disposal by sale.[52] It has already been shown that questions of diet and of cattle lie in core areas, and Lutke-Entrup's evidence supports the hypothesis of stability of attitudes towards cattle in the face of considerable practical change. The same disruptive forces, emanating from the fragmentation of the local economy, have impinged upon the provision of diet, but Table 5, drawn from responses of twenty-five villages founded before 1885, reveals the influence of priorities upon practice. It shows that local exchanges now, which I take as a minimum indication of the situation in our period when the economy was not as nucleated, are what would be expected: an extension of village redistribution.

TABLE 5. *Local exchanges of foodstuffs in four selected locations*

Type of exchange	Location				Total	
	Plain		Bush		Plain	Bush
	Itufa	Sinungu	Mbekise	Liumba		
Fish for starch*	3	3	3†	–	9†	–
Starch for fish	–	1	–	3	1	3
Forest fruits for fish	–	–	1	–	–	1
Meat for starch	–	1	2	–	1	2
Starch for meat	4	2	–	–	6	–
Milk for starch	1	2	–	–	3	–
Starch for milk	2	–	–	–	2	–
Self sufficient	2	–	–	–	2	–
Unknown	2	–	1	–	2	1
No. of villages used	8	5	9	3	13	12

* 'Starch' translates *bupi* or meal, the basic ingredient of *buhobe*. It may be of root or of cereal origin.
† The Mbekise villages, being in or at the edge of the Luandui valley where they have fishing rights, count as plain villages here.

Only two of the twenty-five villages claimed to be entirely self sufficient and, in the opinion of those whose villages are represented in the table, such exchanges were more extensive in the past. Today most of the traffic is monetised; then these exchanges were complemented by the stored surplus from state gardens.

So where does the economic function of the kingship as essential redistributor of foodstuffs from the centre, as postulated by Gluckman in the literature, fit in? I suggest that ignorance of the resilience and organisation of local subsistence production and distribution, compounded by insufficient appreciation of the kingship's other functions, has caused this function to be overstressed in the explanation of why there was a kingship at all. In 1899 Mushukula storehouse, the depot for public tribute, consisted of three huts. The sites of all the former tribute storehouses viewed today are not extensive enough to justify the scale of stockpiling that would have been an essential part of bulk food redistribution. Nor is there contemporary evidence to support it.

Holub in 1880, Coillard's pen in 1886 and his camera in the mid 1890s, and the first detailed Administration description of tribute goods in 1897 all revealed that specialised products formed the bulk of tribute. The observation is multiplied in other sources.[53] But as already mentioned, some sorghum and maize tribute was brought in. It was consumed in the capital or fed to the public in the ways described. In 1899 and 1900 some wheat, introduced by the Mission, was grown by Lewanika on state gardens (*bonamukau*) for sale to the 'line of rail', although the difficulty of transport kept this a small affair, soon made unprofitable when farms began to proliferate along the right of way.[54]

There were three types of redistribution of specialist goods. The first was of items of general use which were rare or strategic and which do not spoil: salt and iron. A faintly salty water, *mukele*, can be obtained by pouring water through the ashes of burned cassava stems, but it is a tiresome and lengthy procedure for little result. In the west, the sap of palm trees was drawn off and boiled until a salty deposit remained. Salt was collected by members of the senior 'regiment' Njeminwa, who delivered it to the capital. This indicated its status in the spectrum of diet. It was eagerly sought from outsiders and rock salt was one of the staples of early white trade; but in 1878 it was a royal monopoly as far as an outsider seeking to buy it was concerned.[55]

Iron goods alone can be seen to have gone in large part through a centralised redistribution. The exchange of iron was carefully controlled. Its power for good and evil was obvious, as the tradition of how Lubindatanga discovered the metal illustrates. Briefly, it tells that he discovered how to smelt nodes of ore which he found in the Zambezi river mud near his home, not far from the capital of the first male king, Mboo. With the iron he fashioned arrow-heads for toy arrows which he gave to Mboo's children to play with. One accidentally killed another and people wanted to kill Lubindatanga for bringing such an evil thing, but he ran away from Nangula, his floodplain home, and eventually settled at the present home of his kin, also called Nangula, near the ironstone outcrops of Ikabako Plain.[56]

107

Families of ironworkers in the south, not far from the Njoko river, whose work Coillard reported in 1886 and where in 1895 A. St H. Gibbons watched Totela smiths of 'Serampunta' village at work, gave testimonies which corroborated those in the north.[57] Iron was smelted under strict observance of sexual abstinence by the ironworkers, in a place taboo to women, in a furnace shaped like the female torso which 'gave birth' to the iron.[58] Ritual objects like *lingongi*, war spears, fishing spears and hoes comprised most of the output and then were taken to the capital. In Sibukali, near the ironstone source of Kakenge (Kachenji as Coillard transliterated it), the tribute collectors Ilinanga and Imatina came to collect the products, but Lubindatanga, Mwanangombe and Simutanyi in the north delivered their tribute themselves. The first two were chiefs in their own right charged with that task.

However, all the sources stated that a limited trade, largely in unworked iron, was permitted.

> They brought cows, clay-pots and would exchange these things for prepared pig-iron which they would take home and fashion into tools there. Some people did not know the skills for getting iron out of the rock and that is why they had to exchange things. Exchange of hoes for cows, spears for clothes and guns. Guns first, because my grandfather was a hunter.[59]

In 1887 Coillard's artisan Waddell saw how the people of Sefula took skins or *porokoto* (calico) earned as wages from the Mission – 'The indispensable money of the Zambezi', as his superior called it – and 'set off on a pilgrimage to the Matotelas to barter for the indispensable articles and in this way the Matotelas got a winter's cloak or dress and the other the implement. . .'.[60] The Katenge/Lumbe region attracted clients from considerable distances. Ila, Tonga and Toka were mentioned at Sibukali.[61]

The second type of distribution was distinctly different. It involved goods that did not originate in tribute: cattle. In 1882 the early trader Westbeech guessed that since his accession Lewanika had obtained 20,000 cattle from raids. In 1888 the Ila were raided for a final time and from these sources Lewanika amassed a fund of four-legged patronage which he used to great effect in the 1890s. But reciprocity was not entirely absent. The Ila cattle which Selous saw being distributed in Bulozi were replaced in Ilaland with long-horned Lozi cattle and with gifts of guns and cloth. The purposes of cementing allegiance and of demonstrating power were clear and successful.[62] Ila were coming 'in great numbers to make their submission and Lewanika has treated them well; we have several of them here', wrote Coillard in June 1889. Groups were seen subsequently in 1892, 1896 and 1897.[63]

There were no illusions about what these contacts meant. The relationship was rooted in *machtpolitik*. On the one hand Lewanika had freely admitted to the missionary Baldwin who hoped to go and evangelise the Ila that their country was no historic part of Bulozi; on the other, the Ila made the same point when, a month later, they refused to permit a Lozi emissary 'Mobdule' to settle in their country because 'They remember the great raids on their cattle Lewanika has made in the past.'[64] The redistributions were mainly manipulative. There was only little evidence of reciprocity there and they are mentioned to contrast with this quality in the third type of specialist distribution and exchange.

The functions of social labelling and group demarcation seen in the feeding of people in the public square were absent from the Ila cattle pacts and so denoted the subject peoples' difference from Lozi. But they were vividly present in specialist tributes from the floodplain hinterland. This was most overt in the symbolic construction of the royal barge *Nalikwanda* with materials assembled from all over the country, described in the next chapter, but it was also there in the issue of implements, fishing nets, canoes and symbolic objects of favour or status. These constituted the material component of a more complex communication. That message was connected with the energising principles of the face-to-face and the wider communities which have been explored in this chapter, but it also contained elements of the deeper intellectual currents from which *likute* arose. This contact came through the involvement of the king in the transaction.

The presence of all three levels (of social labelling, of the energising principle and of deeper intellectual currents) may best be perceived by analysing part of a form of address (*liloko*) used by one seeking preferment. The literal translations of the Luyana phrases are as follows:

1.	*ku amba na Nyambe*	To speak to the king [called 'God' here]
2.	*ni ku mu lamata*	is because you are related to him
3.	*wibi wa ku mona*	He is not to be seen
4.	*ni ulwe ndila*	I lack a road
5.	*kiwe seetete sa liywa*	You are the glare of the sun
6.	*manda na kwangwa*	You fail with your sister [i.e. it is taboo to have sexual intercourse with your sister]
7.	*wa ulwa alume*	If you lack someone to send
8.	*ku tume*	Go yourself
9.	*lishema ka mwanoi*	These are not your children
10.	*Amba na Nyambe*	Amba [chief steward] of the king [again 'God']
11.	*mwana mbuto wa mulae*	Child of seed in the calabash
12.	*u ka ngambe kambo ka wa*	You go and praise good reports [of me] to him

13.	*ii u lya ni ya ku amba anu kame*	What you eat you owe to other people
14.	*wa tuma, u tume*	To send, you send
15.	*Mumbuwa nalishebo*	Mumbuwa of Nalishebo

The interpretation can be given thus:[65]

> 1,2. The fear which respect engenders is only overcome by close relationship.
> 3. Although the king is physically nearby and can be seen, I lack a
> 4. way to penetrate his majesty.
> 5. You, *Litunga*, are the glare of the sun. It is as impossible to look directly at the sun
> 6. as it is for you to break the taboo against having sexual intercourse with your sister.

[The speaker now changes his approach]:

> 7,8. If you have no one to send to the *Litunga*, go yourself.
> 9. You cannot trust these, who are not your relatives, with the message.
> 10. Amba, Chief Steward of the king.
> 11. guardian of all the goods [seed] brought as tribute and stored in the capital [calabash],
> 12. you, go and sing praises of me to the king.
> 13. After all, the patronage you have received you owe to other people having once praised you in that way.
> 14,15. Send Mumbuwa of the royal descent name WaNalishebo [he is a close relative of the king's and therefore best able to communicate with him].

The levels of social differentiation give shape to the address. It opens with them as the primary insight and they recur throughout (lines 1–4, 7–9, 14–15). The attempt to use Amba as intermediary and what he is asked to do are vivid illustration of this (lines 10–13). At the second level these relationships are spoken of in terms of *likute*, the energising principle of social intercourse, but the third and deepest level is also drawn in, for the Litunga is tied to aspects of the wider Lozi cosmos by lines like 1 and 5 whose full significance will become clearer in the next two chapters.

Part III

6

Cosmology: royal rituals

Let us first define our terms. In the literature on ritual I find the terms which Gluckman has offered to be most lucid and therefore a good point of departure. Following the usage of Monica Wilson, he prescribed the adjective 'religious' to be specific to phenomena which had attributed to them 'some mystical power'; following the usage of Evans-Pritchard, he addressed 'ritual' to 'mystical notions' as distinct from 'ceremony' which attached to making social relationships precise.[1] Proceeding beyond this broad division, he distinguished four contexts to which the word 'ritual' was commonly applied; examples of each will appear in this and the following chapter.

He used 'ritual' to describe magical action which involved the employ-ment of material substances. Examples of this are the royal medicine of invulnerability, war medicine, medicine to make rain, to bewitch and to cause metempsychosis and medicine for the non-symptomatic treatment of disease. He used 'ritual' to describe ancestor and other religious cults. The worship of the High God and of the royal ancestors is described below. He saw 'constitutive ritual' such as in *rites de passage*, which alter social relationships. Some of the life crisis rituals and those of name inheritance (*ku yola libizo*) have already been examined; the royal installation (*coliso*) is a special case of this type. Lastly he mentioned 'factitive ritual' which enhances the well-being or increases the safety of a group. Rituals of the royal person, the building and use of the royal barge, *Nalikwanda*, the ceremony of transhumance (*ku omboka*) and forms of the social relief of afflictions show these qualities.[2]

This chapter will show how the kingship was shot through with 'some mystical power', and therefore those ceremonies which defined social relationship with which it was involved, for example all those covered by the concept *likute*, are correctly labelled as rituals within the semantic

113

framework adopted here. So it is odd to find that Gluckman was also of the opinion that 'I happened to study peoples who had little ritualisation: the Zulu had lost theirs, the Barotse never had much ritual' and specifically not much political ritual, because within his own definition of the term this was not so in the case of the Lozi.[3]

The semantic distinctions and the contrast between Gluckman's assertion and the analysis which follows both highlight an old but still very much living dichotomy in approaches to the question of what rituals mean. Most work on the significance of religion in central Africa has offered broadly synchronic treatment. It may be divided into two main camps. In one, we can see religious phenomena explained instrumentally as devices to hold society together and on course. They are allotted the role of 'a sort of all-purpose social glue', in Robin Horton's description.[4] In the other we are offered a more psychological interpretation where religious belief and behaviour are taken seriously as the fruits of mental processes that try to grapple with fundamental cosmological questions.[5] But the sociological analysis threatens to crush the distinctiveness of individual cases, best put in Evans-Pritchard's comment that 'it was Durkheim and not the savage who made society into a god',[6] and the psychological interpretation, whilst paying much more respect to the importance of religious meaning in life, risks overstepping the explanatory potentials of the data. Then it becomes vulnerable to criticism of the 'if I were a horse' variety: where the researcher believes that he can spontaneously think himself into someone else's shoes – or hooves.[7]

Professor Gluckman stands firmly in the sociological camp; but I do not stand in the other because I do not see that the two explanations need be either partially or wholly exclusive. In fact it is when they are made so that the problems I mention arise.[8] I find my definition of religion must contain the two elements of coordination with the social order and an attempt to explain the apparent chaos and flux of sensory experience.[9] In De Craemer, Vansina and Fox's distilled phrase, 'Religion provides an individual and collective self-definition.'[10] This chapter and Chapter 7 will illustrate that, in the Lozi case, these two notions were packed into the idea of mystical power.

The royal rituals described below tend to emphasise the ordering function; the beliefs relating to the High God and his relationship to all aspects of the visible and invisible world sketched out in Chapter 7 stress more the explanatory one. But elements of both qualities were to be seen in each type of ritual and the mixture was essential: links to Nyambe, the High God, gave strength and authority to royal rituals; affinity to royal rituals gave a warmth of familiarity to the mysteries and strangeness of Nyambe's world.

It is logical to begin our exploration of the Lozi cosmos with royal rituals because these link back into the material and social aspects of the society which we have surveyed and forwards into its intangible parts. The division is my interposition; the Lozi concept of history and of the kingship's place in it showed how in that perception there was no break.

6.2 FORM AND MEANING

Describing the derivation of power within the related matrilineal groups which constitute Kongo society, MacGaffey wrote that, in popular opinion, 'whatever the source of his powers, the chief exerted them on two levels, "by day" and "by night" '. All power involved contact with powers of darkness just as all coins have two sides.[11] The two essentials of this view – that witchcraft was an inversion of normal behaviour, and that it was as fixed in the peoples' stock of existential ideas as belief in the continuing repetition of the cycles of Nature – were to be seen elsewhere in different types of African society.[12] Among the Nyakyusa where positive moral restraint of the type attributed here to *likute* was exercised by the 'breath of men', Monica Wilson argued that witchcraft was an inversion of the accepted norms of behaviour and, by virtue of this, was the wilful misdirection of the mystical powers inherent in each man which combined to form the 'breath of men'.[13] A terrible breach of conduct generated dark power. Applying this line of thought to the recurrent rumours and reports of royal incest, could it not be, she suggested, 'the African equivalent to the myth of Faust selling his soul to the devil'?[14] This idea is helpful in understanding the supernatural aspects of Lozi royal power.

In a precarious world, the most immediately comprehensible of the ritual purposes of kingship was to offer a striking assertion of man's power over Nature. Every year the flood rose. It showed its inexorable power as it came silently creeping across the pastures, isolating the mound villages, until by the 'month of much water' men were compelled to move to the plain's margin. The *ku omboka* (literally: to get out of the water), was the central ceremony of the Lozi year.[15]

When the moon was full and the omens propitious, the *maoma*, the great royal drums,[16] thundered across the flooded plain to summon the paddlers to congregate at the capital. The ceremony of the giving of this signal is instructive. The first drumbeats were sounded either by the *Litunga* himself or by a member of the royal family authorised by him, and by two commoner members of the *Mulongwanji* (Council). After this initial beating, ordinary people took turns to drum under the supervision of *Natamoyo*, the chief formally in charge of the *maoma*. When beating

115

Fig. 15 Royal drums, 1886.

Fig. 16 Royal drums, 1970s.

116

the *maoma*, a man was a *bakali*, not just an ordinary drummer. On the morning of the *ku omboka*, the *mutango*, a special drum which is beaten every night of the *Litunga's* life, called the common people to Lealui.

Thus, only when the *Litunga* had given permission, and led by the royal barge, *Nalikwanda*, the nation moved as one to its flood-time residence, the water covered with darting canoes, as Coillard saw it in 1891. The *Litunga* had shown that he was indeed Lord of the Earth, and of the flood, and of men.

The *Nalikwanda* itself was a visible statement of the unifying function of the kingship. The design of the vessel has been unchanged since the early nineteenth century. The description of Mulambwa's *Nalikwanda* which Livingstone obtained from Mokantju, an Mbunda who had been Mulambwa's attendant, was of a boat 'built of planks sewn together, roofed in with white cloth [the *lutanga*] and requiring twenty men to paddle it'.[17]

Fig. 17 Lewanika I's *Nalikwanda*, 1890s.

It was the biggest piece of technology in the land. The construction was 'overseen and in part done by chiefs and stewards. The boatyard near the capital is screened, above all to hide the work from women.'[18] Lewanika invited Coillard to witness the first voyage of the *Nalikwanda* of 1889 (usually a new vessel was built each year): 'Everyone wanted to make me share their admiration and enthusiasm. "Well, *moruti* [teacher], what do you say of *Nalikwanda*? You see what the Lozi can do. The Lozi!" and a clicking of the tongue told the rest.'[19] Coillard observed patronisingly that given the country and the people, it was a masterpiece. Lewanika sensed the disdain and attempted to strike at its source. He got the artisan Waddell to explain to him the principles of European boat building.[20] His

117

later *Nalikwanda*s were larger than their predecessors and, after 1897, there were two *Nalikwanda*s, one made '*ka serotse*' (in the Lozi fashion), the planks bound together with *makenge* (the roots of the *mukenge* tree, *Combretum zeyheri*),[21] the other '*ka sekhoa*' [*ka sikuwa*: in the white man's fashion] using long nails.[22]

But *Nalikwanda* was more than a demonstration of technical skill, it was in a quite literal sense a symbol of unity, a concretisation of factitive ritual which was taught in a question and answer song. Here is a part of it:

> *Nalikwanda* says 'You people, who made *Nalikwanda*? What people contributed the material?'

> 'The timber came from the Matotela; they had to cut the timber and bring it to Lealui. The Kwangwa have collected different kinds of fibre, the roots of trees.'[23]

Each year the cutting of new wood, its transport to the capital, the shaping and building, adornment, launching and the first voyage to be dedicated at the grave-site (*sitino*) of Mboo or of Mulambwa were an object lesson. That was what Coillard saw at Sioma in 1887 and what Waddell saw when in August 1890 he met a fleet of new canoes descending the Lumbe river on the way to Nalolo to be broken up and built into *Nalikwanda*.[24]

But *Nalikwanda* also expressed unity and well-being through what was done in the boat. The song continues, evoking the twin elements of satisfactory diet, *buhobe* and *busunso*, and the behaviour pattern of *likute*:

> 'What kind of boat is this, for it looks like a garden of maize on a *lizulu*? [The image is of the raised paddles which look like maize stalks when the boat is under way.] And what is this remarkable thing? When you look at the boat you see smoke coming out!'

> 'It is from a fire for cooking meat inside that boat.'

> 'Sometimes I see steam there. What is that?'

> 'That steam is from cooking. It shows that all kinds of things are found there in *Nalikwanda*. It is a boat which does not belong to the *Litunga*, it does not belong to any individual, it belongs to all the people. Anyone who wishes to go there to it cannot be stopped. Only if he does not paddle strongly will a man be stopped from going there. He will be thrown overboard.'[25]

In the person of the *Litunga*, the theme of symbiosis, of mutual responsibility expressed in the notion of mutual ownership – the country by the *Litunga*, the *Litunga* by the country – takes a step further from the last

Fig. 18 Lewanika II's *Nalikwanda*, 1970s

part of the *Nalikwanda* song. It is a constant refrain in court praise-sayings, ballads and proverbs. Thus: 'when he is in Kuta, he is like an elephant which is in the thorns. He is a buffalo in the thick forest. He is like a garden of maize upon a mound. . .' Here the praise-saying evokes a volatile balance of forces: the strength of the elephant and the obstructiveness of the thorns may fight each other or the one may protect the other; similarly the buffalo and the forest. The third image stresses the positive potential in the relationship of king and people.

I can demonstrate the durability of this theme over time through a proverb. Here is the fullest modern version I have:

> *Nengo minya malolo wa fulanga mei matanga, musheke ni mu ku onga.*
> The [bull] hippopotamus who leads the herds swirls the deepest waters [in the river], the white sands [of the shallows] betray him.[26]

This was interpreted to me to be an analogy for the *Litunga* (the hippopotamus) and the nation (the deep waters that cover and protect him).

Two forms of the proverb incorporating the basic elements were recorded in the 1890s.

> *Ka tuwa mbu wa Libonda, wa mona tjimba-tjimba; ka mona wato ba lipe, wa fulanga meyi matungu, musheke ni mu k'onga.*

119

> He jumps, the hippopotamus of Libonda, when he swims; he sees a canoe on the riverbank, he swirls the deepest waters, the white sands [of the shallows] betray him.[27]

This material can contain the modern interpretation. The other, interestingly, stressed the idea of dependency by equating the people with the herd:

> *Mbu ku mwan'a lilolo, wa twelanga matungu, musheke ni mu k'onga.*
> The hippopotamus is child of the herd, he dives to the deepest waters, the white sands [of the shallows] betray him.[28]

The image of hiddenness in the depths is potent. We find it in another part of the praise-saying: 'A good chief is hard to find. You have to get nets and a fishing basket, go into the river and catch him at the bottom of the river. . .' But its central message was unambiguous: 'Rule the country well. If the country dies you will be responsible. If it prospers, it will be proud of you and it will do homage to you: "There he is, the son of a brave man. Give him fat meat!. . ." '[29]

Once installed, the *Litunga* ceased to be the 'owner of his body', in literal translation. He had the power of life and death, to distribute tribute, to grant land and cattle. He was spoken of only in a special vocabulary of words reserved for reference to him. As described already, the utmost *likute* was practised in his presence from which all unclean things were barred. Yet he could do nothing for himself. Should a dangerous snake come towards him, it was the duty of the subjects to kill it. Conversely, should the people be displeased with the *Litunga*, it was in their power to kill him. The *lutanga*, the white hive-shaped cabin in *Nalikwanda* whose entrance was guarded, symbolised this power. The authorised formal tradition relates how Yeta Nalute was executed when his *Nalikwanda* was scuttled and he was drowned inside.[30] This action had a double significance, for the sinking of a king's *Nalikwanda* symbolised the end of his reign, whilst Yeta was killed without his blood being shed, which would have released evil. It is an extension of this belief which explains why suffocation and poison are the recurrent ways of committing premeditated murder in Bulozi.[31]

The dual potentialities of the kingship may also be what is reflected in the usual shape given to the royal tradition. Three pairs of kings appear following one another, the one seen as good, the other bad:

Yeta Nalute	(bad)
Ngombala	(good)

120

Mwanawina I	(good)
Mwananyanda	(bad)
Mulambwa Santulu	(good)
The Kololo Interregnum	(bad)

From the standpoint of 1900, Mulambwa was the last king of the Noble Age (*Muluilonga*).[32]

The ritual of *ku omboka* showed the *Litunga*'s power over nature; the rituals of *coliso* (installation) showed his acquisition of those powers from Nature. There were four main stages. After the candidate had been selected and the choice approved by a group of certain chiefs and certain *liñomboti* (priest-guardians), the first stage of the process could begin. Hunters obtained lion manes, leopard skins and eland tails. Bulls' hides were prepared and just before the new moon the future *Litunga* was taken to Makono, village of Mbuywamwambwa. He had to remain there one night and secret rites were performed which invested him with power 'of the night' and 'of the day'. At the *coliso* of Yeta in 1916, the missionaries Burnier and Boiteaux could not persuade any one of their confidants to give them an inkling of 'that mystery which we are not permitted to probe and which leaves some anxiety in our hearts'.[33] The analogy used for it was that Liombekalala (representing legitimation by the royal predecessors) and Lingongole, the huge water snake, spirit of the plain, were involved. The active verb used to describe these rites was *lasa* (Luyana: to lick).[34]

The next morning the *Litunga* went to *Nalikwanda*, and sitting upon one of the drums he took two sticks and made fire which was placed in a pot shard and fed with maize stalks. Then he visited Ikatulamwa and afterwards returned to the capital with the new fire where the second stage of the ceremony took place.[35]

Ngambela lifted the new king up and placed him on a drum before his people: then the men danced the *ngomalume* before the new *Litunga*, with the royal drummer *Itwi* playing the drum *mwenduko* (adverbially: 'downstream'); and they formed into their *makolo* ('regiments'). The people came to do homage (*shoelela*). Meanwhile the women came to collect the new fire to rekindle their hearths which had been extinguished since the death of the previous king. These were all ritual ceremonies.

The third stage occurred some time later (nearly four months later in 1977) when the *Litunga* visited Ikatulamwa and Imwambo, the sites connected with Mboo; last was the ritual hunt at Sanya – ritual in that it was only necessary for the *Litunga* to cast a spear at an animal to fulfil the 'hunt' (see Chapter 4, Section 4 above).

The derivation of royal power from the intertwined forces of Nature and the supernatural was expressed again in funeral rites through their forceful statement of the kingship's ability to defy mortality and to transcend time. Eye-witness reports of Lewanika's burial in 1916 illustrate this. On 4 February, 1916, as soon as the news of the king's death came, the two missionaries Burnier and Boiteaux went to the palace, entering through the rear courtyard and, 'passing beside the medicines and charms, we reached the inner court' where the dead king lay in state in the barge *Indila*.[36] Meanwhile, Lewanika's European-style house at his village, Nanikelako, had been torn down and a huge pit dug in the middle of the mound. Great physical effort, including the digging of a special canal, was vainly expended in an attempt to launch the huge *Nalikwanda* which was waiting at Lealui for the *ku omboka*, so that it could carry the body on the journey from Lealui to Nanikelako before being scuttled. In the event, it had to be destroyed with axes, on dry land.

At the interment, the missionaries spoke to the assembled people and said that they had 'put their finger on the strength of the ties which unite the Mission and people'.[37] But it was the nominally Christian *Ngambela* Mukamba who drove the common people out of the burial enclosure and supervised Lewanika's elevation to deity, and the sacrifice of ten oxen to his spirit.[38]

The ceremonies continued for several days, with the sacrifice of huge numbers of *muhoha* (funeral cattle), 170 on 9 February alone. Thereafter, 'each chief and petty chieftain must provide one head of cattle and all this is noted'. Christians were supposed to abstain from the sacrificed meat.[39]

R. V. Roach, the Administration official present, had possibly a faint idea of what was happening. On the day after the funeral he sent a note to his superior, invalided in bed, to say that the *Ngambela* and Council had to remain at the graveside all night to prevent anyone coming near, thus obtaining 'immense power for good or bad over the natives'.[40]

More detail may be added. Coillard knew that the grave of a *Litunga* was lined with reed mats and that it was dug on an east–west axis. A hut similar in shape to the canopy (*lutanga*) of *Nalikwanda* was erected in its western end. All this is indeed still done today. The body, surrounded by household objects, bowls of food, etc., was placed under the *lutanga* in a sitting position, dressed in white calico and adorned with white trade beads. In more recent years coffins have been used. Coillard was also told that formerly servants and some chiefs were either buried with the *Litunga* or committed suicide by drowning under the *matindi* – the matted floating grass in the plain.

Ngambela forced a strong reed through the roof of the *lutanga* directly above the king's head and then people began to fill the grave. The reed ended a few feet below ground level and when the soil reached that point, a deep wooden bowl with a fitted lid (*tubana*) that had been pierced top and bottom was placed on top of the reed. A further length of reed extended upwards from it above the surface. This formed the channel called the *limbwata* through which communication with the dead king would take place. All this was done before the public gaze. Then, after the grave was filled, all the men worked to build a fence around the site. Once this was complete, only the reigning *Litunga* and the *ñomboti* (priest-guardian) could enter. That night, the first consultation of the king took place to determine whether his spirit rested in peace or not.[41] It will be seen in the next chapter that these rituals were strongly resonant of those whereby a witch (*muloi*) obtains his power. At the completion of these rituals, the grave became a *sitino* and certain senior *liñomboti* who had been called to the capital at the death of the king taught the new *ñomboti* his duties.[42]

6.3 WHITE CALICO AND MILK

The royal grave-sites (*litino*) are one of the most difficult things to study in Bulozi. Because of their continuing importance they can be approached either physically or in questioning only with the greatest circumspection.[43] What follows is therefore a relatively bloodless description of a vibrant, rich and concealed cultural phenomenon.

Dr Mainga suggested that the royal graves stood distinct in form and also to some extent in function from two other strands in Lozi religion: the 'Nyambe cult' and beliefs in witchcraft, sorcery and magic which, she wrote, Lozi claim to have adopted from the Luvale, Mbunda and other surrounding peoples. It is a claim which she does not dispute.[44] Indeed, her work consistently postulated a contrast between Lozi and alien traditions: alien witchcraft was being suppressed while the Lozi cult of the royal graves was being 'revived' during our period.[45] In fact the evidence does not permit the sharp-edged distinctions she made. Far from bypassing the worship of a High God (Nyambe), the grave-sites were part of the same cosmological projection, whilst aspects of dark power were present in the rites connected with them. Nor does even the thin evidence we have support the implication that Lewanika's political decisions expanded or indeed could expand the importance of the royal graves. The idea of revival is argued in the face of written evidence as well as internal suggestions of greater continuity: graves, groves and gravekeepers, and, still less, widespread reverence for them, cannot be quickly conjured up.[46] So what in fact do we know?

There were four types of royal grave-site and we have different sorts

123

and amounts of evidence about each. The first consists of the key ritual sites: Makono, *sitino* of Mbuywamwambwa; Ikatulamwa, capital of Mboo and the place where his body was buried; and Imwambo, the *sitino* without a body to which the spirit of Mboo moved and where it is consulted. We have no eye-witness accounts of the installation rituals connected with these sites, and they have rarely been visited by outsiders. Coillard stopped at Ikatulamwa in 1895 and described a layout much as it is today.[47] He also wrote of Mboo's transmigration without naming Imwambo, although nine years earlier the 'village of Mboho' was named as 'Mohambo' (Imwambo misheard?) in the notes of the first testimony on Lozi dynastic history which he collected from Lewanika and Nalubutu.[48]

The second and largest type are most of the royal graves of traditional time. Of them we have most datable information about Lilundu, *sitino* of Mulambwa Santulu, the last major Luyi king before the Kololo invasion. The information suggests a general image of how the significance of sites changed over time and in response to present circumstance. It shows how the changing perceptions of Lozi society over time, expressed by the waxing and waning of specific grave-sites, can be represented as a series of maps of their locations, for which we possess only the broadest outlines at the moment.

When Livingstone visited Lilundu in 1853 during the period of Kololo rule, it was clearly a *sitino*: the dead king was spoken of in the present tense by priest-guardians (*liñomboti*) who were supported by gifts from Luyi and also Kololo and the site was visited by 'the Cow of God' (*Liombekalala*). But it was initially shown to Livingstone as the late king's village where, in a grove of trees which he had planted, stood the ritual artifacts which Mulambwa had used to invoke his forefathers. Praise stories about Mulambwa were told to Livingstone.[49] I think that here we see the king after the first 'stitching' of his tradition partly in traditional but still partly in historical time.

The next European description of Lilundu does not include the artifacts, and Coillard's photograph taken between 1891 and 1896 shows only the fence around the grave mouth (*limbwata*) and grave.[50] It is the site of the king, now firmly in traditional time, who for the generation of colonial contact most powerfully represented the Noble Age (*Muluilonga*) of which he was seen to be the end but whose qualities were, by implication, sought. In this respect it is significant that *Nalikwanda* was reportedly dedicated at Lilundu as well as at Ikatulamwa at some time during this period.[51] These qualities were described in the praise-saying for Lilundu: 'There is happiness in Luwa [Lilundu], in the past it was greater than other villages, now it has things added to it.'[52]

124

Fig. 19 Lilundu royal grave-site, 1890s.

In the twentieth century, we can see the same process – the transformation of a recently deceased king's village into a powerful ritual site – occur with even greater precision in the case of Lewanika's grave Nanikelako, which was the king's 'country retreat' when Jalla visited him there in the early 1900s, became a *sitino* in February 1916, and has come to occupy in later years the position held by Lilundu in the 1880s and 1890s.

The third type is illustrated by the *sitino* of Mboo's brother, Mwanambinyi, which stands at Imatongo in the south of the floodplain. Like that of Mboo, his burial was not regular. The well known myth tells that he dug a pit and entered it with his soldiers and some cattle; the rest he changed into egrets and to this day egrets are called 'Mwanambinyi's cattle'. It is the first grave encountered upon entering the Valley from the south. For Coillard it was the guardian of the iron gate to the kingdom of shadows,[53] because sacrifice was made here to ask for or give thanks for a successful passage through the Ngonye rapids. This is shown in invocations of Mwanambinyi's help. These texts, separated by many years in their performances, also show that appreciation of Mwanambinyi's power was a consistent theme. I give the more recent text first: the second was recorded in the 1890s:

Mwanambinyi a nañananyi Mwanambinyi of the wagers
Shangwe, shangwe, shangwe, noble lord, noble lord, noble lord,
Moliange yooshoo. Our Master, all homage.

125

The hidden hippopotamus

U tu be ndila, tu ende.	Give us the road, that we may travel.
A mei a ombole wino-wino,	Oh let the water be really placid,
Ku enda wino-wino.	Oh that we may travel really well.
Ku ala tomu, u tunamanine,	Look at the hippo, he is dead,
Nji bali Molietu ky tunda,	For we come from Our Master's dwelling
Nji onge ti ya ti file	For if it is an antelope, it is dead
Nji siaman'e sonje.	Or any other sort of animal.
U ku tu twaka, tu wabelelwe	Oh that we may be really well received
wino-wino	in the place where we are going
A ka tu nyangulukelwe o michima	May hearts melt towards us [those of]
A kwa matunga.	The people of other places.

Ana likanda lia mande,	You who wear a belt studded with *mande* shells,
Ka mu iye mu ngoma;	Come [and beat] the drum.
A muwa-muwa,	You the beautiful ones, beautiful people,
A muwa-muwa a shikalete ngoma.	You the handsome men who carry the drums.
Uy'uto na singi ku yoa,	Whosoever wishes to wash his canoe,
Ni mu ka yoa mu Nalikana wato wa ye.	Let him wash it at Nalikana.
Umukoa no Liambai,	In the brotherhood of the Zambezi,
Ku mu isa silongano umo.	There is not a slothful paddler.
Aya mato oondje ku shweta,	all the boats ascend the river,
Ku ta mutulo sikulo sa Mwanambinyi.	They are heading northwards to Mwanambinyi's mooring . . .[54]

Coillard refused to make the sacrifice demanded of him on his first ascent of the river or thereafter[55] but later white travellers did at least stop at Imatongo.[56] The Methodist missionary Baldwin ascended the river for the first time in 1892 and clearly did not understand what he did: 'At one of these villages the king's father lives and the chief said it was customary for all white men passing to make him a little present, so I cut off about 1½ yards of white calico and sent it.'[57] A missionary who prevented his crew from doing homage reportedly lost his boat in the early 1900s,[58] whilst barge crews employed by the haulage contractor George Sutherland always stopped to give homage (*shoelela*) in the mid colonial period. Dr Mainga witnessed such action during the 1960s, and I met the Nalolo royal establishment at a *mafulo* (camp) near Imatongo in May 1975.[59] Imatongo is a particularly visible special case in the written record. The same cannot be said for the final and most hazy type of royal grave-site where written information is scant and what there is is different from the equally scant oral data.

The *Litaba za Sichaba* records that Nakaywe was the village of *Litunga* Ngombala, who lies buried in the neighbouring village of Ñundu, and that

126

Kusio, ruler of Nalolo, who contested Mulambwa Santulu for the kingship later in traditional time and died in the process, is buried there.[60] Oral information about Nakaywe is not forthcoming. Several times, my request was answered with a proverb: 'A small house does not indicate slavery; the people of Ñundu are not masters of those of Nakaywe.'[61] Then a previously proven source described to me how no one was buried at Nakaywe (*mbumwa milalo*, chief of the graves), where the High God Nyambe was worshipped and *sombo*, the ritual request for fertility of crops and herds was made. This is corroborated in two other sources. Gluckman wrote that after the king had reserved his portion of tribute, 'first, they give to Ilinangana, the priest-caretaker at Nakaywe, the capital of the king Ngombala, near which in national extremity Ilinangana offers prayers to God, Nyambe',[62] whilst informants at a senior grave-site confirmed that Ilinangana played an important role which they were not prepared to specify. And there my information stops.

The proverb may certainly bear the interpretation that the priest-guardian of Ñundu, Nyamanalimweya, was subordinate to Ilinangana, and this was the interpretation given by my proven source. But the full explanation of the mechanics of the royal grave system at any point of time remains unknown to me. So all I can say is that I suspect that the history of Nakaywe may contain direct evidence of the linkage between Nyambe and the royal grave system. This hypothesis is supported by circumstantial evidence from the 1880s concerning rites and purposes of the royal graves.

Coillard learned early in his time in Bulozi that 'the king is Nyambe's servant'.[63] He encountered Mwanambinyi's grave as he ascended the river, but Mataa, *Ngambela* during the period of Lewanika's exile, refused to allow him to visit grave-sites in the heartland.[64] However, in 1889, Nalubutu gave him an account of the relationship between the ancestral spirits (*balimo*)[65] and Nyambe. The vehicle of expression was the myth of genesis of the royal line.

> Above these gods [the *balimu*] there is another god who alone bears the name of Nyambe and of whom the *balimu* are only servants. In the night of time, Nyambe married Buya Moamba [Mbuywamwambwa] who gave birth to the Lozi royal family. He also married a crocodile, a tigress, a lioness – from whom came forth the animals and the different races of men. . .[66]

Recall how the *Litunga* was addressed as Nyambe in the praise-saying which ended Chapter 5. The relationship was made more explicit in his praise-name *kaongolo ka Nyambe* – God's insect. In the passage of the Ngonye rapids Nyambe was thanked through an act of homage (*shoelela*)

127

on the spot and Mwanambinyi was thanked upon reaching Imatongo.[67] In the next chapter, the invocation of Nyambe will be seen to involve several actions common to the royal graves and to 'dark' power.

All four types of grave-site served several functions beyond the specialist ones of specific sites. They offered invulnerability. The warriors who accompanied Lewanika on visits to royal graves in 1886 carried no shields and bore their arms upside down, and were anointed with the royal protective medicine *litsuku*. They formed the advance party of the army, accompanying the *sebimbi*, a virgin who carried a horn of war medicine which had been sanctified and prepared at a grave where also the sacred spears, usually kept in the shelter (*kaolo*) within the courtyard of the palace, were blessed. Coillard saw them all go forth in January 1888 to raid the Ila.[68]

The ancestral spirits (*balimu*) which resided in the graves could restore health. When a member of the royal family fell sick, it was at a grave-site that 'some dignitary, not unfrequently the king himself, will repeat a form of prayer supplicating the departed on behalf of the patient', 'to restore his health through intercession with Nambe'.[69] When George Westbeech lay sick at Lealui in February 1886, Lewanika sent messengers to invoke the 'Dear Departed' to speed his recovery; Westbeech was unimpressed by their help.[70] When most under Coillard's influence, Lewanika's oldest son, Litia, told him how he had been summoned to Nalolo to pray for a relative who was sick, but he had refused.[71]

The ancestral spirits could give rain. Rain is valuable. In Luyana *ku loka* means 'to rain'. The relationship between graves and rain appears in this proverb given to Jacottet:

> *Iwa li ka loko Mulina, isitjima [muchima] sa lio ni ba Liondo li'eñua lia silila ñeke.*

> When it rains in Mulina [translated by Jacottet as 'far removed places', but it is printed with a capital 'M'], its heart is at Liondo where people beseech help and where children cry.[72]

Rain has always to be coaxed; that is what the old rainmaker told Livingstone in their celebrated exchange, and in all rites to make rain the theme stands out.[73] Dr Mainga was told that the sacrifice for rain at a royal grave was always of black cattle, for the black symbolised rain clouds. My information from a senior priest-guardian confirmed this and added that the *ngomalume* was danced by the men outside the enclosure; this was a vital part of the procedure *ku shea pula* (to pray to the royal ancestors for rain).[74]

Within the enclosure, all was and is white. The priest-guardian dressed in white, the gift of a traveller safely returned was white calico, white beads or white *mande* shells. The normal cattle for sacrifice were pure white, the only exception being *ku shea pula*, and the medium of communication with the spirit was milk.[75]

One of the most consistent statements about the royal graves is that concerning the method of consultation. Milk is poured down the reed of the grave mouth (*limbwata*.) If the ancestral spirit accepts the milk, the answer is positive, if the milk is refused and blown back out of the *limbwata*, the answer is negative. If, on the other hand, the milk has been part of a non-oracular libation, its refusal indicates that the spirit is not at peace.[76] Again, it will be seen that there is a resonance with a *muliani* (medicine) 'accepting' or 'rejecting' the person to whom it is administered.

Above all, the ancestral spirits gave advice. Royal graves were visited for advice on major policy decisions, or to find explanations for inexplicable occurrences, like the drought years 1889–91 and the smallpox epidemic of 1892–3. For example, Matauka, Lewanika's sister, was ordered after divination with *litaula* (knuckle bones) to visit grave-sites to obtain approval for the canal construction programme.[77]

Throughout this section I have made innuendo to 'dark' royal powers. Arnot heard of the king's power to make rain, to direct thunderbolts (a witches' speciality) and to avoid thunderbolts;[78] Lewanika claimed his magic powers of invulnerability and his ability to protect his followers in one of his first meetings with Coillard while relating before Kuta the tale of his exile,[79] and elements of the installation rites are designed to invest 'dark' power. But hard evidence is, not surprisingly, elusive. About the most solid is that concerning the royal drums. Holub heard how they contained the amputated fingers and toes of the children of chiefs and whilst Jacottet wondered if this referred to the Subiya fetish drum *Infoma*, his description of that artifact was significantly different.[80] An officer of the Colonial Administration mentioned the 'fingers in the drum' unprompted and added that the matter had been raised formally in Provincial Administration meetings during the 1950s where it was decided that there was little to be gained from interfering and a lot of goodwill to be lost. He recalled seeing chiefs without the top digit of the little finger.[81] Beyond this is speculation. I would only observe that supernatural functions 'of the day' and 'of the night' were not at all distinct.

6.4 A HISTORICAL ACID TEST

So far in this chapter we have carefully uncovered and cautiously fingered fragmentary, difficult, unequally illuminated or mutable data. Because of the nature of these sources, it would be advantageous to be able to view our observations about core areas and what they contain from another perspective. The flow of narrative history in Bulozi offers us such a possibility and the analysis of royal power which I have advanced may be assayed in the acid test of the rebellion of Mataa and Tatila Akufuna of 1884–5.

Gluckman suggested that conflict was built into tribal societies and that such conflict was mediated in different ways. In the Lozi case he thought it was mainly through the existence of 'custom' – a norm of behaviour – that friction was lubricated, that differences of opinion were settled by protracted and secretive negotiation among the elite and that the spear was an exceptional and final resort. But he thought that when violence erupted openly, 'rebellions reassert the values of kingship and restore its power'.[82]

A semantic distinction between 'revolution' as structurally disruptive and 'rebellion' as structurally reinforcing is valuable, but there is a danger of attributing qualities to each word without justification, perhaps thus making the difference too polarised. In other places it seems that real revolutions occurred.[83] What we know of the events of 1884–5 in Bulozi support Gluckman's plain observation, but not the theory which he employed with it.

The reassertion of the values of kingship was achieved in two ways. During the rebellion, a situation of high tension caused superfluities to be shed, leaving the fundamentals exposed; in the aftermath, the reinstated Lewanika relied upon those of his attributes closest to the fundamentals from which he could derive the surest support. But we must be very careful in the implication which we draw from this.

From the evidence I have used above to describe 'core areas', and explicitly in my statements of hypotheses, I have stressed repeatedly two sets of propositions: the difference between 'core areas' and those areas which could be moulded, and the interdependence between the perceived stability of the one and the malleability of the other. In these terms Lozi history is like a spiral: elongated from one dimension, circular from the other. I have argued that to be competent draughtsmen we need to work in both dimensions, and this is why I carefully distinguished the face value of Gluckman's observation from his larger theory.

This theory was a concern with the repetitiveness of social systems which I think is just an optical illusion that results from using a one dimensional viewpoint. His was an equilibrium model; mine cannot be. There is a vital difference between understanding that people believed that their society was unchanging and sharing that belief.

Gluckman was aware of difficulties with his theory and when he wrote retrospectively of the years during which he conducted his work with and did his major thinking about the Lozi, he observed that 'I was thinking in crude functional terms of institutions – even civil war, which can after all be an institution – contributing to the maintenance of a rather rigidly conceived social structure'. But in fact the structural-functional idiom was still that within which his Yale lectures on Lozi jurisprudence, also a product of his later years, were cast.[84]

During the 1960s Gluckman wrote in detail about the equilibrium model which he had used.[85] As a result of his line of explanation I encounter real difficulty. This model, he suggested in 1966, was a mode of analysis, *not* a description of reality: a heuristic device drawn from reality but going beyond reality. The equilibrium assumption was an 'as if' assumption, conspicuously labelled in this way to show that it was abstracted from the full complexity of historical data in order to facilitate analysis of the 'structural duration' of the axiomatic aspects of a society. Such 'structural duration' has a long wavelength of time change and contrasts with what Gluckman called 'actual historical time'. At once the reader will recognise a close affinity between this thesis and the slightly more systematic process model of differential time change which I proposed at the beginning of this book. In his essay, Gluckman continually stressed that the 'as if' equilibrium assumption was not an assertion of stasis:

> The failure to appreciate this when reading an analysis of institutions may give the reader a false impression that the writer believes that the institutional form he analyzes has endured in exactly the same form from far in the past, and will thus endure into the future. This is not always the reader's fault, since often the analyst has not made clear that the time element in analysis is a structural duration, and not actual historical time.[86]

Thus it becomes a moot point when a synchronic analysis is in fact a diachronic analysis in synchronic clothing; that could rapidly become like debating how many angels can dance on a pin head. The reader will now appreciate the fundamental difference between the model that I have used, which does not recognise the distinction between 'as if' structural time and 'actual' time but ascribes reality (and equal concern) to all time-scales, and Gluckman's, which sees no necessary and interactive connection between work at different time-scales, however desirable that might be.

Gluckman suggested wistfully that narrative and clarity in structural analysis sat at opposite poles – it was a dilemma always with us – and the one was only to be purchased through sacrifice of the other. I am more

131

optimistic for reasons which the structure and content of this book, exemplified in the organisation of this present chapter, make plain. I do not agree that the undeniable tensions between the different time-scales of, in Braudel's terms, 'event history', 'trends' or 'the long term' are debilitating; on the contrary, rather are they creative; they help to accumulate expository power, thus giving demonstrable reliability to the analyses which are offered. I do not think that Gluckman's process model, if put into service, would give this reliability, although it must be emphasised that this is because I do not share Gluckman's confidence in the inherent capacities to elucidate deemed to be present in unsupported field data. But more to the point, I cannot discern the caveats of the 1966 paper in the 1950s *Custom and conflict* theory, nor in the exposition of his Lozi materials from the 1940s at about the same time. As used in those years and before, I see his equilibrium model as indeed static and one dimensional, and that is why I wrote of it as I did above. But this is not to say that the structural-functional idiom is devoid of insight. In 1966 Gluckman tartly observed that there was almost an element of abuse in the term by then; that dismissal of a theory teaches nothing and that if we call others 'ass-head' we had better beware in case, like Bottom in *A Midsummer Night's Dream*, we are actually wearing a donkey's head mask! At least the structural-functional insight registered clear awareness of the existence of long wavelengths of time. But Gluckman was right. The clamour of the eager iconoclasts was the shouting of dwarves perched on giants' shoulders, more unhelpful to the cause of understanding in the long run than his own, generously admitted, overenthusiasm for the structural-functional theory when he used it years before; more unhelpful because the dwarves lacked both the data and the charity of the giants, not to mention the height.

But the structural-functional theory is an incomplete and therefore inadequate intellectual tool and so, having distanced myself from that position, still possessed, I hope, of my own head and not that of any other animal, I will use the data about the Lozi civil war to illustrate a less expansive point than Gluckman wished to make: that the kingship evinced both the functional and explanatory roles I proposed at the beginning of this chapter.

We do not know and probably never will know the cause of the rebellion. Four different explanations are to be found. One suggests that it came about because Lewanika was unable to satisfy the demands upon his patronage of Mataa, leader of one of the rival factions who had helped to overthrow Mwanawina in 1878.[87] A second, proposed publicly by Coillard, blamed Lewanika's excessive cruelty.[88] A third, proposed by Gluckman, was akin to a now superseded view of the War of the Roses:

that it was a reaction by overmighty vassals to an attack on their personal retinues and also a reaction to the law of redemption (*Muliu*).[89] The fourth is that given by the rebels themselves to Coillard. Lewanika had broken the rules of kingship by instigating the murder of a chief within Nalolo which was supposed to be a sanctuary.[90] This supports Gluckman's contention through its implicit defence of the kingship against an unworthy occupant. What is significant is not the truth or falseness of the charge, but that this idiom was chosen to express it.

By 18 April 1884, Frederick Arnot, a young missionary then staying in Lealui, smelled trouble and took up Serpa Pinto's offer to accompany him to Bihé in the west. When he bade farewell to Lewanika on 1 May, the king showed that he too had premonitions of what was coming.[91]

The initial coup was apparently a palace affair. Mataa attacked Lewanika's house, and the king, fleeing in the ensuing confusion, seized a loaded gun and a bandolier of the wrong size of cartridges for it. Therefore he was unable to make an immediate counter-attack which might have contained the violence.[92] In the event his capital was reduced to smouldering ruins. His *Nalikwanda* and thus, by symbolic extension, his reign were sunk.[93] But the principle of the kingship itself was reaffirmed because the ritual of usurpation was followed. The rebels sought to legitimate their new regime in the expected ways. Coillard witnessed the full Kuta ceremonial at Akufuna's court, obtained accurate descriptions of the roles of *Ngambela* and *Natamoyo*, saw ñamba (tribute) brought, a

Fig. 20 Akufuna (left) and Mataa (right), 1886.

chief installed, the *shoelela* (homage) given. Akufuna himself was of the royal lineage.[94]

The first reaction of the Sesheke chiefs when news of the rebellion arrived on 1 September 1884 was of worry and fright. Uncertainty about the new regime's permanence, which continued throughout its duration, may have caused some slackening in the degree of forcefulness with which the chiefs ruled. Waddell wrote of a stealing spree and of commoners selling ivory to traders (normally a royal monopoly), but these irregularities were superficial.[95] The day after the news came, the chief Ratau allowed Coillard to go up river and when he did, he found that the main 'state' services and the rites and practices of kingship continued.[96]

Take, for example, the porterage of canoes at the Ngonye Falls. This service had been located at Mukwala village at least since Livingstone's visit, during the period of Kololo rule.[97] Coillard found the 'owner of the name' 'Mokuala' to be Mwauluka, who operated the porterage for him on his way to see Akufuna on 26 December 1884. Coillard liked him and stayed three days with him on his return, when he found that 'Mokuala' was a fierce partisan of Lewanika's. Indeed, this man, who enabled him to visit Akufuna, later became Lewanika's *Ngambela*.[98] Returning from Lealui, Coillard had stayed at the village of 'Mokumandi' who had been a steward to Lewanika and was now a steward to Akufuna.[99] He wrote that 'civil war makes men into madmen, makes savage beasts out of them. Here, as in Paris, it has given birth to the Commune and the Commune has left its marks',[100] but his day to day observations scarcely support the judgment. Violence visited the elite and their families, causing Akufuna's sister MaMochisane to sigh that this was a 'land of blood', but she survived the counter-coup and lived on in obscurity. It was because Mataa killed all Lewanika's immediate kin, except his mother Inonge who was saved by Mwauluka, that Lewanika revenged himself upon Mataa's kin. His purging was selective.[101] Of greater significance although of less dramatic potential is the information that the royal grave-sites were respected throughout the civil war.[102]

In August 1885, Lewanika's *Ngambela*, Silumbu, left the deposed king in his retreat in the Mashi Valley and advanced to Lealui, compelling Mataa and Akufuna to flee to the north to Akufuna's brother, Sikufele. Mataa deposed Akufuna, appointed Sikufele in his stead and returned to Lealui. Meanwhile, Lewanika had arrived with more forces and a pitched battle ensued. In January of that year Coillard had found a Scottish trader called John MacDonald living in the house of the departed English missionary, Arnot, trading with Akufuna and Mataa. 'During his stay, Lewanika returned and he being oblidged to defend his life and property took the side of Lewanika and now the natives boast of his great shooting and having defended himself against so many with a double barreled gun.'[103] Some Mambari traders fought for him also. However, it was mostly close spear fighting. Mataa and the *Ngambela* Silumbu both fell.[104]

News of the battle reached Westbeech at Pandamatenga on 17 October, confirmed on the 29 October. He went to Lusuma (where Coillard had heard the news by 21 October) and there he heard conflicting reports – that there had been no battle and that Lewanika had not returned – from the chief of Sesheke, the *Mulanziane*.[105] Exasperated, Westbeech went back to his base leaving a letter which mystified Coillard:

> I left, but am coming back. . .I'm coming on horseback and before I leave everything must be settled. No trading, no hunting, it is time to bring things to a head so that you can have security and I also. P.S. The natives hide things of importance from you, but fear not, we are coming.[106]

'Bringing things to a head' meant using his hunters as soldiers to restore Lewanika and although in the event this was not necessary, Westbeech used them to make the fact of the restoration very clear to the Sesheke chiefs who at the end of November were indecisive or openly hostile to Lewanika's return.[107] Westbeech received instructions from Lewanika to precede Coillard up river and reached Lealui in late February 1886.

Fig. 21 Lubosi (left) and Matauka (right), 1886.

TABLE 6. *The relationships between the kingship structure and the royal ancestors in Lewanika's reign, 1880s*

Ancestor			Lewanika's representative to ancestor				
King	likolo	sitino	Queen	Chief	rank[a] likolo	Steward	rank[a] likolo
NGALAMA	Kawayo	KWANDU	The Moyo (Ikuma, Ma-Morambwa)	*Ngambela*	1/R1 Kabeti[b]	Imasikwana	3/L2 Njeminwa
YUBYA		NAMAYULA	Lunga ('like a second Ikuma')	Liomba	5/R6 Kabeti as above?	Salali Awami	(?) 7/L7
MULAMBWA	Imutakela	LILUNDU	Mukena	Mukulwakashiku	3/R4 Imutakela-Nandinde[bc]	Wina	6 Njeminwa
				Kalonga Mafwira	8/R15 Njeminwa[bc] (?)	Kabila Runi	(?) (?)
NGOMBALA	Imutakela	ÑUNDU	Kamona Matondo			Mubita- Kalunde Molelenyana	10/L9 (?)
YETA I	Suyaela	NAMANDA[d]	Namabanda	Nalishua	(?) Ngulubela[be]	Amba[f] Lisholi[g]	(?)
				Namunda Waluka	9/R11 Ngulubela[h] (?)		
'MOANA SILUNDU'		'KATURAMOA'[i]	Malundwelo				
'MBOO?' INYAMBO	Ñundwe Kabeti	IMWAMBO LIONDO	Imwambo Maondo	Imukondo	*Sikombwa* 15[j]	Ilikani Walishebo	(?) (?)

Sources: Jalla, *Notes privées*, pp. 93–9; pp. 103–4; Burger, *Notes privées*; Gluckman, *AOBNA*, passim; Mupatu, *Bulozi sapili*, pp. 46–7.

Notes:
a. In rank columns, Jalla's position is given first, Gluckman's second. 'R' indicates right-hand mat in Kuta, 'L', left-hand mat (stewards); (?) shows that no information about the name appears in either source.
b. Head of *likolo*.
c. Jalla calls Njeminwa 'the king's regiment'. Mupatu records that Lewanika's *likolo* was Imutakela. Kalonga is recorded as much more senior in 1890s than 1940s.
d. Jalla: 'Nambwawata'.
e. Gluckman stated that Katema (R10) was head of Ngulubela.
f. Head of royal household staff. Jalla distinguished him from other *likombwa* (stewards).
g. Literally 'thief'. A joke? A misunderstanding?
h. Gluckman stated that Namunda was head of Kawayo.
i. This is a fascinating entry in Jalla's notebook. It refers to Ikatulamwa where the official tradition related that Mboo's body was originally buried. In 1977, a 'northern origin' version of the foundation myth appeared in which Mbuywamwambwa was said to have been married not to Nyambe, but to a Lunda man, Mwana Silundu. Here is perhaps an early indication of a strand of tradition which submerged during the colonial and early independent regimes. The name was added in brackets above the original sentence 'Marund-welo–représente mânes de Katuramoa tomb. de' (incomplete), p. 98.
j. Jalla names him as a chief but records him as the 15th *sikombwa* (steward). The present Imukondo is a chief.

As he set about the restoration, the king concentrated on the funda-mentals. He purged his enemies, killing many on the 'Wizards' Ant Heap', Lwatile, which was to become a Mission Station in 1892, rewarded his friends and seated himself firmly upon tradition, paying great attention to the royal grave-sites, which 'alone offered him security both as a man and king'.[108]

In March 1886, 'the king started on a round of visits to the graves of his forefathers to pray for the welfare of his country. . . He was away four days, returning on the 5th with much beating of drums. . .'[109] In April, when Coillard returned from Europe, he was on another tour. Lewanika did not possess the technology of repression to impose his rule upon an unwilling people; he could massacre huddles of chiefs, and apparently even that only by stages, but it was beyond him to embrace all his far-flung people in a grip of terror.[110]

But there was another logic in his actions. In December 1888 he was called to Ikatulamwa to sacrifice an ox. Coillard scolded him. 'I must yield to the Lozi who do not understand your teaching', explained the king.[111] In 1891 Coillard learned that he had been to the royal graves again. He confronted the king in front of the Kuta whilst he was receiving homage from some of his people. 'You went to pray to the dead?' 'Yes', he said, 'I am a Lozi, what do you want me to do?'[112] From the evidence given already, it should be clear why he gave this reply: his acquiescence was the reciprocal of his people's allegiance. Lewanika had no doubt as to the fundamental derivation of his power.

He placed himself under the special protection of Ngalama, who was represented to Jalla in the formal tradition as the strong-armed conquering and unifying king.[113] The other ancestor to whom he paid special attention was Mulambwa, the lawgiver and last ruler of *Muluilonga* – the Noble Age. We are not obliged to rely solely upon oral opinion in making this observation, for there exist data which reveal very clearly how Lewanika's priorities in this regard were reflected in the structural dispositions of personnel within the royal establishment. These data are presented in Table 6. It shows that Lewanika's senior wife, the *Moyo*, three junior wives, several very senior chiefs, including the *Ngambela* and the stewards attendant upon the queens, chiefs and stewards who together encompassed the headships or were members of the senior 'regiments' (Kabeti, Njeminwa and Imutakela), were focused upon the two rulers, Ngalama and Mulambwa, through their ritual duties. These duties were to invoke the special qualities and aid of the dead kings, and the concentration of high ranking people among those charged with the invocation of these two kings both spotlit them and implicitly stated that at that time they were regarded as pre-eminently important.

'If there is one thing he finds loathsome to see us fight in the breach', wrote Jalla to the Mission supporters, 'it is the worship of his ancestors.'[114] Chapter 8 gives a fuller view of the fight.

7

Cosmology: public rituals and beliefs

7.1 THE LIMITATIONS OF THE EVIDENCE

It is not surprising that it was the kingship and its rituals which were particularly visible to early outsiders. From their writings we have been able to gather sufficient data of sufficient precision to show stability in the institutions and behaviour which they described, often with little understanding of what they saw, in the 1850s, 1880s and 1890s, and which I observed in the 1970s. In this area I have been justified in using field data to fill out and explain often cryptic observations.

But these royal rituals formed part of an embracing intellectual pattern whose seminal expressions were in the foundation myths and myths of genesis which populate that prestigious period in the Lozi perception of the past before the beginning of traditional time. In Western eyes this is cosmology, but to the Lozi it is the vital stuff of history, concerned both with the social order and with questions beyond society, which is why it must concern us. However, these impalpable topics are usually the most difficult to recover from any of the available data and are the most difficult to understand reliably. Vansina wrote a whole chapter on Kuba intellectual history in *The children of Woot* with the primary intention of pointing this out and of facing historians squarely with the consequences of such ignorance.

In Bulozi we are fortunate in two practical ways which make it possible to look at intellectual history inevitably incompletely, but with slightly more precision than is often possible. Firstly, we can use some of our contemporaneous European sources extensively because we can test their reliability. Livingstone and especially Coillard and Jalla were all good observers and extensive note-takers. The last two were not only resident, but also exceptional linguists about whose work we do not need to feel the general pessimism that Evans-Pritchard felt about early white sources,[1] although we need to understand the likely effects of their personal opinions upon their interpretations. Furthermore, for the first time we have the full range of their materials available. Secondly, we benefit from a historical coincidence.

In the same year that Coillard returned to Bulozi with his Mission party, E. Jacottet began his ministry in Lesotho. In July 1885, he moved to the parish of Thaba Bossiu and it was there that he undertook most of his very extensive work on linguistics, folklore and ethnography. His main field was naturally the study of the Sotho, but in 1894 three young men aged about twenty were sent from Bulozi to be schooled in Lesotho. Kasala and Samata were Subiya, Kabuku was a Luyana speaker. They stayed with Jacottet for several weeks and freely dictated to him a mass of cultural material after having taught this remarkable linguist their languages.[2] In 1896 he published formal grammars of Subiya and Luyana as a result of this contact and, in 1899, he published parallel versions of the Subiya texts. In June and July 1900 two more Luyana speakers, Akaende and Wambinji Malumo, stayed with Jacottet, and with their help he

Fig. 22 Jacottet's informant, Akaende (standing).

revised the texts dictated by Kabuku in 1895. Akaende was raised in Lealui and was the purest speaker in Jacottet's opinion; Kabuku had a Kwangwa accent and Malumo was brought up in Makanda, where Kwangwa is spoken. However, three-fifths of the Luyana texts published in 1901 originated from the earliest informant, Kabuku. In his introduction to these texts, Jacottet promised an index which would identify the material given by the later informants, but unfortunately it was not published. Nor were the Mbunda and Totela texts which he had in his files and which he envisaged as a fourth volume.

This is the full extent of the biographical information which Jacottet gives us about his Lozi informants. It is insufficient to give a decisive reply to the first critical question which must be answered if we are to use this collection with confidence to describe the general Lozi cosmology of the 1890s: how representative of the Lozi people were these informants? For example, if they were all the sons of princes and chiefs, we could not feel great faith in generalising from their evidence to the 'average man in the bush'. Thanks to the meticulous research of Rev. J-P. Burger it is now possible to answer this question with a little more accuracy.

François and Christina Coillard made their first exploratory expedition to Bulozi in 1878–9. During this trip they obtained permission to return and establish the Zambezi Mission and so they travelled back to Lesotho on the first stage of a journey to Europe to raise funds for the endeavour. With them they took two young men, Seajika and Kalumba, whose homes were in southern Bulozi. The intention was that they should be converted, made literate and prepared in Lesotho to become evangelists, 'that these two young men may be the means of shedding some light abroad on the banks of that beautiful river among the heathen who live there', as Christina Coillard put it to her niece. They did return to their homeland with the Coillards in 1884, but rapidly became alienated from the Mission. Seajika especially will be encountered in other roles in Part IV of this book. This experience caused Coillard to conclude that the training of African evangelists was best conducted in their home environment and he never repeated the experiment of sending men to Lesotho.

However, in 1894, Coillard's subordinate in southern Bulozi, Louis Jalla, did try again and sent to Lesotho the first three young men who had professed the Christian faith under his tutelage. This was the criterion of selection. Samuele Kabuku was an ordinary man who came from the area of Mabumbu, just north of Mongu in the heartland of Bulozi. He had come south to Kazungula and it was from there that he was sent to the Evangelists' School at Morija in Lesotho in 1894 where he remained until 1898. During 1895 he visited Jacottet. Returning to Bulozi, he became an evangelist first at Sesheke, then at Kazungula. Later he was sent to his home area, Mabumbu, thence to Nakato in Makanda where he died in 1927. Setefana Samata undertook the same course of studies as Kabuku at Morija. He worked for the Mission at Sesheke until 1908 when he was disciplined and does not appear to have reentered Mission service there-after.

Petrose Kasala was, like Samata, a Subiya of humble origin. He first entered Louis Jalla's service as a junior herdboy, in charge of the calves. He attended Kazungula school and made good progress. He confessed his faith in 1894 and was sent to Morija for the same course as the other two. On his return to Bulozi in 1898 he was baptised, married and was placed at the Victoria Falls (Livingstone) Mission Station to assist M. and Mme Coisson. Later he founded a school annex at Siakasipa, but returned to Livingstone to second Louis Jalla. He died there quite suddenly on 22 March 1910.

Jacottet's later pair of informants arrived in Lesotho rather differently. Struck by the double disaster of the rinderpest epidemic in February 1896 and the death of her husband in April, Mme Mathilde Goy decided to go to Lesotho.

> My escort was made up of eight young Zambezians; five of them had to bring the wagon back to the Zambezi with provisions for the missionaries on the return trip . . . The three others had been my pupils for five years and my intention was to take them as far as Lesotho where they would be able to pursue their studies. . .

Of these three, one returned to Bulozi shortly after arrival, another, Moetseko, died. The third was Akaende.[3] He undertook training as an evangelist and it was during this time that he helped Jacottet. However, he does not seem to have succeeded in his studies in Morija, for he returned to Bulozi as an evangelist-aide, i.e. without a diploma. He worked in Sesheke.

Alfred Wambinji Malumo, the last informant, was the most enterprising. He was raised near Lealui and went to Lesotho on his own initiative, travelling south with a Sotho evangelist, Jakobo Moshabesha, who was returning home. On arrival at Morija, Malumo was admitted as a pupil in the Normal School and the director suggested that it would be appropriate for him to be supported financially by the Zambezi Mission, which he was. He returned home with a Sotho wife and a teaching certificate; he taught at the Normal School in Sefula from 1908 until 1912. Eventually, since his salary of £22 per annum was not close enough to the £75 which he sought, he, like many other Mission teachers, left the teaching service to pursue a more lucrative career in the Government administration.[4]

The second critical question to be asked of Jacottet's collection of texts is about the circumstances in which the work was done. Were the informants coerced and frightened or were they open and cooperative? To answer this, we must mingle a little extrapolation with such observations as we now have. What we know of their subsequent careers suggests that the informants were essentially in harmony with their cultural context in Lesotho. I suggest that the circumstance which operated most greatly to our advantage was that when they transmitted these materials, these informants were in a benign cultural limbo. I call it this because although Thaba Bossiu was not Bulozi, and therefore the young men were freed from any local restraint upon their tongues, they were still in a community of Sotho speakers (which was how Jacottet could be taught so quickly). Recall that these were the years during which the techniques of inventing tradition were being discovered in Bulozi and in which a public distinction between 'open' and 'closed' subjects was becoming known. In Lesotho these pressures were absent. We have evidence of this, although admittedly not very full evidence: Jacottet wrote in 1895 that his informants 'gave me all the data of which I had need with intelligence and good-will', which one might expect since their environment in Lesotho was both positive, giving them literacy and learning, and supportive, in that missionaries and their teaching made light of the dangers present in what they related. More encouragingly for us, in 1900, Jacottet revealed that he had been given certain material on condition that it would *not* be published. It was a 'very strange story about an ancient Luyi king . . . it appears that it is forbidden to tell it to strangers'. He could not see the danger in it, but kept his word to his informants.

In fact, we can 'control' these data from another direction. The young men gave Jacottet versions of the myths of genesis, work songs, children's riddles, descriptions of public rituals like the *ngomalume* dance, explanations of witchcraft belief and practice and so on. The striking omission is akin to this curious story which Jacottet was forbidden to publish: there is no continuous form of formal royal tradition.[5] It is striking in contrast with the performances recorded in Bulozi from the elite, including the king, over the same period. There we can watch the emergence of increasingly structured versions of the formal royal tradition which gradually edged out the transmission of most other types of cultural material and culminated in the *Litaba za Sichaba*. I suggested earlier that one effect of this 'authorised version' was to draw shutters over certain areas of Lozi life. So one further circumstance which makes Jacottet's collection valuable is that it was made before Lewanika's visit to England in 1902 which, among other things, taught the king what shape of his society should be projected. The closest and perhaps only comparable situation of which I know was that in which Wilhelm Bleek was taught the Bushman language and Bushman lore by five major informants between February 1871 and January 1875. Like Jacottet's informants, the Bushmen stayed with their pupil away from their people.[6]

It is for these reasons that I think that the Jacottet texts offer us a detailed and datable body of cultural material which I may reasonably use to organise the fragments of our knowledge about the Lozi cosmos. The books have been little used before and being in French, Luyana and Subiya (these rendered in French phonetics), they have remained relatively inaccessible, particularly in Bulozi. Their influence has not been able to 'feed back' into the oral tradition in the manner of the *Litaba za Sichaba*, the English translation of Coillard's book and elements of later writing. But it is legitimate to wonder whether these books have 'fed back', even unconsciously, through my own questioning in the field, thus prejudicing the data I collected. This was not so because the works did not come into my hands until I visited the Doke collection in Salisbury towards the end of my first spell in Bulozi, by which time I had independently gathered much of the basic comparative modern material. But there is a third and rather different reason why we are able to recover a workable quantity of material, and it relates to the nature of Lozi beliefs, a point best understood in contrast to another study.

Nuer philosophy as studied by Evans-Pritchard centred upon the idea of Kwoth, Spirit. The Nuer had no conception of what Spirit's characteristics might be; they only knew that what happens in the world is determined by Spirit, who may be influenced by prayer and sacrifice. Ancestral ghosts played only a small role, animist ideas were almost entirely absent, witchcraft ideas had little scope and magic, less, because human skills and practices could not affect fortune since fortune and misfortune both came from Spirit. Ritual was almost entirely absent and, since Man's role was passive, there were prophets who were more influential than priests. Consequently, to ask for more detail was futile: 'They say, very sensibly, that since the European is so clever perhaps he can tell them the answer to the question he asks.'[7]

It has already been seen that Lozi religious ideas, coordinated with the social order through royal rituals, took, in consequence, more precise forms than the Nuer. The services, needs and potentials of royal ancestral spirits were definable. Below, it will be seen how the High God at the centre of the Lozi cosmos was also much more clearly etched than the Nuer Spirit. Nyambe had defined characteristics, accepted fields of direct and mediated intervention; access was highly ritualised, priestly and other manipulative roles clearly prescribed. Nyambe, like Kwoth, also determined what happened in the world but the methods were less predictable, more open to influence in more ways. In consequence, there were simply more phenomena about which observations could be made. These permit us to describe and to fix chronologically the existence of certain material phenomena – sites, artifacts, etc. – the execution of certain ritual actions and the expression of certain oral data. But although we may make many reasonable deductions about motive and meaning from them, there is finally the limitation that local data is local data. The step from it to a universalist interpretation is also a step beyond the data. It is a step of faith.[8] But whilst it may be impossible to *describe* the spiritual experience wherein the explanatory function of religion takes place, the response of the historian should be not to ignore or deny its existence, but carefully to circumscribe the spot in as much detail as possible, however little that may be.

7.2 RIVER SAND AND WATER

The concept of a High God Nyambe was the hub from which other aspects of the Lozi cosmos radiated and took their bearing. The image and ritual relating to him remain stable throughout our period. Livingstone observed how 'Nyampi' was worshipped and invoked in cases of sickness or failure at the hunt by placing a bowl of water opposite the rising sun.[9] Holub wrote of

> an invisible omniscient being who observes exactly what everyone is doing and deals with everybody arbitrarily. It is feared even to say his name and instead, as a rule, the substitute word 'Molemo' is used...The proper name for this omniscient being is Nambe...They believe that the powerful being is living '*mo horino*' [*kwa halimu*: above, in the sky][10]

The informants of Jacottet elaborated this dour image. Nyambe was cruel,[11] vain[12] and capricious.[13] Men's attitude to him combined love and fear. They strove to follow him into the sky,[14] yet sought to kill him for his pride.[15] God once lived among men and men were like gods, but they lost their immortality.

In the version of this which Coillard learned, God and Kamunu, the first man, were originally together on earth where the animals were man's equal. The estrangement was a result of Kamunu's realisation of his skills: first he cultivated plants, then he discovered fire, then he killed an animal and cooked it, then many other animals. Finally Nyambe decided upon a test. He called all the creatures to his island home where a huge pot sat on a blazing fire. He asked someone to remove the pot. No animal could, but Kamunu and his children brought water, extinguished the fire and could

145

then remove the pot.[16] Then Nyambe was afraid and accompanied by his messenger and adviser *Nalungwana*,[17] he enlisted the help of the spider who spun a thread by which Nyambe escaped to heaven where he founded his village, *Litooma*. Lewanika and Nalubutu described *Litooma* to Coillard in 1888 as 'God's village at the sunrise' in contrast to *Nanjenje*, village of the damned.[18] Implied in the ascension, as in other myths of this type, was an increase of power.

In Jalla's version, Kamunu lost his immortality as he gained his independent skills. Jacottet's informants related that man was condemned to mortality when woman broke a taboo.[19] After this fall, God sent two messengers to mankind – the hare as bearer of death, the chamelion as the bringer of life – and he allowed the matter of man's mortality to be settled by who arrived first. It was the hare.[20]

Nyambe was implored directly at moments of crises or of special need. The individual did this by placing a bowl of water on a small altar of white river sand and green twigs at sunrise.[21] The small community asked blessing on its collected hoes and seed grain when the first rain fell, and at times of national emergency. *Sombo* could be made at Nakaywe as already described.[22] The means of invocation was through the act of homage (*shoelela*).[23] Nalubutu related how Kamunu first rendered homage to Nyambe whilst he was still on earth.[24]

Nyambe communicated with man through the cycles of Nature: of the sun, the moon, the seasons, the menstrual cycle. The taboos which surrounded menstruating women dramatised the dangers inherent in the procreative powers of Nature,[25] while attention to the phases of the moon in particular could release their potentialities. Therefore the *ngomalume* was an act of worship.[26] The timing of military campaigns, the movement of the *Litunga* and, supremely, the *ku omboka* all were controlled by the phases of the moon, coinciding with its rebirth. Consultation at royal graves was also made normally during the waxing moon. All these underlined the *Litunga*'s claim to kinship with Nyambe.

The royal graves were inhabited by the ancestral spirits who were subordinate to Nyambe. The proverbs about Nakaywe where Nyambe was invoked make that clear.[27] The divine origin of the kingship was explicit in the foundation myth, in the funeral rites of the *Litunga* and in the rituals of the royal grave-sites.

In approaching Nyambe or his subordinates, skill and knowledge were important, for, as the myths of Kamunu suggested, they gave man what power he had in the face of a capricious god. The priest-guardians were specialists. Cunning and strength could enable a chief to seize ruling medicine from a supernatural being.[28] An ordinary man could acquire the characteristics of an animal by 'drinking worms' (maggots from the

146

carcase of the animal desired). The worms would accept or reject him. If they accepted him, then after death he would become such an animal by metempsychosis, thus 'defeating' death.[29] Here the line between powers of the day and of the night was shadowy.

On the basis of the thirty or so religious movements of which they collectively have knowledge in a region to the northwest of Bulozi and with which several of the languages of Bulozi have connection, De Craemer, Vansina and Fox distinguished a shared cosmological matrix, probably of great age, from forms of expression shaped by localised cultural influences which were relatively volatile because they related to volatile problems.[30] This hypothesis may serve us here, for the Mbunda divining basket (*ngombo*) and the Luyi divining bones (*litaula*) addressed the same problems. This will become clear when I display the techniques of treating affliction in the next section. The most convincing indication of the superficiality of separating overt magical and religious practices on a criterion of ethnicity is the nature of Nyambe as perceived in our period in so far as I have been able to sketch it.

Nyambe was capricious. He radiated darkness and light. The world and all that happened in it eventually depended upon him. His world was full of resources which were therefore charged with positive or negative potentials, reflecting his nature. Jacottet's informants explained this graphically: nothing in the natural environment was neutral (which is not the same as animism).[31] Skill and faith were both necessary to manipulate the natural environment beneficially. Take the crucial commodity of rain. In their argument, the rainmaker had told Livingstone that 'God alone can make rain, my medicines don't make it. But he has given us the knowledge of certain plants and trees by which we pray to him to make rain for us. We charm the clouds and he makes the rain for us.'[32] Jacottet's informants told him of the powers of the 'old man of the rain and thunder'[33] and of the way that the royal ancestors could be beseeched to intercede with Nyambe to bring rain. The relationship was the same even if the methods were different.[34]

Birds,[35] animals,[36] roots and plants all had these dual potentials. Which was activated depended primarily upon the motive, contingently upon the manner in which they were approached. Human beings had the same potentials but they were controlled differently.

The professions of healer (*ñaka*) and of witch (*muloi*) were very similar in many of their ritual performances. Techniques of diagnosis and divination, of bewitching and of curing, were frequently similar, sometimes

147

indistinguishable. Jalla was given the standard evasive answer in the 1890s: 'According to the Lozi [sorcery] comes from the Mbunda, just like *mwati*' (vegetable poison, of which more below). The real distinction between witch and healer was one of *motive* expressed by certain ritual behaviour, and part of this sense was in Jalla's own observation that 'the *moloi* (sorcerer) is someone who divines with evil intent [*jete des mauvais sorts*] – the *ngaka* (doctors) are entirely different'.[37]

A person could become a witch by choice or by accident. Those who acquired the powers of a witch by choice could do so either to advance a particular comprehensible goal, like despoiling the wealthy and successful,[38] or to satisfy a craving for human flesh, which was unnatural.[39]

The voluntary acquisition of witchcraft (*buloi*) involved one or more of four ritual actions: (1) the drinking of a medicine given by a senior witch. As he gave the medicine, the senior witch would tell the initiate that a very close relative would now die and that if this happened it would be proof that the medicine 'accepted' him – a similar sort of test to that described for voluntary metempsychosis;[40] (2) the killing of this or another close relative whose spirit would then be enslaved as the witch's familiar (*ku swala silumba*);[41] (3) the enslavement of the spirit of any recently dead person by reviving the corpse with medicines,[42] and (4) the eating of human flesh.[43]

Liñaka (healers) who were appropriately skilled could provide protective medicines that would prevent bewitchment. Such medicines were, and are, highly prized. However, the danger was that the healer consulted might be a hidden witch and so the protective medicine might, in fact, capture the spirit of the seeker after protection. Consequently, 'the most sought after doctors are foreigners. One goes to them, or has them brought at great expense'[44] precisely because they would not involve the risk of local healers who might capture and use one's spirit.[45]

Manipulation of medicines enabled suitably skilled men to control the lesser creatures. A healer who had such medicines could control animals beneficially; the most important of such were crocodile doctors who could protect cattle from attack whilst fording a river.[46] A witch, whose motives were evil, would direct his familiars to evil actions.[47] Snake doctors and those with lion magic were especially feared.[48]

However, to beat the witches at their own game was too risky a course for commoners. So before one was bewitched it was generally better to employ a specialist healer with his protective medicines and when it was too late, to consult divination. Techniques of divination have changed more easily than other areas of ritual. For the 1880s and 1890s we can establish the range shown in Table 7, which I divide by general area of application and increasing seriousness of subject.

148

TABLE 7. *Forms of divination*

	Vernacular term	Application
Divining bones	*Litaula* (Luyi)	General minor misfortune;
Divining basket	*Ngombo* (Mbunda/Luvale)	foretelling the future;
Axe/hoe	*Silepe/muhuma*	certain disease diagnosis;
Medicine horn	*Mushengo ('lwiya')**	preliminary witch-hunting
Calabashes	*Lihwana ('tungu')**	
Poison oracle	*Mwati* (fowl as medium)	More serious misfortune.
Dance oracle	*ku bina liyala*	Diagnosis: witchfinding
Boiling water ordeal	*Katjoo ka maoma'**	Specific witchcraft
	(Katulo ka maoma:	accusations
	judgement of cauldron)	
Poison ordeal	*Mwati* (accused witch)	
Dance of the men	*Ngomalume*	Serious communal
Consult at *litino*	*Ku shea kwa litino*	misfortunes (e.g. epidemic disease)

* Jacottet, *Études*, vol. III, pp. 161–2, 155; his transcriptions.

Litaula and *ngombo* were oracular and depended upon the reading of patterns in the fall of the bones or the arrangement of objects in the basket. Luyi used *litaula* and Mbunda used *ngombo*. A small mat held by the diviner and blown upon could, by the way it responded to the blowing, give a yes or no answer to a dubious interpretation of the bones.[49] The use of an axe or a hoe as a localised oracle in which the answer was given by whether the implement could be lifted or was fixed to the ground has remained in unchanged form and use into the present,[50] like *litaula* and *ngombo*. But divination with medicine horns and calabashes, described to Jacottet,[51] has changed. Today the *sikuyeti* is found as well – a gourd filled with latex with a small antelope horn and a piece of mirror implanted in it.[52]

Mwati was a white viscous vegetable poison. It was administered to fowls and the divinatory power of the medicine killed or spared the bird. Because they were used for this purpose, Lozi royals would not eat chicken, as the missionaries found out to their embarrassment when Matauka visited them.[53] This sort of oracle was used for more serious matters like witchfinding. Jacottet and Jalla both received accounts of healers using dancing for witchfinding in order to divine while entranced.[54]

The most dramatic, best documented forms of divination were of the

149

two related ordeals to determine a specific accusation of witchcraft. In the first stage, the accused plunged the hands into a cauldron of boiling water. Arnot witnessed it in 1882 and again at Lealui in 1885 when the victim was unscalded, which was taken by the Lozi as proof of the efficacy of the test.[55] On this point, the Methodist missionary Baldwin wrote most fully in 1892:

> There is a mystery about this boiling pot which puzzles us, for whilst some – as we should suppose would be the case always – are badly scalded, others seem to be able to thrust their hands into the boiling water without any hurt. Mr Coillard says he has known cases where the person after taking out the stones has picked up the pot and poured the water over their heads and down their bodies to further attest their innocence without any apparent hurt.[56]

One of Coillard's evangelists watched the ordeal at Sesheke in 1885.[57] Christina Coillard noted a case the next year where a woman who had quarrelled with a man who died the following day was accused. She failed the boiling water ordeal and died during the second stage.[58] This stage was described graphically by Holub: the accused was stripped of clothing and ornament. His wooden or ivory bracelets, sign of being a high-born Lozi, were symbolically broken. Then he was seated astride a scaffold over a low fire and given *mwati* to drink. If he became unconscious and toppled into the fire, it was a sign of guilt and he perished. If he vomited up the poison it was a sign of innocence and he was released. The test was a direct appeal to Nyambe for judgment.[59] *Mwati* was the medium of communication. It is notable that none of the means of divination were purely psychic; even the entranced dancing of the diviner involved inhalation of smoke from burning medicines. In complementary form, the act of bewitching also always involved a material substance. A spell could be 'thrown', but first it had to be made. The same conception underlay ideas of disease.

7.4 THE RELIEF OF AFFLICTIONS

Afflictions are of two sorts, physical and psychological, and therefore they are often psychosomatic. They form a very immediate concern and people everywhere tend to make it a high priority to get rid of affliction once it is perceived. Therapy presupposes explanation of causes. Such explanation is frequently indicated in the form of therapy and, because of the immediacy of the problem, the explanation (hence therapy) will often expose core values more explicitly than other sorts of behaviour. The more intensely the problem is perceived, the quicker will recourse be made to what is considered to be most reliable.

I began this chapter by commenting on the usual difficulty in obtaining data on intangible matters in the African past. It seems to me that the historical study of therapeutic thought and practice offers one way into the subject, for just as the civil war of 1884–5 offered us an opportunity to view royal rituals in action, so does the treatment of affliction offer a test of our other information about cosmological ideas. Such work is in its infancy. What follows is a sketch for the Lozi case.[60]

In the last section I suggested that the relationship between the conceptual matrix represented by ideas of the High God and magical practice was one of continuing stability and superficial alteration and variation. The same may be said of the relationship between theories of disease causation and therapeutic techniques.

All the good and evil in the world was the creation of Nyambe. He placed a fixed quantity of disease in the world and all that an individual could do was to observe certain taboos and practices in an attempt to avoid contracting disease or, once infected, to exercise *butali* (skill, cunning) to rid himself of the affliction and place it somewhere where the next passer-by would pick it up; the devils could not just be cast out, they had to enter the unfortunate and innocent Gadarene swine. This cyclical view of disease had two significant pivot points: that the total quantity of disease could not be diminished by man's agency – in case of epidemic such as the smallpox one of 1893, appeal was made via the royal ancestors for Nyambe to act – and that the acquisition of a disease normally could be traced to a physical action or material object.

Illness could come from breaking the menstrual taboo or from breaking the post-parturition taboos. The ease with which the latter might accidentally be broken can be seen from this description: Kanoti Nalumango's wife miscarried at Nakonga, their village near Sefula, in late March 1890. She was confined to a small hut outside the village, he to the village itself where he had to avoid crossing the tracks of cattle or going near growing crops. After the new moon, his wife was entirely shaved and the hair was burned along with her previously broken cooking pot and calabash plate and the shelter where she had stayed.[61] Equally, a thief might become ill with colic if he ignored a *sifunda*, which might be a line drawn in the sand to make a magic circle (*lishengo*), or some knotted grass near a field of grain to indicate that the property was protected. The unfortunate Nalumango infringed a *sifunda* soon after his wife's miscarriage and he told Coillard that only the person who had made the charm could give him medicine to cure him.[62]

The worst *sifunda* to infringe was one established after someone else had been freed of a disease. In many forms of individual, but especially communal, treatment the sequence ended at a crossroads where the

151

medium into which the disease had been transferred from the patient was deposited; this might be some medicine sticks or a bowl of water.[63] This ritual idiom, recorded in the 1970s, has been peculiarly resilient over time. Here is Coillard's account from 1887:

> At the crossing of two paths in the wood I noticed three stakes with magic grasses where someone had boiled medicines and close by a sefunda, a circle traced in the sand with the foot. Nguana Kwai [Mwana Kwai = son of tobacco!] and Libonda let out a shout of fear seeing me put my feet inside the magic circle, touch and examine the little shelter. 'Teacher! You'll die from it! Here is where the ñaka has disposed of someone's disease and if you even only approach it, you are sure not only to catch it, but to die from it! When we see such things, we make a large detour.'[64]

This was the end and the beginning of many types of disease, notably those involving washing or leaving some substance at the end of the procedure. Why should such a theory of causation and a related form of therapy persist in such detail? Tylor suggested several basic 'intellectual conditions for the persistence of magic' which Skorupski has more crisply labelled as 'blocks to falsifiability': ways in which 'facts and theories lose their potential for coming into direct opposition'.[65] Tylor saw the majority of the successes of magic, which he regarded as a 'sincere but fallacious system of philosophy', to be the result of 'natural means disguised as magic' coupled to an 'incapacity to appreciate negative evidence'.[66] Skorupski observed that both these blocks are the result of attitude, since they could be removed by the experimental approach. Tylor suggested a third block of interest to us: that failure may be blamed on neglect of the conditions imposed or upon improper execution of the rites. Skorupski observes that this sort of block to falsifiability is different, deriving from the logical structure of the beliefs themselves.

Thus we may see that the theory of causation *per se* was protected by an 'attitude' block and reinforced by an established pattern of therapy which, along with the deployment of substances, was protected by a 'structural' block to falsifiability. This pattern included the non-symptomatic treatment of affliction. It may be covered at first by the same 'attitude' block common to most therapy in human history: a link to natural effects (natural recovery indicates success of therapy). If the patient worsens or dies, i.e. if one moves from 'low' to 'high' intensity, then the 'structural' block comes into play. But this does not account for symptomatic treatment with specifics, for in the 1890s, whilst Jalla was of the opinion that physiological knowledge was rudimentary, there being

152

no concept of the function of organs, the circulation of the blood, etc., he also noted the presence of effective purgatives and emetics.[67]

In fact there seems to have been quite a range of specific treatment, most administered in the village on the basis of folk knowledge. Table 8 sets out information about afflictions and therapy in two dimensions. One axis ranges from individual to communal treatment, the other from specific symptomatic treatment to non-symptomatic divination. On the basis of the close parallels in the descriptions of causation and mode of therapy already seen, I am prepared to suggest a broad stability in method, even if details have changed.

In support of this, I cite the pattern in which new modes of explanation and therapy have been handled during the twentieth century.[68] Allopathic medicine has been insulated by 'attitude' blocks which have prevented it colliding with the ideas set out above. One has seen that its curative potentials have been used without accepting the premises of the therapy. From this response has arisen the phenomenon of shuttling between hospital and traditional healer, especially in towns.[69] Another response has been simply to exclude allopathic medicine from certain areas, mainly of psychiatric and psychosomatic disorder, designating these *matuku a sintu* (African diseases). These afflictions are especially treated communally and are of particular interest to our present purpose. The converse of this block by selective application is that therapy is not claimed for afflictions where it would be hard to claim an effect. The most important area here is of broken bones and accident injury. No remedies are shown in the accompanying table because I have never collected or read of treatment for this most painfully specific sort of affliction. So it is interesting that doctors think that injuries of this type are perhaps the only class of affliction which will pretty reliably be brought straight to hospital.

I do not have information from analysis of the active principles and properties present in the treatments prescribed for specific symptoms although I have lists of such prescriptions for Bulozi and there are published lists for two neighbouring areas sharing basically the same botanical resources as Bulozi.[70] Simply to look at the lists and prescriptions is to gain two impressions. Firstly, they would not have been recoverable in this form if much of it had not worked; secondly, with no notion of dosage, the risk of failure even if the active principle was right was thereby increased.[71] But here, as in those cases for which the prescription was wrong, there was a sequential series of blocks to falsifiability: if the specific treatment failed, this would be a sign that the affliction was not simple and it therefore required specialist treatment. If the healer's specifics failed, this was a sign of evil interference which had to be

153

TABLE 8. *The relief of afflictions*

'LOW' INTENSITY →

Individual/'Folk'		Ñaka		Communal	
Symptom	Therapy	Symptom	Therapy	Symptom	Therapy

Symptomatic treatment

Symptom	Therapy	Symptom	Therapy	Symptom	Therapy
Minor body aches	Herbal infusions, drunk and applied			Depression	*Liyala*
Wounds, Swelling, Skin-scaling	Animal fat and plant preparations, usually applied			Evil dreams	*Siyaya*
Snake and dog bites	External washing, wound suction, emetics			Insanity	*Maimbwe, Muba* and modern derivatives
Accidental poison	Emetics			Body pains (often in conjunction with depression)	
Leprosy, Smallpox, Measles	Herbal infusions used to wash external symptoms	A skilled *ñaka* would have available similar types of treatment for any case listed to the left where the condition became more serious than village lore could handle, or if village applied remedies seemed to produce no response. Especially likely to go to the *ñaka* were:		Severe headaches	Involve inhalations, washing, sweating
Constipation	Purgatives				
Colds, minor coughs	Inhalation of steam from boiling herbal medicines				
Headache	Cupping with horns				
Evil dreams	Herbs chewed, spells recited, sitting in the sun	Abscesses	Lancing		
Mild aphrodisiac	Herbs chewed	Love potions, stronger aphrodisiacs	Herbal and animal preparations, spoken spells		
Abortion	Abortifaciant suppositories	More difficult obstetrics	Vaginal incisions		
Simple obstetrics	Uterine contractant, post partum vaginal anaesthetic from herbs	Venereal diseases	Infusions applied and taken, applied via steam or smoke, scarification		
Gynaecological	Various suppositories				

Divination and symptomatic treatment

			Cause (Muloi)*
Headaches	Standing in the wind of a felled tree as it falls	Difficult obstetrics	Bewitching
		Infertility	Taboo breaking, bewitching
		Paediatric illness	Ancestor unquiet, spirit enslavement
		Severe coughing	Sign of cannibalism
		Poisoning	Muloi, direct action
		Depression ⎫	
		Evil dreams ⎬	Attempts at spirit enslavement
		Insanity ⎭	
		Control of wild animals	Evil metempsychosis, familiar
		Acute forms of common complaints (eg. indigestion)	Taboo infringement etc.

Divination and non-symptomatic treatment

Depression ⎫	Liyala	
Evil dreams ⎪	Siyaya	
Insanity ⎬	Maimbwe	
Body pains (often in conjunction with depression) ⎪	Muba and modern derivatives	
Severe headaches ⎭	Involve inhalations, washing, sweating Disease disposal as described in text **'HIGH' INTENSITY**	

* Because specific therapy ends and is replaced by identification of cause (witch) as a form of therapy, it therefore logically takes its place in the therapy column.

identified by divination, and in this way a structural block could be invoked, even if the patient died. Thus a difficult case would move along one axis of the table from individual to communal and the other from symptomatic to non-symptomatic treatment, hence diagonally. The line could be extended off the table since for affliction beyond the norm, such as the early 1890s smallpox epidemic, recourse could only be through appeal to the unseen powers and there divinatory practice merged with the other functions of the royal graves.

Communal healing sessions of the type mentioned in the right-hand column of the table have had the same format in their essentials since the 1880s and 1890s, involving the patient lying prone while others dance and sing around him, led by the presiding healer, and drummers beat their drums.[72] Outsiders have called such sessions 'cults of affliction', but the generic Lozi term is *ku folisa mwa milupa* (to heal with drums).

In these cases, the affliction has a broad name, *'liyala', 'siyaya', 'muba'* etc., hence the names which distinguish the cults. From analysis of the song sequences of specific sessions, I have demonstrated elsewhere how the cults accumulate over time in a series of strata all founded upon a common cosmological viewpoint. The first stage of the healing sequence is to discover with which stratum one is dealing. This divination/diagnosis is effected by singing the songs of each cult until the patient responds by twitching and shuddering. Then the second stage occurs and as more songs of the identified cult are sung the healer may dance around, fan or wash the patient or put him under a blanket with a steaming pot of aromatic herbs to inhale. Cure is demonstrated when the patient can stand upright again and then can carry the herbs or other substance to a crossroads with the healer, who can ritually conclude the seance by depositing the disease there. The disease is from God and the cure comes from God also. This is made clear in the first song of a *siyaya* sequence recorded in 1977:

> *Pataule, pataule mbala Nyambe kuwa ba!*
>
> Cut, cut the medicine of God (Nyambe)!

sung antiphonally over and over again whilst the medicines were chopped up.[73]

But reasonable proof of the close intertwining of these visibly stable sedimentary cults, as I prefer to call them, with the fundamental dualist perception of the cosmos and the nature of Nyambe, can also be found in a precisely datable source which thus supports the inference I would wish to make from the content of cult songs. Like the theory of causation and mode of disposal of disease, the myth of Muba after whom the *muba* cult was named has remained extraordinarily intact over time.

Muba or Mwendanjangula or Mwendalutaka, as he is also called, was and is a monster who inhabited the deep forest. He was described as a man made half of wood and half of wax, divided vertically, or just half a man – one eye, one arm, one leg. He sang like a bird and his victims were drawn irresistibly to the sound. Once he appeared before them, they were lost, for like his human brothers the *baloi* (witches), Mwendanjangula enslaved their spirits. The symptoms of possession by *muba* might be high fever and loss of consciousness during the time that the spirit was being dragged forth to act for its master.[74] As well as illustrating the partisan nature of the environment, the myth also went on to show directly how power to rule both Nature and men – to be healer or chief – was linked to 'dark' sources. The theme is common to many mythologies: the ogre is vanquished in battle by the ordinary man who spares the ogre's life in return for magical ruling powers.[75] The version transmitted to Jacottet stressed the Promethean strain latent in it. Whilst such power could make men mighty, it could also break them. Hubris is never far from Nemesis. These powers could only be released in controlled surroundings if they were to be harnessed and were not to run amok. That was the purpose of Pandora's box and I suggest it was also a purpose of the purity and exclusivity seen in royal rituals. Thus in our survey of Lozi cosmology, our path has brought us a full circle.

Part IV

What next?

So far in this book my guiding intention has been to describe the core areas of Lozi society and culture in the late nineteenth century. I gave an outline of the rationale for doing this in Chapter 1; in the subsequent chapters I have approached the task circumspectly by attempting to present a comprehensive survey of what are commonly considered to be the important material, social and intellectual component parts of any society. The needs for food, shelter, society and intellectual security – the broadest determinants of the human condition – gave an outline shape to my investigation. This was the limit of the external definition which I consciously imported. Then I uncovered the energising indigenous Lozi concepts within each broad area.

When I had done this and had thus displayed the core areas and concepts of Lozi culture, I noticed that the pattern which they presented was not very comfortably contained within any narrowly deductive, formalist explanatory framework, Marxist or not. Such a framework seemed to be unhelpfully constrictive because of the expansive embrace of the initial materialist assumptions upon which it was erected, and therefore I discarded it. Instead I found congenial a notion which permitted scope for a more inductive approach. This was the 'subsistence ethic'.[1] In Chapter 1 I stated my intention to let the paradigms look after themselves for a time while always recognising the unrealism and danger of a troglodytic empiricism. After the experiences of the intervening chapters, the 'subsistence ethic' still appears to be fairly serviceable. However, it should be added that the idea is stronger in its defensive armour which protects it against other, over-precise theories than it is in its offensive armament: more like a troop-carrier than a tank. But that is as it should be because, as I observed in Chapter 1, we have to be careful not to crush our specific data by the weight, momentum and innate destructiveness of our preconceptions in the interests of our own intellectual security.

However, finding a helpful label was only a minor concern. More important was the attempt to defend the propositions about core areas. These propositions were identified in phenomena with long wavelengths of historical time; some were longer than others, all were longer than the rapid oscillations to be seen in the narrative flow of events. But, I suggested, since such historical data have a low 'scientific' status (lacking replicability and the power of accurate prediction: what Professor Hesse called the 'pragmatic criterion'),[2] some other test of the reliability of such propositions was needed, a test beyond that technique of making detailed comparison between nineteenth-century material and a modern template of the society constructed from first-hand field research by which I had identified core areas in the first place. We needed to test these ideas in another sort of medium than that of their origin. This medium was that of narrative history.

This I tried to do, in particular with regard to one historical episode, a *coup d'état* in the mid 1880s. But that is not enough. We need a fully extended examination of the narrative history of our entire period. Not only will this help us to judge whether my identification of core areas in Lozi culture remains intact under the highest magnification of detailed evidence; but since this is inevitably a two-way test, we shall also see to what extent our knowledge of core areas is helpful in activating the fullest explanatory potential latent in the narrative record. This is the best test of reliability in both sorts of history that we may hope for. It is admittedly a modest aspiration, but that cannot be helped. It is conspicuous among our tasks in the next pair of chapters.

162

8

The meaning of contact

Olunde [western educated son of the chief]: Yet another error into which
your people fall. You believe that everything which appears to
make sense was learnt from you.

Jane [wife of the District Officer]: Not so fast Olunde. You have learnt to
argue I can tell that, but I never said you made sense. . .[1]

This chapter and the next one first describe and explain the partial mutual
misunderstandings between Lozis and Europeans and then the fruitful
consequences of those mutual misunderstandings. The most important
sustained contact which Lozi in Bulozi had with Europeans during the
crucial years preceding formal colonial rule, which began nominally in
1896, was with the members of the Zambezi Mission of the Société des
Missions Evangéliques de Paris. Therefore these chapters concentrate
upon the history of that Mission. Given the nature of the Mission, much of
the tone of that contact was determined by the founders François and,
until her death in 1891, Christina Coillard. Therefore it is important to
understand these people well, removing the patina of hagiology which has
settled upon them over the years, and I devote adequate space to this task
in the narrative which follows.

I shall argue that in March 1886, Coillard assured the defeat of his own
long-term objective. He would never see a 'real, deep and vast awakening
among these dear people'.[2] Instead, without fully realising his contribution in it, he saw a heathen chief adapt himself and his people to face a
new world. I do not think that he ever fully realised why or, if he did, was
not prepared to admit it to himself. The central purpose of this chapter is
to document and explain how this defeat came about.

A common approach in the first generation of African historiography
seeking to explain the reasons for chiefship has been to see it linked to
developments in trade and exchange.[3] This material argument has been

used in Bulozi also, but already in Chapter 5 I have shown that the data cannot bear the weight of explanation which a theory centred upon the economic functions of the kingship places upon them. Instead, in Part III, I demonstrated that the gap in our explanation made by the removal of this untenable economic overemphasis was in fact filled by hitherto little understood and less tangible ordering and explanatory functions. These chapters rested upon much less accessible data and a considerably more guarded use of assumptions. I consider that the earlier model of Lozi kingship was the product of three converging methodological mistakes: too rash use of an 'if I were a horse' assumption about the primacy of economic considerations with, as a consequence, a failure to explore these other data and a failure to understand what the superficial economic data did *not* explain. This blindness was itself the result of an imbalance in the energy devoted to theoretical and methodological issues.

An extension of the 'trade and empire' view of African chiefship has been a ranking of assumed African priorities in the colonial encounter which placed highest the extraction of material benefit from the whites – guns, cloth, technical help, literacy and so on. This interpretation has been placed upon the events of 1888–91 in Bulozi. Chapter 9 shows that it was certainly true that Lewanika and his Council sought to obtain material things as well as diplomatic, secretarial and technical aid from the Mission, that to a smaller degree than they hoped they did obtain some of these things, but that all of them were subordinate to the most important commodity which Lewanika sought and obtained – the rein-forcement of Lozi self-confidence in the face of the white encroachment – which resulted from the ritual location of the Mission below the king which this chapter describes.

This is not just my opinion. As will be shown, re-examination of the detailed sequence of the events of the Concession Crises underpins this interpretation in the clearest possible way. When Coillard's ex-aide George Middleton presented Lewanika with a direct choice between those things which previous authors have assumed that he wanted most and Coillard, who basically offered the other less obvious commodity, the king chose Coillard. It is not my argument that the material aspects were absent from the pattern of contact, but that they were subordinate to this more nebulous commodity of cultural reinforcement which, in the light of the earlier chapters of this work, we are now able to perceive and understand.

To sustain my argument, I begin the first section of this chapter with a presentation of the actors; I trace the early history of their Mission, showing its nature and problems. Then I describe closely one sequence of

164

events in its foundation and argue a localised interpretation of its significance. Its wider importance is illuminated in the third section by situating it in the context of inter-racial perceptions. I argue that Lewanika had to locate the missionaries below himself because the missionaries were perceived by ordinary people as having two qualities akin to (and therefore potentially threatening to) his own: they were seen as magicians and, since magical and chiefly qualities were closely intertwined, also as chiefs. If the technologies and powers thus explained could be harnessed, they would thus implicitly boost self-confidence in Lozi powers and therefore be powerful aids in aligning Lozi culture in relation to the colonial intrusion into central Africa which was by then clearly beginning. The efficiency with which the culture's core areas could be defended was in direct proportion to success in this initial positioning. Conversely, if the Europeans ran amok, were seen to be superior to the kingship and unaffected by it, then they had the potential to do great damage. Lewanika's actions in late 1886 after Coillard established his mission at Sefula, described in the first section of Chapter 9, underscored the point made by the events of March.

For their part, the Mission members were sharply divided. They were divided in their perception of their impact on the people and divided in their conceptions of what their role should be, so to understand the interaction properly we must delve into their preoccupations also. The series of internal crises which preoccupied the Mission in its early years meant that an effective and coordinated campaign of any type in relation to the Lozi could not be mounted, and so during those years Lewanika was well placed to draw advantages with minimum risk. Since these divisions have not hitherto been documented, I am obliged to do this also.

The second part of Chapter 9 demonstrates that what has usually been considered to be the Mission's historically most important contribution – as arbitrator of the 1889 and 1890 Concessions – recedes in significance, both because the absolute importance of the Concessions has been overstated in the past and because this contribution stands relative to others, hitherto undervalued, which we have been able to illuminate; for example in the history of agricultural improvement in the 1890s. However, within the confines of the issue of the Concessions, Lewanika is seen to have been heavily dependent upon Coillard. It was the other side of a symbiotic relationship, and when Lewanika suspected that he might have been double-crossed his vacillation and his fury both revealed the extent of his trust in this prescribed area. However, the crisis of confidence was resolved in Coillard's favour and, as I have already suggested, tends to support the basic argument of these two chapters.

But the Concession Crises and their immediate aftermath also showed signs of the second stage of technique in Lozi/European relations – the subtle art of inventing traditions. This was to be the dominant tactic of the colonial era, but could not have been developed so successfully without the substantial achievements of the first stage – that of ritual location – which this work shows.

8.1 PREPARATIONS, 1876–FEBRUARY 1886

Coillard was an enthusiastic photographer and the now tattered pages of his personal album document the journey of the Mission party northwards from Lesotho in 1884. Photographs of the wagons on the dry wastelands of the northern Transvaal and the Kalahari desert show the party's hardship and the difficulty of their route. One page is worth closer attention; it bears four photographs, two of which are of the Mission party. Both are posed and both give an insight into the group.

One is of a night-stop camp (Fig. 23). Mme Coillard dominates the picture, seated beside a collapsible table with her work basket set upon it, defiantly domestic in the wilds. Her husband stands at the other side of the table, his hand tucked into his jacket in Napoleonic fashion; the others are positioned as appropriate to their social stations. The second picture shows the hierarchy of the party even more explicitly (Fig. 24). The two senior white men stand behind, the evangelists and their wives squat or sit on the ground in a half circle around the two white women, and the retainers, Middleton and Waddell, sit on stools on either flank, looking out to the left and right like the lions at the base of Nelson's column.

Fig. 23 1884 Mission party: night stop.

166

Fig. 24 1884 Mission party: posed group.

There is no question of who are the dominant personalities of the party, nor of the ranking of the others. The pictures suggest the tension between members which their journals often confirm and show the potential for future explosion within the Mission; potential which was to be realised. The Coillards' single-mindedness and insistence upon absolute discipline led to a series of crises with white and black personnel throughout our period, but especially in the critical first years. The origins of this divisiveness, the other side of the breathtaking perseverance with which Coillard fought all-comers to preserve his Mission, lie on the first page of the album in photographs of Coillard's home town.

François Coillard was born in 1834, by nine years the youngest of the eight children of a moderately prosperous vine grower, petit bourgeois, a pillar of the Protestant church of Asnières near Bourges in Berry. Calvin had lived at Bourges and had often walked near Asnières, and in that split community the Catholics called the bridge which the future reformer had crossed 'the Devil's bridge', the Protestants, 'Calvin's bridge'. Coillard was proud of his lineage from old Huguenot stock. His father died in 1837 and creditors threw the widow and her baby into poverty. Coillard remained her baby. He was always small of stature and thought to be frail. At school 'I was *little* Coillard; in the village among the Protestants, I was *little* cousin and my mother always called me her *little* child. *Little* I had to

167

be since everyone gave me this epithet.' His childhood has hard. When he was fourteen, the events of 1848 burst upon Bourges: 'it was a time of complete anarchy. Bands of socialists roamed the countryside, ransacking the chateaux and mills and setting them on fire. . .'[4] They left an abiding impression which can be seen in his descriptions of the Paris Commune, the Lozi civil war or anything else deserving the highest opprobrium. These were his 'years of slavery', culminating in a spell as a junior gardener at the Chateau of Foëcy, where he was taunted and finally resigned because of the Catholic head gardener.

In 1852, during lunch at the Institut de Glay where he was studying, he experienced his conversion. He volunteered to go to the Basutoland mission field and in 1859 was given the task of founding the parish of Leribe. In Paris, during preparation for the missionary career, he had briefly met Christina Mackintosh. She was five years his senior and had come to France from Scotland to stay with one of her sisters and to be a governess and teacher of English. Like Coillard, she came from a strict and devoutly Protestant family where she had lived an austere but not poor life, and like the early years of her future husband, it had been full of Bible study and Missionary tracts.

In fact, despite their geographically separated upbringings, their specifically Protestant heritages derived from a common source in the work of two Scottish brothers, James and Robert Haldane, both former naval officers, who in 1796 sold up their estates to devote themselves to evangelism. In the course of their travels through Scotland at the turn of the century, Christina Coillard's father, Lachlan Mackintosh, was brought into the ministry; under James Haldane's preaching in Edinburgh the Mackintosh children were brought up.

In 1816, Robert Haldane visited the continent. In Switzerland, he inaugurated informal Bible reading sessions which developed into the Société Evangélique de Génève. Haldane travelled on to Montauban in post-revolutionary France where he saw to the printing of new bibles to replace those destroyed by the revolutionary regime. He was followed later by members of the Geneva Society, travelling preachers who helped to stimulate the French Protestant revival. In 1828 the Société des Missions Evangéliques de Paris was founded. Among its preachers was Ami Bost, originally one of the Geneva group. He became the pastor of Asnières and the young Coillard was greatly influenced by him.[5]

However, the recombination of these two streams of evangelical Protestantism was not instantaneously achieved. Coillard proposed to Christina Mackintosh by letter when he was but newly arrived in the mission field in 1858, and was refused. In 1860 he tried again through the good offices of a mutual friend in Paris, and she accepted. He recorded that her first words to him upon disembarking in South Africa were, 'I have come to do with you the work of God, whatever it may be, and always remember that wherever the Lord calls you to go, you will never find me blocking the path of duty.'[6] This was not necessarily an idealised recollection of his wife after her death. Their letters to each other and journals are full of similar language. Their marriage strikes the modern reader as exceptionally formal even for its time. From the proposal onwards the Coillards expressed their deepest feelings and made their major decisions on paper. The oral tradition of the Mission is that Coillard was intimidated by his wife and found it hard to talk to her directly.[7] Whether that was so or not, she was evidently a woman of ferocious will-power. She kept her word and put duty first. They never had any children.

In the mid 1870s white and black members of the church of Lesotho began to discuss the idea of sending a mission from the south to territories beyond the Limpopo. In February 1875, the synod decided to send an expedition to the Banyai, in Ndebele territory. Hermann Dieterlen, a young missionary, accompanied four Sotho catechists northwards but they were stopped and arrested by the Boers near Pretoria. Clearly such a task demanded someone of greater experience. In 1876, the Coillards were due to return to Europe on leave and Christina Coillard's letters home show how much she looked forward to it. In November, her husband attended an extraordinary Conference of the Church at Thaba Bossiu, which was to be his last function before departure. The question of the Banyai Mission was raised and in a letter to his wife, Coillard wrote: 'then eyes were turned towards me ... not to abandon our return to Europe but to go and found the Banyai Mission first which would take a year or eighteen months at our discretion.'[8] This letter stunned his wife in Leribe. However, it concluded with advice to her to pray for divine guidance. 'Now my beloved, you are, like I am, a servant of JC – let us forget men and let us compose ourselves to hear His voice. If he says to us *go*! we will go *without second thoughts*.' She wrote the next month to break the news to her family that 'it was only after a hard struggle and great suffering of mind that I was able to see that it might be God's will that we should undertake this long and perilous journey'.[9] By the same post, Coillard wrote to his brother-in-law to explain their decision, in so doing touching on a powerful and continuing theme of the next fifteen years: 'it is a *submissive* suffering – the suffering of the victim laid out already on the altar of God'.[10]

Christina Coillard was forty-nine when their great travels began and already in poor health. Particularly after they reached Bulozi, she suffered almost continually from recurrent fevers, crippling headaches, and increasing physical weakness that drove her more and more to her bed.

Fig. 25 François Coillard.

Fig. 26 Christina Coillard.

She and Coillard talked much about healing by faith in those later years, but this progressive martyrdom for the sake of people whose souls she loved and whose persons she endured must have made the early years of the Zambezi Mission extraordinarily stressful for all concerned.[11]

The Banyai expedition took longer to prepare and longer to execute than they had anticipated. However, even before departure, Coillard was looking beyond, towards the Zambezi. In March 1877 he wrote to his brother-in-law again and commented that, were it not for the tsetse belt near the river, they would go to Sotho-speaking Bulozi for preference.[12]

For three months, the party waited for permission from Lobengula, king of the Ndebele, to go to his tributary area. While waiting, Coillard met traders who 'urged us to look across the Zambezi to the Barotsi'.[13] Eventually on 2 March 1878 Lobengula informed the Mission that it was forbidden to establish itself anywhere in his domains because it came from the Basuto, who were 'traitors, they had betrayed Langalebalele a Zulu chief who had come to seek protection from them and the odour of Molapo was so strong that the Matabele could not bear to look at them, much less consent to see them settle in their lands'.[14] So the party proceeded to Bechuanaland and to the capital of the Tswana chief, Khama, at Mangwato. There they met George Westbeech, an ivory hunter, who 'gave me all sorts of information about the Barotsi ... Apart from Livingstone he is the only European to have visited the valley. They allow no other European to penetrate it.'[15] He also promised Coillard that he would help him to enter Bulozi and establish his Mission, a promise that was to be vitally important.[16] Coillard and his party established a base at Lusuma just south of the Zambezi; and on 1 November at Sesheke, Coillard received a message from the newly enthroned King Luboshi Lewanika:

> The king greets you much. He is pleased by your arrival in Bulozi. But you find him only recently installed on the throne, he is still living in the fields. Now he must build his capital. He has not yet a house. He cannot receive anyone at present. Leave the country before the rains, depart in peace but return in the winter.[17]

Encouraged, the party retired to Lesotho. On the way Mme Coillard commented acidly on the Ndebele that it could not be long before this 'obstacle to Christianity' was removed and this 'fortress of heathenism burst open'.[18] Certainly Lobengula had denied himself the chance of gaining the advantages that Lewanika was to reap from Coillard.

For nearly four years Coillard campaigned widely for funds to launch his venture. Support for a Zambezi Mission was lukewarm in Lesotho. It was far away and expensive to reach. In Paris Coillard encountered similar opposition. His official biography records that permission was given to Coillard to attempt to raise funds in the francophone Protestant churches, but here there was considerable doubt as to the wisdom of the enterprise (which hardened into opposition once Bulozi fell within the British sphere of influence). [19] As a local Swiss newspaper put it in 1897, recalling Coillard's previous visit to Lausanne, 'the Paris committee, paralysed by a chronic deficit, short of men and of money hesitated. In human terms the Paris committee was right and M. Coillard was wrong; that was the impression of more than one of his audience [at that time]'.[20] However, Coillard was a distinguished orator and he did obtain funds from other than central Mission sources. But the 1884 expedition set off without the whole-hearted support of either Paris or Lesotho. In late 1884 Coillard felt that all the world was against him: he received a letter 'full of fire' from Boegner, director of the Mission headquarters in Paris; the hostility is implicit in a joint appeal of 1885 from Coillard and Jeanmairet, his subordinate missionary, for funds: 'we cannot stress too much that your contributions bear the special designation "Zambezi Mission" since, as you doubtless know already, our work has to depend solely on special gifts and we have no claim upon the general funds of our Society'.[21] His Mission seemed to be what the photographs suggest: a one-man show on a shoestring budget. But this would not be entirely correct. Two people, each of whom made essential contributions to the foundation of the Mission, are not in the picture.

The first of these was Khama. I have been unable to discover the full extent of Lewanika's diplomatic dealings with the chief of the Tswana. One elite informant told me that contact was first made between the two men when Lewanika was in exile in the west in 1884.[22] However, in May on his way north with Coillard the artisan Waddell wrote of Lewanika that 'He must be a terrible beggar as he asked Khama to send him a horse, a plough, a black dog and a Weslyricard [sic] gun and to crown all he wants Khama's daughter for his wife',[23] so the contact preceded the rebellion. But whoever ruled Bulozi, Khama favoured a Mission presence there and he sent an envoy, Makuatsa, to the new regime of Mataa and Akufuna. Of him, Jeanmairet wrote that 'We count also on Khama's envoy who is at the moment in the Valley to explain the true nature of our Mission to the Barotsi. . .'[24] Makuatsa returned rejected from the Valley;[25] but this was not to be the last intervention by Khama in Lozi affairs.

Coillard needed results quickly. Anxious to set off from the southern region of Sesheke, he was doubly impatient to get to the Court in person, whoever ruled there (which was immaterial to him), firstly because he had actually travelled a day north of Sesheke on 1 September 1884 before being recalled because of news of the *coup d'état*, and now because

Khama's envoy had failed in his mission.[26] The last months of 1884 saw him eating up funds to no visible purpose in Lusuma, his base camp to the south of the Zambezi. He compared himself to St Paul in prison. 'It is impossible that so many sacrifices, delays and deprivations should be lost.'[27] Eventually he got transport to visit Lealui in December 1884/January 1885. It was a huge tactical blunder to visit so soon those who had driven Lewanika out of Lealui – it could not possibly be clear then whether or not the new regime would endure – and displayed a lack of political sensitivity scarcely designed to endear the missionary to Lewanika when he was eventually restored. Nor did it win Coillard any practical advantage, for he spent the rest of 1885 champing at the bit back in the south. His mistakes were only retrieved through the good offices of George Westbeech, the second person whose help was essential to the Mission.

'Jolosi' (George, i.e. Westbeech) remains a shadowy but evidently important figure.[28] He promised to help Coillard enter Bulozi in 1878 and while the missionary was overseas raising funds, Westbeech refused an offer of £500 from Jesuits wishing to take the region for themselves[29] who sought his help, for between 1876 and 1886 he was indisputably the most influential European in Bulozi. He was recognised as headman of Pandamatenga and chief of that region and sat as a member of the Kuta when he visited Lealui. As he wrote himself, 'I have lived among the natives here for fifteen years, and . . . those who were boys when I arrived are now men, and trust me.'[30] Furthermore, before coming to Barotseland in 1871, Westbeech had traded in Matabeleland and retained his links with Lobengula which 'had kept their drifts [crossing places] free from Matabele through my friendship with that king whose no was NO and yes was YES. . .'.[31] He wanted the Mission to settle in the country to blunt the savagery of the people, as he saw it. Once Lewanika was restored, the king sent word to Coillard to remain at Sesheke

> until I have been to the Valley as all his overtures have been made to the king who has fled, viz Wa-ga-Funa and I must first make things agreeable for C before he will be permitted to go on; which means simply that he won't see the Barotse before next winter. So much for being strong headed and refusing, or at all events, not taking my advice.[32]

It will be seen below how Westbeech saved Coillard in some respects.

The relationship between missionary and ivory hunter was one of convenience, not of warmth. Westbeech wrote of Coillard:

> although he does not listen to my advice . . . I suppose I must now help C to get to the Barotse. It's a thankless office, for missionaries

as far as I know them, with very few exceptions, generally when they have got all they can from one, throw you away like one throws away a fruit-skin after having sucked out all the fruit. However we shall see.[33]

Coillard wrote of Westbeech as an unsaved soul, doubly compromised by having a black mistress. The Coillards refused to shake hands with her, lectured him to no avail and gave him Cambridge Tracts to read.[34] 'M.W. . . . is a man who I cannot prevent myself from liking despite his licentious life. I think that his goodness and natural generosity are the cause of his moral and financial ruin.'[35] Coillard found his manner to be correct but 'cold' after January 1886. Throughout his life, Coillard recorded his repeated surprise and sadness when he found that other Europeans were not exactly of his opinion.[36] His writings also showed a ferocious attachment to those who he thought did share his views.

In the case of his employees, he brooked no question. So long as Middleton was 'his' man, he was 'much loved' and his 'dear Middleton'.[37] Waddell was in the long term the only person prepared to give this slavish submissiveness. He idolised Mme Coillard, sometimes to her irritation. He always referred to Coillard as 'the Master' and Coillard always addressed him as Mr Waddell. But he was an unusual sort of man. The Methodist missionary Baldwin wrote thus of him in his journal: 'He has no mental ability – never opens a book save his Bible and even troubles little about the newspapers. He is without aspirations save to do his work well . . . He is very susceptible in his feelings – is encouraged by a word and equally soon depressed.'[38] The consequences of so polarising a view of relationships will appear below.

Mme Coillard was equally intolerant of other opinions. Her journal of August to November 1886 when Coillard was away and she alone at Sesheke with Jeanmairet and his wife Elise (who was François Coillard's niece) is a chronicle of extreme tensions. For a month she did not enter the other whites' house and then only after a formal invitation to meet Mr Westbeech at lunch.[39] Eventually she could not speak to Jeanmairet who did not run the station to her liking and who she thought was stealing her meal. Elise she found cross and exacting. Such interpersonal tension, compounding the fever, the heat and the worries about gaining permission to settle, about reactions in Paris and in Lesotho, is strong evidence of the Coillards' faith and single-mindedness. Without those attributes, they might not have survived psychologically. The Mission party entered 1886 divided and tense.

8.2 ENCOUNTER, MARCH 1886

Westbeech's meeting with the Coillards at Sesheke had been chilled by the presence of his mistress and also perhaps by the fact that Lewanika had instructed Coillard to wait until Westbeech had gone up river to meet the king. The merchant was 'thoroughly sick of this place' (Sesheke) and set off early on Monday 25 January 1886 despite continuous rain.[40] Coillard could only fume: the chiefs controlled the canoes. On 9 February he wrote in his journal, 'I shall wait until March 1st and if canoes have not materialised, I shall start out on foot.'[41]

Westbeech had a difficult journey with high winds, leaking boats and frightful headaches. Through all of January there were only two dry days. He reached Nalolo on Tuesday 9 February but was so sick that he had to rest several days before going on to Lealui at the weekend (13–14). His spleen was swollen and his headache debilitating and Lewanika was alarmed. It was a sign of how much he valued Westbeech that 'the king keeps sending to the graves of the old departed Barotse kings to pray for my recovery'.[42] He recovered between 9 and 15 March, having been 'doctored and plastered by the king's M.D.'s to their hearts content and my intense disgust, but to please the king, who is really anxious, I grin and bear it'. He buried the potions and, clandestinely, he took his own medicines.[43]

For weeks after Westbeech's departure, the Sesheke chiefs procrastinated, putting Coillard off with excuses or with vague promises and no canoes appeared. Then, quite suddenly, the missionary was provided with two boats, ten well built Subiya paddlers and, as escort and captain of the expedition, a minor Subiya chief, Mukumwakumwa ('Mokumoakumoa'). Coillard attributed this change of affairs to his own blustering, but this seems unlikely.[44] Westbeech had reached Lealui on 14 February and therefore had ample time to discuss Coillard and his Mission with a king whose actions showed the extent to which he valued the trader. Evidently he had persuaded Lewanika to overlook Coillard's gaffe of consorting with the king's enemies. A maximum of just over a fortnight for reflection could then have elapsed before the next move had to be made, for the early morning of Wednesday 3 March was probably the last moment at which a messenger could have been dispatched from Lealui and hope to arrive at Sesheke on 5 March, the day that canoes and escort were presented to Coillard.[45]

I argue that a specific royal directive is the only reasonable explanation of all that happened: the sudden change of attitude among the Sesheke chiefs, the nature of the escort, the quality of the paddlers, the attitude they all showed to Coillard:

176

> I didn't delude myself over my Subiya. They showed themselves to
> be animated with a good-will which is not to be denied. They vied
> with each other to give me pleasure. Mukumwakumwa, the chief,
> set the example. When we disembarked, he used to be the first to
> pitch my little tent, to build a shelter, to look for wood. . .[46]

This air of cooperation continued throughout the voyage. A month later
when Coillard paid off the paddlers upon his return to Sesheke there was
'not a single bitter word', a forceful contrast with his previous journey of
early 1885 when his paddlers had gone on strike.[47]

There was a further and persuasive reason why the Sesheke chiefs
would have been unlikely to take such a decisive action unilaterally at that
particular time. Less than four months previously, an execution squad
had surrounded the village of the senior Sesheke chief, the *Mulanziane*,
who had favoured the rebel cause against Lewanika, and on the night of
26–7 December 1885, during the dark last quarter of the moon, they had
launched a commando raid on the village, purging the *Mulanziane* and his
people.[48] Just before that action, the Sesheke chiefs had received a
pointed reminder of the reality of the restoration from the tongues and
guns of Westbeech and his hunters; and just after, royal power was seen
when the *Mulanziane* herds were redistributed.[49]

In fact, I would go further and suggest that we can deduce what the
original message probably was that was sent to the Sesheke chiefs: it was
that Mukumwakumwa, his boats and crews should be prepared and that
they were to convey Coillard up river, exercising the greatest care to
deliver the goods undamaged, setting out on the day of the new moon.
Coillard later had cause to accuse Mukumwakumwa of treating him like a
parcel when he was not consulted over a decision to camp.[50] The new
moon was on 6 March, the day that Coillard and Mukumwakumwa set
out from Sesheke.[51]

They made slower time than the paddlers or the king would have liked
because, since the flood was very late that year, the water in the plain was
still high and the lower river was running fast against them.[52] They were
further slowed because Coillard 'conscientiously set foot on the shore at
each dangerous place', faithful to a promise to take care made to his wife
and 'to those Sesheke chiefs, who seemed so preoccupied with the safety
of my person',[53] which suggests the other clause in the orders they had
received.

About midday on Friday 12 March the party reached Matome's village
at the Kaale rapids (16°49′S 23°47′E).[54] The paddlers stopped and went
off to look for Matome himself, pilot of the rapids between Kaale and the
Ngonye Falls. He was away cutting wood for canoes for the king and

Mukumwakumwa flatly refused to budge. He ordered camp to be pitched despite Coillard's heated protestations; but the missionary had to accede, 'and to tell the truth I was mortified and deeply humiliated. What a lapse after the good journey that I've had!'[55] Mukumwakumwa was most apologetic. He explained that before leaving Sesheke the chiefs had taken him aside and told him that under no circumstances was he to attempt the passage of the rapids without Matome. Not only were the waters dangerous, but the Lingongole was reputed to live near the Lumbe confluence. In fact Coillard was not too unhappy that they had stopped, for the skies were threatening.

At dusk, two messengers from the king arrived. Lewanika had evidently decided that royal paddlers would bring Coillard more speedily, for they told him that two barges were en route to collect him. They also brought a letter from Westbeech. Coillard decided to go on with his Subiya paddlers rather than wait for the royal boats and, on the Saturday, Matome's sons piloted the party through twenty miles of rapids.[56] Coillard walked; one boat was lost.

Coillard always tried to avoid travelling on the Sabbath and stopped to hold his service and to rest at Sioma where he found the king's boats waiting for him. On Monday, the reinforced party set off and managed to travel about twenty miles a day that day and the next, reaching the mouth of the plain on Tuesday evening. But the southern floodplain, although covered so that they could take a direct course towards Nalolo, presented problems that made progress slow. It was choked with floating rafts of vegetation that collect there each flood, and also the course to Nalolo does not permit one to escape entirely the influence of the river current without very lengthy detour. So it was on Saturday that they reached Nalolo, having managed about sixteen miles a day from the Wanyau plain.[57]

The *Mulena Mukwae* Matauka received Coillard royally.

> From the moment that she saw me she began to laugh; she offered me her hand and made me sit down opposite her. She looked at me intently for several moments, always smiling, and at last, betraying the direction of her thoughts, she shouted in a tone that made me quake, 'Mataa! Mataa! We have killed him and all his relatives!'[58]

She was mightily impressed by Coillard's photographs of the rebel chiefs of Sesheke. On the Sunday she attended what Coillard considered was the best service that he had yet had in Bulozi, and in the evening she invited him to her palace again and proffered an old accordion which Coillard played for her; then she played it for him and returned his visit by coming to his camp.[59] Crowds of other people clamoured to see the photographs of the dead Sesheke chiefs also. Coillard had a dreadful night. His tent was invaded by warrior ants (*sului*). They climbed all over his mosquito net, got inside and forced him to leap out of bed and rush into another courtyard.

Meanwhile in Lealui, Westbeech had recovered and, his business done, he made preparations to depart on Tuesday 23rd, taking Lewanika's eldest son, Litia, with him to see Pandamatenga. The king sent messengers to Matauka to tell her to prepare for Westbeech's visit; they must have arrived in Nalolo between the 18th and 22nd.[60] It would have been extraordinary if Lewanika had *not* known Coillard's whereabouts, since I argue that he had set the date for his departure, knew approximately how long it took to ascend the river, had become worried that the missionary was taking too long and had sent extra boats to collect him and speed his passage, and from Westbeech we know that messengers went to Nalolo around the weekend that Coillard arrived. Presumably they returned, for 'as we heard the Rev C. was close by, the king asked me to stay a few days',[61] which he did.

Coillard was not rested when he set out on the last stage of the journey which is shown on Fig. 27. Dawn was at 6 am.

We left around 7 am. . .we glided rather swiftly over the grasslands, crossing bends of the Zambezi from time to time. Soon we heard the muted sounds of the great war drums of the King – the *maoma*. They couldn't be at Lealui, the sound reached us too strongly for such a great distance. Around 2 pm we approached Masheke village when we noticed a number of men and canoes. Soon one of these canoes came up to us like an arrow, carrying three men, and one of these men was Mokano,[62] the famous Mokano in person! A bad omen. 'The King asks who you are?' Mukumwakumwa: 'It is the *moruti* [teacher] and Mukumwakumwa who accompanies him.' Soon another message comes via Mokano, this bird of misfortune: 'The King says that the *moruti* must land, take a piece of white calico and come and pray at the tomb of – – – (the name escaped me).' 'Tell the King that I pray only to God, who is the only true God and that I have come to introduce you to Him.' Some time after, 'The King understands. If the *moruti* doesn't pray to our Gods, let him give a metre of calico which is sufficient.' 'Tell the King that he may ask anything else of me, but that I can do no other in this type of affair. I do not pray to the dead and know of only one God.' Soon another message: 'The King requests a little fabric from you.' I refused. My people were furious. A new message: 'The King insists.' Now it was a battle. I would have liked to see him and to talk to him myself. But

I could not see him before having given the cloth. I wished that I had someone through whom I might have communicated a little with him. My only intermediary was this Mokano who I knew was ill disposed towards me and who would be only too happy to entangle me in a quarrel with the King. Moreover, my obstinate refusal had protected a principle that no-one could understand.

The canoe had scarcely disappeared into the thickness of the vegetation when we heard the air resound with 'Lôche! Lôche! [Yooshoo! Yooshoo!]' and a few moments after there was a commotion at the shore which announced the King's departure. We were soon surrounded by a little flotilla. A canoe elegantly covered with mats and manned by paddlers sporting brilliantly coloured kerchiefs glided alongside mine. From the cabin there emerged a person whose sole attire was made of wildcat skins around his waist. It was the King. At the sight of him, my Subiyas fell to their knees as if struck, clapping their hands, murmuring their 'shangwes'. Mukumwakumwa raised his hands, cried his Yooshoo, fell to his knees in his turn, sprinkling his body with water while clapping his hands and firing off a salvo of praise-sayings. All smiles, the King extended his hand to me, we exchanged some words of greeting, he said that he was happy to see me. He offered me half a roast goose then, arranging a meeting for that evening in the capital, he took his leave. Then it was a real race. My men didn't want to be left behind, tired as they were. There were about fifteen boats. The Queen's was manned by nine paddlers. In the rear-guard, that is to say with us, sometimes beside us, sometimes behind, sometimes in front, was the boat carrying the three vast drums which three men beat powerfully, but in cadence. This lugubrious sound which the natives say can be heard all around for ten leagues or more wasn't exactly agreeable. Furthermore, was I not angry when we saw the royal procession steer towards a village, the tomb of some ancestor. All the inhabitants had come out, letting out piercing cries to acclaim their sovereign, and when he went to the tomb to pray there and make an offering of calico and white beads, all the women standing outside the village sang a well modulated song in honour of the King. 'Yooshoo's' resounded in the air and soon the deep notes of the great drums announced that the royal cortège was off towards another of these sacred places.

We rushed on [*filâmes*] ahead and at 4 pm we disembarked at Lealuyi. . .There is no longer [tall] grass through which [on Coillard's previous visit] one had had to tread a path with difficulty from one part of the village to another. One only senses from the appear-

180

ance of the place that the master is there. Mr W. and a young Portuguese trader of the name of Philesburt S. Gabes[63] welcomed us, a good number of people came to greet me. But *Ngambela* is ill and cannot see me. He sends his greetings, indicates our lodgings and my people prepare our installation there. Drums, shouts and songs announce the King's arrival, but I am too exhausted to go to the Kuta. Mr W. came to see me and we sat chatting beside the fire until 10 pm. He has a lot to say. I think that he stakes his heart and honour on the success of our enterprise.[64]

Thus Coillard wrote privately: he did not like getting involved with native idols and ancestors, but in the circumstances he had no alternative and since no one understood why he was refusing, it made the argument in favour of acceding more powerful. In any case, what was the alternative? To turn around and go back? By the time he returned to Sesheke in April he had convinced himself that what had happened was justified by the results. The day after his return (18 April), Waddell confided to his journal his understanding of what 'the Master' told them of his travels.

The Barotse Valley was flooded being the annual innundation and he was met by Makano (the man who was impertinate at Lushuma) in a canoe who was sent by the King to salut Mr C and ask a piece of cloth but he at first refused the cloth not knowing the object but afterwards yielded to Lewanika's demand he sent back Makano to say he would not see him without he sent the cloth. His Majesty had been a few mls. from the capital on a pilgrimage to the graves of his fathers. But after his return the evening he received Mr Coillard very warmly.[65]

The following day Coillard wrote his report to Paris in similar vein. Mokano was described more specifically as having once behaved in an extremely coarse way to the white women and the actual incident in a bantering tone thus: 'I gave the metre of calico. Soon noisy "Yooshoo's" which resounded in the air told me what had been done with it. The gods of the Barotsi are content with little, a length of calico, a necklace of pearls [beads]; but it must be white; it's obligatory. No other colours are tolerated in their Elysium.'[66] This view was percolated into later writing. Favre's popular edition of the biography of Coillard condensed the incident into a sub-clause: 'The 22 March, Coillard, who had already met the King on the way, arrived at Lealui.'[67]

Were Coillard and those who have followed his interpretation right? I shall argue that they were not. To do this, we must answer three questions, two practical, the third embracing them both. The larger question

181

is, why did Lewanika wish to compel Coillard to be seen to sacrifice at a royal grave-site? It is answered throughout the rest of this chapter. The practical questions which increase the precision and reliability of our general answer and of the detailed account of Coillard's voyage given above, are: why that particular grave, and why at that particular moment? Let us take them in turn.

Coillard did not catch the name of the grave-site to which his piece of calico was taken and where, patently, Lewanika was lying in wait for him. The only geographical clue is the name of the village, Masheke, which is, unfortunately, rather difficult to use.[68] Luckily the journal gives us other clues: we have Coillard's timetable.

From other evidence, we were able to see that on the first leg, Sesheke to Matome in the faster running lower river, the paddlers were making about 1¾ mph against a current of around 7 mph.[69] Goaded by knowledge of the king's impatience and then reinforced by new paddlers, they made 2 mph to the entrance of the plain and fell back a bit in the difficult Sudd-like lower plain, narrower and following a course nearer the main river. Above Nalolo, Coillard comments on the increase of speed and mentions crossing river bends (which would agree with the courses indicated on Fig. 27). The current in the plain was likely to be about half that in the lower river. So if we take 8 mph to be the top speed that paddlers in such canoes can maintain,[70] then, given that after the meeting Coillard went faster than before, speeds over the ground of 3 mph between Nalolo and the place of meeting and 3½–4 mph thereafter seem most reasonable, because they enable him to complete the journey within the timetable:

> 7 hours paddling Nalolo to meeting place
> approximately one hour at meeting place[71]
> maximum of one and a half hours paddling from the meeting place to Lealui

This would put the possible place of meeting within the cross-hatched area between the intersects on Fig. 27. Within that area, easily the most prominent grave-site which is also the one situated closest to Coillard's direct course from Nalolo to Lealui is Lilundu, *sitino* of Mulambwa. Although in the *Tableau Synchronique* and the *Litaba za Sichaba*, Jalla states that the meeting occurred at the tomb of Ngombala, i.e. Ñundu, close to the important site of Nakaywe (15°11′S, 22°58′E),[72] there seem to be three material reasons to suspect Lilundu was the *sitino* and not Ñundu.

The first is one of timing. To reach Ñundu by 2 pm Coillard's paddlers would have had to maintain a steady 4 mph over the ground. With a main river current in spate at around 7 mph, the current in the plain, experience

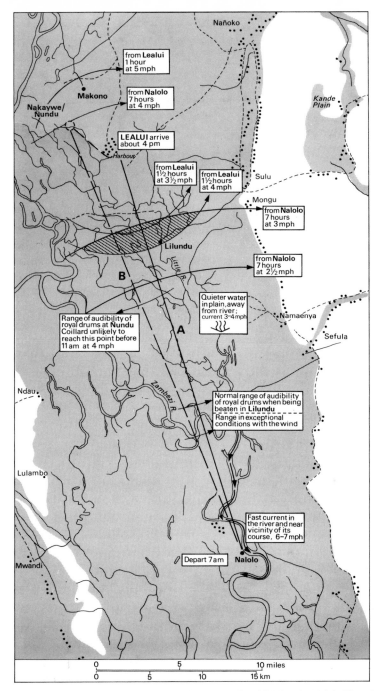

Labels within the map:

from **Lealui**
1 hour
at 5 mph

Nañoko

Makono

Nakaywe/
Nundu

*Kande
Plain*

from **Nalolo**
7 hours
at 4 mph

LEALUI arrive
about 4 pm

Harbour

from **Lealui**
1½ hours
at 3½ mph

from **Lealui**
1½ hours
at 4 mph

Sulu

Mongu

from **Nalolo**
7 hours
at 3 mph

B

Lilundu

Little B.

from **Nalolo**
7 hours
at 2½ mph

Quieter water
in plain, away
from river;
current 3–4 mph

Namaenya

Range of audibility of
royal drums at **Nundu**
Coillard unlikely to
reach this point before
11 am at 4 mph

A

Sefula

Ndau

Zambezi R.

Normal range of audibility
of royal drums when being
beaten in **Lilundu**
Range in exceptional
conditions with the wind

Lulambo

Fast current in
the river and near
vicinity of its
course, 6–7 mph

Mwandi

Depart 7 am   **Nalolo**

0   5   10 miles
0   5   10   15 km

Fig. 27 The voyage of François Coillard on Monday 22 March 1886. The shaded
area represents the floodplain.

suggests, was unlikely to be less than 3 mph. So if we assume that as a minimum, Coillard's paddlers would have to sustain pretty close to maximum speed for seven hours without let-up. Then, since Coillard suggests that the next leg was faster still, we should consider a cross-current speed of say 5 mph, which would be easy to achieve, giving a passage time of about thirty-five minutes from Ñundu to Lealui. So our timetable would look thus:

> seven hours paddling Nalolo–Ñundu
> minimum of one and a half hours meeting
> maximum of thirty-five minutes, Ñundu–Lealui

In favour of Ñundu is that it is closer to other royal graves to which we know that Lewanika then proceeded. But if, for instance, the sacrifice described by Coillard took place at Makono, then he would have approached Lealui from the *north*. In any case, there was ample time between 2.45 pm and dusk when he returned to Lealui for Lewanika to have visited Ñundu, Nakaywe and Makono, for example, from Lilundu.

This leads to the second objection. Coillard had been to Lealui before during the flood and, if he had gone to Ñundu, his course would have taken him abeam of the capital which, even given his known tiredness after his sleepless ant-bitten night at Nalolo, would surely have aroused his suspicion and, given the meticulousness of the rest of the journal entry, we may think that such suspicion would have been reflected on the page. There is no indication that he approached Lealui otherwise than the way common sense would dictate: directly.

The last objection is connected to the drums. Coillard wrote that the *maoma* had a range in excess of ten leagues.[73] He wrote that they could hear the *maoma* for most of the morning.[74] 'They couldn't be at Lealui, the sound reached us too strongly for such a great distance.' Therefore they could not have been at Ñundu either.[75] So we are left with two alternatives. If the meeting took place at Ñundu, Lewanika first sailed *south* from Lealui,[76] and then the king must have sailed parallel and ahead of the missionary. The second alternative is that Lewanika sailed down to Lilundu before mid-morning to wait for Coillard to arrive and that the drums were stationary there throughout the morning, the sound strengthening as Coillard approached.[77]

Therefore in my reasoning Lilundu was on balance the most likely place for the encounter. However, if the meeting was at Ñundu, it is likely that Lewanika first travelled at least five miles south of Lealui before mid-morning. If he did this, there are other strong reasons why he should have visited Lilundu at that time. Conversely, for similar reasons, if the meeting was at Lilundu, Ñundu was a prime candidate for one of the subsequent visits of the afternoon. So I suggest a probability, asymmetrically favoured by an encounter at Ñundu, that both sites were ritually visited in the course of 22 March.

A glance back at Table 6 and the argument about Lilundu advanced in Chapter 6 show powerful reasons why Lewanika should favour a meeting there. Mulambwa was the king whose special protection Lewanika sought; Table 6 showed structural evidence of this. To make Coillard sacrifice to the royal spirits would ritually locate his power below that of the kingship; to make him sacrifice to Mulambwa was a much more precise communication. It was to call on Lewanika's particular supernatural ally, but further, it was to invoke all that Mulambwa represented: the best of the Noble Age (*Muluilonga*) which Lewanika sought to revive, but also the skill to deal with and to control white technology – and by implication other things too – for the Lozis' benefit, which Mulambwa had been the first to do. Collateral support for this argument is that Coillard was subsequently 'adopted' into Mulambwa's descent group (*mushiku*), WaNdandula.

However, there are cogent and slightly different reasons to recommend Ngombala, whose *sitino* is Ñundu. While he was not one of the two kings to whom Lewanika was especially attached, he also projected a significant message. He was a *Litunga* who had succeeded an evil chief and who thus brought better times. He came to power overcoming the disability of having only one eye, and by the exercise of great magical skill doctors transplanted a child's eye into his head; Lewanika had also overcome difficulties in establishing his rule. Ngombala was a unifying king. He reincorporated Sesheke into the kingdom, he established the Nalolo dynasty with his daughter Notulu; Lewanika sought to unify his people again in the 1880s. Even so, the choice of the most suitable site seems to me to fall upon Lilundu, for the message of Mulambwa was most relevant to the event and Mulambwa was to the 1880s what Lewanika is to the 1970s, the most immediately meaningful of the past kings.

The evidence has suggested that the meeting was not accidental. If the drums were stationary at Lilundu, then Lewanika was waiting; if they were audible all morning, yet the meeting was at Ñundu, the probability is that preparatory visits were being made, perhaps to Lilundu. Furthermore the king had 'the Queen' with him. If the meeting was at Lilundu, the likelihood is that this was Mukena, if Ñundu, Matondo. But any queen at a royal grave is there for a purpose, namely, to participate in the ceremonies with the priest-guardian. So if a queen was brought, a sacrifice was planned. But this is flimsy evidence at best. The case for premeditation is strengthened when the timing of Coillard's voyage is examined in conjunction with other events we know about.

In Chapters 6 and 7 above, I explained the significance of the moon in certain important rituals involving royal grave-sites. Put simply, the time which was most auspicious for consultations was at the new moon; the time of the waxing moon was the positively charged part of the month, that of the waning moon, the time of increasing inauspiciousness. Only the *Litunga* himself had the power to operate at the royal graves safely in the dark nights immediately before the new moon; for example, the installation rites began during those days. They are the days when witches are at their most powerful and misfortune is abroad. We have already seen that considerable pains were taken, and explicit orders were given, to ensure that Coillard made a safe passage up river. So it would not have been prudent to have allowed the missionary to set out on such an important journey during the evil days. That in itself is a sign of the seriousness with which the Lozi elite treated the appearance of the Mission. But I suggest that there was another reason.

On the evening of 5 March, Westbeech wrote in his journal, 'King started on a round of visits to the graves of his forefathers to pray for the welfare of his country, but being too weak could not accompany him. He was away four days, returning on the 5th with much beating of drums and acclamations of the crowds.'[78] I think that we can elaborate this slightly. The powers of the missionaries were known, impressive and, unless contained, a threat to the welfare of Lewanika's country. This 'round of visits', probably to the most powerful of the graves, was, I suggest, the ritual involvement of the powers of the spirits to enhance and to stand beside the powers of the king in the coming encounter. The timing of the visits underscores the seriousness of the matter, for dark and light powers were usually sought when the *Litunga* made sacrifice *before* the new moon appeared.

Let me now deduce Lewanika's logic with regard to Coillard. If the missionary was to be harnessed, it was imperative that the first thing to happen should be an act ritually locating him below the combined human and spiritual powers of the kingship. Moreover, by ensuring that the act occurred at Lilundu, the intentions of the king would be instantly and quite precisely clear to all his people. To ensure success, everything had to be arranged as auspiciously as possible. Thus it would have been theoretically possible for the messenger to Sesheke to have been dispatched directly from one of the grave-sites early during the tour of 1–5 March. The new moon both indicated the beginning of the auspicious time of the month and enabled all actions to be synchronised. The intention was to get Coillard to Lilundu on a waxing moon. This was rather important and so, for safety's sake, the king dispatched more boats to ensure that there was no delay. In this, the king only just succeeded, for whilst he knew how long his paddlers might take,[79] he perhaps did not allow for Coillard's refusal to travel on Sundays. Had he not stopped, Coillard would have reached Lealui on Saturday 20th, the night when the moon appeared at its fullest.[80] In fact that was the day he reached Nalolo. However, the moon would not have begun to wane appreciably by the 22nd, so effectively the missionary arrived at full moon.

Before accepting the interpretation which I place upon this sequence of events, it is good historians' craftsmanship to posit the null hypothesis: to suggest that any circumstantial cultural evidence aside, this coincidence between the progress of Coillard's journey and the phases of the moon was, in fact, no more than coincidence. Unusually for a historical hypothesis, we can examine the supposition of premeditation by Lewanika and his councillors, a supposition supported by the evidence of the moon, in the context of another case. The event under scrutiny is a canoe voyage up the Zambezi and it imposes an inescapable structure upon any who undertake it. Therefore we have the best conditions of replication which may be hoped for in historical data. The case at issue is that of the Jesuit mission attempt of 1881 and 1883.

When the French Protestant Coillard left central Africa after his exploratory journey of 1878–9 during which he obtained permission to return and found his Mission, the English Protestant trader George Westbeech gave Coillard his word that he would help him when he came back. During Coillard's absence, a Catholic expedition led by Fr Depelchin came north to the Zambezi, and Depelchin asked Westbeech for his help in entering Bulozi and in establishing his mission there. Westbeech wrote in his journal that he was even offered £500. He claimed that he refused the bribe and refused to help the Jesuits because he had pledged his word to Coillard. But Depelchin wrote that Westbeech offered to render his best services to the Catholic missionaries.

It was also repeatedly affirmed in writing by Westbeech himself and other Europeans, and by requests such as Depelchin's that the trader was powerful in the councils of the Lozi. But these were mostly just opinions expressed, no more. However, if I am correct in suggesting that the phases of the moon have significance, we may use the timetable of the two expeditions to test these opinions. From the timetable we may deduce three things.

In the first place it suggests that Westbeech in fact kept his word to Coillard, did not accept the Catholic advances, but urged the Lozi to reject their mission; secondly, that Westbeech was indeed influential with the Lozi elite as he and others had said because, finally, even if there were other contributory reasons also, the Lozi elite put into practice the policy which Westbeech had said that he would favour: they decided that they did not wish to welcome the Catholic mission even before it had entered the country. However, following standard Lozi practice, the Catholics were not presented with a forthright rejection and forbidden to enter Bulozi. The hippopotamus did not stand exposed and bellowing in the shallows, it manipulated the situation far more delicately from its hiding place in the depths.

First of all, Fr Depelchin was kept waiting for a month in Sesheke. 'Ratow, the intractable chief who defends the route restrains us here as if in prison' he wrote. But then, on 15 August 1881, two ill constructed and leaky boats were made available and the party set off, starting on the first day of the last quarter of the moon, passing the most dangerous series of rapids, where they narrowly avoided shipwreck, during the darkest days (22 to 24 August). Their meetings in Lealui were inconclusive and their return journey took place at exactly the same phase of the moon during the next month, their departure being at the beginning of the last quarter, its exact date being fixed by the hosts, not by the guests. During 1883 Fr Berghegge returned to Lealui. Again Ratau controlled the departure. Again they travelled up and back on a waning moon; at Lusu rapids, in the dark days, Br de Vylder drowned. The Mission was abandoned.

These deductions from the timetable of the Jesuits' voyages correspond neatly with our information from other sources. So in three examples there is a clear correlation between the voyage and the phases of the moon. When we then pick up again the circumstantial cultural evidence for the hypothesis, I think that together these data give us reasonable confidence in rejecting the null hypothesis. It would appear that the Lozi behaved in these cases exactly as one might expect them to do.[81]

Thus encouraged, let us return to Coillard. He was for the Lozi king a quite different proposition from Depelchin and his priests, none of whom spoke any of the languages of the country; fluent Sotho was only one of Coillard's attractions. So the confrontation had to be arranged to maximise the chance that Coillard would accede to the demand. We may deduce that Lewanika did the most obvious thing. He demanded the sacrifice as the price of seeing him, the thing which Coillard had been straining to do for months, and ensured that Coillard had 'no-one through whom I might have communicated a little with him. My only intermediary was this Mokano who I knew was ill disposed towards me.' Notice that Westbeech, who evidently had accompanied the king to royal graves on other occasions, was not in the welcoming party. He was left at Lealui. Coillard was faced with an entirely stark context in which to make a very simple decision.

Once the ritual location had been made, it was then possible for Lewanika to see the new arrival and indeed, it was in his interests to demonstrate clearly and repeatedly that the Mission and all its works were his and under his care. When he met Coillard on the water, he gave him a gift of half a roasted goose as sign of welcome and during the following days, the king went to considerable lengths to lavish patronage on the Mission.

The formal session of introduction took place on the Tuesday. Lewanika took his seat in the Kuta, whose members were all present, and a messenger was sent to summon Coillard. Westbeech accompanied him. Mukumwakumwa made a brief introduction and then Coillard launched into a lengthy statement of his intentions. Lewanika replied with an equally lengthy statement of how it was only with difficulty that he had persuaded the chiefs to permit Coillard to come, but that now he received him with joy; he had only to say where he wanted to settle – Lewanika favoured Mongu or Sefula. Westbeech suggested that the king order the Totela to cut a wagon road for Coillard from Sesheke to the Loanja river and the king readily agreed, sending off messengers that very afternoon.[82]

For the rest of the week, Coillard observed life in the capital: seeing cases being tried, talking with Westbeech, talking with his old acquaintance the *Ngambela* Mwauluka. On Sunday 28 March, *Ngambela* gathered crowds of five to six hundred people in the public square to attend the morning and evening services. Westbeech did not kneel down to pray and Coillard commented that 'he weighs on my heart'.[83] The trader left on Monday morning with Lewanika's son Litia, made a leisurely downstream passage, stopping to do a bit of hunting, and on 10 April reached Sesheke 'where I visited the Mission party, who were well, but anxious about Mr C. who was still at the King's. However, as I had left him in good health and could assure them that they might expect him any day as he was to have left Li-a-Liue shortly after me, that comforted them.'[84] Meanwhile in Lealui, on 3 April Coillard was taken by *Ngambela* to visit the old and extremely powerful chief Nalubutu. On the 5th, he attended the Kuta and heard Lewanika graphically recount his flight from the capital in 1884 and how by virtue of his medicines of invulnerability he vanquished the rebels, how foolish the rebels had been to oppose him and how they had paid the price of their folly. Coillard did not like such talk: 'I took up my chair and departed.'

On 6 April he watched the *ngomalume* – the Dance of the Men – and also on that day when the new moon was visible, Lewanika related to him the first connected dynastic history of the Lozi through the time of tradition that Coillard had recorded. On 7 April, Lewanika questioned the missionary closely about Lobengula of the Ndebele and Khama of the Tswana. Why, he asked, was Lobengula not like Khama? He also demanded European medicines. On 9 April, Coillard set off back to

Sesheke. When he reached Nalolo, he found the village almost deserted since Matauka was on a 'pilgrimage to the tombs of her ancestors'. He waited, and at about 4 pm the war drums announced her return. After seeing her, he went on, stopping for the night at Itufa, eighty miles from Lealui. By the next night-stop he had learned more about the operation of the royal graves and specifically about *lizuku*, the royal medicine of invulnerability which Lewanika had described the previous Monday. He reached Sesheke without further incident on 17 April and paid off his paddlers with no friction. They, for their part, had delivered the package back to Sesheke the day before full moon; both voyages had been made during the auspicious times of month.[85]

Coillard now set about preparing for the overland journey to Sefula which could not begin until winter when the rivers had fallen so that they could be forded. Meanwhile, Lewanika summoned all the Sesheke chiefs to Lealui in mid June to receive the new *Mulanziane* Kabuku who Lewanika hoped would be more pliable than his rebellious predecessor. At about the same time, to the south of Sesheke at Pandamatenga, Westbeech's people held a big beer party to say goodbye to Lewanika's son Litia at the end of his holiday. He and Westbeech set out together, the one to return to Lealui, the other to go hunting elephant in Linyanti. On the way, the trader stopped at Sesheke to see Coillard,

> who begged my acceptance of a silver watch as a recognition of his thanks for my endeavours in furthering his mission among the Barotse, which is now a settled thing. I accepted it with suitable words, which pleased him, and I was pleased, not on account of the watch, but simply because he evidently appeared grateful for my services. I have done much for my countrymen in this and other countries (Kafir) but it is the only time I have received a little gratitude.[86]

In what ways does the received interpretation affect that which I have just advanced? Coillard and subsequent writers have viewed Lewanika's behaviour as entirely self-interested. He was portrayed as an African chief who had climbed to power on a mountain of corpses, whose grip on his throne was tenuous at best and who sought the presence of a trader like Westbeech and a missionary like Coillard as a shield to defend himself against his own people and who, to obtain that shield, had to override substantial opposition among his chiefs and council, led notably by Nalubutu. I shall argue that there was indeed a sense in which Lewanika was dependent on his whites, and I shall document that relationship in the next chapter, but he was not dependent upon them in the way that has been suggested by earlier writers. This is

190

shown by the evidence already adduced and which I shall briefly rehearse now.

I showed in my account of the civil war of 1884–5 given earlier that the purging was by no means indiscriminate. The commando raid on the *Mulanziane*'s village was closer to the norm. But Coillard had a great deal of trouble with the Sesheke chiefs who would not do what he wanted (indeed his complaints against them came early in his speech before Kuta on Tuesday 23 March),[87] and his public writing consistently suggested that they were a bloc opposed to the restored king. His private writing, and Westbeech's evidence, showed the fissures in their allegiances more clearly; the implication of the foregoing narrative has been to stress the degree to which they were actually responsive to the royal will. The persistent image in the literature of this opposition bloc has been a result of taking Coillard's political judgments (as distinct from his observations and immediate experiences) too literally. However, the coordination of events was not the only evidence which resists the received interpretation. Notably there was the massive and systematic mobilisation of the apparatus of supernatural and communal power represented by the involvement of the royal graves and their inhabitants. The king could not have done this on his own, a view supported by concrete evidence, for the events of Coillard's stay in Lealui showed how fully the elite and the people were involved: the people attended the Kuta sessions (and Coillard's services) in large numbers and *Ngambela* took the new arrival to see Nalubutu. Here and subsequently, in the development of the trunk canal system described above, Nalubutu's actions contradicted the interpretation of his role which Coillard publicised.

The intention of the events of this carefully planned seven weeks was to ensure that contacts between the Mission and the Lozi in the immediate future took place within a precisely defined cultural context. It was defined by complex statements about Lozi intentions, the missionaries' supernatural and material powers and their relative subordination, statements which were distilled and thus made both simple and explicit through an interrelated sequence of symbolic actions. Simplification was a product of the symbolic content of those actions and, thus condensed, knowledge of the actions – and hence the meaning they contained – could be widely and easily broadcast. This has been my argument in this section and I have suggested that the evidence accepts this interpretation of intention at the highest magnification of detail and without violence being done to the data. We also have evidence of its effects.

Winter came and with it the falling of the rivers which would have to be forded by the wagons as they travelled up the east bank of the Zambezi after leaving Lewanika's wagon trail through the forest. Coillard completed his preparations in the congenial surroundings of Sesheke. 'Mukumwakumwa', he noted, 'is decidedly our friend since our voyage to Lealui.' He brought them gifts of meat which he had shot, but asked for the bullet back so that he could use it again.[88] Coillard, Waddell and Middleton set out in the middle of the month on what was to prove to be a long and hazardous trek. Mme Coillard was left at Sesheke with Dorwald and Elise Jeanmairet.

She was awakened by a noise on Monday 23 August and, throwing on a shawl, ran to find her herdsmen giving precious lumps of dried cattle dung from the Mission cattle to a couple of girls. She upbraided them and they said to the girls, 'Certainly you shall have cow dung for it belongs to the chief and this cattle too.'[89] This was the message intended by Lewanika from the events of March and here it was from the mouths of simple herdsmen. The Mission cattle were *za mbuwa* cattle – royal gift cattle, given in trust – and their employer was Lewanika, not Mme Coillard. Why should the king have bothered to go to such lengths to make this point? The answer lies in an understanding of how the missionaries were perceived, to which we now proceed.

8.3 MUTUAL PERCEPTIONS, 1884–1891[90]

Travellers from Livingstone onwards noticed how they were explained by the people in terms of magic and chiefship. Holub, who was not a missionary but a doctor, recorded how Sipopa ordered his paddlers to ensure that on no account was this powerful magician to die within Bulozi,[91] whilst Coillard heard of Livingstone's supernatural reputation soon after he first visited southern Bulozi. A chief he met thought that Livingstone had used magic to induce the fall which caused the Kololo chief Sebitwane's accidental death.[92] When the young English missionary Arnot stayed at Lealui during Coillard's absence in Europe, he was called *Monare* or *Monare nyan (sic) (*i.e. *nyinyani)*: Little Livingstone. He found that people recognised the explorer's portrait and one old man recited one of Livingstone's sermons from memory.[93] Livingstone was described to Coillard and to Baldwin, the Methodist, as a magically successful hunter, a man of great generosity and as the controller of inexplicable phenomena like fireworks and his magic lantern: the attributes of a chief. Men who had travelled with him spoke of him to Coillard and 'always ended by saying Ngaka [Healer, magician] ah! He was not a man like others. He was a God!'[94]

However, such a display of power had its dangers. In the tense period before the rebellion, Lozi who got too close to Arnot were under suspicion and of Arnot's acquaintances, one was banished and one burned.[95]

Lewanika told Coillard years later that the *mwati* poison oracle was consulted in 1878 to decide whether to take Khama's and Westbeech's advice to allow Coillard into the country and that since the verdict was not definitive, as a precaution none of the gifts which the missionary sent to Lewanika were permitted to reach him because they might have been bewitched.[96] People were unsure who Coillard was. Some asked if he was Livingstone's brother.[97]

Many things about the whites were strange but to their African audiences some were more so than others. When Waddell built a log cabin at the Victoria Falls, the people were amazed that it stood and 'said we white people were wizards as we could make houses stand on trees [i.e. foundation logs] instead of planting them in the ground'. When Waddell asked them to help plaster the house, they asked for 'medicine' to enable them to do it. 'They think that all our wisdom and skill comes to us by taking medicine.'[98]

Means of communication caused more consternation than the Europeans' odd buildings. Writing was equated with divination.[99]

> Sebofo said, 'Missionary, you haven't written for him' (the sick man) 'What do you mean? I have given him some medicine', I replied. 'Yes, yes, but you know you haven't written in your book, you haven't divined. . .that is the white man's way of divining and you must divine in order to help him to get better.'[100]

'They are never tired of seeing my pen run over the paper', wrote Coillard. 'It is marvellous they say, and ask themselves what might be the mysterious medicine which initiates you into this strange art.'[101] Messengers carrying a letter from Coillard to his wife whilst he was visiting Tatila Akufuna were thunderstruck when she addressed them individually, having read their names on the back of the envelope.[102] Westbeech's post caught up with him near Sioma as he descended the river after the meetings of March 1886. As he devoured his letters, his people were 'quietly remarking to one another, "Look, he's laughing again. How wonderful! What can he see in that thing that he's looking at that causes such pleasure? For he does not speak, neither does it. Surely there's only one thing that beats white men and that's death. See how they cure sickness. . ."[103] Although letters were treated with respect, the power of the word was not unknown. However, it was a royal possession; the vast majority of the population lived on the margins of literacy where the word could be absorbed into an eclectic cosmos and where its power to heighten an individual's identity did not have rein.[104] 'The *lengolo* [*liñolo*, word] is a thing of the [royal] courtyard; cattle are of the public square', was how one speaker put it in debate in 1887.[105] The written word had mysterious power and the concrete achievements of people who possessed that power were highly visible; therefore it was not so surprising that illiterate heathen parents willingly provided cattle to enable their children to buy bibles.[106]

Still more powerful than the word was the photograph. A picture of a white girl on a calendar was saluted as if it were a live person.[107] It was convenient that photography was Coillard's hobby. He photographed the Sesheke chiefs who joined the rebellion against Lewanika. After the rebellion was over, these photographs affected *Mulena Mukwae* Matauka visibly: 'These people are dreadful. They carry the living and the dead in their pockets.'[108] Even in 1890, the showing of these pictures as slides caused consternation.[109]

Events only confirmed the impression of power. Once Waddell fell off a roof he was building but escaped injury; he was observed by an old chief and, as he soon learned from rumour, the incident was taken as proof of his supernatural power.[110] More bizarre and impressive yet was when the artisan killed an ox for the celebration of the Coillards' silver wedding in 1886. The bullet passed through the animal, ricocheted off a tree behind it and landed in the sand at the feet of a rather shaken Waddell who picked it up and put it in his pocket. An old man witnessed the freak shot and soon it was known that Waddell was a *moloya* (witch) who could call back his bullets.[111]

Some attempted an ideological counter-attack against that aspect of the Mission. In September 1884, the old *Mulanziane*, soon to be murdered, barged into the Sunday service in Sesheke. He began to talk very loudly to drown the sermon which Jeanmairet was preaching; what he said was a recital of the Lozi myth of creation – of Nyambe and Kamunu. Coillard told him to be silent but it was only after considerably stronger words that he went away, grumbling. After dark he returned. 'Teachers, you have scolded us, but God will strike us because of you, someone in the village will die during the night!'[112] It was precisely to resolve such problems as these that the events of March 1886 were so necessary. Even so, there was an understandable residual popular suspicion. In mid October 1886, Westbeech returned again to Lealui and noted that 'The King has taken to him [Coillard] but the people want to know what he wants there, and he won't trade with them. . .'[113] Kanoti Nalumango was deputed by the king to be Waddell's apprentice, to learn European technical skills, so it is not surprising to find that the man sent to obtain new sorts of power was a healer, a man of certain powers already – Waddell watched him treating people with cupping horns, medicines and the inhalation of infusions of herbs – who could therefore face the whites from a position of strength.[114] Indeed, during the later part of 1886, there had been one specific event which was taken to show the power of the missionaries and which showed how essential it was to bridle such terrifyingly powerful people.

In the early afternoon of Sunday 29 August there was a total eclipse of the sun. Coillard, Waddell and the trekking party viewed it encamped at the Seboya stream. Coillard thought how the event put him in touch with his wife since he thus knew exactly what she would be doing at that very moment.[115] What actually happened in Sesheke, the travellers learned only weeks later. Mme Coillard wrote that, as Waddell reported it,

> the Chiefs of Sesheke had been in a plite on the Sunday of the Eclypse as they thought the Missionary had darkened the sun because they had not been to the morning service and they went in the afternoon and apologised to Mr Jeanmariet for not attending and asked him to show them how they had done it.

Mme Coillard told the new *Mulanziane* Kabuku that it was his sin that made him afraid.[116]

The supernatural attribution of their power made the missionaries more like chiefs, and therefore more of a threat to chiefs, than their trader predecessor Westbeech. African magicians did strange things and behaved in strange ways within the material and cosmological resources of Bulozi. The missionaries were unlike them in that their odd social values, style of living, food, etc. were not related to the scale of those resources. Theirs was not a familiar oddness and their technology and ideology laid claim to previously unencountered sorts of power. However, the events of March 1886 showed that the most effective idiom within which to locate the missionaries was the existing one and further, that once harnessed, the more that those powers were seen, the more they redounded to royal credit. One example illustrates this well. It will be recalled that the power to make rain was one of those in the chiefly arsenal. In reply to the question, how did Coillard win converts, it was said:

> There was no rain; the land was dry. The Mbunda cast their bones in vain. Then *Mungole* [Coillard: 'the man who talks a great deal'] called Lewanika and the people into the church at Lwatile. Before them all, he preached and preached and preached. As he preached, a cloud no bigger than a hand appeared on the horizon. Then *Mungole* began to sing a hymn. By the time he had reached the second verse, the sky was dark. By the time he ended, the rain fell so hard that people could not return at once to Lealui but had to remain waiting in the Church. Alas, there are not such men of power nowadays![117]

If missionaries had the status of chiefs, it was not surprising that they were expected to have the ambitions of chiefs also. In April 1891, the Primitive Methodist missionary Arthur Baldwin, who was seeking permission to open a station in Ilaland, was at Sesheke at the same time as it was being visited by Matauka. One moonlit evening, he and Ward, his artisan, took a walk near Matauka's camp:

> We spoke to several persons as we passed and to the enquiry made once or twice 'what are you seeking?' we replied 'Nothing, we are simply taking a walk'. . . On returning as we were crossing [on a path] a piece of cleared yet unoccupied ground near to the Queen's enclosure. . . [Ward showed Baldwin how he had seen one of the Sesheke chiefs walking]. . .he walked backwards drawing his right foot along making a pretty straight mark. . . as a means of being able to retrace one's steps.[118]

The next day they were summoned to the camp and accused of trying to bewitch the queen. Their protests were in vain. 'They said they couldn't see how we could be merely taking a walk. We must have intended in some way to harm the Queen and her people.'[119] Baldwin was forced to sit in the sand. 'They refused to believe me. . .it was a case of witchcraft – we were wizards seeking to kill the Queen, her chiefs and ultimately we intended to become masters of the country.'[120] Auguste Goy, now in charge of the Sesheke station of the Paris Mission, tried to stand up for Baldwin, but he was vilified also as the 'father of wizards'. In the heat of the moment all these latent fears spilled out. The Sesheke chiefs forbade Baldwin to go 'a yard in the direction of the King', for fear that he might try to bewitch him too. Throughout this, Baldwin was forced to kneel hatless in the sand under the full sun. Then Matauka herself came. She restored him to his stool in the shade and told him not to worry but to pay a fine, which Lewanika eventually waived.[121]

The incident was revealing not only of the fears, but also because it showed how essential it was to locate the whites ritually so that fears like these could be suppressed and a productive relationship established. In Baldwin's case, the ritual location was to take place without his understanding what he did when he made sacrifice at Imatongo, grave of Mwanambinyi.[122] Once the supernatural sting was drawn the humbler practical functions of chiefliness posed no threat. Some years later, Baldwin noted that 'It would be easily possible for me to play the part of a big chief if I gave encouragement to the idea, but I again and again tell the folks I am not their chief but their missionary. Sometimes however I interfere in the interest of right. . .'[123]

Coillard had been aware from the outset of the value of his status as a

196

chief and a magician. In 1884 at the first service he held at Lusuma, 'Mr C. made them repeat over and over again the first verse of the hymn in Seruto "The Great Physician now is here"'.[124] Its significance was evidently not lost on the audience, for the next year a visitor showed Waddell a song he had heard in the night and jotted down; it was the same hymn.[125] In September 1884, Coillard observed that Livingstone's visit had left a supernatural reputation. 'What a beautiful testimony! What footsteps to leave behind!' he commented.[126] When he disclaimed supernatural power to cause the eclipse of the sun in 1886, no one believed him. So long as their power was undefined, people feared the missionaries. In December, those who attended services feared to close their eyes in case they were taken by surprise and bewitched.[127] As Coillard ascended the river in December 1884 to meet the rebels Mataa and Akufuna, his retainer Walubita announced the new regime at each night-stop by explaining that now one should not work on Sundays – the 'Sunday law' of these new chiefs. Coillard was meanwhile reading Livingstone's biography 'with an intense interest'[128] as he travelled. At the first service which he held in Lealui, on Sunday 28 March 1886, Coillard employed the same tactic of promulgating law, reading the ten Commandments – the 'law of God' which, he later told his artisan, appeared to affect Lewanika.[129] His predecessor had used a magic lantern with good results and Coillard did the same. At the party held to celebrate the marriage of Elise to Dorwald Jeanmairet the next year, the magic lantern and fireworks caused frenzied excitement.[130]

Coillard realised how the Christian God had been absorbed by Lozi as yet another deity to placate or to beguile and he sought to make his God appear the most powerful in the pantheon. He preached that the Kololo invasion had been a punishment from his God for the wickedness of the Luyi.[131] For their part, after his return from the Valley, the position of that God and his servant was clear to the Sesheke chiefs. Once they had returned with Kabuku, the new *Mulanziane*, a new site for Sesheke had to be chosen:

> They have consulted the *litaula* – thrown the dice as we say in French; they have sacrificed oxen to the spirits of the former chiefs of Sesheke; at dawn they have gone in procession, ceremoniously led by a woman, to pray at the important grave sites and then, on Sunday afternoon, they came in a body to pray to the God of the missionaries. Thus nothing now lacks to assure the prosperity of the new capital of the Province![132]

But Coillard persisted. He pointed to the European buildings as proof of the Mission's power,[133] used spectacles like his photographs, magic lantern and fireworks – called 'the Gun of God' by the Lozi[134] – as well as less exotic bribes like food and cloth to draw people to the Mission, for they were all 'powerful lessons to give them faith in the missionaries' teachings'.[135] A most deliberate trial of strength was in selecting the sites for the stations. Sefula had material attractions – the stream, its position relative to Nalolo and Lealui – but it was also in 1886 'nothing short of a Golgotha; skulls and bones of unfortunate wretches resently [*sic*] burned for witchcraft are scattered up and down'. Lwatile, the station at Lealui, was also an execution ground.[136]

Although Coillard understood and used peoples' reactions to his supposed magic, neither he nor his wife seemed to appreciate that the constant stream of beggars and sellers who came to the door were also showing normal behaviour towards a chief. Tribute was a reciprocal arrangement and that was not understood. At Lealui in 1884 Arnot had discovered that until he had lost or given away his possessions, begging was continuous and only after he was destitute did he feel that he had any success in evangelisation.[137] The article he wrote stating this in the *Missionary Echo* infuriated Coillard, who was bringing goods with him that Arnot had requested, but the same happened to them. For example, a man came to Mme Coillard with maize to sell and could not understand that even though at that moment she did not need it, she would not buy it. 'It's corn, I want a cloth, you have plenty', he kept repeating.[138] He expected the missionaries to dispense their patronage in the same way that the *Litunga* controlled the flow and direction of his; for whilst people attempted to wheedle from him as much as they could, they also expected him to draw a line. But in this case, Mme Coillard was seen to be hoarding an unreasonable surplus of desirable rare goods.[139] Similarly, service for the chief was rewarded. Thus service for his white subordinates should also be rewarded, but attempts to wheedle things by obsequiousness in the accepted Lozi way were merely seen as deception. Mme Coillard wrote to her sister of these 'despairingly non-inquisitive people': 'One day after the preaching, a man came and said, "Have I not listened well? Give me a handkerchief!"'[140] Waddell also recalled incidents when payment was required for listening.[141] A little later, a missionary at Sesheke had three enquirers to whom he explained the Gospels for five consecutive days after which, to his disgust, each demanded five days' pay.[142]

9

The consequences of contact

9.1 SYMBIOSIS: THE ZAMBEZI MISSION, 1886–1891

When Lewanika visited England in 1902, the *Manchester Guardian* correspondent dubbed him a 'dusky Disraeli, for he is wonderfully like Lord Beaconsfield', and added that 'if Lewanika has a curious likeness to Lord Beaconsfield, he is also no mean diplomatist'.[1] It was this deftness of touch which was most evident in the late 1880s, for after the events of March 1886, Lewanika's main priority with regard to the Mission changed. Now he had to capitalise on his new possession and to do this well his proprietary interests had to be made plain.

Coillard had a long and expensive trip to Sefula with his wagons, losing a lot of goods through accidents on the road. He finally reached Sefula on 11 October and sent Aaron, one of the Sotho evangelists, straight on to Lealui to inform Lewanika. The king came to see the Mission the very next day, riding a horse and dressed in European clothes. Both, but especially the horse, were symbols of royal intention and the swiftness of the visit also made clear an interest further confirmed by later actions.[2] Patronage flowed. By November, when Coillard went down river by canoe to collect Mme Coillard, Lewanika had given him a total of six oxen.[3] However, there were things which Lewanika wanted in return in areas where he lacked expertise. His desire to obtain formal protection under the British Crown was expressed first in the interval before Coillard went to collect his wife. He desired British protection so that Bulozi would be closed to 'other nations such as the Portuguese and the Boers, the latter Khama was affraid [*sic*] of and now he has nothing to fear'.[4] Here was the clue.

The missionary had come to Bulozi with Khama's recommendation and Khama was Lewanika's friend with whom he sought the closest ties. Khama had a settlement with the whites that had left his state intact. Therefore if Khama had missionaries and soldiers who gave this desirable

Fig. 28 Lewanika in later life.

result, Lewanika should use the medium – Coillard – that Khama had sent. For his part, Coillard advised Lewanika 'frankly that it was not likely that the British government would extend their dominions so far north'.[5] The matter was taken up again when Coillard returned in December. He decided that the king was acting entirely in his own interest – 'to shelter himself from another revolution'. Coillard wrote a letter to the Governor of the Cape, but would not send it until he satisfied himself that the king had popular support for his policy. He told Lewanika so.[6]

A few weeks later the king provided evidence of his mandate and, at the same time, further evidence of the perceived position of the Mission, in a form which made Coillard most agitated. On 1 February, the king called people to Lealui to discuss whether to raid the Ila that year. They decided against it. Then *Ngambela* asked bluntly whether they wanted the Mission.

> 'Don't say that the King is imposing on you something that you don't want. Speak! Speak!' The silence didn't last long and in the space of three hours, eighteen speakers made speeches successively. Hearing *Ngambela* put our stay here in question in such a crude fashion, we were not exactly without anxiety. . .If they were publicly to declare that they didn't want us, what a prospect. Would we then have to pack off out of the country like the Jesuits?
>
> First speaker: 'What? Does the King ever give us bad things? If he has found these teachers for us, isn't it because they are a good thing? Don't we hear tell of all the black nations, all the chiefs having their missionaries to teach the young people and the Kings the wisdom of the white nations?'[7]

Coillard reported more detail to his retainer when he returned home:

> Some spoke in our favour and promises were made to learn and to do as their father the Missionary would tell them. . .Others said, 'No we do not need these teachers unless they know and teach us to make powder and such like things. . . One man said the missionaries were bad. . .and not long ago they caused the sun to rot (meaning the eclypse [*sic*]) and they chased away the rain. . .'

Liomba, who had seen Khama and his missionaries, then spoke. He told the assembly that 'on the day of the iron bell Kama [*sic*] and his people go to here [*sic*] and be taught'.[8] The outcome was that the Mission was publicly confirmed, although fear of expulsion remained for several more years.

The raid on the Ila in fact took place the next year. While Lewanika was away, he heard a false rumour that Sefula had been pillaged. He imme-

diately sent a message to Coillard which again showed his hand. He told
the missionary to go to the capital and wait there for his return when he
would reinstate him at Sefula. What bothered Coillard most was that the
idea had been put around that they could be pillaged or the station set
alight.[9]

The Mission opened its school and Litia and other children of the elite
dominated it. In May 1889, Coillard visited Nalolo paddled by his noble
pupils and people muttered about him making the king's son his slave,[10]
but in August, Auguste Goy the canal builder wrote that the king 'protects us with all his authority'.[11] In September Lewanika agreed without
conditions to the foundation of a new station at the strategic site of
Kazungula, leaving all arrangements to Coillard's discretion – 'which is
thus remarkable!'[12] On return to Sefula, Coillard had problems with his
paddlers. A message to the king produced an instant remedy: 'Seajika
came back with Mosala [who] ordered everyone to go away at once which
they did in good humour.'[13] In November, women cultivating near Sefula
hemmed in Coillard's fields. He mentioned it to the king who ordered
everyone to move. This led to a mass exodus leaving the Mission isolated.[14] Why such concern? The next month gave a sign of the answer.
The king sent parties of Ila who had come to render homage to visit
Sefula. The reason, I suggest, was to let them see for themselves the sort
of power which the king controlled.[15] Coillard was special. A few years
later Baldwin noted that whilst others were robbed, Coillard never locked
anything and never lost anything either.[16] But as the assembly of February 1887 had made quite plain and as subsequent events had confirmed,
the Mission was a particular royal asset before all else.

Undoubtedly, the most easily visible region in which Lewanika drew
benefit from the Mission was in the diplomatic negotiations of 1887–91;
this area of symbiosis is examined in more detail in the next part of the
chapter. However, there were two other parallel ways in which he
deployed his Europeans' skills. The most important has already been
closely described. In 1888 the idea of a trunk canal network was sown and
during the years when the Concession Crises were at their height, this
huge mobilisation of public labour to put into effect an alien idea for the
public good was undertaken. What it also showed about the real power of
the king and the real relationships within the Kuta cause us to regard with
scepticism the opinions of Coillard and those who have followed him
uncritically in seeing the king's actions as entirely selfish and a response to
his personal weakness and precariousness.

The other way was his personal involvement with white technology and
white goods to show his control over such things as well as to gain the
benefit of them. His clothes and his horse showed very clearly to his

people where he stood in this respect. As already seen, he made the same point in the most dramatic way possible by incorporating white techniques into the state barge *Nalikwanda* to the extent of having two, one built with Lozi techniques, the other with European, in the later 1890s. Within a month of the Mission party's arrival at Sefula, Lewanika sent '12 elderly Barotse to learn, or watch us building'.[17] But they were useless as apprentices, and so he sent Kanoti Nalumango and Samoinda to Waddell, but as soon as they had sufficient training they were recalled to the capital to build the king a large European-style house.[18] But when, encouraged by Waddell, Nalumango began to build a European-style house for himself, his temerity evoked a swift reaction and, on the orders of several chiefs, his house was pulled down.[19] The artisan commented on Lewanika and Litia's inventiveness, their use of European tools and of models to try out ideas. The king tried to get Waddell to move his sawmill to Lealui. The reason for keeping so tight a rein on these things was shown to Waddell in an overhead conversation. 'One of the Mambari traders was standing gaping at the roof of the church [at Lwatile, then being built] and a Marotsi said to him, do you see that is what our *likoa* [*mukuwa*: white man] can do, your *lekoa* is no good (meaning the Portuguese).'[20]

Lewanika's problem was to obtain the maximum profits from Coillard without causing him to feel too disheartened to wish to remain. His relationship with Coillard showed the contradictions of this position. Waddell described it eloquently: 'He is either all honey or all durt [*sic*].'[21] On the one hand there was his wrath; in fact Coillard refused to have any financial dealings with the king after difficulty over a wagon ordered for Lewanika in the south.[22] There were boycotts. In September 1887, Litia and his noble-born schoolmates waylaid and threatened people coming to sell produce at the Mission which was then under royal displeasure.[23] In May 1891, there was a fortnight's food and labour boycott of Lwatile in punishment because Coillard had lent a canoe to the Methodist Buckenham whom the king was trying to compel to pay dearly for transport.[24] In May 1892, there was another blockade: 'All the boys. . .were terrified and some had already asked for their pay and gone.' It began on 26 May; on the 30th, Coillard shrewdly told Lewanika that it was bad politics to blockade an old man because it might give others ideas! It was lifted on 4 June.[25] In November, the king 'laid siege' again to force Coillard to barter some shirts, but it was only a token gesture.[26]

On the other hand there was an almost child-like dependence on the missionary. One incident serves to illustrate it. Towards the end of the early Concession negotiations, Lewanika broke his watch. Coillard gave him another and the king thanked 'his father' profusely. However, the next day the secretary Seajika came to the missionary with a long face.

Getting up that morning, the king had knelt on his new watch in his waistcoat pocket. Therefore he fined himself £5 which he sent to Coillard. The missionary called Lewanika to come and see him and returned the £5, but the watch was very thoroughly broken.[27]

Coillard also held ambivalent views. On the one hand, after Litia and his mates established a blockade in 1887, he wrote, '*borena* [*bulena*: the kingship] is brigandage'.[28] In large part, he attributed his failure to spark off wide-scale conversions among ordinary people to the oppressive hand of the rulers. [29] Lewanika consistently refused to convert, producing over the years many variations on the theme voiced in 1890: 'I am too evil, I've spilt too much blood, I have been too immoral.'[30] But Coillard had to work through the *Litunga* and over the next years his writings show that a real concern for Lewanika developed, and he continued to hope for his conversion throughout his life. The king and his missionary came to know each other very well and the evidence gives a strong impression that the verbal battles and the physical sanctions which the king and Coillard levied upon each other were more like the lunges of fencers than of soldiers. Coillard's attitude to the king, as indeed to everyone else, was primarily determined by his conception of his aims and his role which consequently conditioned his view of the people.

In May 1893 a severe gastric infection sent Coillard into a semi-coma during which he dreamed. As he later recalled it, he and Adolphe Jalla, his second-in-command since 1890, were showing magic lantern slides to a noisy African audience. Coillard told Jalla to search for a slide of Peace, which he did, only to find that it was broken. 'There is another, better yet', said Coillard and when it was found intact and was projected, the audience fell silent; then he heard the whispered word 'Peace' roll over it.[31] This was his aim: to see peace, through Christianity, reign in Africa. His motives were equally clear. On the one hand, 'we pay the debt of centuries past of Europe, Christian Europe; we atone for her crimes, past and present'. On the other, and more fundamentally, 'At His bidding, as Moody so beautifully said, millions of angels would fly down to work, to suffer and to die for the salvation of sinners in benighted Africa. But that glorious privilege is ours, not theirs!'[32] He and his wife were called to bear suffering submissively, as he had written before they left Lesotho.

It was expressive of both his motives and his view of Bulozi that he saw his role to be similar to that of St Paul. Frustrated by delays in Sesheke, he felt like Paul in prison; 'betrayed' by one of his European retainers, he compared him to Alexander the coppersmith (who did Paul 'a great deal of harm'); two years later, when he met two of his apostate converts, he wrote in his journal, 'It is curious that I undergo so many of the experiences of St Paul.' Earlier that year, Jalla had preached on the persecution of Paul at Ephesus, which Baldwin had thought was ill advised since it might give the people a precedent for persecuting the missionaries. Baldwin himself would have tried to frighten the people.[33] But like Paul, Coillard felt that he moved among heathens who resisted his message with vigour. 'These poor Barotsi!' he wrote, 'What an abstraction one has to make in order to love them!'[34] His wife was more direct. 'I have not yet seen any natives so callous and so utterly indifferent to anything outside their world!' she wrote to her sister.[35] Both she and Coillard despaired of their moral qualities. In May 1885, he wrote how little one could trust a Lozi's word, wondering if he had been wise to return on the basis of Lewanika's message of 1878; she, alone to face them whilst Coillard was taking the wagons up to Sefula in 1886, wrote despairingly in her journal, 'Oh! I am tired of these peoples' lies.' She felt that there was 'a wall of brass between me and the people. . .I don't live here, I languish'.[36] Their opinions changed little with time. In 1889, Coillard asked himself if there were any Lozis in whom he could have confidence and Mme Coillard felt that 'they would see us die sooner than help us if we were in want'.[37] In 1893, Coillard told Baldwin, the visiting Methodist missionary, that 'he has never preached a single sermon on "Love" since coming into the country, for this side of the peoples' nature is so dead that an appeal to it at present would be useless'.[38] Yet the same observer noted that Coillard was very lenient with his workers, far more so than with his whites, and Baldwin could not understand why.[39] The agonies of mind which Coillard went through on behalf of his Lozi converts are some indication of what Baldwin could not understand, for they reflected differences of attitude and of approach from those of the other members of the Mission which displayed themselves in deep divisions over techniques and goals, divisions which split the Mission throughout most of its early years.

The relationship between Dorwald Jeanmairet and the Coillards was always formal, although after his marriage to Elise, their niece, he was promoted to being addressed by his Christian name, an event of sufficient note to warrant special mention.[40] In the years before 1886, Jeanmairet's differences of opinion were submerged by Coillard's enthusiasm. Coillard was decisive because he was convinced of the correctness of what he did and how he did it. He was a strict and paternalist leader who basically liked Africans[41] – I have the impression that he was the only member of the early Mission party for whom that was true – and who believed that the Zambezi Mission should be conducted by Africans as much and as soon as possible (under his firm direction) for both moral and financial reasons.

As early as August 1885, Jeanmairet registered his disagreement with this policy to Paris. He criticised the laxity of indigenous Christians and stated firmly, 'I do not subscribe to the evangelisation of Zambezia by Basutos, I would be really *frightened* to see them arrive in great numbers.'[42] However, he signed his name to Coillard's joint appeal of 1885 for the subscription of special funds. Later that year he wrote to Boegner again describing his disillusionment with the lack of moral fibre (*manque de coeur*) which 'seems to me to be a distinctive characteristic of these people', adding, 'My picture isn't very pretty, but M. Coillard is the best qualified to complete it and add to it more sparkling colours without which my account, doubtless, lacks impartiality.'[43] These latent differences came out into the open in late 1886. Jeanmairet refused to take Mme Coillard's 'advice' ('qu'on lui fasse la leçon', as she wrote), and she disapproved of the way he ran the Sesheke station; 'There is nothing being done, literally nothing, not even a passing word to those who sell corn.'[44] By late November, just before Coillard returned, 'D says every day that he will leave the country, for the insecurity makes him so miserable. . .Add to this the utter indifference of the chiefs who will not move a bit and you n[ow] [w]onder that D. says we have never been rec[eived].'[45] This unhappy interlude was to have lasting consequences.

Coillard had a busy year of travelling in 1886–7: a return canoe trip in March and April 1886, a wagon trek from August to October, another return canoe trip to collect Mme Coillard from November 1886 to January 1887. Then the next winter, news came that the first reinforcements were on the way, so he travelled to Pandamatenga in July to collect Louis Jalla, Dr Henri Dardier and Auguste Goy, the agricultural aide. Jalla stayed at Sesheke with Jeanmairet, and the others all reached Sefula in October. The end of this voyage marked the beginning of five years of almost ceaseless crises from several different sources. Coillard had to contend simultaneously with problems arising in his relations with his European staff, with his Sotho evangelists, with the threat posed by the arriving Methodist Mission, with shortage of funds and suspicion from Paris, and with hostility from the Church in Lesotho, quite apart from the better known problems posed by his dealings with Lewanika, with the British South Africa Company and the British Crown. Therefore, before these latter events are re-examined in the next section, we must explore the full context of these stressful years. This is best done in a simple chronology.

On his way up river, Dardier lost his parasol overboard and so became badly sunburned. The party reached Sefula at the end of October and he was already unwell.[46] Coillard now had the two specialist reinforcements he wanted, but the financial position of the Mission was precarious. In November he wrote beseechingly to a leading Glasgow Protestant businessman, Richard Hunter, asking for help in cash and kind.[47] However, his new staff turned out to be less than what he had hoped for: 'They expected to find things differently, they thought that the natives would be friendlier and more desirous to hear the Gospel.'[48] Dardier refused to help in the school or at any other tasks while he was healthy ('Never dream of sending a doctor who is only a doctor', Coillard wrote later), whilst Goy 'has good qualities [but]. . .He, accept a hierarchy? He is the most independent man in the world. . .He wasn't two weeks here before he declared to Waddell that he would have nothing to do with me.' It made an impossible situation and Coillard wrote to Boegner, 'I beseech you not to send young unmarried people to the Zambezi. It inflicts a heavy cross on a certain lady who finds hers already heavy enough.'[49]

Christina Coillard was the nub of the problem for the young men. 'It is sometimes too humiliating to bear it all. It isn't possible by patience or any other virtue to live in peace with her', wrote Goy, adding that the most disagreeable thing was the Coillards' close supervision of food.[50] In December, Dardier, who had become ill again, decided to return home. Middleton, the English retainer who had been with Coillard throughout the expedition had, since June 1887, had it in mind to leave also and the two left Sefula together. Even this was the occasion for a final row between Coillard and Dardier because Coillard put the more experienced bush-hand, Middleton, in formal charge of the passage.[51] Dardier's hasty departure was explained publicly to be solely because of his health. 'Will he ever come back to Sefula? Our sadness and disappointment are great; they are in proportion to the immense joy that the arrival of this rein-forcement had given to us.'[52] To Boegner, Coillard wrote that it was 'a true deliverance, but he has been here long enough to do much harm'.[53]

Middleton went on south alone and Dardier reached Kazungula and a very sick Westbeech on 1 February. The two men cared for each other, but on 23 February Dardier died in Westbeech's arms.[54] The news reached Coillard on 7 April. He was shocked that Jeanmairet had not even been to see the grave. 'It's incomprehensible. The impression in Europe will be undesirable.'[55] To Boegner, he wrote, 'Alas, he was only a straw! For goodness sake do not make a martyr of him.'[56] But the living were proving to be more troublesome than the dead.

In February, Goy wrote that although he did not approve of Dardier's departure, he understood it: 'it was difficult for him to live here, in two months he had had as much as he could take of it [*il en avait fait plein la coupe*]'.[57] On 15 March, Goy's cup of grievances was overflowing. He told Coillard that he did not wish to be his personal workman and asked, 'Is it a man like Waddell that you need? And he replied to me in the affirmative.'[58] To ease the tension, Coillard sent Goy off to Sesheke on a routine supply run with the wagon. Soon after he left, another crisis broke.

About a fortnight ago, I thought to reclaim and cultivate a piece of land. I offered a patch of ground to Aaron [one of the two Sotho evangelists] thinking that he would accept it gratefully. Not at all. He pocketed the trade beads that I gave him to cultivate it but did nothing. . . Today. . . he ended by saying, 'You'd do better to let me go home at once. I shall not lift a hoe here, I shall do nothing further'. . .we parted, I deeply hurt, he in a temper. 'Is it a sin to return to one's home?' 'It is a sin', I said to him, 'to abandon the work of God when there is no-one else to do it.' There is a bad spirit in him, very bad. He never greets my wife.

Coillard had appealed to Paris for support.[59] He asked Boegner to instruct Goy to remain, but to forbid him his independent ideas. He complained also that the Conference of the Church of Lesotho had itself complained about his references to it in his letters. 'We haven't received an obol since we left', he commented.

Yet another crisis now loomed. The threat of the Methodists was first revealed in the issue of *The Christian* of 11 November 1887 which published their intention to send a Mission to Bulozi. As soon as he received his copy, Coillard wrote a guarded letter to England to warn them off his patch,[60] but fear of being out-manoeuvred became a growing concern. A few days later he wrote to Boegner, enclosing a copy of his letter to England and revealing his worries about four converging threats. There was that of the Methodists; there was a lively fear that 'the Zambezi will pass into the shadow and be forgotten' because after the delineation of spheres of influence the interest of the Direction of the Mission was, Coillard feared, focused on the francophone Congo; there was the deficit, 'our dreadful expenses, our cattle disasters', and there was the crisis of discipline. Goy and Aaron intended to leave Sefula. If they were not replaced, Coillard wrote, it would be proof that the Zambezi Mission was not supported. 'To open the door [to the Methodists]. . .is to cede them our place.'[61]

Goy arrived in Sesheke with the wagon on 28 July, 'happy to leave and to leave behind Mme C.'.[62] He, Jalla and Jeanmairet talked together and the two Sesheke missionaries sent a letter at once to Coillard basically supporting Goy, opposing the use of Sotho evangelists and favouring the centring of the Mission at Sesheke. Coillard replied to them on 24 August in firm terms: Goy was a *missionary-aide* to concern himself with agricultural *work on the station* under the *'fraternal control of the chief mission-ary'*; the Sotho evangelists had proved their role and whilst Sefula was geographically 'eccentric' viewed from Sesheke, 'after all, it is here in the Valley that the nation is. Must we open the door of the Valley to the

Methodists who are coming?'[63] Coillard followed this up with a long and reasoned rejection of their scheme for a model farm that would provision all the Mission Stations, an unequivocal statement that he desired a farmer aide to grow Mission food and who *'identifies himself with us in the work of Sefula'* and an anxious observation that at that moment they had a possibly unique opportunity to root themselves firmly in the country.[64] Goy had now returned from Sesheke, and in a postscript added to the letter, Coillard told Jalla and Jeanmairet that conversation with Goy revealed that a reconciliation of their divergent views on the Mission's tactics was not to be hoped for.[65]

Goy and Aaron set off to Sesheke again with the wagons, and made good time, getting there by early February. Goy had left despite Coillard's opinion that to do so in the face of the Methodist threat and with Aaron also going was a sin.[66] In the meantime, the Sesheke missionaries had put their case to Paris. They described Goy's frustration at being denied all initiative and registered their own feelings about Coillard's style: 'Is it to say that when M. Coillard as chief of the Zambezi expedition requests an agriculturalist, he requests him for himself personally?'[67] Coillard took this letter as 'an act of accusation' and so, in April 1889, set out his case for the committee.[68] By June Coillard felt 'humiliated' by the need to defend himself in this way and hurt by a venomous letter from Mme Dardier basically accusing him of killing her son. He felt that it was extremely possible that they might be expelled from Bulozi altogether.[69]

Coillard felt that the only way to keep the Mission together was to go personally to Sesheke and settle all their differences. He went down river, reaching Sesheke on 25 July. Aaron, who was still there waiting for transport to go south, was silently hostile, but 'a half-hour of conversation has swept away all misunderstanding' with Jeanmairet.[70] It was an example of Coillard's exceptional diplomatic skills. By 18 August, they had reached a compromise on sites. Louis Jalla would go and found a station at Kazungula; on the 26th, Coillard, Jeanmairet and Jalla wrote jointly to Paris to inform the Committee of their accord, to tell of the Kazungula decision and to announce plans for stations at Sioma and Lealui as soon as there were sufficient personnel.[71]

For the moment, the problems with the European staff seemed to be solved. In October Goy, who was on his way to Lesotho to collect his bride before returning in the newly defined role of white evangelist, met the hitherto unknown and therefore feared Methodists and reported that they 'seemed to be disposed to agree with us'.[72] In fact the two Methodists, Baldwin and Buckenham, could not agree with each other and Buckenham spoke no Lozi (as Coillard was to note with some relief), and so another threat diminished.[73] Middleton had meanwhile evidently

209

changed his mind about leaving and decided to return to Bulozi as a trader. Coillard commended his services to the king when he visited Lealui after returning from his journey of reconciliation to Sesheke.[74] There was no further mention of suppressing a French Mission in Bulozi in favour of one in the Congo, but the financial problems continued.

The Coillards were overworked early in 1890 as they held the fort alone until Adolphe Jalla, brother of Louis at Kazungula, arrived in February. There was a sizeable financial deficit, in part due to the unexpectedly large expense of canalising the Sefula stream,[75] although benefactors had paid off the outstanding debts. But Boegner was 'stiff' in his letter which arrived in early June 1890. He suspected that Coillard disposed of Scottish and English funds which Paris did not know about.[76] In July and again in November, Coillard demanded to see the accounts for 1888–9 to discover what caused this attitude.[77] It was against this background that the public events of the Concession Crises took place. With Coillard's other preoccupations in view, we are now in a position to examine it, and his part in it.

9.2 SYMBIOSIS: THE CONCESSION CRISES, 1888–1892

So far I have shown that the symbiotic relationship between Coillard and the Lozi ruling class was deep and important to both sides, that the actual mutual benefits were considerable and that the whole phenomenon was delicate and rather difficult to perceive. We have discovered reliable criteria of the real nature and extent of Lewanika's power during these years and seen the constraints upon Coillard's mind and person. Because of this, the more conventionally documented sequence of events usually taken to represent the substance of the inter-racial encounter, namely the 'Concession Crises', sinks into context even before we examine it in any great detail.

Unlike the trunk canal programme or the spread of new fruit trees, the diplomatic negotiation of the Ware and Lochner Concessions (described below) – negotiations, as distinct from ritual public assent in the Kuta – concerned only very few Lozi and involved fewer. Consequently, given his publicly demonstrated control over the Mission and his use of its skills, knowing Coillard's dependence upon him if he wished to remain in Bulozi and realising that, for whatever reason, Coillard favoured what he also desired, namely British protection, Lewanika thought that he could afford to trust his missionary who had the expertise he lacked in these matters. A detailed examination of the negotiations will show how total his trust was. When he feared at one stage that he had been misled, his fury was mountainous. But the resolution of those doubts in Coillard's favour revealed at a superficial level an awareness that he was the best of the available media of communication, as the king had earlier thought, but more profoundly, that this was not his primary value; this was in those attributes of the Mission which have already been described above.

In the event, the actual content of the Concessions was to prove to be relatively unimportant. What was significant in them was that they did eventually lead to a form of colonial administration beginning nominally in 1896 and more seriously in the early 1900s without the prior intrusion of large numbers of white men as soldiers. By that time, Lewanika and his people had profited from their years of experience with Coillard and as migrant labour respectively and were able to design ways to explain, locate, control and thus detoxify these new forces as they had done with the Mission. The final section of this chapter on the one hand provides the coda to the first stage of Lozi/European relations by describing the continuing and paralysing difficulties of the Mission, and on the other prepares the scene for the next movement by recapitulating the circumstances of the mid 1890s in which the Lozi were to face their next challenges from outside Bulozi. Hence it is an entr'acte.

At some time after the assembly of February 1887, when the value of the Mission had been extensively debated before being confirmed (Section 1 above), Coillard evidently decided to send his letter enquiring about British protection. The message seems to have been transmitted via Khama. The British response was torpid. Only in late 1888 did the Foreign Office advise the Colonial Office of the request ('The Chief I allude to holds sway over the Berutsi country. . .'), and the Colonial Office replied that 'The proposal to take a chief living north of the Zambezi under protection is one which cannot, for obvious reasons, be entertained.'[78] Meanwhile Coillard was becoming increasingly immersed in the mounting internal problems of the Mission but Lewanika, back from raiding the Ila for their cattle, after distributing the booty and thus strengthening his patronage ties was ready to turn his mind again to the matter.

On 20 September (while, in fact, the Colonial Office was cogitating), an assembly was called. *Ngambela* put the case for requesting protection skilfully.

> Barotsi. . .enemies menace us within and without. You are brave, I know, but the danger is great. I sought missionaries for you so that you should not be behind other peoples. Have you welcomed them? Are you grateful for them? Khama has missionaries, but he also has

masole (soldiers). The one goes with the other. So if you keep the missionaries, ask Satory [Victoria] to send us her *masole*. The missionary will do it for us. To hesitate is to reject the missionaries themselves.[79]

Of course the benefits of the missionaries meant one thing to Lewanika and the Lozi audience, another to Coillard. When we are in a position to catch a little of that Lozi resonance, the skill of attaching the two issues together becomes apparent. Yet there was a vocal opposition to the move, fearing that the king would be enslaved. The king turned the threat neatly. Liomba, the chief who had visited Khama and who had spoken out strongly for accepting the Mission in February 1887, was seized, bound, threatened, given sanctuary by the *Natamoyo*, pardoned, fined an ox and reinstated. The ox was donated to the people and after this drama had been played out over three days, people had had time to reflect and Lewanika's view prevailed. Dr Caplan suggested that the show trial was intended to intimidate the opposition. If that was so, why choose Liomba? It was done in order to outflank them.[80]

Lewanika's motives and timing are plain. His domestic position was strengthened; he had just completed a large and successful exercise in reinforcing his patronage ties; he was worried about the threat of Ndebele attack across the Zambezi and had just lost his mediator with the Ndebele, for Westbeech's illness of February 1888 proved to be fatal and he died of liver disease while travelling south on 17 July 1888.[81] Furthermore, the threat of Portuguese and Boers which the king had mentioned in 1886 had not diminished and since he had heard nothing as a result of the earlier enquiries, from all points of view now was a good time to try again.

Coillard's motives for cooperating were different. He knew from his experiences in Lesotho what the effect of encroaching white settlement could be if not properly controlled – which he took to mean controlled by the metropolitan power.[82] But he also hoped to see the removal of royal power as an obstacle to the advance of Christianity. As he wrote when he discovered that the British South Africa Company might not be effective as the Crown's agent, 'I was anxious to see this unhappy country, a hotbed of constant intrigues and revolutions. . .pass under the protection of a strong but wise and humane government.'[83]

The internal disputes of the Mission were at their worst in late 1888 and it was not until the New Year that Coillard wrote again on behalf of the king. On 8 January 1889, he sent a letter to Sir Sidney Shippard, Administrator of Bechuanaland, and about the same time another letter to Khama asking for more advice.[84] He then returned to his own troubles.

On 9 June, he was seriously worried that his Mission might still be expelled.[85] Thus the appearance about ten days later of Harry Ware, an accident-prone game hunter now turned concession hunter,[86] seeking a concession to prospect in Tokaland on the eastern periphery of Bulozi, seemed to offer a modest start on the path towards controlled European entrance to the country. Coillard wrote privately to Boegner:

> They [the chiefs of the Kuta] naturally look to me. . .You may believe that I shall do my level best to make the transactions succeed, whilst always watching over the interests of Lewanika and the nation. Great changes that will bring into the country! But in waiting, we must be calm so as not to be disappointed.[87]

A week later, although ill, Coillard went to Lealui to be present at the finalisation of the concession. Ware made free with his gifts and the people thought that he would be a good replacement for Westbeech. Coillard reflected, 'I suppose that Mr Ware congratulates himself on his success and he is right to do so. For my part, I did my best for Lewanika and I think that there is nothing to regret.'[88]

On 10 July, Coillard and Ware left Sefula to travel down river together. While Coillard began to resolve his differences with his subordinates, Ware travelled south and fairly soon sold his Concession to a man called King, who by November was offering the Concession to Rhodes for what Rhodes considered was the ridiculous price of 1,600 Chartered Company shares.[89] Meanwhile, during Coillard's absence in Sesheke, Lewanika may have received a letter with a very positive reply from Khama who was clearly well satisfied with what had been done.[90]

Coillard went out to Lealui on 8 November for the first time since his return from Sesheke, so Lewanika certainly received Khama's letter by then. The missionary probably also had another communication which would have heightened the king's pleasure. Sir Sidney Shippard wrote to Coillard to tell him that the request for protection had been forwarded to England and that in the meantime, Rhodes would send Lewanika a mission from the new Chartered Company – the British South Africa Company.[91] Coillard returned to the capital later in the month and the king asked for shirts; Coillard replied that his ex-artisan George Middleton would have them to sell since he was soon returning as a trader.[92]

Middleton sacrificed himself for Coillard beyond the demands of service in the early years of the Mission. He had accompanied him up river in 1884 to meet Mataa and Tatila Akufuna, lacerating his feet so that he became gravely ill. But he grimly hung on, attending the Kuta session when they reached Lealui although sometimes doubling up with pain. On return to Lusuma, he went south by wagon to Pretoria where damage to

213

his lungs was also diagnosed, but he returned to the Zambezi in time to trek north to Sefula with Coillard and Waddell in the winter of 1886. Coillard wrote glowingly of his exertions on that difficult and long journey.[93] At Sefula, Middleton began making bricks and while Coillard was away collecting Mme Coillard, since he spoke passable Sesuto Middleton took the Sunday service.[94] But during the early months of 1887, his sentiments changed, swinging from the loyalty and devotion which the charismatic missionary had inspired in him, to the other extreme. In June, Coillard's own choice of image revealed why it was so hard to have neutral sentiments about him: 'I thought I had conquered him, but his heart is no longer here.'[95] Middleton left with Dardier in December.

Musson, a Mangwato trader, was the Mission's freight forwarder.[96] It was therefore not surprising that since Middleton went south with the Mission wagon he saw him. Evidently their conversation changed Middleton's original plan to return to England, for in December 1889 he returned to Lealui as Musson's agent.[97] Middleton brought 'a number of porters carring [*sic*] goods which Lewanika ordered through Mr Selous a year ago who handed the order over to Mr Mussan [*sic*] now successor to the late Mr Westebeech [*sic*]'.[98] Middleton was clearly regarded as Westbeech's successor as 'trader to Bulozi', his nickname being 'Jolosi nyinyani' (i.e. 'little George' (Westbeech)). Of this visit, Coillard wrote,

> Middleton came the day before yesterday to spend the night and part of yesterday. He has returned to the King. The poor man speaks angrily [*il parle haut*] and I think that he'll be a thorn in my path. He purchases popularity at any price. He deluges the people with presents from left and right. . .He speaks angrily against the concession.[99]

Middleton stayed at Lealui until late February or early March 1890. He presumably communicated his suspicions to the king, but they did not sway Lewanika's judgment. On 6 January he and Matauka converged on Sefula for two days of school fete. Waddell taught the children to play cricket and Coillard spoke to the king about conversation.[100] However, Coillard worried about the effect Middleton might have. In guarded tones he told Boegner that 'there are evil influences upon the work – intriguers who do all they can to spoil our influence. . .we are accused of selling the country and what do I know?'[101] He had earlier heard from Louis Jalla at Sesheke, who complained of Middleton as he passed through. 'He is our enemy, that man', wrote Coillard. The pendulum had swung to the other extreme for both parties.[102]

It had been on the evening of Friday 12 January 1890 that Coillard first heard in detail about the British South Africa Company and the Mission headed by Lochner which was on the way to Bulozi. Letters from Ware and Heany explained that,

> He is coming to treat with Lewanika in the name of the new *Chartered South African Comp.* which is to extend from the Zambezi to the Nile and from the Lakes to the Congo Free State. It would appear that the Lakes Company (of the Moir brothers), that of Ware and others as well have amalgamated themselves with this great company which already has a capital of more than a million pounds sterling and which promises to be for Central Africa what the Indian Company has been for India. In fact it has great privileges and powers – to conquer, rule, administer justice, levy taxes, build roads and railways.
>
> The news has caused Lewanika some consternation. He fears being too precipitate and thus compromised in writing to the Governor of Bechuanaland and he has sent express messengers to intercept the letter he sent on the 2nd or 3rd of January.[103]

This journal entry makes it perfectly clear that from the first, Coillard understood that the Company was *not* the same as the Crown, but believed that its powers were *as good as* the Crown. When later it seemed as if he had miscalculated Coillard claimed that he was duped.[104] But it was a fundamental quality of the Company that it was all things to all men. At its inception, it had appealed to Salisbury's administration as the best sort of imperialism – imperialism on the cheap.[105] Once the bait was taken, the charter was swiftly and secretly drafted along the lines proposed by the petitioners giving vague and sweeping powers and little tangible Governmental constraint.[106] The parliamentary permission was tacked on to the end of the Colonial Office vote and, without the opportunity of debate, the package was pushed through the lobbies at 2 am at the end of the 1889 session on the grounds that 'it was most important on public grounds that the Charter should be granted without delay and its issue cannot be postponed until the next session'.[107] It was made to seem a sound investment by the provision of what an opponent of the Company, during the debate upon the Select Committee report into its affairs after the Jameson Raid, called 'The ornamental class [of directors who] consisted of Dukes and other people of high social position who were generally attractive to the gullible investor.'[108] It was made attractive to rulers like Lewanika, who desired British protection, by making it look like the British Government.[109] It was, in the judgment of its historian, an 'engine without a governor', 'characterised from its origins by institutionalised irresponsibility', a vehicle for Rhodes' ambitions made possible by the failings of imperial policy.[110]

Company interest in Bulozi fell into two distinct phases in these years. In 1891 Captain William Stairs took possession of Katanga after the murder of Chief Msiri. Although he was a Canadian, the annexation was under the Belgian flag. His action thus emptied Rhodes' Barotseland strategy of its major purpose, which was to secure the gateway to the north and Katanga. Thereafter Stairs' name was mud in Northern Rhodesia.[111] Once this *raison d'être* had been removed, Rhodes was extremely reluctant to incur the expenses of administering a territory, Bulozi, from which he could expect no return. As I shall later describe, it was eventually Colonial Office pressure which compelled the Company to send a Resident to Bulozi six years after the Concession had been signed.

However, Stairs had not scooped Rhodes in 1889. The aim of the Lochner mission was to cut off the Portuguese advancing from Zumbo, obtain the Barotse treaty, then advance northwards to Arnot's mission station to negotiate a treaty to prevent the Lunda of Chief Msiri from falling to the Congo Free State, and then press on and link up with Joseph Thomson who was coming from Nyasaland. As Rhodes expressed it to Lochner in his instructions via Rutherfoord Harris, 'There is no doubt that your combined expeditions could secure the whole stretch of country between the Nyassa, the Barotsi and Lake Bangweolo and Moero.'[112] This last clause was to be Rhodes' residual interest after 1891, for then he saw little value in Bulozi except that it 'completed our area' and since 'land is the only thing in the world apart from the precious metals which always has a certain value and in this country you never know what it may contain', his inclination was that more of it was better than less.[113]

Before Lochner reached Bulozi, Rhodes had enquired whether Coillard would be prepared to serve as Resident. The missionary politely declined ('I cannot serve two masters'), but offered his services as intermediary.[114] Rhodes instructed Lochner to decide with Coillard the size and method of payments to Lewanika, the timing of a Resident's arrival and the nature of his escort, and indeed generally to put himself in Coillard's hands.[115] This he was compelled to do quite literally.

At the end of March, whilst Lochner was struggling to ascend the Valley, two 'interior men' reached Lealui. One, Jan Weyers, was an Afrikaner who had been one of Westbeech's elephant hunters throughout the 1880s; the other, Sells, had been employed and dismissed by Lochner. They set about blackening Lochner's personal reputation and that of his mission, and were supported by a messenger sent from Sesheke by Middleton with a warning for the king.[116] Coillard went to see Lewanika – who was delighted to see him – and explained the nature of the Company's charter as he understood it, apparently to the king's satisfaction. Then Coillard went down to Nalolo, where he found a weak and bedraggled Lochner whose 'head and hands are full of the Weyers and Sells business'.[117]

The Company agent reached Sefula on 7 April. On the 9 April Coillard wrote, 'we find that it is a pity that such a man was chosen for such a mission. He lacks the requisite qualities. Furthermore he has an invincible aversion for natives.' By the 19th, 'he doesn't even have the manners of a gentleman. . .and to think that we must lodge him for some months yet. What shall we do?'[118] Circumstance dictated. Reporting to Boegner, Coillard rationalised his role: 'Refuse my services in such serious circumstances, I cannot and I must not do so. But it is certain that I shall do my level best to see that my role as ambassador of JC is displayed in full light. . . .Let God give me wisdom! Please don't publish anything of this.'[119] His subordinate, Adolphe Jalla, only four months in the country, had written to Paris the previous month outlining their fears. Lochner, 'the British government representative', had arrived and 'above all we fear that they [the Lozi] will identify us with M. Lochner. God watch over our Mission.'[120] Lewanika did not make this assumption.

Early in May he 'pestered me [Coillard] to have the translation of all the Company documents' and at the same time told Coillard that he was sending messages to Mosidi (Msiri, the Lunda chief) and to Arnot. He pledged Coillard to secrecy, 'and that above all Mr Lochner should know nothing of it. Why?. . .' But Coillard kept his word.[121] It was presumably because he waited on replies to these messages that Lewanika compelled Lochner to cool his heels until June. While waiting, Ratau, one of the senior Sesheke chiefs, came with fresh warnings to the king from Middleton. Lochner wrote to Lewanika demanding a date for the assembly to discuss the Concession. The king replied haughtily, telling Lochner that he was trembling at the stories told by Weyers and reproaching Coillard for having abandoned his interests to make common cause with Lochner. This was the effect which Middleton had: Coillard described his role at that moment as that of 'a sworn enemy who has done much harm. He has now thrown off his mask which is for me a bitter disappointment and a painful thorn in my path. . .[but] he is not difficult to demolish.'[122] He replied firmly to Lewanika, telling him that he was mistaken and had better watch his language.[123] The effect was immediate. Four days later Lewanika wrote to Coillard that 'I am the only one who can advise him and that all his affairs were in my hands. . .that he was sad that the other day he didn't have more confidence. . .'[124] These vacillations were a sign of the truth of the last admission. But for the next few months the opinions of Weyers, Sells, Middleton, Ratau and other critics were all suppressed. The king had committed his judgment and stuck to it. We

217

cannot know whether Lord Knutsford's dispatch of 14 September 1889 with its promise of British Government interest had arrived and helped influence this, although it was physically possible that it could have done so. Nor do we know what Lewanika heard from Msiri and Arnot, but in late May and early June he was writing Coillard 'very flattering letters, very honeyed, too much so. In all these affairs', the missionary observed unhappily, 'I feel myself to be between the hammer and the anvil.'[125]

24 May was very conveniently Queen Victoria's birthday and to make the identification of his mission with the Crown quite clear to everyone, Lochner staged a party at Sefula. Lots of roasted meat, games, magic lantern shows and a large firework display, including the first rocket that had been seen in Bulozi, prepared the way for the assembly later in June.[126] Lochner decided that the king was personally weak and that he needed to win over the chiefs (which he tried to do with huge bribes when he went to Lealui later in the month). Coillard, he wrote, 'is doing everything in his power for the success of my mission'.[127] Lochner went to the capital ahead of the missionaries on 17 June. Coillard heard that Jeanmairet was seriously ill and made plans to go to Sesheke after the assembly. He arrived at Lealui on the 21st. The assembly lasted four days and began on Tuesday 24 June.[128] Its conduct revealed Lewanika's total dependence on Coillard and is therefore worth following day by day.

On the Monday, the Kuta had wished to question Coillard alone on his role in the Ware Concession. They accepted his explanation and Coillard had a long private talk with the king in the evening. On the Tuesday, Lochner made a 'frank, concise but clear' speech, in Coillard's opinion. He began by reprimanding the detractors of the mission and then 'declared himself to be sent not by the Queen but by the Chartered Company for the Queen. He undertook certain obligations and made certain promises.' Coillard translated. Makuatsa, Khama's usual envoy to Bulozi, arrived a bit late and made a speech which Jalla condensed thus: 'Be members of our family. Friendship of Khama. Brought M. C. [Coillard] here in 84. Prepared to intervene with arms for Lew. No welcome.' Lochner had also travelled up the Valley with 'Macquatsie' and had promised him a wagon if he helped the Company cause. The agent thought that the speech 'seemed to go a long way towards convincing them', but on the basis of Khama's known position previously on similar issues, it would not be correct to assume that the promise of reward motivated Makuatsa's speech, although it may have added zest to it.[129] In any case, we may doubt Lochner's judgment, for Jalla noted further that the chiefs were absent from these opening formalities. However, Mokumba made a speech approving the idea of the agreement: it was like putting one's hands out in front so as not to tumble on one's nose.[130]

On Wednesday, Coillard awoke with a terrible headache and vomiting. 'The King delayed the assembly as much as possible [in fact until 10.00 am: Jalla], then sent Seajika [the royal secretary] to see how I was. It was to beg me indirectly to not – if possible – abandon him.'[131] Coillard went, but was compelled to withdraw leaving Jalla to mediate. The king said 'Question', and a barrage of questions followed. Ratau from Sesheke said that these were nice promises, but that they would see the results. The morning session ended with a general rendering of homage in a half circle around the king. In the afternoon they all discussed the treaty. Lochner was 'like a man who had received an electric shock' when Coillard suggested an annuity of £2,000 for the king rather than the £500 proposed in Lochner's instructions. He, for his part, wrote that Coillard seemed to be 'feverishly anxious that the King should have his full rights', but agreed.[132]

The final treaty was ready by Thursday evening. 'We were sitting in the Kuta discussing the boundaries of the country when Mr Lochner arrived with the 2 copies of the treaty. "What!" shouted the King, "He has made these letters? Not you?" "He's only made copies. We have already discussed them together after your own comments." '[133] The king was not satisfied, adjourned the session until the next day and came late on Thursday evening to seek reassurance from Coillard.[134] The missionary had a sleepless night and on Friday the signing took place in full public view in the Kuta. 'First the King, then his son, then his ministers, then his stewards, then the chiefs of Nalolo, then those of Sesheke, those of Mambova, those who came from the extremities of the country, more than 40!' (The unremarked presence of the Sesheke chiefs in this list contrasts interestingly with the representation in recent literature.) Coillard was obliged to limit the number of others who wanted to make their marks on the paper, which gave rise to murmurs of discontent.

There is visual evidence to corroborate Coillard when he writes, as here, of a general acceptance of what was done. At about midday on one of the days during the negotiations (most likely the Tuesday or the final morning), Coillard took photographs of the assembly. One, which has been reproduced a number of times before, shows a posed scene with Lochner facing Lewanika (Fig. 29). Adolphe Jalla made in his notebook a sketch-plan of the seating arrangements for the Lochner negotiations, and so we know that the stewards and state officers are seated to the king's left (right of the picture), the Lealui chiefs to his right, and that the people seen behind the royal musicians are inhabitants of Lealui and its environs. The royal family members (*linabi*) were directly behind the photographer and behind them again, phalanxes of people from Libonda and the north, Nalolo and the southern floodplain, Sesheke and the far

219

south, in that order. But, as can be seen, in this photograph the faces of the senior chiefs are not distinct.

Hitherto unknown, another photograph was taken moments before (Fig. 30). The band appears still to be playing (their xylophone (*silimba*) beaters are in the air, whereas in Fig. 29 the players' hands are folded in their laps; one leans forward to whisper to the others; a drummer stares at the camera). Lochner has not yet taken his seat and more people can be seen still joining the assembly in groups. Importantly, the faces of the two most senior chiefs are not blurred. They are *Ngambela* Mwauluka and *Mutompehi* Nalubutu. Both wear stocking caps and are seated immediately next to the king. Given the very considerable significance for status which attaches to exact seating in a formal Lozi assembly, this close physical proximity also associates the two chiefs with the king in their opinions, for given their undoubted power in the land, if they were in disagreement with what was happening, as some modern historians have suggested, they would not be there. It is therefore instructive to recall that these are precisely the two men dubbed as leaders of the 'Conservative Pagan' opposition to the Zambezi Mission and to the treaty negotiations in Coillard's published exhortatory works – although not in his private writings, as we have seen – and that it was the published opinion which was embraced by later historians.

The signing of the concession was followed by an exchange of gifts – cases of gunpowder, cartridges, muskets, rifles, lead, caps, wire, blankets and a saddle from Lochner, a distribution of some of this as royal patronage and two huge elephant tusks for Queen Victoria from Lewanika.[135] Lochner went down river on 4 July a little ahead of Coillard.

The conduct of the negotiations consistently showed Lewanika's reliance on Coillard. A final incident made the king's gratitude plain. Lochner left on the 4th; on the 5th the king sent a gift of geese to Sefula and arrived there himself later in the afternoon. He stayed until the 8th and Coillard wrote of the visit, 'I have never seen him so at ease and apparently so happy with us.'[136] He was especially touched that after having provided so many boats at one time, some to take Lochner down river and twenty sent to Sesheke to collect Middleton and bring him up to continue in his new role as Westbeech's replacement, the king had nevertheless reserved his personal boat for Coillard's use. Both Jalla and Lochner individually confirmed that Coillard's role was absolutely central to the success of the exercise.[137]

They parted, the king to go north to organise labour for the first major season of arterial canal construction, the missionary and Waddell south to see their sick colleague Jeanmairet. As they descended the river they picked up Lochner's trail. 'He's not a man, he's a lion!' they were told at

Fig. 29 1890 Lochner negotiations, Lochner present.

Fig. 30 1890 Lochner negotiations a few moments before.

Sioma.[138] The agent went off to Pandamatenga without bidding Coillard farewell, and without a word of thanks. 'And people still tell me that the Zambezians are ungrateful – and Europeans? To buy one's enemies and to exploit friends is an odious principle. But it was not for him that we have done what we have done.'[139] Other missionaries understood in simple terms why it had been done. 'God has answered our prayers and rewarded our efforts: the Protectorate is accepted and many of the rights of Lewanika and the Barotse are safeguarded',[140] wrote Jalla, for whom the difference between Government and Company was negligible (he had referred to it earlier as the 'Governmental South African Company'). On his way to Bulozi the Methodist, Baldwin, met Lochner on his way south. The Company, he explained to his mother, was organised 'on Christian lines to civilise the natives'. The success of Lochner 'will be a good thing for us, at least when they come to develop the country, for we shall have British protection'. Lochner told Baldwin that since poor health and low supplies prevented it this year, he would return in 1891 to go to Garenganze to visit the Lunda.[141] Captain Stairs made that unnecessary. But in any case, the agents who did come up to the Zambezi in 1891, Bagley and Frazer, found a quite different atmosphere awaiting them.[142]

Coillard met Middleton on the lower river as the one was going to Sesheke, the other returning to Lealui. They discussed two outstanding problems. One was that Middleton had delivered in poor condition a team of oxen and harness which Coillard had bought from Musson; 'as to the calumnies, he denied them formally'. Coillard sent letters via Middleton to his wife at Sefula and they went their separate ways.[143] Middleton dropped off the post at Sefula on 5 August and went on to Lealui. He soon fell sick with dysentery and was out of action for much of August.[144] Once recovered, he spent the winter trading. It was only after Coillard's return to Sefula that he really began to attack the Concession, for in late September Coillard, returning with Buckenham, the Methodist, who was harmless to the Zambezi Mission if he was dominated by it, had found a friendly letter of welcome from the king awaiting him. But soon the king was getting worried.

Coillard, Jalla and Buckenham went to Lealui on 26 September for three days. Coillard found that Middleton had been 'making quarrels again about the concession. The King said he has pelaelo [doubts] and begged me to bring him the contract.' Coillard met Middleton there and 'this poor prodigal child' seemed 'very ill at ease – and yet he is a man who I loved greatly'.[145] By the end of the month, Lewanika was 'bowled over, another man': 'What storms! My God! Middleton has done his work. . . [illegible]. . .He has succeeded in goading the King on the subject of the Concession to the point where he is mad with anger.'[146] In fact, Middleton drafted a long, sober and extremely clear letter to Lord Salisbury on Lewanika's behalf in which he repudiated the Ware and Lochner Concessions, representing the Lochner Concession as 'nothing less than a gigantic monopoly of the entire natural resources of his country'. He denounced Lochner's representation of himself as the queen's envoy and repeated Lewanika's desire for a real Protectorate, ending with the hope that Lord Salisbury would see fit to reassure the king that 'neither British Queen, her Government, nor her people will take from him by deceit that which he is not prepared to give'.[147]

Middleton's analysis of the nature and motives of the Company was quite correct, as we can see with hindsight. Coillard's judgment that the Company was as good as the Crown was wrong. However, it was immaterial either to the immediate situation or to the long-term consequences of these years that Middleton was right. Jalla and Coillard went to Lealui at the end of the month summoned by a brusque note from the king.[148] As a result of the discussions, another letter was written in the king's name, this time by the missionaries. It asked whether the Company had the right to use the queen's name. Lewanika signed it on 2 November. On the 3rd, Jalla had a talk with Middleton and then left for Sefula to prepare his departure for Italy in order to be married. He left for Sesheke on 5 November.[149]

Lewanika continued to veer violently from one opinion to another, a sign of his deep confusion. In mid November he summoned Coillard again and wanted to stage a public debate between him and Middleton. In early December. he was again suddenly friendly, sending Waddell his tools to sharpen.[150] Middleton (and his letter) left Lealui around Christmas Day, reaching Sesheke on 2 January where he fell sick and had paddler problems. But he had traded successfully and had ten boatloads of ivory. He rested in Sesheke until the end of the month and then went on south ahead of Jalla.[151]

On 29 January 1891, word of the new Company agents, Bagley and Frazer, reached Lealui. Lewanika refused to allow them to cross the river. In view of Middleton's letter, which he had evidently seen, Coillard declined to write for the king to tell them this. He felt compromised and was beginning to disengage himself from any overt political negotiations.[152] Indeed, he did not send the letter signed by Lewanika in November 1890. However, Middleton returned to Lealui in March and again trouble stirred. Prodded by this, in April Coillard wrote a covering letter and sent the November letter off to England.[153]

The *ku omboka* of 1891 was to a camp close to Sefula. Coillard went over to visit the king who tried to get Coillard to come to Lealui to confront Middleton, who had been recalled by his employer, Musson.[154]

223

This was on a Friday. The following Wednesday, Coillard received a verbal summons to Lealui that he felt should not be refused. That same evening, the post brought news of the witchcraft accusation against Baldwin in Sesheke (Chapter 8, Section 3) which gave him another reason to see the king. Writing after the event, Coillard described this not as an ordinary visit, but as a command appearance *('une sommation')*. 'Middleton, who poses as the champion of the natives has raised a storm that it is no longer in his power to quell, even if he wanted to, which I doubt.' Coillard went to Lealui on Friday 29 May. The king came to see him in the evening. On the Saturday, a confrontation took place, lasting from 9 am to 4 pm. Lewanika attacked the Company for trying to drive Middleton out of the country; Coillard replied that his employer had recalled him. The king refrained from a frontal attack on Coillard, but the missionary felt 'like a fly fallen into the web of two spiders. . .the weak point is on my side, alas'.[155] Presumably that evening, Coillard wrote to the Government again: 'What he [Lewanika] wanted and still wants, nothing more or less, is the Protectorate of the Queen's Government and not that of a mere goldmining company.'[156] He was stealing Middleton's thunder.

The next day was the Sabbath and so no business could be transacted. However, exceptional circumstances demanded exceptional measures and so Coillard continued the battle by other means:

> His text was now we are ambassadors for Christ. After explaining what an ambassador is to a nation and what it is to insult him. He said the missionaries are ambassadors or servants of Christ sent with his message to the nations and woe be to the nation that rejects or maltreats them for it is God they will have to answer to. . .[157]

Middleton returned to the attack with conventional arms the next day, Monday 1 June. He tried to blame Coillard for everything by getting the king to pay over to him the £200 received as the first annuity under the Ware Concession. But things were calmer than the previous Saturday and Middleton shook hands with Coillard who then returned to Sefula, where Mme Coillard was waiting for news 'on hot coals'. However, the missionary had had enough of politics.

On Friday 5 June, he composed a careful and rather bitter letter to Rutherfoord Harris, the Company Secretary in Kimberley, washing his hands of its business: 'if the British Protectorate has been used simply as a blind, I emphatically protest against it and regret if I have been made a dupe and an accomplice in such transactions. . .I must decline in the future any more to do in these matters.'[158] He sent one copy of the letter to Lewanika at Lealui on 8 June and enclosed another to Boegner in Paris on 16 June. His public report was that 'those recent events (which have whipped up a storm in a tea-cup, as the English say) confirm me more and more in the conviction that the Treaty made last year with the Company was a sure foothold as much for the nation as for Lewanika himself'.[159] For Boegner's eyes only, he added that the enclosed letter was written because 'I could not remain silent without risking a compromise of the advantage of the Mission and my image as a minister of JC. The King has declared himself satisfied. Is he really?'[160]

Evidently he was, for Lewanika turned his mind to other things. The second season of trunk canal construction was approaching and the king began to assemble labour to dig the Mwayowamo canal. Coillard also looked to other problems because the Methodist threat had been resurrected in a new form. Whilst Buckenham and Baldwin were at odds with the people and with each other, Coillard feared that Lewanika would plant them somewhere in Bulozi instead of letting them go to Ilaland.[161] Middleton went south sometime in July or August and, feeling that he had been defeated in that round by Coillard, refused to carry any of the missionary's letters when he left Sesheke at the end of the month.[162]

Meanwhile other odd things had been happening to the post. Coillard's letter of 10 April 1891 enclosing Lewanika's letter of November 1890 reached London in late July. Middleton's letter of 27 October 1890 was somehow delayed and did not reach the Colonial Office until 10 October 1891, not that that mattered much since 'No notice was taken of Mr Middleton's letter, an answer having already been sent to the similar one from Lewanika himself.'[163] Lord Knutsford, Secretary of State for the Colonies, had already, it will be recalled, taken a positive line on Lewanika's request. He now recommended that 'Lewanika should be informed that he is under the protection of Her Majesty and that Lord Salisbury should approve the Concession.' Salisbury agreed with the sentiment but did not consider formal approval of the Concession to be necessary, 'as it was proposed that the powers of Government and administration should be exercised by Her Majesty's Commissioner and not by the Company'. Therefore Loch in South Africa was directed to inform Lewanika 'that he was under Her Majesty's protection and explaining to him the position of the Company'.[164]

In the Valley, Coillard and the king were again on the best of terms. So far no official confirmation of Coillard's view of the Company had yet arrived except Lord Knutsford's first dispatch of 14 September 1889, so this restoration of harmony and the rejection of Middleton's views had been achieved simply on the basis of the king's view of the personalities involved. On 16 October, M. and Mme Coillard paid a visit to the capital and the king was most friendly with them. On the 23rd, Coillard received news that Middleton was on the way back. On the 28th, Mme Coillard died. *Ngambela* and others of the Kuta came to Sefula. The king himself could not come because the *Litunga* may have nothing to do with the dead. However, he sent a message: 'I would like to come myself because you are my brother and you are in mourning. My tears are this ox [a beast of mourning] and *Ngambela* is the Nation. She was our mother. We all weep.'[165]

On 7 November, the first of the monthly postal deliveries inaugurated by the Company arrived. It brought Loch's dispatch. 'The governor of the Cape writes to certify the thing. What a relief. How will the King take it? Middleton his evil genie has returned, but the final result will be the same.'[166] On the 9th, Coillard sent the dispatch and a translation to the king. On the 16th he wrote a note to Middleton appealing to his conscience and received a rude reply on the 18th. It 'made a pair' with the letter from Mme Dardier. 'Before I saw young Dardier and Middleton, I didn't know what it was to have an enemy', Coillard wrote.[167] Meanwhile he also wrote to Paris to tell Boegner.

> It's what we were waiting for for such a long time, everything necessary to disperse our political fogs. The Lord himself has taken our cause in His hands. . .It isn't to say that we shall enter the golden age. . .There will be evil, much evil beside a little good. But if that little good is the salvation of this tribe by the establishment of firm and equitable government, it's a lot.[168]

On 23 November, Coillard rode over to Lealui and delivered a long and sober speech, telling Lewanika the history of his quest for protection, his feebleness in the face of false counsel and so on. 'I spoke without bitterness, but the occasion was unique.'[169] He returned to Sefula feeling that he had been vindicated, only to find a new and for him far more terrible crisis arising which was to occupy his thoughts above all else for the next two years, and which is described in the next section. However, on the political front, he was essentially correct. Middleton had lost, although during December 1891 and the early part of 1892 he made a final attempt to force the issue.

In the first week of December 1891, Dr James Johnston, a Scots missionary who had worked in Jamaica, arrived in Lealui on a visit. Lewanika and presumably Middleton explained all the problems of the Concessions to him. The king had been especially incensed to learn that the tusks presented to Lochner to convey to the queen adorned the Company boardroom.[170] Johnston came on to Sefula and he and Coillard instantly became friends. He warned Coillard against the French traveller Dècle and against his own new recruit Vollet, both of whom were in close correspondence with Middleton.[171] On 20 December, Coillard went to Lealui. Lewanika rushed to see him. Johnston had already alerted the missionary that the king 'doesn't get along with Middleton any more, and that he [Middleton] is so annoyed that he speaks of leaving the country'.[172] The king showed Coillard letters from Vollet telling him to trust Middleton and not Coillard. Johnston continued his journey downstream in mid January, taking with him a letter whose style and content suggest that its author was Middleton. It was another protest against the Company. Johnston himself was furious about the Company and incorporated this letter in a spiced and very effective account of his time in Bulozi which, when it was published in 1893, became a powerful weapon for the anti-Charter lobby in England.[173]

Middleton was to Lewanika the ideal replacement for George West-beech. He spoke the language, was a good and proven trader. His nickname was 'little George'. But he was not Coillard. Thus when in February 1892 he tried to force the king to choose between himself and the Mission, it was he who went. He had done little trading since his return and was living on the king's charity. In April, Lewanika cut his rations and by the end of the month, Middleton was gone.[174] He returned again in August having gone into partnership with another trader called Frost, but was sent away.[175] He disappeared from Lozi history.

Looking back over all of 1891, Coillard asked himself, 'Is it really possible that I was able to survive all that? . . .I shall try to cast a veil over the most painful period, the most anguished of our years of life and labour together.'[176] Indeed, he had lost his wife, but he had survived the Concession Crises and had been vindicated in Lozi eyes, his European staff now followed his lead, and the Methodist threat had finally dissolved. However, 1892 was to bring what were in many ways his bitterest disappointments.

9.3 ENTR'ACTE, 1892–1896

Seajika and Kalumba, two young men who had been taken to Lesotho by the Coillards in 1878 with the hope of training them as evangelists, never formally converted to Christianity and as soon as they returned to Bulozi they distanced themselves from the Mission, but without losing touch. Seajika became Lewanika's literate secretary and has appeared from time to time in the narrative of high politics. Despite their proven obduracy, Coillard continued to hold out hope for their conversion. That being so, it is not hard to imagine how much more intense his feelings were for those who showed more promise of redemption.

Upon Coillard's return to the country in 1885, Lewanika arranged for a slave to be presented to Coillard to be his servant. Mwanangombe lived with the Coillards as their body servant throughout the early years. In 1888 he spoke to Coillard of conversion. The missionary warned him to look carefully at Seajika and Kalumba who had made similar statements in Lesotho and had since lapsed. A month later Mwanangombe told Coillard that his faith was no illusion. He had been given as a servant and had become a believer.[177] For the Coillards, it was a ray of light in the gloom of their other difficulties, but they insisted on a strict probation. He became like a son to the childless missionaries. 'Splendid Mwanangombe, he is one of the greatest blessings that God has accorded us in this country. We feel it more every day.' At the New Year 1890, Coillard tried to get his servant/adoptive son/potential convert to name a higher wage, but Mwanangombe said that he lacked nothing. They called him into the house: 'Your mother and I have been thinking that we would give you something in recognition of your services. Here is £15. The dear child was speechless.' He left the money in Christina Coillard's safekeeping.[178] He became increasingly indispensable, protecting Mme Coillard during her husband's absences and continuing the work on the Sefula canal after Goy's unhappy departure.

The day of his baptism was fixed for 25 May 1890, Pentecost. Coillard sent invitations to the king and to the *Mulena Mukwae*, but they excused themselves. Mwanangombe chose Andrease (Andrew) for his Christian name, 'since Andrew was the first who followed Jesus'. It was a moving occasion for all at Sefula, ending with the first celebration of the Communion in the church.[179] In July, just after the end of the Lochner negotiations, there was a fire at Sefula and it was Andrease who climbed up and with buckets of water saved the house and, in consequence, the station.[180]

Things began to alter during 1891. In April, Andrease was accused of making a girl pregnant and Coillard thought that he did not seem to be himself; it bothered him that the young man seemed to be increasingly in Seajika's company.[181] In June he went on holiday to see his parents at Kazungula. But other circumstances offset these worries.

Mme Coillard had been unwell for many months, but she decided that she should make her annual visit to the capital and on 16 October she, Coillard and the newly arrived Mlle Kiener went to Lealui in a light wagon. At the Sunday service on the 18th, the king's son Litia, who on returning from his visit to the Christian chief Khama had already announced his intention to do so, stood up and confessed his faith. His speech moved to tears his friend Mukamba, nephew of the late *Ngambela* Silumbu who had died in the battle to restore Lewanika in 1885. 'What a rare sight it was said Mrs C to see a Morotsi weep and weep for his sins.

Why I thought a Morotsi had no tears. Not long ago I would have gone some hundreds of miles to see a Morotsi weep.'[182]

Later in the month, Mme Coillard died. On 27 November their Lozi son came to Coillard's office to see him. He asked to look at his money, which totalled £31.10.0d. In his journal, Coillard wrote, 'I feel that he has yielded to influences, that he doesn't belong completely to me.' He sensed that he was about to lose Andrease. He had a series of difficult interviews with him during December. Coillard wondered whether Lewanika, who had been flattering him greatly, 'wanted to create a position for him over there [in Lealui]'.[183]

On New Year's day 1892, Litia was married in the first Christian Lozi marriage. James Johnston who was then at Sefula photographed the marriage party. Coillard looked morose. He had had another interview with Andrease a few days before. Another followed on the 4th and then on the 14th, while he and Andrease sat reading the Bible together, paddlers came from Lealui, prearranged by Andrease, to collect him. From the 14th onwards, Coillard's journal for January was dominated with agonised entries. On the 25th, Coillard meditated on the theme of the pruning knife. Two days later he had rationalised further. The lapses were God's indication that he should go and establish himself at Lealui where he could be near his apostates and where he could hope to influence them.[184] On 4 February, Andrease came to see Coillard who offered him substantial wages to return as an evangelist. He read Andrease his baptism declaration which moved the man deeply. He confessed that in fact he was not free to be apart from the king in whose service he now was and he returned to Lealui on the 10th. In May, Lewanika sent him to Mangwato to buy tools, which showed which of his attributes were valued; recall that the king was in the midst of his public works programme and, as Waddell observed, he needed foremen. Concern with Andrease continued as a theme through the journal for May. Coillard never really recovered from the shock. He moved to Lwatile to be near his fallen boys.

In December 1892, Mukamba, who had cried and thus moved Mme Coillard, came to announce his lapse from faith. In January 1893, again the apostates dominated Coillard's concerns. Litia took a second wife, Andrease married a pagan. On 3 February, Coillard's evangelists Pauluse and Jacob confronted Andrease and questioned him on his faith. They received insolent replies. With a heavy heart, Coillard publicly denounced his first baptised Lozi.[185] For their part, the Sotho evangelists were restless. First they refused to do any work except preaching, then Pauluse refused to interpret for the Methodist Buckenham in an interview with the king in March. Coillard apparently took this badly also. Baldwin wrote that 'The treachery of his two evangelists has pained him far more than all the insults of the king. He had trusted them fully and had made an especial confidant of Pauluse. He knows everything about Mr Coillard's matters here.'[186] The following day there was a stormy scene between Coillard and his subordinates. As with Aaron before, Coillard had expected extremes of obedience, energy and devotion and faced with such an uncompromising stand, the evangelists were driven to an opposite reaction. Nor was this to be the last crisis between Coillard and his black subordinates. The 'Ethiopian' church episode at the end of his life had its roots in one of these incidents.[187]

This sombre picture of scrabbling for the allegiance of a few potential converts in an atmosphere of tension and some bitterness was, occasionally, relieved. These were those welcome gaps in the clouds which gave Coillard the will to continue when he felt 'so useless, good for nothing'.[188] The balance between those events which engendered depression and optimism in the missionary was in the main held by the king. Baldwin suggested that the disaffection of the two evangelists had been with Lewanika's covert but concrete support (he gave them favourable trading terms), but on the other hand throughout 1894–5, Coillard felt optimistic about the king's personal stance.[189] In February 1894 he wrote to Baldwin in Ilaland that 'the King at times seems very near the Kingdom of Heaven. But he is terrified for the Barotses and that keeps him back.'[190]

Two events in particular gave Coillard hope. In January 1895, some chiefs accused Pauluse of disrespect towards the king when he pointed a finger during a sermon, but the king defended the interest of the Mission by making light of the incident.[191] The early months of 1895 also saw many enquirers and some converts at the Mission[192] and above all, in July, Lewanika permitted his wife Nolianga, titled *Ndundano ta Katongo*, to leave the royal household and to convert to Christianity. Nolianga's conversion was taken and presented as a great advance, clear evidence of a softening in the king's attitude, of the retreat of the 'Conservative Pagan' forces before the onward march of the forces of light and further reason to hope for Lewanika's own eventual salvation:[193]

> She sat down. After a moment of deep silence Lewanika stood up and said, 'Don't stare at that woman, what she has just done, she did with my approval. The movement goes forward and will no more stop.' After a pause, he added, 'whoever amongst you feels the power of what the missionaries declare to us is free to reveal himself. Let it not be said that I prevent people from converting!'[194]

Nolianga's conversion serves as a classic illustration of how Lewanika coordinated all his goals.

The king had originally had three good reasons for his marriage to

Nolianga: she was the daughter of the late King Sipopa and thus he might hope to satisfy the patronage demands of Sipopa's kin; she was from Lewanika's household and by tradition one of the *Litunga*'s wives should be closely related, and she was the great grand daughter of Nolianga, mother of the last king of the Noble Age and Lewanika's special protector, Mulambwa. Mulambwa's mother had been starved to death by the 'evil' King Mwananyanda who preceded the 'good' King Mulambwa[195] and she was buried at Katongo. Nolianga's *libizo la buoli* (royal wife name) showed that she had responsibility for that royal grave. Thus for reasons related to the status of Mulambwa in the 1880s and 1890s, her ritual role was rather important. By her conversion, she forfeited all this former identity. How should we interpret this?

Lewanika's first hope, to assuage the jealousies of Sipopa's kin, was not realised. In June 1891, Coillard heard of a plot to put one of the ousted lineage on the throne[196] so we know that this was a live fear. After making her profession of faith, Nolianga had to flee to Lwatile Mission for protection from hostile people, but it is not correct to assume that this was a clear logical sequence. In fact she was suspected of attempting to bewitch the king in the interests of her paternal kin.[197] Therefore Lewanika had to get rid of her anyway and made a fourfold use of the opportunity. Simultaneously, he heartened Coillard and the Mission, cleansed the important ritual offices close to Mulambwa, outmaneouvred Sipopa's kin and delivered a very clear message to his people. Jalla's report of his speech might be rephrased thus:

> Don't stare at that woman. She has offended against *sizo* (tradition) and me; therefore she has forfeited her rights, duties and powers and she has my permission to do what she likes. I have shown mercy and permitted her the harmless alternative of conversion to the missionaries' beliefs. Anyone who wants to do so may follow suit for, as you see, these beliefs are no threat to the nation. And you, the kin of Sipopa, take heed of my warning!

In fact they did not stop intriguing. Nolianga went to live at Likapai with her brother Mboo Fwabi and in 1911 Lewanika confronted Sipopa's children again. This time the Colonial Court was his chosen instrument. He accused Mboo Fwabi of sedition for refusing to *shoelela* (do homage) to him and for allegedly speaking of restoring the long vanished Mwanawina to power. During the trial, evidence was given of this idea being mooted in 1906 also.[198] The Lozi chiefs, sitting as assessors, all found against Mboo; the Resident Magistrate Mackinnon agreed to exile Mboo, but the case was eventually overturned for lack of evidence. In his review of the case, the Secretary for Native Affairs, Worthington, gave another interpretation of Nolianga's conversion. He believed that she calculated that Lewanika would convert and therefore to ensure that she became his senior wife, she decided to convert also. In the event, Lewanika decided not to proceed but compelled her to do so and then divorced her, having neatly finessed her hand.[199] This interpretation is entirely compatible with the one I have produced from other sources.[200]

Nolianga's conversion may stand as an eloquent example of the Mission's genteel bondage, of the reason for the frustration of its objectives in these years and of Lewanika's political sophistication. The game was as much played between as on the lines. The incident also illustrated the degree of skill available for the future challenges which would be confronted in the colonial era proper.

This era was some time in coming, six years in all from the receipt of the Loch dispatch in November 1891 which had effectively ended the last Concession Crisis. After all, the British South Africa Company had every reason to drag its feet. Captain Stairs had pre-empted Rhodes by seizing Katanga for the Belgians in 1891, the British Government had repeatedly made it very clear to Rhodes that the Company should bear all expenses in connection with Bulozi[201] and, as Harry Johnston was to observe to the Foreign Office, Bulozi was 'scarcely worth opening up, as it is marshy and exceedingly unhealthy'.[202] In fact the best use for Bulozi that the Company Secretary could think of in 1892 was as a bait for the Ndebele. 'I hope they do raid the Barotses', he wrote, 'so that we may always be able to prove justification and their being a cruel damnable race.'[203]

The Ndebele obliged. It appears that earlier in 1892, some Ndebele raiders in Ilaland encountered some Lozi soldiers. One of the Ndebele was killed and others taken as prisoners to Lealui. In August an Ndebele force raided near Kazungula in revenge and in late November another force set out towards Bulozi.[204] Early in 1893, Coillard wrote to Loch to say that Lewanika was frightened by these raids and he strongly urged immediate action to fulfil the undertakings that had been made. 'No one can believe in promises, however sincere on the part of Government.'[205] Other bodies were also clamouring for action for their own reasons.[206]

In July 1893, news of further Ndebele incursion reached Lealui. Lewanika ordered the war drums to be beaten for a general mobilisation and wanted to march south in strength. Interestingly, it was the Kuta that disagreed and therefore, as a compromise, an expeditionary force was sent to 'Lesikili' in Batokaland. However, again the seemingly bad had a good effect for the Lozi, because the Ndebele were actually halted by smallpox; the epidemic brought into Bulozi from the north by the Lozi armies that had attacked the Luvale had now swept through to the south of the country.[207] Meanwhile Lewanika went to inspect the valley of the

Lui river with a view to flooding it as a strategic barrier lest the Ndebele return.[208] They did not, for the Company had its excuse, if it ever needed it, and in January 1894, Loch replied to Lewanika's letter with news of the conquest of the Ndebele.[209]

The news reaffirmed Lewanika's faith in Coillard which had clearly been strained in 1892–3 as the first part of this section showed. He had been saved from impetuousness in July 1893 by his Council and now it appeared that the Company meant business. From this time we can detect his returning warmth towards Coillard as described earlier in the chapter. The defeat of the Ndebele also had an effect upon the Foreign Office which had hitherto ignored requests to see the terms of the Lochner Concession fulfilled.

In April, the British South Africa Company was officially informed of the Foreign Office view that the defeat of the Ndebele made proper relations with Lewanika more urgent: 'It is undesirable that this state of uncertainty should be allowed to continue.'[210] The Company replied that arrangements for Bulozi were in hand in the overall context of administration north of the Zambezi. But there was another line of pressure on the Foreign Office. The two years *modus vivendi* agreed with the Portuguese in June 1893 was about to expire, there were rumours of Portuguese moves and the Colonial Office felt that Lewanika should be visited 'as early as possible by some representative of British Authority'.[211] There was a general unease in Government that all their field information came from the Company whose word had to be trusted and already the anti-Charter lobby had established that the queen's name had been illegitimately used during the Concession negotiations.[212]

It was decided to send Major Goold Adams to examine the western border area for the Government, and the Company was told that since the delimitation Commissioner would be in Bulozi in 1896, it would be good to see evidence of administration by then.[213] News of Goold Adams' mission reached Bulozi on 11 May and the man himself arrived on 5 October. The king had earlier asked Jalla, in charge of the Mission whilst Coillard was on leave in Europe, to give the Major hospitality. Jalla took him at once to see the king but two days later heard that Lewanika doubted the Major's credentials. The next morning the missionary went to advise the king and in the afternoon, Lewanika relented.[214]

Lewanika's suspicions were understandable in view of the long delay. Most recently in 1895 both he and Coillard had written directly to Jameson, Rhodes' confidant, requesting a Resident to come and control the white prospectors entering southern Bulozi.[215] Coillard wrote more graphically to Loch at the same time that 'the boat, to use a Zambezian illustration, is about to shoot down the rapids'.[216] He took up the case in

233

person whilst on leave, visiting the Colonial Office in November 1896 to press for two Residents – one for Lealui and one for Kazungula – and the Foreign Office in 1897 to repeat this request and to ensure that the Company did not exceed its powers to grant land.[217]

At about the time that Coillard was in London, Goold Adams sent a preliminary report confirming that there was a Portuguese fort at Kakenge[218] and suggesting that Lewanika's writ indeed ran west of the *modus vivendi* line.[219] The Lozi also benefited from the growing cloud of suspicion which surrounded the Company, for it caused the Government to look all the more carefully at its actions and promises. In January 1897, the Colonial Office told the Foreign Office that 'Mr Chamberlain believes it to be doubtful whether the British South Africa Company are anxious to carry out the terms of the Lochner Concession in their entirety', that the Resident should be an imperial police officer to control whites and that the Company should be permitted no more administrative responsibility until the House of Commons Select Committee on its affairs had reported.[220] Indeed, in two letters of the same day in April, the Colonial Office indicated preparedness to allow Lewanika even to repudiate the Concession whilst retaining imperial protection, although the king never did this.[221]

In March 1897, the Company nominated Robert Coryndon, one of Rhodes' 'Twelve Apostles', to be Resident, replacing their first nominee, H. J. A. Hervey, who had just been killed in Matabeleland.[222] Suspicion of the Company was prominent in Coryndon's instructions from the Foreign Office: they stated bluntly that 'the South African Company has no rights of government in the Barotse country'. Therefore Coryndon was made a magistrate and a major in the British South Africa Police. He was not to attempt to obtain administrative power for the Company from the king; he was to do his utmost to maintain friendly relations with the king; he was to report Lewanika's objections to the Lochner Concession and alterations that the king might wish to see made to it; he was to impress upon the king that he represented the British Government; on all matters he was to communicate with the Secretary of State for Foreign Affairs under flying seal to the High Commissioner in South Africa; on matters of expenditure and related issues alone might he communicate with the Company. Coryndon interpreted his brief widely but the general inhibition upon his actions was effective. To make the point about the nature of the new era quite plain to Lewanika, Milner wrote to tell him that the Resident now on his way was bringing him a portrait of Victoria.[223]

10

Conclusion

In 1897 the rains came early to the capital, in the middle of October, and the long awaited Resident arrived a few days later.[1] The day after he reached Lealui, Coryndon was given a formal reception in the public square before the full assembled Council; seven *makolo* (as regiments) paraded and executed the ceremony of homage to the king. During the subsequent three days of meetings, Coryndon was questioned intensively about his mission, Jalla acting as his interpreter only; he did not appear to exercise any of the formative influence which he and Coillard had possessed seven years before. The king behaved as he had done during the Concession negotiations of 1890, on the first day acting warmly, on the second suddenly announcing that he did not trust the replies he received and then, equally suddenly, becoming effusive again. But it was a sign that this disconcerting behaviour was used as a tactic to extract the fullest information and was not simply evidence of confusion that on the third day Lewanika, now warm again, shrewdly requested Coryndon to put down a statement of his purposes in writing![2] For his part, the new Resident presented the king with the portrait of Queen Victoria and the king declared that he was very pleased to receive it.[3]

In addition to his new picture, Lewanika had several other reasons to feel pleased at this time. Some are evident in the details of Coryndon's arrival. First, Lewanika was welcoming a Resident, not resisting regiments of white soldiers as had recently been the lot of his neighbours across the Zambezi. Secondly, he was visibly a king in control of his kingdom, able to mobilise quite a substantial display of his formal power and of the assent of the nation's councillors when it was required. This did not look like an unpopular tyrant seeking the support of alien forces to bolster a narrowly based and precarious regime.

In fact his nation had just weathered the combined assault of flood, pestilence of man and beast and plagues of locusts in a remarkable way. Lewanika had been able to derive advantage from these apparent disas-

235

ters to reinforce his patronage network, as argued in Chapter 4. But much of the success which the Lozi had had in avoiding mass starvation came from one aspect of the ruling classes' astute mobilisation of benefits brought by the Zambezi Mission. The previous seven years had seen not only the education of the king and his entourage in the niceties of diplomatic negotiation, it had also seen the deployment of the concept of trunk canal construction, learned from the Mission, within the existing robust and flexible indigenous system of production and distribution. The coordinated drainage system thus created was fundamentally buttressing Lozi society during the 1890s. Its construction was both proof and consequently reinforcement of the cohesion of the nation.

Finally, Coryndon's arrival revealed the extent to which the Mission had been successfully harnessed. It no longer stood centre stage; Coillard was absent in Europe and the pattern of acquiescent behaviour seen here was a foretaste of the norm of the future. The scene was now set for the next act of the colonial encounter in which, given those fluid qualities of the Lozi state explained in Chapter 3, a sequence of elaborate and detailed invention of tradition for the benefit of colonial authorities and using the Mission as the medium could take place. A purpose of this book has been to explain how we reached this position.

In the beginning I suggested that without an understanding of the longer term dynamics of society we had little cause for confidence in our interpretation of the flow of events; that when we had armed ourselves with such knowledge our interpretation of these twenty years in Bulozi would be considerably altered. How far this has been true and convincing is the most vivid test of reliability in both aspects of the book.

I have employed our new insights to free us from bondage by the contemporaneous observers' natural emphasis upon the importance of the Concessions and their negotiation. A study of the narrative of the Concession Crises alone proved insufficient to explain the nature of the narrative, because this nature was predicated upon an earlier stage of the inter-racial encounter, hitherto concealed because the contemporaneous sources did not emphasise it. Chapters 4 and 5 explained, among other things, the material context of royal power in Bulozi; Chapters 6 and 7 gave its supernatural setting. Together they gave us both understanding of the different types, fields and uses of royal power and fairly precise guidance about its cultural manifestations. Thus equipped, in Chapter 8 I was able to locate, enlarge to maximum magnification and explain the events of March 1886, showing why I considered them to be so crucial. The key was our awareness of the different properties of royal power. It was also axiomatic to understanding how Lewanika could afford to rely so completely upon Coillard during the Concession Crises.

Our understanding of royal power in its indigenous setting converged with a revised assessment of the absolute significance to the Lozi of the Concession negotiations. We saw that indeed Coillard miscalculated the power and influence of the British South Africa Company, that as earlier authors have documented, the Concession copies were indeed inconsistent, but we also saw that this did not matter. Further, we saw that Lewanika was by no means staking all his power and reputation in the negotiations.

Aware of the broader form of royal power, we placed the 'trade and empire' explanation of Lozi kingship in correct proportion relative to other hidden facets. The detailed narrative of the Concession negotiations offered a splendid opportunity to test this altered perception and, again at the highest degree of magnification possible in the data, we found that Lewanika's behaviour over the George Middleton affair was entirely consistent with this revision.

A foundation has now been provided whose strengths and weaknesses have been probed, tested and mapped. In future work I shall place upon it the history of Bulozi through the following eighty years and, as I shall show there, the explanations laid out here prove to be both illuminating of and compatible with our very different types and qualities of data for the colonial and post-colonial eras. Added to the tests of reliability built into this work, it is encouraging. The answers these data provide turn out to be as much at variance with most received interpretations of the later years as this work has been with those directed at the later nineteenth century.

From time to time in the course of this work I have been obliged to consider alternative interpretations of aspects of Lozi history. In every significant case I have reported differences too great to be ascribed to divergent readings of the same evidence. I have suggested that fundamental conceptual and methodological flaws in earlier work are the cause of these contrasts. But these works which I have found to be unreliable utilise assumptions and approaches to questions and data which are common to very many works of history that deal with the period of the scramble for Africa and its consequences. I draw my own conclusions from this and do not find them at all disheartening, for knowledge of ignorance is the beginning of wisdom.

Towards the close of his long ministry in Bulozi, Adolphe Jalla was struck by a saying attributed to Bishop Knight Bruce and he jotted it down inside the back cover of what proved to be the final volume of his daily journal: 'The more one knows of the natives, the more one finds consistently they keep on concealing from strangers what they really think.'[4] The language may be dated but the perception is not. It is simply

237

the corollary of what the Lozi themselves have always said: the hippopotamus swirls the deepest waters in the river; the sands of the shallows betray him. It forms a good starting assumption for research. It is a good way to end.

Appendix

About the fieldwork

The foundation of this book is what I have learned from people now living in
Bulozi. This knowledge has underlain and supported whatever I have been able to
do subsequently with the various written sources which I used. In the notes I have
tried to give full attribution of data from the archival record, but I am unable to do
the same for my field materials and oral sources because I have given my
informants an assurance of anonymity. I regard this as basic politeness – to put it
no more strongly – in this type of work. In the few cases where it has not been
possible to conceal identities, they are revealed with the consent of the individuals, or because of intervening death. This being so, the reader has every right to
expect information about how the field research was conducted so that he can thus
be helped in deciding whether and why he wishes to trust what I say. This
Appendix is a brief attempt to meet that demand.[1]

After spending a fortnight with me in the field early during my research, my
father commented that if he stayed a month, he would understand everything,
after six months it might begin to look a bit more complicated and after a year,
incomprehensible. I suspect that few people who have done fieldwork would
disagree. In my case it took a further two years before the incomprehensible
began to gain any satisfying resolution, and by that time I was writing about quite
different things from what I had originally intended, which had been solely
concerned with the local effects of mid-twentieth-century labour migration. The
new topics defined themselves but, as Table B indicates, that did not begin until
eighteen months had been spent in the field. However, lest this sound too smug
(always a danger with this sort of retrospective comment), in fairness I must add
two other observations. When I reread my daily journal even for productive
periods, the spells of uninspiration and tedious motor mechanics look appalling. It
is also sobering to see how much of what I argue in this book was originally the
product of accident or stimulated by a hunch rather than by cool reflection. I spent
a lot of time flying blind and often to destinations which were eventually not very
helpful.

What were these new topics? Most often they arose from grappling with the
problems of controlling colonial written sources. Like other historians, I found
that reminiscences by (usually elite) informants were not much help. In Bulozi
these people are mostly literate, many have read or absorbed popular

239

accounts of the period of contact; some are bilingual and they are well accustomed to 'handling' visiting researchers. I was compelled to adopt a radical solution.

My initial problem was to know what I could believe and what I should mistrust in various written sources for the period 1876 to 1916, the two generations of the initial colonial encounter and the creation of the colonial *modus vivendi* in Bulozi. The solution was twofold. First, I classified the written data and exercised internal cross checks between the various types; this meant mainly between easily accessible archival sources, printed contemporaneous books and more obscure private journals, correspondence and the like. This can be seen in more detail in Table A. But in turn this exercise was informed by field data which gave, among other things, practical guidelines of what different writers might and might not have known so I could distinguish observation from inference more accurately. My approach is no different from that of the potter who tells his pupils that they must get the feel of the clay before they try to work it. Therefore, here in Table A is some clay in the form of a consumers' guide to sources for the study of the history of Bulozi. It shows how fieldwork was integrally part of the undertaking in two ways. First, the columns of crosses headed C (privately held) and D (lost or discarded and found) indicate material which has been undervalued and which I, sometimes literally, tripped over. This included some critically important sources: the private papers and journals of the most acute pioneer missionary (in a cupboard in Switzerland); the papers and accounts of a pioneer trader (in the hands of a relative in London); large quantities of original tax registers for the late colonial years (in outhouses and dusty cupboards on Government stations throughout Bulozi); volumes of Tour Reports for the same period (in similar places); a District Notebook (in Nottinghamshire); extensive detailed statistics of recruited and deserted labourers (under a table in a Johannesburg suburb). Finding and copying this material consumed a good deal of time, but these were clearly valid field activities.

Secondly, there are the 'control' properties of different types of field data. I have already mentioned how participant observation and personal recollections give a knowledge of likely constraints upon early white observers, but recollection is often (perhaps usually) imprecise. Therefore the checking should be a two-way process. For example, aerial photographs can be used to check recollected accounts of the physical extent of agriculture, as I showed in Chapter 4; or quantitative field data collected under known conditions may be used to assess the reliability of official statistics. But conversely, detailed periodic data offer a vital complement once an opinion has been formed.

One type of written source is frequently rather difficult to deal with. The historian has to decide how far he is willing to accept the data and the analyses of his anthropologist predecessors, if he has any. I suggest that such sources should be scrutinised in the same way as missionaries' letters or administrators' reports, unless the previous researcher has shown open awareness of methodological problems. Two possible objections to this immediately arise. One is that *ad hominem* assessment of a formal, analytic argument is somehow vaguely improper; the other, that it is in any case difficult to find out how someone else did his work because direct questioning of the sort of easily accessible people who might know – for example, former research assistants – would inspire little confidence.

Field materials are located, defined, collected and preserved at the behest of one individual. His personality and methods of work obviously influence how this is done; therefore they are perfectly legitimate objects of interest for the historian. However, the second objection has greater merit. The difficulties may be overcome only through using less accessible information. Knowledge of techniques used or of informants tapped can only be successfully mobilised within a wider understanding of the society. It is carping to say that someone's field situation was bad; it is useful to explain how that situation affected the subsequent analysis.[2] But direct questions about anthropologists are not the only ones to be shunned. The productivity of interviewing is deeply influenced by what is *not* asked. How is the historian to know what to avoid?

Questions which raise suspicions or doubt about the researcher's motives in the informant's mind are obviously one category to be avoided. However, in my experience such questions *must* often be answered because they address important areas of society and culture – witchcraft, magic, traditional medicine and cosmology are good examples. Questions in these areas cause suspicion in Bulozi because there is a well established pattern of what whites should and should not be interested in which was part of the colonial *modus vivendi*. Oral data on the deeds of kings, on political organisation or on the beneficial effects of the Missions are easily procured and belong to areas where tradition has been most thoroughly processed for external consumption. The first task is to realise this. For example, in Bulozi, to conduct a study of witchcraft, divination and magic openly would be, by definition, to fail. Therefore a strategy for interviewing is required whereby what is overheard and observed silently may guide what is actually asked. In this endeavour, speed kills. How it may be put into practice is most conveniently illustrated visually. Table B shows the allocation of time to different activities during my work on Bulozi.

Four points in the table provide the necessary illustrations: first, the long period labelled 'Bureaucracy', which consisted of obtaining approval from the Zambian and the traditional authorities. It was clearly foolhardy to try and rush this. Second, I chose not to go to the official archives until I had had my initial exposure to the society and had begun to search for data of the 'Lost and found' (Table A, column D) variety. This was because I felt that without some taste of the place and people I would be both inefficient in selecting material, and thus waste a lot of time in the archives which could be better employed doing other things, and defenceless against the biases in the material. Third, I did not begin systematic interviewing until I had been in Bulozi for slightly over a year, by which time I had grasped the beginnings of the language, knew what to mistrust and had begun to know what I could and could not ask openly. This all sounds too full of reason and hindsight to be credible, of course, and so a fourth point must be added. Earlier I mentioned the role of luck and intuition in the development of technique and it was during the first year that its influence was greatest. This was also a time of low productivity of material which I was subsequently able to use; but it was also the

TABLE A. *Sources for the study of Lozi history*

Source description	Period				
	1876–96	1897–1916	1917–45	1946–64	1965–
Travellers					
published	very good*				
letters/journals	good*				
Missionaries					
published	fair*	good	very good	poor	
private	excellent*	excellent	very good	very good	
periodic			fair	fair	
photographic	excellent*	fair			
Administrative					
high level	good*	very good			
policy	good	very good	good	poor	
court cases		excellent	excellent post 1928		excellen post 19⁻
low level		very good*	good	excellent	
private	very good				
Department papers					
agencies					very goo
periodic		fair	poor	excellent	poor
photographic				excellent	excellen
Traders					
accounts		very good			
private papers		very good	poor		
External statistics				excellent	
Anthropology	fair/poor* →		→		
Technical studies					good

* Main types of written source used in writing this book

	Location					Ranking of relative ease (1) to difficulty (3) in locating and/or using a source	Control field data
Official archives	Secondary archives	Privately held materials	Materials lost or discarded and found	Published sources	Data in government and parastatal offices		
A	B	C	D	E	F		
				+		1	Rec
	+			+		1	Rec
	+			+		2	Rec; PO
		+				3	PR;EI;PO
	+					2	EI;PO
	+	+				2	PR
						1	EI;PR;Rec
						1	EI;PR;Rec
	+					3	EI;PR;Rec
		+	+			3	EI;PR;Rec
		+	+			2	EI;PO
					+	3	QS;EI;PO
			+		+	3	PR;EI
		+			+	2	
		+				3	
		+				3	PR;EI
		+	+			3	PR;QS;EI;PO
				+		1	PR;Rec;QS;EI
		+		+	+	1/3	AS;PO

ec = recital of a formal tradition   PR = personal recollection of the informant
QS = quantitative study (sets of contemporary studies)   PO = participant observation
AS = area studies (statements of village origins etc. made through village history questionnaires)
EI = European informant

TABLE B. *Distribution of field activities*

Months	-3 -2 -1 0 1 2 3 4 5 6 7 8 9 10 11 12 13 14 15 16 17 18 19 20 21 22 23 24 25 26 27 28 29 30 31 32 33 34 35 36 37 38 → UK
Locations	UK Transit Bulozi ——→ SA / Zim —→ Bulozi UK Transit Bulozi ——→ UK

Eighteen months interval

Activities
Waste (illness etc.)
Bureaucracy
Motor mechanics
Official archives
Searching/
 secondary archives
Formal interviews
Personal recollections
Formal traditions
European interviews
Area studies
Village histories
Participant observation
Writing

Language
Comprehension begins
Halting speech
Relative fluency

Productivity
Low
Medium
High
Very high

* Work done without an interpreter as an essential third party.
SA = South Africa   Zim = Zimbabwe

time of highest personal stress. The dash in month seven of the 'Waste' line was a period of stress-related illness.

It was during the first months that decisions began to be made on four rather mundane matters central to the fieldwork: whether or not to be mobile; what sort of research assistance to seek; who to pay (and how) for what, and the expedients to be adopted in undertaking different investigations. It is incidentally in these practical matters that it is easiest to see where the tasks of a historian converge with and diverge from those of an anthropologist.

The historian requires synchronic and diachronic field data. The former show convergence with the anthropologist, since they call for participant observation and for quantitative small-scale studies, preferably more than one and in different places. The latter diverge and require wide-ranging collection of oral data and a mixture of chosen and random informants. I noticed a positive correlation between the specificity of informants – highest when collecting 'Formal traditions' – and the miles I drove. In seeking to identify and to explain the nature and purpose of invention in formal tradition, the Land Rover is a powerful tool in the historian's collection of equipment. In a well structured society like Bulozi it gives him several valuable assets. For instance, it enables him to travel faster than the bush telegraph. In Bulozi there is evidence of how a desired pattern of invented tradition may be sent ahead of the plodding, paddling and accompanied researcher. Sometimes this does not matter; for example, recitals of royal history can only be decoded through rigorous examination of the texts afterwards. But if one seeks recollected accounts of political and economic organisation then, as I suggested when discussing the difference between my views and Gluckman's in Chapter 5, it does. Once, when I entered a new and remote area to obtain village histories of origin, I stumbled upon an aged chief whose account of political structure was quite new to me; it introduced me to the role of the clapperless bell (*ngongi*) and provided the catalyst I needed to stimulate a much more critical awareness of mutability in such data than I had hitherto entertained. So my car both taught and facilitated systematic suspicion! It also enabled me to travel and research in areas of the country previously little represented in the literature or the received analyses. Away from the rivers and wagon trails of early travellers I discovered empirical evidence of economic institutions (the state gardens, *bonamukau*) which altered my view of the political economy of late-nineteenth-century Bulozi, as I explained in the final section of Chapter 5. Lastly, transport is a most useful currency to be able to exchange for services.

Mobility also affects the sort of questions that are asked on tour. Most visibly, it makes it important to try and construct a body of common reference so that particularly in collecting personal recollections, there may be possibilities for easy comparison. For the researcher, this can be a blessing and a bore – boring in its repetitiveness, a blessing in that it gives a bridge-head into the language fashioned out of a few areas of vocabulary.

But the general does not march alone. In learning the language and in most types of fieldwork, some sort of assistance is used. The specific form which it takes will be dictated by circumstance. In Bulozi, my fear of being 'run' by an assistant (which I think in retrospect was perhaps exaggerated but not entirely unfounded) caused me to adopt an extreme solution. I had no employees during my initial field trip. Let me set this out more broadly. Research assistance seems to be of two types. There are secondary services such as transcribing and translating tapes and notes. The personal relationship involved is relatively easy to handle and cash payments present no problem. However, such services are usually second in task and second in time, sought later during the research.

Primary services are first in importance, task and time. I see four categories. There is interpretation. Here the raw researcher is most at his assistant's mercy. After some early experiments, I did not attempt formal interviewing again until I understood a bit of Lozi. Ideally the historian should set independence from a third party in interviewing as a high priority. However, even as my command of the spoken language improved, I continued to have interpreters present for some formal interviews, especially when entering a new area. Sometimes I would choose a community leader who would be informally appointed 'interpreter' for a group interview from which I tried to decide who might be helpful informants for subsequent conversations. This then is the second function of an assistant – to set the minds of the informants at rest and to make the researcher's presence legitimate.

Again, Bulozi being a structured society, it demanded a special response. When I began formal interviewing widely during months thirteen and fourteen, I was initially accompanied by a well known royal adviser who had been a colonial law court interpreter before his retirement, by the second ranking chief of the relevant traditional royal establishment and by a letter of introduction from the *Litunga*, the late Mbikusita Lewanika, which bore his seal; I had my Zambian government credentials as well. From my assessment of the contemporary mix of power and influence, I concluded that without both sorts of approval, my scope would be considerably restricted; so I sought the help and presence of these particular men because I knew them and because of who they were. This tactic is open to the criticism that it associated me undesirably closely with the traditional royal establishment. To an extent this is true, but such association is unavoidable. What is really at issue is how the royal connection is handled, which means making conscious efforts to explain to oneself what the expectations of helpers and permission granters are so that compensation may be made if necessary. This is akin to the third type of assistance, which is the negative side of the second.

Research assistants may simply be there to supervise the researcher and to inhibit his informants. Fortunately, the sort of crude tactics with soldiers, Special Branch agents and stool pigeons have been uncommon in Zambia to date. As I indicated in the Preface, I have rarely encountered anything other than interest and cooperation from the large number of Zambian officials with whom I have had cause to deal, and so I cannot suggest from my experience how to overcome such difficulties, if indeed they can be overcome at all.

The fourth sort of assistance is rather different. When conducting quantitative or questionnaire studies, someone has to ask the questions and fill in the replies. My policy has been to seek this sort of help from the people themselves. In the various area studies which I have done, I saw my role to be that of a catalyst, to explain to the people why the study was worth doing and if after discussion they agreed that it was valuable, to show them how to study themselves, for each area contains sufficient literate people to do this. Of course, I had a high failure rate. Only one in ten of the questionnaires on village history which were distributed was subsequently returned in a usable form. In area studies based on the individual, the failure rate and the scale of the undertaking were both much smaller.

During my first field trip I never paid anyone in cash for either assistance or information. My assistants helped me because of other motives, notably wanting to be sure that I got their history 'right'. I felt that I could more easily identify and compensate for their biases if their motivation was in no way financial. Since the Lozi elite are relatively wealthy and since my first helpers were older men, they could afford the time; I provided transport and food. Younger friends travelled with me in their free time on the first trip. On the second trip, one was released to me from his Government job and then I paid his salary without hesitation. Naturally, I paid my translators and transcribers. I never had one established assistant.

The reason why I never paid for information except in unsolicited ways with transport, food or medical treatment was that, again, I felt that non-monetary motives were the easier ones to comprehend. In particular, I was frightened by the career of one of my predecessors in Bulozi who reportedly paid freely for information. In consequence he received a great deal from needy and greedy people, cooked to his taste as they understood it; he was also given a Lozi nickname which means, in free translation, 'the recklessly generous giver' (*Makapweka*).

The answers given to the three problems above – of mobility, of assistance and of payment – together compose the answer to the fourth – of the guise to be adopted. By pursuing several different tasks simultaneously, it was possible to pursue them all. Thus for example the 'cover' of the village history questionnaires sheltered the collection of migrant labourers' recollections and of certain formal traditions; the 'cover' of small-scale area studies did the same thing for other sorts of reminiscence and some unofficial formal traditions. Only with mainstream formal traditions was no 'cover' possible. This was in any case the most taxing single project and I deliberately left it for the final months of the second trip.

This is no advocacy of mystery. At once it must be said that complete frankness about all openly conducted work is mandatory. I always assumed that I could hide nothing of what I did and so I revealed all. But the researcher will put to work some of those things which inevitably he will learn silently from observation and casual chatter. Probably there will be information gathered in this way which he will never reveal because to do so would be counter-productive; but most of it he will introduce into open interviewing through leading questions as part of the way in which he seeks to make an encounter most productive.

The use of leading questions is ticklish. The problem is to let the informant know that you know enough for him to consider taking you seriously without telling yourself, through his lips, the answer that you expect. As a general rule, as in surgery, adequate antisepsis is the goal but, unlike surgery, some degree of contamination is necessary. The practical test to see whether an informant was speaking for himself or for the interviewer is to revisit the person after a good lapse of time and conduct a second interview. This is a counsel of perfection, for frequently it is not physically possible; death, pressure of time, or of budget, can easily intervene. However, I think that testimonies which seem to be at all pivotal should be checked thus. I revisited after several months the aged chief with the novel version of political organisation just to be certain that his initial testimony was not adventitious.

Revisitation also features in the other tactic. This is simply to make some friends and, if you trust them, to get them to help you to hone the amount of edge that different leading questions require by trying them out in completely frank conversation, where your friend will say 'no' if you are wrong. In my work I have a handful of friends with whom I can do this and I cherish them.

Notes

The following abbreviations are used in the notes and bibliography:

AOBNA	M. Gluckman, *The administrative organisation of the Barotse native authorities with a plan for reforming them*
CO	Colonial Office
DC	District Commissioner
DEFAP	Département Évangélique Français d'Action Apostolique
DNB	District Note Book
ECBP	M. Gluckman, *The economy of the central Barotse plain*
ELLRP	M. Gluckman, *Essays on Lozi land and royal property*
FO	Foreign Office
GRZ	Government of the Republic of Zambia
HMC	Historic Manuscripts Collection
IBJ	M. Gluckman, *The ideas of Barotse jurisprudence*
JPB	M. Gluckman, *The judicial process among the Barotse of Northern Rhodesia*
LM	Livingstone Museum
MMS	Methodist Missionary Society
NAZ	National Archives of Zambia
NAZim	National Archives of Zimbabwe
NC	Native Commissioner
PRO	Public Record Office
RCS	Royal Commonwealth Society
SAHCNR	South Africa, High Commissioner, Northern Rhodesia
T/R	Tour Report

1 Introduction

1 Gluckman, *ECBP; ELLRP; AOBNA; JPB; IBJ;* M. Mainga Bull, 'Lewanika's achievement', *Journal of African History* XIII, 3 (1972), 463–72; *idem, Bulozi under the Luyana kings* (London, 1973); G. L. Caplan, *The elites of Barotseland, 1878–1969* (London, 1970); G. C. R. Clay, *Your friend*

Lewanika: The life and times of Lubosi Lewanika, Litunga of Barotseland, 1842–1916, Robins Series 6 (London, 1968).

2 E. Stokes, 'Barotseland, survival of an African state', in R. Brown and E. Stokes (eds.), *The Zambezian past* (Manchester, 1966); T. O. Ranger, 'The "Ethiopian" episode in Barotse history, 1900–1905', *Rhodes-Livingstone Institute Journal* xxxvii (1965), 26–41; *idem*, 'Nationality and nationalism – the case of Barotseland', *Journal of the Historical Society of Nigeria* iv, 2 (1968), 227–46; M. Mainga, 'A history of Lozi religion to the end of the nineteenth century', in T. O. Ranger and I. N. Kimambo (eds.), *The historical study of African religion* (London, 1972); S. Shaloff, 'The Kasempa salient: the tangled web of British–Kaonde–Lozi relations', *International Journal of African Historical Studies* v, 1 (1972), 22–40; A. D. Roberts, 'Pre-colonial trade in Zambia', *African Social Research* x (Dec. 1970), 715–46; J. S. Galbraith, *Crown and charter* (California, 1974), Ch. 7; L. Van Horn, 'The agricultural history of Barotseland, 1840–1964', in R. Palmer and N. Parsons (eds.), *The roots of rural poverty in central and southern Africa* (London, 1977). Other unpublished or technical works appear as required in the notes.

3 For the onslaught: T. O. Ranger, *Revolt in southern Rhodesia* (London, 1967); the dream: Galbraith, *Crown and charter*, pp. 31–2, pp. 87–9; both: J. R. D. Cobbing, 'Lobengula, Jameson and the occupation of Mashonaland, 1890', *Rhodesian History* iv (1973), 39–56, p. 41.

4 In contrast, I. Wilks, *Asante in the nineteenth century* (Cambridge, 1976), describes a well articulated African kingdom with, apparently, well developed divisions of opinion in its elite; the importance of timing is stressed in J. M. Lonsdale, 'The politics of conquest: the British in western Kenya, 1894–1908', *Historical Journal* xx, 4 (1977), 841–70, p. 844.

5 Lonsdale, 'The politics of conquest', p. 841.

6 *Ibid.,* pp. 866–70; D. A. Low, *Lion rampant: essays in the study of British imperialism* (London, 1973), pp. 30–3.

7 Cf. J. Skorupski, 'The meaning of another culture's beliefs', in C. Hookway and P. Pettit (eds.), *Action and interpretation: studies in the philosophy of the social sciences* (Cambridge, 1978); B. Nathhorst, *Formal or structural studies of traditional tales*, Stockholm Studies in Comparative Religion 9 (Stockholm, 1970), pp. 38–45.

8 M. Hesse, 'Theory and value in the social sciences', in Hookway and Pettit, *Action and interpretation*; C. Coquery-Vidrovitch, 'L'histoire vivante', *Cahiers d'Études Africaines*, lxi–lxii, 16 (1976), 67–73; J. H. Hexter, *The history primer* (London, 1972), esp. Ch. 10.

9 *E.g.* J. Vansina, *The children of Woot: essays in Kuba history* (Madison, 1978), Ch. 11.

10 The words of two other, rather different, critics of that position: S. Young, 'Fertility and famine: women's agricultural history in Southern Mozambique', in Palmer and Parsons, *The roots of rural poverty*, p. 66; A. G. Hopkins, *An economic history of West Africa* (London, 1973), p. 10.

11 I have borrowed and slightly altered this phrase from J. Berque, 'Vers une

étude des comportements en Afrique du nord', *Revue Africaine* IV (1956), 523–36, p. 529.

12 I think that the only historians' models with a bright future are those which address primarily the question of change. The one used here is found in F. Braudel, 'Histoire et sciences sociales: la longue durée' which was first published in *Annales*, IV (Oct.–Dec. 1958), 'Débats et combats', pp. 725–53, republished in F. Braudel, *Ecrits sur l'histoire* (Paris, 1969), pp. 41–83. An example of these insights at work is in W. De Craemer, J. Vansina and R. C. Fox, 'Religious movements in central Africa: a theoretical study', *Comparative Studies in Society and History* XVIII, 4 (Oct. 1976), 458–75.

13 Therefore this passage deliberately echoes E. P. Thompson, *The making of the English working class* (London, 1963; 2nd edn 1968), p. 13.

14 J. Goody, *The domestication of the savage mind* (Cambridge, 1977), esp. p. 37.

15 R. Horton, 'African traditional thought and Western science', *Africa* XXXVII (1967), 50–71, 155–87. The particular example of medical practice in this debate is central. For the Lozi case, see Chapter 7 Section 4 below and 'Disease at the crossroads: towards a history of therapeutics in Bulozi since 1876', *Social Science and Medicine* (Spring, 1980); cf. E. R. Ackerknecht, *Medicine and ethnology* (Baltimore, 1971), *passim;* J. Janzen with W. Arkinstall, *The quest for therapy in lower Zaire* (Berkeley, California, 1978), *passim.*

16 Horton, 'African traditional thought', p. 155.

17 T. S. Kuhn, *The structure of scientific revolutions* 2nd edn (Chicago, 1970). the thesis is brilliantly illustrated in A. Koestler, *The sleepwalkers* (London 1959; 2nd edn 1968), especially the biography of Kepler, pp. 227–427.

18 Gluckman, *JPB*, p. 28; Sir Henry Maine, *Ancient Law* (1861; Everyman edn 1972), p. 100; E. Gellner, *Legitimation of belief* (Cambridge, 1974), pp. 158–67, whose categories I take here in a different order.

19 Here is a brief guide to some literature that addresses these questions: A. V. Chayanov, *The theory of peasant economy,* American Economic Association Translation Series (Homewood, Illinois, 1966); M. Sahlins, *Stone Age economics* (London, 1972); Barrington Moore Jnr, *Social origins of dictatorship and democracy* (Harmondsworth, 1966), esp. pp. 453–83.

   For England: K. Polanyi, *Origins of our time: the great transformation* (London, 1945), *passim*, but especially the discussion of the Speenhamland relief system; Thompson, *The making of the English working class, passim*, but especially analysis of 'A journeyman cotton spinner's address' (1818), pp. 218–22; *idem*, 'The moral economy of the English crowd in the eighteenth century,' *Past and Present* (Feb. 1971), 76–136; E. Hobsbawm and G. Rudé, *Captain Swing* (London, 1968).

   For France: R. C. Cobb, *The police and the people: French popular protest movements, 1789–1820* (Oxford, 1970).

   For the ante bellum southern United States: E. D. Genovese, *Roll Jordan roll: the world the slaves made* (New York, 1972).

For southeast Asia: J. C. Scott, *The moral economy of the peasant: rebellion and subsistence in Southeast Asia* (New Haven, 1976).

20 The phrase used in Gellner's earlier version of these ideas in R. Horton and R. Finnegan (eds.), *Modes of thought* (London, 1973), pp. 162–81.

21 M. Rader, *Marx's interpretation of history* (New York, 1979), p. xx.

22 The translation in T. B. Bottomore and M. Rubel (eds.), *Karl Marx: Selected writings in sociology and social philosophy* (London, 1956; 2nd edn 1961; Penguin edn 1970), p. 67.

23 Rader, *Marx's interpretation*, p. 185.

24 *Ibid.*, pp. 14–18. Rader asserts that *bedingt* should be taken to mean 'conditions', not 'determines', which would be *bestimmt*. Starting from a reconsideration of this one word, he proceeds, by examining other fundamental concepts used in the Preface, to offer a non-reductive interpretation of this piece which, above others in Marx's corpus, is so often used to support the 'fundamentalist' reading of Marx's thought.

25 Unsurprisingly, this discussion of false consciousness is obliged to cover much the same ground as Scott's in *The moral economy of the peasant*, pp. 159–60.

26 W. Soyinka, *Death and the king's horseman* (London, 1975), author's note, p. 7.

2 Contexts

1 For details of relevant maps, see list of illustrations and elsewhere in the notes.

2 E. Jacottet, *Études sur les langues du Haut Zambèze* (3 vols., Paris, 1896–1901), vol. II, pp. 143–5; vol. III, pp. 135–7. For discussion of the nature, sources and value of this work, see Chapter 7, Section 1 below; F. Coillard, *Journal intime*, DEFAP, Paris, entry of *vendredi soir*, 12 *mars* 1886. As a general rule I use the closest source to the original observation that I have available, usually the journal Mss.

3 D. Livingstone, *Private journals*, ed. I. Schapera (London, 1960), p. 238; A. Jalla, *Notes privées*, privately held, p. 38.

4 This was the usual pattern of rainfall for 1886–96 also. F. Coillard, Lecture to an unidentified audience, draft notes, 23 *fév* 1898, DEFAP, Paris.

5 Parsons Corporation, *Final report, the water resources of Barotse Province, Zambia*, Job No. 4229 (New York and Los Angeles, August 1968), p. 53, pl. 9 for rainfall; pp. 65–80 for evapotranspiration and aquifers.

6 W. C. Verboom, soil and vegetation map of the floodplain near Mongu, drawn from infra-red aerial photographs, at Agric. Research Stn, Mongu; information at Limulunga, Feb. 1974; W. Waddell, *Diary*, 28 Oct. 1891, NAZim; Livingstone, *Private journals*, p. 203; A. St H. Gibbons, 'A journey into the Marotse and Mashikolumbwe countries', *Geographical Journal* IX (Feb. 1897), 121–45, p. 126.

7 Published in W. C. Verboom, *An ecological survey of Western Province, Zambia*, vol. I, *The environment*, Land Resources Study No. 8, Directorate of

Overseas Surveys (Tolworth, 1968), pp. 60–1, Map 5; further description D. U. Peters, *Land usage in Barotseland*, ed. N. Smyth, Rhodes-Livingstone Institute Comm. 19 (Livingstone, 1960), pp. 9, 15–26; and G. G. Trapnell and J. N. Clothier, *The soils, vegetation and agricultural systems of North Western Rhodesia* (Lusaka, 1937).

8 Livingstone, *Private journals*, 19 July 1851, p. 30.

9 It is odd that he should have thought this since the 336 item wordlists which he made, even though not under the best conditions, clearly show the differences reflected in later work. Schapera mentions the vocabularies and that he obtained photocopies of them from the South African Library, Cape Town (Livingstone, *Private journals*, p. 31, n.1). Livingstone describes how he collected the lists from named individuals (pp. 30–4). Mr M. Mann of SOAS alerted me to an entry in the SOAS library catalogue which proved to be typed transcriptions of the lists.

10 Coillard, who had a generally low opinion of Holub's abilities and good sense (see his *Journal intime*, 31 *août* 1886), made the same point against Holub's observations without mentioning him by name in the definition of 'Ma-Mbunda' in the English translation of his edited letters. F. Coillard, *On the threshold of central Africa*, (London, 1897; repr. 1971), Glossary, p. 651; E. Holub, *A cultural survey of the Lozi—Mbunda kingdom in south central Africa* (Vienna, 1879), translated by Dr L. Holy (typescr.), pp. 2–3. The Jesuit, Fr Depelchin, showed a copy of Holub's work to the trader George Westbeech in 1881 and translated sections of it for him. Westbeech, at that time the dominant European in Bulozi, expressed an opinion similar to Coillard's. H. Depelchin and C. Croonenberghs, *Trois ans dans l'Afrique australe* (Brussels, 1883), pp. 285–6.

11 Coillard was given a skeletal version of the legend by Lewanika and Chief Nalubutu at Lealui, *Journal intime*, 3 *nov.* 1893. The fuller account given here derives from performances recorded in the later 1890s and early 1900s by Jalla in *Notes privées*, p. 71 and *Litaba za Sichaba sa Malozi* (Oxford 1909; 5th edn, 1969), pp. 8–9. These are consistent with versions I have heard and with Gluckman, *ECBP*, p. 89, and M. Mainga, *Bulozi under the Luyana kings* (London, 1973), p. 24.

12 In 'Reasonable Order' of 1925 under Proclamation 8 of 1916. See Sesheke DNB, privately held, p. 13, p. 100 (Notes by R. O. Ingram, 16 Oct. 1929).

13 F. Christol, *L'art dans l'Afrique australe* (Paris, 1911), pp. 107–15.

14 Face markings were intended to gain the person entry to Litooma, the village of the High God Nyambe, after death, hence their name *muamuhelo* ('the welcomer') from the verb *ku amuhela* (to welcome).

15 Mainga, *Bulozi under the Luyana kings*, Ch. 1; G. L. Caplan, *The elites of Barotseland, 1878–1969* (London, 1970), p. 1. The problems of using oral traditions in conjunction with other material are discussed in D. W. Phillipson, 'Iron Age history and archaeology in Zambia', *Journal of African History* xv, 1 (1974), 1–25, pp. 17–18; A. D. Roberts, 'The age of tradition', in B. M. Fagan (ed.), *A short history of Zambia* (Oxford, 1966); S. Feierman,

The Shambaa Kingdom (Madison, 1974), pp. 40–3; T. C. Weiskel, 'L'histoire socio-économique des peuples baule: problèmes et perspectives de recherche', *Cahiers d'Études Africaines* LXI–LXII, 16 (1976), 357–95, pp. 358–73.

16 J. O. Vogel, 'Some Early Iron Age sites in southern and western Zambia', *Azania* VIII (1973), 25–54, p. 53; J. D. Clark, 'The Bushman hunters of the Barotse forests,' *Northern Rhodesia Journal* I, 3 (1951), 55–66, pp. 56–7; Phillipson, 'Iron Age history', p. 12.

17 J. D. Clark, 'A note on the pre-Bantu inhabitants of Northern Rhodesia and Nyasaland', *Northern Rhodesia Journal* I, 2 (1950), 42–52, p. 45; Fagan, *A short history of Zambia*, p. 61, Fig. 16, p. 58.

18 B. M. Fagan, *Southern Africa during the Iron Age* (London, 1965), pp. 52–3; D. W. Phillipson, 'The Early Iron Age in Zambia – regional variants and some tentative conclusions', *Journal of African History* IX, 2 (1968), 191–211, p. 200.

19 J. D. Clark and B. M. Fagan, 'Charcoals, sands and channel decorated pottery from Northern Rhodesia', *American Anthropologist* LXVII (1965), 354–71, p. 365.

20 Proposed *ibid.*, p. 369; questioned, Phillipson, 'The Early Iron Age in Zambia', pp. 207, 209.

21 Phillipson, 'Iron Age history', pp. 1–11; Vogel, 'Some Early Iron Age sites', p. 53; D. W. Phillipson, 'An Early Iron Age site on the Lubusi River, Kaoma district, Zambia', *Zambia Museums Journal* (1971), 51–67, pp. 51–7; Fagan, *A short history of Zambia*, pp. 88–90.

22 N. Katanekwa, 'The Iron Age sequence in the Machili Valley of southwestern Zambia', MA thesis, University of Birmingham 1977; conversation in Livingstone 28 Sept. 1977.

23 The best documented sequence is that of the Dambwa, Kalomo and Kangila traditions of southern Zambia. Both Vogel's work and the intersextile range of radio-carbon dates show an overlap of the two former and a distinct break between the two latter. Work on the Tonga plateau puts this 'interface' at around AD 1080. Phillipson, 'The chronology of the Iron Age in Bantu Africa', *Journal of African History* XVI, 3 (1975), 321–42, pp. 324–7; *idem*, 'Iron Age history', p. 16.

24 A. D. Roberts, *A history of the Bemba* (London, 1973), pp. 46, 49–50; *idem*, 'The age of tradition'; *idem*, *A history of Zambia* (London, 1976), pp. 63–6. The same point is made by Weiskel, 'L'histoire socio-économique des peuples baule', pp. 387–90.

25 Phillipson, 'Iron Age history', pp. 17, 21–4.

26 *Ibid.*, p. 16.

27 Roberts, *A history of Zambia*, p. 71; M. A. Bryan (ed.), *The Bantu languages of Africa* (Oxford, 1959), pp. 70–1.

28 The seminal discussion of time is E. Evans-Pritchard, *The Nuer* (Oxford, 1940), pp. 107–8. J. Vansina, *The children of Woot* (Madison, 1978), Ch. 1 and *idem*, *Geschiedenis van de Kuba van ongeveer 1500 tot 1904*, Wetenschappen van de mens 44 (Tervuren, 1963), pp. 7–31 and Pt IV C offer a

sensitive treatment of the problem. J. C. Miller, *Kings and kinsmen* (Oxford, 1976), esp. pp. 11–28, gives a sophisticated dissection of the 'coded' content of traditional myth.

29 Y. W. Mupatu, *An autobiography,* ed. G. Prins, Zambia Past and Present Series 4 (Lusaka, forthcoming), Editor's note to genealogical table. For a discussion of list-making in an oral culture, see J. Goody, *The domestication of the savage mind* (Cambridge, 1977), Ch. 5.

30 A. Jalla, *Tableau synchronique,* retyped and revised by J-P. Burger (1970), privately held typescr.; information from Miss G. Jalla, Mongu, 22 Aug. 1977.

31 M. F. Ribeiro, *Homenagem aos Heroes que precederam* (Lisbon, 1885), reference to 1795, pp. 30–1; A. Baldwin, *Journal,* MMS, ?26 June 1893, p. 281.

32 Coillard, *Journal intime,* 7 av. 1886; 8 nov. 1886; 12 déc. 1892.

33 D. P. Henige, *The chronology of oral tradition: quest for a chimera* (Oxford, 1974), p. 7. Valuable studies which grapple with this problem are: D. C. Dorward, 'Ethnography and administration: a study of Anglo-Tiv "working misunderstanding"', *Journal of African History* xv, 3 (1974), 457–77; D. P. Henige, 'Kingship in Elmina before 1869; a study in "feedback" and the traditional idealisation of the past', *Cahiers d'Études Africaines* LV, 14 (1974), 499–520; Weiskel, 'L'histoire socio-économique des peuples baule'; and in East Africa, M. Twaddle, 'Ganda receptivity to change', *Journal of African History* xv, 2 (1974), 303–15, and *idem*, 'On Ganda historiography', *History in Africa* I (1974), 85–100.

34 In Jalla, *Litaba za Sichaba;* Gluckman, *ECBP*, pp. 89–90; and Mainga, *Bulozi under the Luyana kings.*

35 Mainga, *Bulozi under the Luyana kings*, pp. 66–7; G. Prins, review, *African Social Research* III (1976), 89–92. The data on the Kololo period are unusually consistent for political traditions, a form of material where it is surprising not to find change. In Mainga's reconstruction, in my oral materials and in the private notes of Jalla (after Coillard the most important missionary of his generation), the theme of Lozi disunity recurs. My 1977 testimony is almost a paraphrase of Jalla's *Notes privées* (pp. 65–6). One wonders why. There is certainly not enough work done to support the weight which Mainga places upon a theory of structural weaknesses.

36 E. Holub, *Seven years in South Africa* (London, 1881), vol. II, pp. 284–5; *idem, Cultural survey*, p.1.

37 Quotation from descendant, Sefula, 17 Feb. 1977; other information at Limulunga, March 1977.

38 Coillard, *Journal intime,* 11 mars 1887; 10 juill. 1890.

39 C. Coillard, *Journal*, DEFAP, Paris, 18 Aug. 1878. Today, a palm tree which stands near Kashembe, Mongu District, is said to commemorate the unburied Sipopa.

40 *Luboshi* derives from the verb *ku bosheka*, used especially of a grip on an opponent's forearm when wrestling. In modern Lozi, the 'h' has been dropped and the name is written as 'Lubosi'.

41 Literally 'The Earth of the South', i.e. chief of the south. Usually colloquially called *Mulena Mukwae.*

42 *Na-lolo*: place of the hippopotami. Also called Lwambi. The first ruler there in traditional time was Notulu, daughter of Ngombala (sixth in king-list), but all successive rulers until the Kololo invasion were men. However, Sipopa installed his sister Kandundu (eighth in Nalolo list) and since then the ruler of the south has been a woman. Lists: at the Palace, Nalolo, 9 Sept. 1977; F. Suu *et al.*, 'The Barotse form of government' n.d., p. 4, privately held.

43 The rebellion is described in detail in Chapter 6, Section 4 below; information from Sikufele, at Mulobezi, May 1975; at Sefula, Feb. 1977.

44 Early uses of the name Lewanika: Coillard, *Journal intime*, 6 *jan*. 1885; 8 *jan*. 1885; 1 *fév*. 1885.

3 Boundaries

1 J. Vansina, 'A comparison of African kingdoms', *Africa* XXXII, 4 (1962), 324–35, p. 333; cf. T. W. Weiskel, 'L'histoire socio-économique des peuples baule: problèmes et perspectives de recherche', *Cahiers d'Études Africaines* LXI–LXII, 16 (1976), 357–95, pp. 385–6.

2 See also Lewanika's sworn affidavit detailing his tributaries in F. Worthington *et al.*, 'Notes and documents, 1900–1936', KDE 2/44 (NAZ); A. Jalla's (less expansive) statement of the position as of 11 June 1891 made in Bulawayo on 10 June 1903: 'Memorandum concerning the Award of King Victor Emmanuel III (1905)', privately held; King of Italy's Award, 30 May 1905 in Cd. 2584 (1905).

3 Lewanika's reaction to 1905 Award: Dispatch 812, SANWR, 32434 and Dispatch 864, SANWR, 33473 (appended comments in both cases) in CO 417/409 (PRO); S. Shaloff, 'The Kasempa salient; the tangled web of British–Kaonde–Lozi relations', *International Journal of African Historical Studies* V, 1 (1972), 22–40, illustrates this convincingly for the northeast. W. van Binsbergen proposes a theme of consistent Nkoya enmity to the east.

4 Sikongo from the Ñinda river to the line of the present border; Ilukuyi from Kutiei river to Lealui, later to Lukwakwa; Itondo-Mukena from Litabwa to Kalenga. Machalo remained at Tundombe; information at Sikongo, 16 May 1977.

5 E. Jacottet, *Études sur les langues du Haut Zambèze* (3 vols., Paris, 1896–1901), vol. I, Preface, p.i (*août* 1895). See further Chapter 7, Section 1 below.

6 G. Fortune, 'The languages of the Western Province of Zambia', *Journal of the Language Association of Eastern Africa* I, 1 (1970), 31–8. I am indebted to Mr M. Mann for this reference.

7 A. D. Roberts, *A history of Zambia* (London, 1976), p. 68.

8 D. Livingstone, *Private journals,* ed. I. Schapera (London, 1960), 19 July 1851, p. 34.

9 F. Coillard, *Journal intime,* 22 *juin* 1888; Jalla to C. Mackintosh, 25 Nov.

1913, Lealui, DEFAP, Paris; A. Jalla, *Sikololo dictionary* (1914), Preface, and *Silozi dictionary*, 2nd edn (London, 1936), Preface.

10 A. Jalla, *Silozi dictionary*, 3rd edn (1970), typscr.; information from its compiler, the late Rev. E. Berger, Feb. 1977.

11 The best technical study of linguistic interrelationship is J. J. Hoover, 'The seduction of Ruwej: reconstructing Ruund history (the nuclear Lunda: Zaire, Angola, Zambia)' PhD thesis, Yale University, 1978. The only extended linguistic study of Luyana is T. Givón, *The Siluyana language*, University of Zambia Communication 6 (mimeo), (Lusaka, 1970).

12 Mwene Kandala, 'The beginning of Mwene Kandala's chiefship' (typescr.), privately held; information at Yuka Palace, Mabumbu, 27 July 1977; at Kataba Valley, June 1973.

13 C. Coillard, *Journal*, 11 Aug. 1878, NAZim and DEFAP; Jacottet, *Études*, vol. I, pp. vii–viii; Jalla, *Sikololo dictionary*; information at Sefula, 25 Feb. 1977.

14 Phillipson, 'Iron Age history and archaeology in Zambia', *Journal of African History* xv, 1(1974), 1–25, pp. 12, 21–4.

15 Cf. Fortune, 'The languages of Western Zambia', p. 33.

16 Information at Sibukali and Lumbe, Aug. 1974; at Lui River dispensary, Aug. 1974 and Lui Wanyau, May 1974. Awareness of the different qualities of traditions available in different types of oral source is illustrated in J. Vansina, *Geschiedenis van de Kuba van ongeveer 1500 tot 1904*, Wetenschappen van de mens 44 (Tervuren, 1963), esp. Pt I C and Pt II A; *idem, L'évolution du royaume rwanda des origines à 1900*, Académie Royale des Sciences d'Outre-Mer, Sciences Morales et Politiques xxvi (Tervuren, 1961); Weiskel, 'L'histoire socio-économique des peuples baule', pp. 359, 362–3.

17 Information at Yuka Leprosarium, Kalabo, Aug. 1973; Limulunga, March 1974; Senanga Hospital, May 1975; Shekela, May 1974.

18 Information at Sibukali, Aug. 1974; Siloana Plains, Oct. 1973. This is a widely current theme.

19 Gluckman in particular projected a rather immobile picture, *ECBP*, pp. 28–9; *IBJ*, p. 118. D. U. Peters followed him in this: villages in the floodplain 'were originally sited where they are found today', *Land usage in Barotseland*, ed. N. Smyth, Rhodes-Livingstone Institute Comm. 19 (Livingstone, 1960).

20 A. Jalla, *Notes privées*, privately held, p. 53; F. Worthington, the early administrator, concurred: 'The ruling class is much mixed' (retrospective n.d.) in 'Notes and documents, 1900–1936', KDE 2/44 (NAZ).

21 *Mo liange njimulianu, wa Tonga na Totela. A Tonga ka ile ku bika, ayia ku linde ngwane Mulonga;* collected at Mwenyi, 19 May 1977.

22 Information at Ikatulamwa, 15 Sept. 1977; at Yuka Palace, Mabumbu, several visits, July–Sept. 1977.

23 Information at Mabumbu, 11 Aug. 1977. Strictly speaking, *mushiku* translates as 'totem', but is colloquially used to describe the whole concept of

descent group (a better rendering than the more common and potentially misleading 'clan').

24 Gluckman, *ECBP*, p. 86; *IBJ*, Chs. 3 and 4.

25 Gluckman, *ECBP*, pp. 84–5 describes *mishiku*. Coillard's work also does not support Gluckman's view. He wrote in general terms (e.g. to A. Boegner, *août* 1889, *Lettres à la direction*) of the instability of residence. But the comment is not tied to specific observations; I see it more as the projection of a Hobbesian view of Bulozi and therefore place little weight on it. It offers no alternative explanation.

26 Information near Mabumbu, 5 June 1977; at Namaenya, 20 Aug. 1977.

27 Information near Mabumbu, 5 June 1977; at Mabumbu, 11 Aug. 1977. Rev. J-P. Burger, *Notes privées*, privately held (circa 1930), pp. 46–51. The informant was the late Thomas Mwandawande. For biography see M. Mainga, *Bulozi under the Luyana kings* (London, 1973), p. 248.

28 Information at Sibukali, 14 Aug. 1974; Siloana Plains, Oct. 1973; Shekela, May 1974; Salunda, Kalabo, May 1977; Y. W. Mupatu, *An autobiography*, ed. G. Prins, Zambia Past and Present Series 4 (Lusaka, forthcoming); information at Sioma, 24 May 1977 and 25 May 1977.

29 Gluckman, *IBJ*, p. 147; Jalla, *Notes privées*, pp. 113, 117; E. Holub, *Seven years in South Africa* (London, 1881), vol. II, pp. 314–15; Gluckman, *IBJ*, pp. 79–85. Seminal papers on this issue are P. Bohannan, ' "Land", "tenure" and land tenure', in D. Biebuyck (ed.), *African agrarian systems* (London, 1963) and R. E. Frykenberg (ed.), *Land control and social structure in Indian history* (Madison, 1969), especially the essay by W. C. Neale, 'Land is to rule'.

30 The principle of occupation is still recognised and judgment made upon it, e.g. Gluckman, *JPB*, 'The case of the Headman's fishdams', pp. 178–87; Masunga Kabika v. Situhu (a case disputing rights to fish lakes in the Luena Flats), Case 74/ITA/24, appeal from Kangoti Kuta to Mongu Magistrate's Court, 1974. On Lewanika's use of granting powers, see Chapter 4 below and Mupatu, *Autobiography*.

31 E.g. Case 106/71 before Saa Siikalo, Lealui, 15 Nov. 1971: Imongu Tabu attempted to claim ownership of Silimanwikalo, a title land traditionally owned by *Ngambela*. Although Tabu had lived unmolested on the land for five years he lost at first trial and on appeal (SSTA/1/72). Large areas of the Kataba valley are vacant title lands.

32 E.g. at Sianda, Senanga District, the respondent attempted to take advantage of the senility of the local chief to obtain land by misrepresentation. Prosecuted on the principle of *muliu*, Nalolo Kuta, 10/1972. Upheld on appeal when the non-culpability of the chieftainess was heavily stressed by the magistrate.

33 Sefula, 25 Feb. 1977.

34 Mainga, *Bulozi under the Luyana kings*, p. 136 and M. Mainga Bull, 'Lewanika's achievement', *Journal of African History* XIII, 3 (1972), 463–72, p. 469 only mention the introduction of the law, which is linked to a hypothesised revival of the *lilalo* administrative units that I

question on other grounds. The interpretation does not distinguish law and principle.

35 Mongu DNB, vol. II, KDE 10/1/1² Sect. 'R' (NAZ). Gluckman's interpretation of the repeal in *IBJ*, p. 122 and the 'Case of the Prince's gardens', *JPB*, pp. 56–61, mention a provision which barred suit to free land on ancestral title after 27 April 1928. This clause cannot be found. Cap 3(a) of Barotse Native Government Proc. No. 6 of 29 Oct. 1927 only states that claims would not be entertained 'on the grounds that it belonged to his ancestor before the Makololo invasion' and this is certainly the interpretation of the *muliu* repeal remembered by contemporary informants.

36 Gluckman, *JPB*, pp. 287–8.

37 Jalla, *Notes privées*, p. 84; F. Coillard, *Sur le Haut Zambèze: voyages et travaux de Mission* (Paris, 1898), pl. xxv (opp. p. 356) (reproduced here as Fig. 6).

38 E. Holub, *A cultural survey of the Lozi–Mbunda kingdom in south central Africa* (Vienna, 1879), trans. Dr L. Holy (typescr.), pp. 63–4, 68; information at Mabumbu, 11 Aug. 1977.

39 Jalla, *Notes privées*, p. 84; Holub, *Cultural survey*, p. 67; *idem, Seven years*, p. 140; W. F. Fairlie, Sketch No. 65 showing thatching at Sesheke, 1876, in G. Westbeech, *Trade and travel in early Barotseland*, ed. E. C. Tabler (London, 1963), p. 69; F. S. Arnot, *Garenganze or seven years pioneer missionary work in central Africa* (London, 1889; repr. 1969), 18 Oct. 1882 at Lusuma, p. 60; Coillard, *Photograph album*, 'Hunting party Sesheke, 1884 or 1885', HMC/LM.

40 Jalla, *Notes privées*, p. 84; Holub, *Cutural survey*, gives a step by step account of construction; *idem, Seven Years*, pp. 163–7; Fairlie, Sketch No. 66 (Sipopa's House) in Westbeech, *Trade and travel* p. 69; Coillard, *Photograph album, lapa* of Mataa and Akufuna, Lealui, 1885. See below on the fate of commoners who attempted to copy superior houses: information at Mabumbu, 11 Aug. 1977.

41 Coillard, *Photograph album*, 'Sioma ?1886'; *idem, On the threshold of Central Africa* (London, 1897; repr. 1971), p. 637; information near Libonda, Sept. 1977; F. C. Selous, *Travel and adventure in South East Africa* (London, 1893), p. 253; information at Nawinda, Senanga, 7 Sept. 1977.

42 J. Stevenson-Hamilton, *The Barotseland journal*, ed. J. P. R. Wallis, Oppenheimer Series 7 (London, 1953), pp. 201–2, and pl. v; Jalla, *Notes privées*, p. 85.

43 See Chapter 9 below; in the 1920s Yeta ordered that all houses should henceforth be square and since then, especially since the arrival of the corrugated iron roof corner-pieces, the style has become almost universal. Round huts are to be seen in the deep bush and the deep plain. The burning of the thatches of overambitious commoners still occurred in the 1930s.

44 Livingstone, *Private journals*: 'The villages and cattle stations appearing as walls of high reed, which indeed forms the only enclosure', p. 200; Coillard, *Photograph album*, 'Hunting Party at Sesheke', 'Mwandi 1887' esp. 'Loca-

tion unknown, probably near Sefula 1887'; *idem, Sur le Haut Zambèze*, pl. xxiv, opp. p. 340; pl. xxviii, opp. p. 396; pl. xxix, opp. p. 412; pl. xxx, opp. p. 428; pl. xxxiv, p. 484; cf. Westbeech, *Trade and travel*, Feb.–March 1886, Lealui, p. 48; Holub, *Cultural survey*, p. 67; *idem, Seven years*, p. 140; On layout: R. Luck, *A visit to Lewanika, King of the Barotse* (London, 1902), p. 53.

4 Production

1 D. Livingstone, *Private journals*, ed. I. Schapera (London, 1960), p. 203; cf. A. St H. Gibbons, 'A journey into the Marotse and Mashikolumbwe countries', *Geographical Journal* ix (Feb. 1897), 121–45, p. 126.

2 Livingstone thought that the Kololo capital, Naliele, had less than 1,000 inhabitants in 1853 (*Private journals*, p. 203); Coillard's photographs of the early 1890s show Lealui as it was described in 1899, 'a large native town of rather a scattered character' (J. Stevenson-Hamilton, *The Barotseland journal*, ed. J. P. R. Wallis, Oppenheimer Series 7 (London, 1953), p. 201. In 1902 R. Luck estimated that Sesheke had 4,000 inhabitants (*A visit to Lewanika, king of the Barotse* (London, 1902), p. 37).

3 F. Coillard, *Photograph album*, HMC/LM: the interrelationship of *malapa* is most clear in 'Location unknown 1887'; also in a Totela village photographed by A. Bertrand in 1895, 'From the Machili to Lialui', *Geographical Journal* ix (Feb. 1897), 139.

4 Information from numerous sources, notably at Katongo, Sefula, Namboata, Nasiwayo, Lui Wanyau, Lui Imalyo, Mapungu (Senanga), Liumba Hill, Ushaa. In some floodplain villages the location of slave huts is still reflected in the relative positions of those of their descendants.

5 I have never witnessed this ceremony. This account is made from information gathered in Ushaa, April 1977; Limulunga, Feb. 1974; Nasiwayo, May 1974 and from a musicologist working in Senanga whose own observations confirmed the essentials of the other sources, Aug. 1977.

6 E.g. case recorded by F. Coillard, *Journal intime*, DEFAP, Paris, 25 *août* 1892, Lealui; Gluckman, *JPB*, 'The case of the violent councillor', pp. 83–90.

7 D. Livingstone, *Vocabularies of eight East African languages*, xiii, L255, Acc. No. 34105, SOAS, p. 12A; C. Harding, *Far bugles* (London, 1933), writing of 1900, p. 106.

8 A. de Serpa Pinto, *How I crossed Africa from the Atlantic to the Indian Ocean*, trans. A. Elwes, 2 vols. (London, 1881), vol. ii, p. 36, writing of 1878; *mafi* gave Coillard indigestion, *Journal intime*, 4 *janv*. 1885; Stevenson-Hamilton, *The Barotseland journal*, 3 Sept. 1899: 'The national sour milk', p. 207; Luck, *A visit to Lewanika*, p. 43.

9 Livingstone, *Private journals*, p. 210 lists relish foods.

10 C. Coillard, *Journal*, DEFAP, Paris, 11 Aug. 1878.

11 Cf. E. Holub, *Seven years in South Africa*, vol. ii (London, 1881), pp. 307, 309; Luck, *A visit to Lewanika*, p. 43.

12 F. Coillard, 'Notes pour conférence à la Faculté de Théologie', 16 *déc* 1896, DEFAP, Paris.

13 Coillard liked *ilia* greatly (as do I also). *Journal intime*, 25 *mars* 1886.

14 Own observation; A. Bertrand, *The kingdom of the Barotsi of Upper Zambezia*, trans. A. B. Miall (London, 1899), pp. 90, 103–4; J. H. Venning, 'Notes on native diets', Lealui (1908) G31/4, HMC/LM; Holub, *Seven years*, p. 309.

15 Information at Sefula, Jan. 1974; Sibukali, Aug. 1974; Katongo (near Mongu), Sept. 1974; Sefula, Sept. 1977. Lists of introduced fruits and vegetables, A. Jalla, *Notes privées*, privately held, p. 50.

16 This change of emphasis from the received description is discussed more fully in Section 4 below; Serpa Pinto, *How I crossed Africa*, p. 35.

17 D. W. Stirke, *Barotseland: eight years among the Barotse* (London, 1922), p. 72.

18 Holub, *Seven years*, p. 313. The distinction in decision making is now quite blurred. The cultivator decides in a fragmented economy.

19 Information at Sabelele village, Kataba, 15 June 1973.

20 The fine was one beast; *Litunga* Mwanawina III to Provincial Commissioner G. S. Jones, 30 Dec. 1950; meeting at Kataba, 14 Dec. 1950, verbatim notes by DC J. Blunden. File 5/7/4 'Kataba Project, Development', Mongu Boma.

21 Use of *makolo*: at Sefula, 25 Feb. 1977; Jalla, *Notes privées*, p. 110; M. Sahlins, *Stone Age economics* (London, 1972), Ch. 2; a comparable mobilisation is described by R. Szereszewski to explain Ghana's cocoa take-off: 100,000 man-days in 1891 to 37 million in 1911 (*Structural changes in the economy of Ghana, 1891–1911* (London, 1965), p. 75).

22 Information at: Sefula, 25 July 1977; Sefula, 24 Feb. 1977; Sioma, 25 May 1977; Mabumbu, 11 Aug. 1977. The observation about the bottleneck is based on watching three seasons through in the area around Sefula. An example of a seasonal bottleneck is given in J. Tosh, 'Lango agriculture during the early colonial period: land and labour in a cash-crop economy', *Journal of African History* XIX, 3(1978), 415–39; Gluckman spelt *namukau* as *namakao* ('a person who owns many hoes', from Luyana *likao* – a hoe), e.g. *IBJ*, p. 82.

23 First explained to me by an old lady near Sefula, Feb. 1974; subsequently confirmed by women throughout the country. Clay pot cooking described by E. Holub, *A Cultural survey of the Lozi–Mbunda kingdom in south central Africa* (Vienna, 1879), trans. Dr L. Holy (typescr.), p. 26. On possible patterns of climatic change, see H. H. Lamb, 'Climate in the 1960s', *Geographical Journal* CXXXII, 2 (June 1966), 183–212; S. E. Nicholson, 'The methodology of climate reconstruction and its application to Africa', *Journal of African History* XX, 1 (1979), 31–49.

24 Information at Nasiwayo, 9 March 1974. This informant dated ploughs becoming common in Senanga District to 1932. The 1934 DC's report recorded hire charges of 10s. an acre, ZA/7/1/17/5 (NAZ).

25 Livingstone, *Private journals*, 19 July 1853, p. 191.

26 *Ibid.*, 15 Aug. 1853, p. 210; *idem, Missionary travels and researches in South Africa* (London, 1857), p. 215.

27 Livingstone, *Missionary travels*, pp. 495, 498.

28 Livingstone, *Private journals*, p. 210.

29 W. Waddell, *Diary*, WA/1/1/1–5, HMC (NAZim), 25 July 1887.

30 E. Jacottet, *Études sur les langues du Haut Zambèze*, 3 vols. (Paris, 1896–1901), vol. III, p. 119; information in Kataba Valley, Lipaa village, May 1973; Livingstone, *Vocabularies*, p. 12A; *idem, Private journals*, p. 316; Holub, *Seven years*, p. 304; Bertrand, *The kingdom of the Barotsi*, p. 103, and *idem*, 'From the Machili to Lialui', p. 146; '*Lukonga siwa ku mbuto wa mashaka*', Y. W. Mupatu, *Bulozi sapili* (Oxford, 1959), p. 4.

31 Information at Mabumbu, 3 Aug. 1977; Livingstone, *Private journals*, p. 210. This disagrees with M. P. Miracle, *Maize in tropical Africa* (Madison, 1966), p. 157.

32 F. Coillard, lecture to an unidentified audience, draft notes, 23 *fév.* 1898, DEFAP, Paris.

33 W. O. Jones, *Manioc in Africa* (Stanford, 1959), pp. 65–7.

34 Gluckman, *ECBP*, Chart 2, after p. 132. I will describe the twentieth-century agricultural history of Bulozi in future work. The present-day (1970s) spectrum of crops is also described in a forthcoming local study by N. Eijkelhof. I am indebted to R. Billington for discussion on this point.

35 Waddell, *Diary*, 28 Jan. 1886. W. G. Clarence-Smith, 'Climatic variations and natural disasters in Barotseland, 1847–1907', University of Zambia seminar paper (1977), where Tables I and II show this to have been a year of moderately high flood and of few other 'disasters'. If that was so, the planting described here was late, even given that Sesheke is usually four to six weeks behind the season in the plain. It should probably be attributed to the disruptive effect of the political unrest of the preceding winter and spring; Coillard, *Journal intime*, 24 *janv.* 1886.

36 Clarence-Smith, 'Climatic variations', p. 6.

37 M. Mainga, *Bulozi under the Luyana kings* (London, 1973), p. 195; a seminal work for this approach was C. van Onselen, 'Reactions to rinderpest in Southern Africa, 1896–7', *Journal of African History* XIII, 3(1972), 473–88, whose influence is to be seen in several contributions to R. Palmer and N. Parsons (eds.), *The roots of rural poverty in central and southern Africa* (London, 1977).

38 Coillard to Mssrs Jamieson and Co., Seedsmen, 10 Nov. 1886, Sefula (a loose letter found tucked into a volume of Coillard's journal), DEFAP, Paris.

39 See Ch. 9 below for the fuller significance of this conflict within the Mission; Goy *à* Boegner, 10 *fév.* 1888, Coillard *à* Jeanmairet *et* Jalla, 2 *nov.* 1888, Sefula, *Lettres à la direction*, DEFAP, Paris. Information from the family of the first market-gardeners, Namboata, 18 Feb. 1977; Jalla, *Notes privées*, p. 50.

40 C. Coillard, *Journal*, 1877–9, 1886 (parts), 1889, DEFAP, Paris, and CO5/1/1, NAZim.

41 *Ibid.*, 3 Aug. 1886; 8 Aug. 1886.

42 Coillard, *Journal intime*, 26–30 *mai* 1892 (boycott of Lwatile station), 24 *nov*. 1892 (another boycott).

43 Information from Mlle G. Jalla, 22 Aug. 1977. The incident she remembered occurred on 5 January 1897; the seller was Chief Kalonga. Jalla, *Journal quotidien*, vol. IV of that date.

44 Jalla, *Notes privées*, p. 49; *idem, Litaba za Sichaba sa Malozi* (Oxford, 1909; 5th edn 1969), pp. 88–9; Mainga relied almost exclusively on published public mission sources intended for European readers in making her judgment. *Bulozi under the Luyana kings*, pp. 194–5, notes 95, 96. The exception was reference to *Litaba za Sichaba*, p. 87.

45 Information at Nasiwayo, Feb. 1974; Nalolo, Aug. 1977; Namboata, 10 Sept. 1977; Sioma, 25 May 1977; Sibukali, 14 Aug. 1974.

46 I discovered it when my Land Rover sank into it up to the axles and subsequently confirmed it from the aerial photographs. Rev. J-P. Burger, 'Notes on the Sefula Canal', cyclo. 21 March 1959, p. 2, in my possession; *idem*, pers. comm. 6 April 1978 recalling conversations with Matauka.

47 Information in Kataba valley, May/June 1973. A very similar story was told during a more recent area study in Ushaa, sixty miles to the north (April 1977) and also at Mwenyi to the west of the floodplain. There people explained the drop in productivity by a loss of soil fertility since their parents' time (May 1977). In fact the newly drained land in the 1890s may have been very productive in the first years of use; it is the logic of peaty soils (see further below).

48 Coillard, *Journal intime*, 24 *janv*. 1885.

49 The Coillards' body servant Andrease Mwanangombe (literally 'son of a cow') was the son of an Ila father and Toka mother near Kazungula. He was a slave presented to Coillard to be his servant. In 1888 he first spoke to his employer about conversion and in 1890 became the first baptised Lozi convert. He became the Coillards' Lozi son. However, he lapsed in his conduct in 1891, became apostate in 1892 and went to serve Lewanika as a steward. Eventually he was made headman of the strategic border village of Imusho near Sesheke. (Sources: Coillard, *Journal intime*; Jalla, *Notes privées*, p. 103.)

50 Burger, 'Notes on the Sefula Canal' recording the testimony of Kanoti Nalumango of Nakonga village. He stated that transport was an important objective of the work; Goy *à* Boegner, 10 *fév*. 1888, *Lettres à la direction*.

51 Coillard à Boegner, *nov*. 1887, *Lettres à la direction*.

52 Others have continued the assumption, e.g. G. L. Caplan, *The elites of Barotseland, 1878–1969* (London, 1970), pp. 62, 89 despite discussion at p. 235.

53 Coillard, *Journal intime, vendredi soir, 6 janv*. 1888. My emphasis.

54 Goy *à* Boegner, 10 *fév*. 1888: 'It is not possible either through patience or any other virtue to live in peace with her', *Lettres à la direction*. See Ch. 9 below.

55 Goy met Lewanika returning with 'uncountable herds' between the Lui and Lumbe rivers as the missionary was on his way south. Goy *à* Boegner, Sesheke, 13 *août*, 1888, *Lettres à la direction*; *Nalikwanda*: Coillard, *Journal*

intime, Lealui, 13*av*. 1889; Burger recalling testimony of A. Jalla, 'Notes on the Sefula Canal', p. 2.

56 Coillard, *Journal intime*, 20 May (*sic*) 1889; Coillard *à* Boegner, Sesheke, *août* 1889, *Lettres à la direction*.

57 C. Coillard, *Journal*, 14 July 1889.

58 Coillard *à* Boegner (*Privée*), Sefula, 8 *av*. 1890, *Lettres à la direction*.

59 Waddell, *Diary*, 15 May 1892. I preserve his spellings.

60 Oral sources of course cannot provide the chronological precision we require here. Mupatu, *Bulozi sapili*, p. 52 suggested that work on the trunk canal complex began in the 1889 dry season, as did Jalla in *Litaba za Sichaba*, pp. 88–9. This may be true of small experimental digging, but contemporary writing, including Jalla's own notes of that time, indicate that major construction began in 1890. The most definite indication is that the big Lealui canal was begun with 500 labourers in October (Jalla, *Notes privées*, p. 91).

Coillard (*Journal intime, dimanche 9 nov*. 1890) recorded his first visit to the capital since he was there for the Lochner negotiations in June (see Chapter 9 below). Works had been done 'since we have been to the capital', but their location is not immediately obvious. However, Waddell's retrospective passage of 1892 clearly stated that 'the rute of their canal was peged out from the river to the capital *and thence* [my emphasis] far into the hills'. Now Coillard's November 1890 description cannot apply to the Namitome canal (see below) because there are no lakes there of the type he describes. However, it fits the Sikalongo section, Waddell's description and also that of another eye-witness. James Johnston visited in December 1891 and also made clear that the waterway he saw was cut to the river first: 'Lealui is situated about five miles from the river. . . [the waterway was cut] *not only* [my emphasis] to the capital, but extending northwards' (J. Johnston, *Reality versus romance in south central Africa* (London, 1893; 1969), p. 178. *Contract 70/5* (1:30,000, Mongu District, GRZ), the 1970 Air Survey, Run 5, Frames 110, 111, 112 reveal the construction of the Sikalongo canal and the lake tapped. Recall that 1888–92 were exceptionally dry years with low floods which would have the two edged effect of impeding water-flow but at the same time making canal digging easier than normal.

61 Coillard, *Journal intime, 9 déc*. 1890; cf. his public eulogising of this diligent and prayerful workband, *Sur le Haut Zambèze: voyages et travaux de Mission* (Paris, 1898), p. 330.

62 Coillard, *Journal intime*, 27 *mars* 1891; *idem, Sur le Haut Zambèze*, p. 365.

63 Coillard, *Journal intime*, 1 *av*. 1891; Coillard *à* Boegner (*Privée*), 10 *av*. 1891, *Lettres à la direction*; Waddell, *Diary*, 7 July 1890.

64 Coillard, *Journal intime*, 22 *mai* 1891, *à* Sana; *ibid.*, 15 *juin* 1891.

65 Johnston, *Reality versus romance*, p. 178.

66 This may be deduced thus: in May 1892 Waddell described the Mwayowamo: 'it receives its supply of water from various small lakes and marches the latter *will now be drained* [my emphasis] and made into mealy fields' (*Diary*, 15 May 1892). By October 1893 at the end of the next season that work had substantially been done: 'Today, not only has the canal put the

264

capital in communication with the river, but it has been extended draining marshes *which are become* [my emphasis] fertile fields', Coillard, *Sur le Haut Zambèze*, 13 *oct*. 1893, p. 461. On his trip to visit the Luvale in June 1895, reference is made to continuing work on the Mwayowamo/Namitome system, *ibid*., p. 541.

67 Coillard, *Sur le Haut Zambèze*, 2 *mai* 1894, p. 487; Plate xxxv shows the 1894 flood at Lwatile. This may be confirmed retrospectively from the testimony of a colonial officer involved in the post Second World War canal programme. He writes: 'There was in my time . . . a large water furrow that ran at least from Mabumbu to the foot of Mongu hill . . . The furrow was large enough for canoes. . . . My point is that the line was known and it had only to be enlarged [to make the post-war Musiamo (North) canal].' Pers. comm., 2 May 1978.

68 Information at several villages in Ndanda on several visits; at Nangula, 10 Aug. 1977; at Nasiwayo, May 1974; at Luandui, April 1975; at Imalyo, Jan. 1975; Coillard, *Journal intime*, 20 *sept*. 1893; information at Limulunga, May 1974.

69 Burger, 'Notes on the Sefula Canal', p.2; information at Ndoka, May 1977; contract 70/5, Run 5, Frame 125; information at Lukona, May 1977; 'Kalabo rural development', File RUR/3T/2/3/KAL (Mongu Boma), Tour report 5/51; DC Kalabo to DC Mongu, 29 Feb. 1956 (Mongu Boma).

70 Johnston, *Reality versus romance*, p. 178; Coillard, *Journal intime*, 9 *nov*. 1890; Waddell, *Diary*, 15 May 1892.

71 Waddell, *Diary* 15 May 1892. See Ch. 9 below for the full importance of the Mwanangombe episode; Coillard, *Journal intime*, 24 *fév*. 1892.

72 Details of Fig. 11: base map: Lealui SD–34–16, GRZ 1:250,000 Series (Lusaka, 1966); other sources: Mongu District map (1954) by C. G. C. Rawlins, G. R. C. Merry and D. Freeman-Greene; Northern Rhodesia Government, *Gazetteer of geographical names in the Barotseland Protectorate* (Lusaka, 1959). Lealui area: own oblique angle photographs and air reconnaissance, October 1974 (rising flood); informants at Mombo, Namitome, Limulunga, Ikabako, Mabumbu, Kande, Lealui, Malengwa, Mweke, Katongo, Namaenya, Sefula, Nomai, Namushakende (1973–7) and own observations in these places; 'Sishanjo crops and food', File 3/4/4/vol. ɪ (Mongu Boma): Meeting of 15 Aug. 1950; Canal Induna M. J. Mayungu's Report, 5 July 1950; 'Water development and irrigation: general', 38/1/vol. ɪ (Mongu Boma); J. G. Lawrence, 'Miscellaneous notes', Mss Afr. s.1180, f.160–2 (1956 Canal report with mileages) Rhodes House, Oxford).

73 Mupatu, *Bulozi sapili*, p. 52: '*Ya sa tapi mwa teñi h'a na ku fela masila*'.

74 Cf. Y. W. Mupatu, *An autobiography*, ed. G. Prins, Zambia Past and Present Series 4(Lusaka, forthcoming), on how his father, a *libuto* (bodyguard) of Lewanika's was given such a village, Sifulelwa. Coillard, *Journal intime*, 22 *fév*. 1904, mentions that all the women of Lealui are away in the fields, 'that is to say, Namitome'.

75 On the effect of smallpox brought by the soldiers who raided the Luvale in 1892 in reducing the labour available in the 1892–3 planting season, see

Waddell, *Diary*, Nov. 1892 and Coillard, *Journal intime, août* 1892. For a dramatic example of the catastrophe interpretation of the 1890s, see H. Kjekshus, *Ecology control and economic development in East African history: the case of Tanganyika, 1850–1950* (London, 1977) and the review of this work by J. Iliffe in *Journal of African History* XIX, 1 (1978), 139–141.

76 For example, a recent article is fundamentally vitiated from the title onwards by, among other things, an inability to define basic concepts with any defensible claim to relevance in the Lozi context. W. G. Clarence-Smith, 'Slaves, commoners, and landlords in Bulozi c.1875 to 1906', *Journal of African History* XX (1979), 219–34.

77 B. Hindess and P. Q. Hirst, *Pre-capitalist modes of production* (London, 1975), p. 127; E. D. Genovese, *Roll, Jordan, roll: the world the slaves made* (New York, 1976), esp. on paternalism, pp. 3–112.

78 D. A. Strickland, 'Kingship and slavery in African thought: a conceptual analysis', *Comparative Studies in Society and History* XVIII, 3 (July 1976), 371–94, p. 383; M. I. Finley, 'Slavery', *International encyclopedia of the social sciences*, 17 vols. (London/New York, 1968), vol. XIV, p. 307.

79 These passages are from *Notes privées*, p. 109; they were the basis for the last two paragraphs of A. Jalla, *Pionniers parmi les Marotse* (Florence, 1903), p. 223. There he edited his prose to sharpen the line of continuity in the description.

80 F. Worthington (retrospective, n.d.) in 'Notes and documents, 1900–1936', KDE 2/44 (NAZ); A. Jalla, 'Rapport de station de Lealui, 1905', 9265, M/73/25, HMC/LM.

81 Coillard used the term 'Lefunga' for all sorts of enslavement. He represented it in early references as 'the royal press-gang' (*Journal intime*, 11 and 15 *juin* 1891).

82 Witnessed at *coliso* of Ilute Yeta IV, 8 April 1977; *maloko* at Mwenyi, Kalabo, 19 May 1977; also Limulunga, Jan. 1975.

83 *Lya ulwa ñete li iba ndambo.*

84 On language, Mupatu, Limulunga, Sept. 1977; Finley, 'Slavery', p. 308.

85 Information at Namboata, 10 Sept. 1977. The wife's testimony is corroborated by Luck's observation in 1902; 'Women at work all day supervised by the Queen's police armed with sjamboks . . . most of these police were dressed in old military greatcoats or tunics', *A visit to Lewanika*, pp. 56–7. Further, in P. A. T. Simey (NC Nalolo) to Resident Magistrate Hall, 15 Dec. 1920, BS3/166 (NAZ). There he quoted the verbatim testimony of a woman Namangolwa, describing the year's cycle of work for the *Mulena*. Induna Sitondo told him that there were 300–400 such women. The fields they worked, now abandoned, can be seen near Nañula village, across the Zambezi from Nalolo.

86 This observation is made from villages near Sefula, near Nalolo and near Mombo.

87 P. Hill, 'From slavery to freedom: the case of farm slavery in Nigerian Hausaland', *Comparative Studies in Society and History* XVIII, 3 (July 1976),

395–426, p. 398. See also *idem, Population, poverty and prosperity. Rural Kano 1900 and 1970* (Cambridge, 1977).

88 Information at Namboata, 10 Sept. 1977; near Sefula, Jan. 1974; *Mubika ni likumba ka li fula ba meyi li oloka;* i.e. his own will becomes malleable when exposed to his master's. T. Givón, *The Siluyana language*, University of Zambia Communication 6 (mimeo), (Lusaka, 1970), also gives a version of this proverb (no. 83, p. 105) where he translates *ku oloka* as 'straighten', thus completely changing the meaning. I checked my interpretation with Induna Mupatu, who was also Givón's informant, and he supported the sense used here.

89 Jalla, *Pionniers*, p. 224.

90 Coillard, *Journal intime*, 7 *sept.* 1885 (visit to Andrease's parents); 10 *juin* 1892 (Ila origin of Nyondo). More detail appears in Ch. 9.

91 *Buñ'a* is sensitively analysed by Gluckman, *IBJ*, Ch. 5; A. Jalla, *English–Lozi dictionary* (typescr.) (1936–9), p. 381, privately held. Interpretation corroborated, Sefula, 25 July 1977. Note, however, that *buñ'a* as an abstract noun is not colloquially used in Bulozi.

92 F. Worthington, 'Notes and documents, 1900–1936'.

93 F. Worthington, 'Memorandum on slavery', 26 March 1913, BS3/166 (NAZ) (benignity); Jalla, *Pionniers*, p. 224 and *idem*, 'Rapport de station de Lealui' (horror).

94 Quoted in Selborne to Sec. State, 11 Nov. 1907, No. 186 in CO 879/95/872, p. 3 (PRO).

95 Case 21/1927, 26 April 1926, Rex v. Kapata, KDE 3/2/1/21 (NAZ).

96 Information at Namboata, 10 Sept. 1977.

97 This statement may be amply buttressed from the instances of 'heart failure' or 'disappearance' of defendants and witnesses in cases which entered Government courts by accident, e.g. due to an over-zealous policeman.

98 This is close to Strickland's point about the hierarchy of kingship, 'Kingship and slavery in African thought', p. 375.

99 Clarence-Smith, 'Slaves, commoners and landlords', p. 227.

100 E. Le Roy Ladurie, *Montaillou: Cathars and Catholics in a French village, 1294–1324*, trans. Barbara Bray (London, 1978), pp. 60, 77–102.

101 E. Evans-Pritchard, *The Nuer* (Oxford, 1940), p. 16; cf. Gluckman, *ECBP*, pp. 20–1.

102 Livingstone, *Private journals*, Libonta, 21 Aug. 1853, p. 213; F. Coillard, 'Memorandum aux jeunes lecteurs des "Petits Messages du Mission"', Sesheke, 27 *sept.* 1885, *Lettres à la direction*; cf. Holub, *Cultural survey*, p. 118.

103 Gluckman, *ECBP*, p. 18.

104 Re crocodile hunting: Docs. 383 (23/7/59) and 457 (18/3/64) in 'Correspondence about Crocodiles', File GAME/12/2/A, Mongu Boma; Report by Chief Fisheries Research Officer (1961); J. J. Soulsby, 'Tour of the Upper Zambezi fishery' (May 1962), p. 2; FAO Fishery Investigation, D. Kelly to M. A. E. Mortimer (Chief Fishery Officer), 15 Oct. 1966. All in File 'FISH/6', Mongu Boma.

105 Waddell, *Diary*, 27 Oct. 1885; 28 Jan. 1886; 15 Feb. 1886; 6 Jan. 1889; Jalla, *Notes privées*, p. 92.

106 The names of the most important nets, fishing verbs and the parts of the fish (scales, fin, etc.) are also largely Luyana words. The best description of fishing practice is Gluckman, *ECBP*, pp. 52–66. Cases involving fish dams illustrating appeal to folk memory: Case 105/1925 Masheke v. Mukumbuta, NC and Assistant Magistrate's Court, Criminal Cases, Nalolo, KSR/1/3 (NAZ); Gluckman, *JPB*, pp. 178–87 (1940s).

107 　　　　'Fish! Fish! What animal ate my child?
　　　　An animal with a noisy tail! Fish, Fish, with a noisy tail!
　　　　What animal with a noisy tail shall I eat today?'
　　　Jacottet, *Études*, vol. III, p. 189.

108 *Njinji lu kulela mu siko ku mana, ku kula, ku ta mu ngambii*: 'Bream grow large in the lagoon and when they are big return to the river.' The proverb is allegorical in intent.

109 *Mbumu a tanga Sanya, na mano kolwe minwe*: 'When the chief has hunted [lit: danced] at Sanya he has full power'; see Chapter 7, Section 2 below for further analysis of installation sequence. Information at Limulunga, 1 Aug. 1977. Hunts: Coillard, *Journal intime*, 24 *oct.* 1886; Coillard *à* Boegner, 25 *mai* 1887, *Lettres à la direction;* Coillard, *Journal intime*, 1–18 *mai* 1891, Lewanika on a long hunt; Jalla, *Notes privées*, p. 93; *idem, Pionniers*, p. 174, again, a major royal hunt in March 1896.

110 Livingstone, *Missionary travels*, pp. 191–2.

111 D. E. Faulkner and H. Epstein, *The indigenous cattle of the British dependent territories in Africa* (London, 1957), pp. xvi, 63–5, 68, Plates 60–4; J. Chapman, *Travels in the interior of South Africa, 1849–1863*, 2 vols. (Cape Town, 1971), vol. II, p. 179.

112 Coillard, *Photograph album*; see Chapter 5, Section 4 below for more on Ila cattle.

113 Faulkner and Epstein, *Indigenous cattle*, pp. 148–52; J. Ford, *The role of the Trypanosomiases in African ecology* (Oxford, 1971), pp. 475–6, 481–4, 486–7.

114 Chapman, *Travels*, vol. I, Sunday 28 Aug. 1853, p. 114.

115 Livingstone, *Missionary travels*, p. 215.

116 Serpa Pinto, *How I crossed Africa*, vol. II, p. 35.

117 F. S. Arnot, *Garanganze or seven years pioneer missionary work in central Africa* (London, 1889; repr. 1969), p. 65; Coillard, *Journal intime*, 21 *janv.* 1885; A. Baldwin, to his mother, 2 Oct. 1890 (MMS).

118 Johnston, *Reality versus romance* 2 Dec. 1891, p. 137; Bertrand, *The kingdom of the Barotsi*, p. 106; Sesheke DNB, privately held, p. 122; A. Goy *au pasteur* Ch. Schroeder, Sesheke, 30 *oct.* 1895, *Lettres à la direction*, DEFAP, Paris.

119 Coillard, *Sur le Haut Zambèze*, 25 *janv.* 1888, p. 262; *idem, On the threshold of Central Africa: a record of twenty years pioneering among the Barotsi of the upper Zambezi* (London, 1897; repr. 1971), pp. 297–8. Original: Coillard *à* Boegner, 26 *janv.* 1888, *Lettres à la direction*, DEFAP, Paris.

120 On the nature of the readership, see Coillard's comments to Boegner throughout their private correspondence on who has written, for example, to complain of not receiving their copies of the *Journal des Missions* and also descriptions of the Mission's supporters groups ('Zambezias'), e.g. *Journal Suisse*, 12 *av*. 1897, DEFAP, Paris; quotation, letter 16 *fév*. 1888, *Sur le Haut Zambèze*, p. 269; cf. Coillard, *Journal intime*, 20 *sept*. 1884; cf. Gluckman, *ECBP*, 'Lozi were not a real cattle-people. . .', 'one told me that it was the Kololo who taught Lozi to value cattle properly' (p. 20). J. Lutke-Entrup, *Limitations and possibilities of increasing market production of peasant African cattle holders in western Province, Zambia*, IAS Communication 7 (Lusaka, 1971), pp. 10, 36–7.

121 M. Herskovits, 'The cattle complex of East Africa', *American Anthropologist* XXVIII 28 (1926), 230–72, 361–88, 494–528 and 633–64; *idem*, 'The culture areas of Africa' *Africa* III, 1 (1930), 59–77.

122 P. T. W. Baxter in T. Monod, *Pastoralism in tropical Africa*. (Oxford, 1975), pp. 206–7; A. H. Jacobs, 'African pastoralists: some general remarks', *Anthropology Quarterly* XXXVIII (1965), 146–9; both cited by R. Waller, 'Change and variation in the pastoral economy: the Maasai of Kenya' (typescr.), p. 1.

123 I borrow the distinction from E. P. Thompson, 'The moral economy of the English crowd in the eighteenth century', *Past and Present,* I (Feb. 1971), 76–136; see further Chapter 5 Section 1 below.

124 Cf. R. J. Fielder, 'The role of cattle in the Ila economy', *African Social Research* XV (June 1973), 327–61. The post-rinderpest cattle sale boom of the 1900s will be described in future work.

125 A loose paraphrase of the praise-saying. Collected at Mwenyi, 19 May 1977.

126 Coillard, *Journal intime*, 3 *nov*. 1893; Jalla, *Litaba za Sichaba*, p. 8; Gluckman, *ECBP*, p. 21.

127 The association of well-being is reflected in part of a healing cult song, from the Kwangwa:

> Chorus: Liombekalala!
> *Ñaka*: Lick!
> Chorus: Liombekalala, bring my child!
> *Ñaka*: Lick her today!

Siyaya session, 29–30 April 1977; see Chapter 7, Section 4 below.

128 Coillard, 'Conférence à la Faculté de Théologie', 16 *déc*. 1896.

129 See Chapter 6, Section 3 below; information from royal grave keepers, dry season 1977.

130 Information at Limulunga, 25 Aug. 1977. Notice that the sacrifice for fertility and good harvest involves elements of *buhobe* and *busunso*.

131 Re Lewanika's funeral, see Chapter 6, Section 3 below; Waddell, *Diary*, 31 Oct. 1891.

132 Coillard, 'Conférence à la Faculté de Théologie', 16 *dec*. 1896.

133 *Ngombe fungwa*: both parts Luyana, meaning literally 'cattle are tied'. Observed by Livingstone, *Private journals*, Thursday 14 July 1853, p. 189.

The operation of the system is confirmed from observation, aerial reconnaissance and examination of aerial photographs.

134 Taken from the explanation of the ballad after performance by Y. W. Mupatu, August 1974. A further praise song of Yeta I, also referring to royal herds, was given by Mupatu in *Mulambwa Santulu u amuhela bo Mwene* (London, 1958), p. 2, part of which is cited by Mainga, *Bulozi under the Luyana kings*, p. 38.

135 Names from several sources. Interpretations at Limulunga, 11 Aug. 1977 from three informants.

136 On *Imutongo* and *Isikeme*, Mupatu, *Autobiography*; idem, *Bulozi sapili*, p. 49; brands, tribute information, at Sikongo, 16 May 1977; other informants at Shekela, Kaunga, May 1974; Siloana Plains, Oct. 1973; Sibukali, Sioma, Aug. 1974. See above, Chapter 3, Section 1.

137 Westbeech to Arnot, 5 Oct. 1882, in Arnot, *Garenganze*, p. 62.

138 A. Goy à Boegner, Sesheke, 13 *août* 1888, *Lettres à la direction*.

139 Waddell, *Diary*, 10 July 1892.

140 I owe this information to papers given at the 1978 ASA conference in Baltimore by Drs Rowe and Carlson. It differs from the view given in van Onselen, 'Reactions to rinderpest', p. 473.

141 Seen by Sharpe. Van Onselen, 'Reactions to rinderpest', p. 473 gives Lugard as his Northern Rhodesian source. I am indebted to Andrew Roberts for pointing out this error to me.

142 L. H. Gann, *The birth of a plural society: the development of Northern Rhodesia under the British South Africa Company, 1894–1914* (Manchester, 1958), p. 152; van Onselen, 'Reactions to rinderpest', p. 484, n. 72.

143 M. Goy, *Dans les solitudes de l'Afrique* (Geneva, 1901).

144 *Ibid.*, p. 48; Confirmed by Jalla's daily diary. It shows that travellers brought news, confirmed by letter shortly afterwards, of the 'extermination of cattle in Seseheke', *Journal quotidien*, 11 *fév* 1896; 28 *fév* 1896.

145 Goy, *Dans les solitudes de l'Afrique*, p. 50.

146 *Ibid.*, pp. 63–4.

147 Major H. Goold Adams to Lord Rosmead, 21 Oct. 1896, Enc. 2 in No. 38, FO 403/6968, p. 56 (PRO); van Onselen, 'Reactions to rinderpest', p. 473.

148 She left Seseheke on 15 December 1896; Coillard, *Sur le Haut Zambèze*, p. 335n.

149 Seseheke DNB, p. 122 (privately held).

150 A. Goy à Ch. Schroeder, Seseheke, 3 *juill*. 1894, *Lettres à la direction*; A. Jalla, *Tableau synchronique*, retyped and revised by J-P. Burger (privately held), p. 11; cf. Mainga, *Bulozi under the Luyana kings*, pp. 134–5.

151 Information especially in Kataba Valley, May/June 1973 and at Nasiwayo, April 1974.

152 Waddell, *Diary*, 19 Nov. 1886; Bertrand, *The kingdom of the Barotsi*, p. 106.

153 Case 21/1929, Mongu-Lealui Native Commissioner's Court, Criminal Cases, KSO/1/2/4 (NAZ).

154 *Ku funda* described in early 1900s, Mongu DNB, p. 64, KSO 3/1 (NAZ); in

early 1920s, Stirke, *Barotseland*, p. 112; oral information from many sources.

5 Distribution and exchange

1 F. Coillard, *Photograph album*, HMC/LM; E. Holub, *Seven years in South Africa*, vol. II (London, 1881), p. 303.

2 Accounts contributing to this description from: Nasiwayo, 5 March 1974; Sefula, 24 Feb. 1977; Sefula, 25 Feb. 1977; Limulunga, Aug. 1977; Tuuwa, Kalabo, 15 May 1977; observed at Shekela, May 1974; D. Livingstone, *Private journals*, ed. I. Schapera (London, 1960), p. 212 described a specific distribution of food and the pleasure a headman took in it. *Silyela* is also used as the translation of Holy Communion.

3 N. Eijkelhof, in forthcoming work about Lui Namabunga area.

4 Details at Kanyau, Siloana, Oct. 1973; information at Livingstone, 23 Feb. 1975; cf. P. M. Ngonda, 'The system of cattle ownership and the cattle industry in Barotseland', privately held (typescr.), p. 4; information at Livingstone, 23 Feb. 1975; D. C. Hazell, 'Notes on native diet', G31/4 HMC/LM; Holub, *Seven years*, p. 307; *idem, A cultural survey of the Lozi– Mbunda kingdom in South Central Africa* (Vienna, 1879), trans. Dr L. Holy (typescr.), p. 26; C. Coillard, *Journal*, DEFAP, Paris, 11 Aug. 1878; F. Coillard, *Journal intime*, DEFAP, Paris, 2 *juin* 1890.

5 In Chapter 1 I introduced the idea of a 'moral economy' in as much detail as is appropriate for a book of this sort, so here is not the place to enter into a lengthy defence of the utility of the concept for studies of basically non-scientific societies. It is done with great eloquence by J. C. Scott, *The moral economy of the peasant* (New Haven, 1976). The first chapter is especially relevant. It includes an example of what I shall argue in later work is precisely the Lozi relationship to the market: Moerman's study of the Thai village, Ban Ping. It shows how the villagers had one field– the Great Field – where they grew 'eating rice', which was of a glutinous variety. They used traditional techniques which involved intensive labour but had a low risk of absolute crop failure. However, in another field – the Thunglor field – when the subsistence needs of everyone in the village had been met, they grew 'selling rice' which was of a variety that the villagers would not think of eating themselves. Modern technology and paid labour was used for a less stable form of agriculture which, if it did not fail, was much more financially profitable than growing 'eating rice'. But the villagers always grew their 'eating rice' first. M. Moerman, *Agricultural change and peasant choice in a Thai village* (California, 1968), cited by Scott, *Moral economy of the peasant*, p. 23.

6 These thoughts are sharpened by contact with those of B. Hindess and P. Q. Hirst, *Pre-capitalist modes of production* (London, 1975), pp. 24–8; but also cf. R. C. C. Law, 'In search of a Marxist perspective on precolonial tropical Africa', *Journal of African History* XIX, 3 (1978), 441–52. See also Gluckman, *ELLRP*, pp. 34–7; *idem, IBJ*, p. 141. The involvement of the unseen

powers in questions of subsistence at times of dearth was illustrated by the ceremony of *sombo* executed at Nakaywe by the priest guardian Ilinangana. See pp. 81 and 127; E. P. Thompson, *The poverty of theory and other essays* (London, 1978).

7 At Mabumbu, 11 Aug. 1977.

8 Clarence-Smith, 'The Lozi social formation, 1875–1906', University of Zambia seminar paper (1977); Gluckman, *IBJ*, pp. 154–5, describes the division of tribute goods in the capital, but with some differences of detail and nomenclature. Dr Clarence-Smith has subsequently had second thoughts, qualifying, but not making more usefully precise, his use of the notion of private ownership. W. G. Clarence-Smith, 'Slaves, commoners and landlords in Bulozi, c. 1875 to 1906', *Journal of African History* xx (1979), 220–1.

9 Re Royal distributions, Gluckman, *ELLRP*, pp. 85–92; re hippo meat tribute, E. Holub, 'A journey through central South Africa from the diamond fields to the Upper Zambezi', *Proceedings of the Royal Geographical Society* iii (1880), 166–82, p. 175; A. St H. Gibbons (referring to 1895), 'A journey into the Marotse and Mashikolumbwe countries', *Geographical Journal* ix (Feb. 1897), 121–45, p. 128; Gluckman, *ELLRP*, p. 42.

10 Y. W. Mupatu, *An autobiography*, ed. G. Prins, Zambia Past and Present Series 4 (Lusaka, forthcoming); A. Jalla, *Journal quotidien*, privately held, vol. viii, 29 *nov.* 1905 described an 'abundant distribution of food in the Kuta square (21 flayed oxen)' following the king's return from a journey.

11 At Sioma, 25 May 1977.

12 Cf. W. MacGaffey, *Custom and government in the lower Congo* (California, 1970), p. 302.

13 Coillard, *Journal intime*, 12 *août* 1893, re Litia's baby daughter; information at Ushaa, 18 April 1977; Sefula, 9 May 1974; A. Jalla, *Pionniers parmi les Marotse* (Florence, 1903), p. 334; O. F. Raum, *Chaga childhood* (Oxford, 1940; repr. 1967), p. 228.

14 *Mwanuke ni ka yunyi, ku mona mukulu ku ituka*; Jalla, *Pionniers*, p. 335; *idem, Notes privées*, privately held, p. 116. A similar situation described and its behavioural implications discussed in M. J. Field, *Search for security: an ethno-psychiatric study of rural Ghana* (London, 1960), pp. 28–9.

15 Information at Sefula, 5 Aug. 1974.

16   *Litimbwalume ka meme mulepu a akulu ku muyakamena.*
     Ku kandula mukulu ni koto kono ingaluko.
     Ikanwa mei ba ndambo, matunga onje ni afubalume.

17 F. Fanon, *The wretched of the earth* (London, 1965; repr. 1968), p. 43; Holub, *Cultural survey*, pp. 21–2; (quotation) Coillard *à* Boegner, 4 *mai* 1886, *Lettres à la direction*, DEFAP Paris.

18 Jalla, *Notes privées*, p. 137; Barotse Courts, Criminal Cases 1906 onwards, KDE 3/2/1 (NAZ). The contrast is equally forceful today. I suspect that it may be linked to the manner of socialisation. The most striking common social factor among in-patients in the Psychiatric Ward of Mongu Hospital in 1977 was rejection by the family.

19 Holub, *Seven years*, pp. 142, 226; Coillard, *Journal intime*, 5 *nov*. 1884 *à* Sesheke; at 'Ali Ka Soga Bonki' (the place where Sipopa died), C. Coillard, *Journal*, vol. II, 18 Aug. 1878; after safe passage through the Lusu rapids ('the rapids of death'), Coillard *à* Boegner, 5 *mars* 1886, *Lettres à la direction*; at Imatongo, grave of Mwanambinyi, Coillard, *Journal intime*, 2 *janv*. 1885; before Tatila Akufuna at Lealui, *ibid.*, 9 *janv*. 1885; at Lilundu, grave of Mulambwa and before Lewanika *ibid.*, 22 *mars* 1886; full description in Coillard, 'Notes pour conférence à la Faculté de Théologie', 16 *déc*. 1896, DEFAP, Paris; on Lewanika's return home from England, *idem, Journal intime*, 1 *janv*. 1903.

20 Holub, *Cultural survey*, pp. 41–2 ('*Tau Tuna*' only recorded before Sipopa); Coillard, *Journal intime* ('*Tau Tuna*' before Maibiba), 6 *janv*. 1885; ('*Tau Tuna*' and '*Yooshoo*' before Matauka), 20 *mars* 1886; *idem, Photograph album*, 'Shoelela before Matauka, 1886'; Jalla, *Pionniers*, p. 32, '*Tau e Tona*' and '*O! Sho!*', salutes when he was presented to Lewanika, 22 *mars* 1890 (cf. *idem, Journal quotidien* of even date).

21 J. Soane-Cambell, 'Reminiscences of Makwengula', Liuwa, April 1913 (typscr.) loose in KSO 3/1 (NAZ), published subsequently as 'I knew Lewanika', *Northern Rhodesia Journal* I, 1 (1950), 18–23.

22 G. Westbeech, *Trade and travel in early Barotseland*, ed. E. C. Tabler (London, 1963), August 1886, p. 73; other observations: Coillard, *Journal intime*, 22 *sept*. 1889; *idem, Photograph album*, 'Lochner with Lewanika, June 1890'; witnessed and photographed at the *coliso*, 1977.

23 Coillard, *Journal intime*, 24 *oct*. 1886, Lealui.

24 Coillard, *Journal intime*, 3 *av*. 1886; *idem*, 'Conférence à la Faculté de Théologie', 16 *déc*. 1896; *idem, Photograph album*, 'Sefula 1887' (kin greeting); J. Johnston, *Reality versus romance in south central Africa* (London, 1893; repr. 1969), p. 138; Jalla, *Notes privées*, p. 124; J. Stevenson-Hamilton, *The Barotseland journal*, ed. J. P. R. Wallis, Oppenheimer Series 7 (London, 1953), 17 June 1899, p. 169.

25 Information at Senanga, 10 May 1977.

26 Coillard, *Journal intime*, 23 *nov*. 1892.

27 Coillard, 'Conférence à la Faculté de Théologie', 16 *déc*. 1896.

28 Witnessed at the *coliso*, Lealui, 8 April 1977; information at Imwambo, 15 Sept. 1977; near Sefula, Jan. 1974; Coillard, *Journal intime*, 23 *nov*. and 22 *déc*. 1892.

29 E. Jacottet, *Études sur les langues du Haut Zambèze*, 3 vols. (Paris, 1896–1901), vol. III, p. 173; Coillard, *Journal intime, mardi* 6 *av*. 1886; *ibid.*, 3 *av*. 1886 (edited down to three sentences in *idem, Sur le Haut Zambèze: voyages et travaux de Mission* (Paris, 1898), p. 196); Jalla, *Notes privées*, p. 123; F. C. Selous, *Travel and adventure in South East Africa* (London, 1893), Sept. 1888, p. 253; Stevenson-Hamilton, *The Barotseland journal*, 8 Aug. 1899, p. 204. Women's dance observed at *ku omboka* ceremonies 1974 at Limulunga and Muoyo, *ngomalume* at *coliso* 1977, photographed and recorded.

30 M. I. Finley, *The world of Odysseus* (London, 1956), Ch. 2.

31 Coillard, *Journal intime*, 'Liaruyi', *dimanche* 11 *janv*. 1885. *Ngambela* is linguistically linked to *ñamba*; therefore at one plane there is a logical link betwen the concepts: chiefship with tribute.

32 Jalla, *Notes privées*, pp. 97–8, 102–7; Mupatu, *Autobiography*, offers a recollected but more selective account.

33 Holub, *Seven years*, pp. 238–40; Jalla, *Notes privées*, pp. 97–8; Gluckman, *AOBNA* (1940–3), p. 19.

34 Jalla, *Notes privées*, p. 96 and *idem, Pionniers*, p. 38 give the seating plan for an important assembly 24 June 1890; Coillard, 'Conférence à la Faculté de Théologie', 16 *déc*. 1896; Jalla, *Notes privées*, p. 106 and *idem, Pionniers*, p. 333 list the hierarchy of title names as it was in the late 1890s. *Notes privées*, pp. 98–9 gives some functions of stewards and councillors (see Chapter 6, Section 4 below). The *Kwandu* takes its name from the *sitino* of Ngalama, the king under whose special protection Lewanika was. His senior wife, the *Moyo*, had special responsibility for Ngalama's *sitino*.

35 Only elements of these have been collected. In particular the origin and history of the Ngambelaship is inextricably intertwined with that of the king.

36 Coillard à Boegner, 16 *fév*. 1888 (Ila raid), *Lettres à la direction*; Jalla, *Pionniers*, pp. 333–4, *idem, Notes privées*, p. 104; Y. W. Mupatu, *Bulozi sapili* (Oxford, 1959), pp. 46–8.

37 Holub, *Seven years*, p. 238; Coryndon to Selborne, 6 Dec. 1905, A1/1/2/14/15 (NAZim). Schedules in CO 879/91/802, No. 243, pp. 417–19 (PRO); Resident Magistrate MacKinnon (1907), Mongu DNB KSO 3/1 (NAZ).

38 Notably E. Holub, *Travels north of the Zambezi*, 1885–6, ed. L. Holy (Manchester, 1976); Gibbons, 'A journey into the Marotse and Mashikolumbwe countries'; Selous, *Travel and adventure*; H. Goold Adams, 'Report on Barotseland' (1897), G40, HMC/LM and elsewhere; C. Harding, 'Reports and notes on expedition to the west' (1900), KDE 2/33 (NAZ); *idem, In remotest Barotseland* (London, 1905).

39 This view is based on extensive conversations with participants in the affair, substantially confirmed in Neuchâtel, 4 Oct. 1977.

40 At Limulunga, Feb. 1975.

41 Gluckman, *AOBNA* (quotation), p. 18; *idem, ECBP*, p. 126. Impact of these views recalled at Wiveliscombe, Somerset, 15 Nov. 1976; Gluckman worked closely with Suu. His opinion of him at the time was put plainly in the caption to a photograph of Suu in a popular magazine article: 'Progressive Councillor. This is Councillor Francis L. Suu. . . one of the most powerful and progressive men of the Barotse Nation.' M. Gluckman, 'Zambezi river kingdom', *Libertas* (1945), 20–39, p. 21.

    A similar situation has been described for the ethnography of Torday among the Kuba. There Vansina was able to interview his predecessor's main informant. I was never able to interview the late *Mwanamulena* Mwendaweli Lewanika or the late ex-*Ngambela* Wina because I had not realised the value of doing so whilst they were still alive. Cf. J. Vansina, *The children of Woot, essays in Kuba history* (Madison, 1978), Ch. 4, p. 79.

42 Many people suspected him of complicity. Particularly full accounts from

participants obtained at Mutuiwambwa, 29 June 1977; Sefula, 25 Feb. 1977; Sefula, August 1974.

43 M. Mainga, *Bulozi under the Luyana kings* (London, 1973), pp. 49–51; Gluckman, *AOBNA*, p. 16.

44 The following paragraphs attempt to condense parts of J. Cobbing, 'The evolution of Ndebele amabutho', *Journal of African History* xv, 4 (1974), 607–31.

45 Holub, *Seven years*, facing p. 147; J. Walton, 'Iron gongs from the Congo and southern Rhodesia', *Man* LVI, 20 (1956), 16; J. Vansina, 'The bells of kings', *Journal of African History* x, 2 (1969), 187–97.

46 A. Jalla, *Lozi–English dictionary* (typescr.) (1936–9), p. 212.

47 Gluckman, *AOBNA*, p. 14; information at Imalyo, Jan. and May 1975 (same informant revisited and testimonies cross-checked); Sefula, 17 Feb. 1977; Ushaa, April 1977; Mainga, *Bulozi under the Luyana kings*, p. 35, also explained the origin of *makolo* in this way.

48 Information at Nangula, 10 Aug. 1977; at Sefula, 25 July 1977; at Ikabako, 10 Aug. 1977; at Sioma, 25 May 1977; at Limulunga, Aug. 1977; at Nalolo, 8 Sept. 1977; at Sikongo, 16 May 1977.

49 Information principally from: Sefula, 17 Feb. 1977; Limulunga, Aug. 1977; Mabumbu, 11 Aug. 1977; Ushaa, April 1977; Mombo, 9 Aug. 1977.

50 This list given at Limulunga, Aug. 1977.

51 Gluckman's translation of *linto za silena* is used, *ELLRP*; cf. Goold Adams, 'Report on Barotseland' (1897), p. 7.

52 J. Lutke-Entrup, *Limitations and possibilities of increasing market production of peasant African cattle holders in Western Province, Zambia*, IAS Communication 7 (Lusaka, 1971), p. 43.

53 Coillard, *Journal intime*, 9 janv. 1886, Lealui; Jalla, *Notes privées*, p. 102; field observation; Holub, 'A journey through central South Africa', p. 175; R. T. Coryndon, *Reports on the administration of Rhodesia for the information of shareholders* (1898), Rhodes House, Oxford, p. 94; R. V. Roach, 'Notes on industries', Mongu DNB, 1, p. 62, KSO 3/1 (NAZ); Coillard, *Photograph album; Annual reports*, Barotse (1907), KDE 8/1 (NAZ).

54 On grain: Holub, *Seven years*, pp. 146–7; A. Bertrand, *The kingdom of the Barotsi of Upper Zambezia*, trans. A. B. Miall (London, 1899), p. 103; *idem*, 'From the Machili to Lialui', *Geographical Journal* IX (Feb. 1897), 145–9, p. 146; recollection of Eli Susman, a trader who usually acted as Lewanika's agent, related by a relative, Livingstone, 7 March 1977.

55 Information at Nasiwayo, Jan. 1974; at Nalolo, Aug. 1977 (corroborates Mainga, *Bulozi under the Luyana kings*, p. 37); R. Luck *A visit to Lewanika, king of the Barotse* (London, 1902), p. 42; A. de Serpa Pinto, *How I crossed Africa from the Atlantic to the Indian Ocean*, trans. A. Elwes, 2 vols. (London, 1881), vol. I, p. 371; Susman relative, Livingstone, 7 March 1977.

56 Tradition related at Mabumbu, 11 Aug. 1977; at Nangula, 10 Aug. 1977; at Ikabako, 10 Aug. 1977. N. S. Ikachana wrote down two versions of the tradition in *Litaba za Makwangwa* (Lusaka, 1952); this book is widely used as a primary reader and so the stories are well known.

275

57 At Sibukali Pan, 14 Aug. 1974; Mwanawalie, Lumbe, 16 Aug. 1974; South Lumbe, 16 Aug. 1974; Coillard, *Journal intime*, 8 *sept*. 1886; Gibbons, 'Journey', p. 134, Map p. 248.

58 Coillard, *Journal intime*, 8 *sept*. 1886, corroborated, *Nouvelles du Zambèze*, 29 *mai* 1916. Filmed in 1950s 'One hoe for Kalabo' – rushes in private possession.

59 Sibukali, 14 Aug. 1974; cf. Coillard, *Journal intime*, 8 *sept*. 1886.

60 W. Waddell, *Diary*, WA/1/1/1–5 (NAZim), July 1887; *porokoto* is onomatopoeic for the tearing sound of unbleached calico. Coillard, *Journal intime*, 2 *juill*. 1888; Coillard à Boegner, 29 *juill*. 1886, *Lettres à la direction*.

61 T. Matthews has kindly confirmed from his work among the valley Tonga that they speak of obtaining iron from Bulozi.

62 Westbeech to Arnot, 5 Oct. 1882, cited by F. S. Arnot, *Garenganze or seven years pioneer missionary work in central Africa* (London, 1889; repr. 1969), p. 62; Selous, *Travel and adventure*, p. 253.

63 Coillard à Boegner (*Privée*), Sefula, 20 *juin* 1889, *Lettres à la direction*; Johnston, 'Reality versus romance', p. 175; A. Baldwin, *Journal*, 8 July 1892 (MMS); Jalla, *Journaux quotidiens*, 21 July 1896, 1 June 1897, 27 July 1897.

64 Baldwin, *Journal*, 26(?) June 1893, p. 281; *ibid*., 9 July 1893, pp. 304–5.

65 Collected near Mombo, 9 Aug. 1977; interpreted with Induna Mupatu, Limulunga, 11 Aug. 1977.

6 Cosmology: royal rituals

1 M. Gluckman, 'Les rites de passage', in M. Gluckman (ed.), *Essays on the ritual of social relations* (Manchester, 1962; 2nd edn 1966), p. 22.

2 *Ibid*., p. 23

3 *Ibid*., pp. 51–2; *idem*, 'Rituals of rebellion in South East Africa', Frazer Lecture, Manchester 1952.

4 R. Horton, 'Ritual man in Africa', *Africa* xxxiv, 2 (April 1964), 85–103, p. 87.

5 The two other discussions of this apart from Horton's (*ibid*.) which I have found helpful are E. Evans-Pritchard, *Theories of primitive religion* (Oxford, 1965) and J. Skorupski, 'The meaning of another culture's beliefs', in C. Hookway and P. Pettit, *Action and interpretation: studies in the philosophy of the social sciences* (Cambridge, 1978).

6 E. Evans-Pritchard, *Nuer religion* (Oxford, 1956), p. 313.

7 Applied to this debate by Evans-Pritchard, *Theories of primitive religion*, e.g. at pp. 24, 43, 47. As befits an anthropologist's analogy, this one can be traced back to its original oral transmission. It refers to a Mid-Western farmer whose horse had strayed, so he stood in the middle of the empty paddock, chewed some grass and wondered where he would go if he were a horse. Via A. R. Radcliffe-Brown, presumably during his time at Chicago, to M. Gluckman. Gluckman, *Politics, law and ritual in tribal society* (Oxford, 1965), p. 2, n. 5.

8 Cf. J. Skorupski's plea that 'this whole investigation needs to be set free from the straitjacket of "ritual = sacred = symbolic" versus "practical = profane = instrumental", *Symbol and theory: a philosophical study of theories of religion in social anthropology* (Cambridge, 1976), p. 173, and his conclusion in 'The meaning of another culture's beliefs', p. 106.

9 I borrow the first phrase from Evans-Pritchard, *Nuer religion*, p. 320, and the second from Horton, 'Ritual man', p. 97.

10 W. De Craemer, J. Vansina and R. Fox, 'Religious movements in Central Africa', *Comparative Studies in Society and History* xviii, 4 (Oct. 1976), 458–75, p. 459.

11 W. MacGaffey, *Custom and government in the lower Congo* (California, 1970), p. 247.

12 Among the acephalous Amba: E. H. Winter, 'The enemy within: Amba witchcraft and sociological theory', in J. Middleton and E. H. Winter (eds.), *Witchcraft and sorcery in East Africa* (London, 1963); in Shambaai where the myth of Mbegha, the first chief, revealed the same sort of dual potentials: S. Feierman, *The Shambaa Kingdom* (Madison, 1974), pp. 63–4; in the geographically closer Kuba kingship: J. Vansina, *The children of Woot: essays in Kuba history* (Madison, 1978), esp. Ch. 11.

13 M. Wilson, *Good company: a study of Nyakyusa age villages* (Oxford, 1951), pp. 101–2; amplified in *idem*, 'Divine kings and the breath of men', Frazer Lecture, Manchester 1959, and *idem, Religion and the transformation of society* (Cambridge, 1971), pp. 85–6.

14 Wilson, *Religion and the transformation of society*, p. 89.

15 Witnessed by F. S. Arnot in 1883; he estimated that 2,000 canoes took part: Arnot to his mother, 15 March 1883, cited in E. Baker, *The life and explorations of F. S. Arnot* (London, 1921), pp. 68–9; by F. Coillard in 1891 – hundreds of canoes – *Journal intime*, DE FAP, Paris, 27 *mars* 1891; in 1894, *ibid.*, 19 *mai* 1894. The *ku omboka* was 'colonialised' by the addition of a Union Jack beside the *Litunga*'s flag in *Nalikwanda, ibid.*, 16 *mars* 1904 (this first happened in 1896, A. Jalla, *Notes privées*, privately held, p. 95).

16 Frequently described, e.g. Coillard, *Journal intime*, 6 *janv*. 1885; *idem, Photograph album*, 'Lewanika's Maoma 1886' (visibly identical to those of the present day), HMC/LM.

17 D. Livingstone, *Private journals*, ed. I. Schapera (London, 1960), 19 July 1851, vol. I, P. 32. A modern *Nalikwanda* has about forty paddlers. Livingstone's thirty-four foot canoe had six, Sekeletu's forty footer, eleven. That suggests that this early *Nalikwanda* was between forty and fifty feet long (*ibid.*, p. 195). Cf. Coillard's description of 1889: sixty foot in length, ten foot beam, forty to fifty paddlers, *Journal intime*, 13 *av.* 1889; *idem, Sur le Haut Zambèze: voyages et travaux de Mission* (Paris, 1898), pl. xxxix, p. 556; Jalla, *Notes privées*, p. 95 also stated about fifty paddlers.

18 Jalla, *Notes privées*, p. 95. His first wife, Emma, was permitted to see it.

19 Coillard, *Journal intime*, Lealuyi, 13 *av.* 1889.

20 W. Waddell, *Diary*, WA/1/1–5 (NAZim), 8 Jan. 1893.

21 O. Coates-Palgrave, *The trees of Central Africa* (Salisbury, Rhodesia, 1956), pp. 135–9.

22 Jalla, *Notes privées*, p. 95.

23 A free translation from Luyana into English by Y. W. Mupatu, who performed the song for me.

24 Coillard, *Journal intime*, 27 juill. 1887; Jalla, *Notes privées*, p. 95; Waddell, *Diary*, Aug. 1890.

25 The paddlers, wearing lions' manes, have always been members of the elite since at least 1889. Before then, we have no direct evidence. Coillard's description contains the observation of failing paddlers being pitched overboard. Jalla's much fuller passage does so also, giving further description of the special body movement of the paddlers and in particular the bow and stern paddlers, all of which can be confirmed from my own observations. He also mentions the fire.

26 Collected at Sefula, 1974. The proverb exists in other 'stripped down' forms with different ornamentation, but the contrast of deep water and shallows is always there.

27 E. Jacottet, *Études sur les langues du Haut Zambèze* (Paris, 1896–1901), vol. III, p. 188, No. 2.

28 *Ibid.*, No. 6, p. 189. The equation of *Litunga* and hippopotamus is amply visible. Hippo are royal animals and Jeanmairet, the first missionary at Sesheke ('place of the white sands') recorded how certain hippo were addressed respectfully as the metempsychotic form of deceased chiefs. *Ibid.*, vol. II, pp. 158–9, n. 3.

29 Performed at Mwenyi, 19 May 1977.

30 A. Jalla, *Litaba za Sichaba sa Malozi* (Oxford, 1909; 5th edn 1969), p. 17.

31 This may be voluminously confirmed in the verbatim transcripts of cases before the Resident Magistrates' Courts, 1906–27, KDE 3/2/1–21 (NAZ) as well as from Coillard and Jalla's writings. More recently, the death of the *Litunga* Imwiko under unclear circumstances in 1948 drew forth a torrent of suspicions, particularly when his *Ngambela*, the late Kalonga Wina, was unable to give a wholly satisfactory public report of them. J-P. Burger *à* La Direction, 27 *juill.* 1948, p. 3 (privately held). Cf. G. L. Caplan, *The elites of Barotseland, 1878–1969* (London, 1970), p. 169.

32 The threshold of the Noble Age moves, of course. Today Lewanika is represented as the resurgence of its qualities. The testimony of an informant nominated by the Kuta illustrated this graphically, jumping from the pre-traditional period straight to Lewanika, omitting all between (Limulunga, 14 July 1977); cf. also Y. W. Mupatu, *An autobiography*, ed. G. Prins, Zambia Past and Present Series 4 (Lusaka, forthcoming). A similar interpretation of paired kings is given by Vansina in *The children of Woot*.

33 Boiteaux *à* La Direction, 9 *fév.* 1916, *Nouvelles du Zambèze* (a journal for supporters of the Mission), 1916, p. 35.

34 In this description, and in what follows, I draw on material gathered between February and April 1977, between the funeral of the *Litunga* Mbikusita Lewanika and the installation of *Litunga* Ilute Yeta. The *actual* rites of

Makono remain a secret; however, I consider the idiom chosen for the public analogy to be instructive. The brief account given to Jacottet contained the main elements present here, but in a rather garbled form which Jacottet could not disentangle, *Études*, vol. III, p. 136 and nn. 1 and 2.

35 T. Burnier, Lealui, 30 *mars* 1916, published in *Nouvelles du Zambèze,*1916, describing the *coliso* of Yeta; details added from my own participation in 1977.

36 Boiteaux and Théophile Burnier sent separate eye-witness accounts of the funeral, written on 9 February and 7 February respectively. Published in *Nouvelles du Zambèze*, 1916, pp. 28–51.

37 *Ibid.*, 26 *mars* 1916, p. 50.

38 *Ibid.*, 7 *fév.* 1916, p. 38.

39 *Ibid.*, 10 *fév.* 1916, p. 40.

40 Roach to MacKinnon, n.d., Buxton 251, SAHCNR, 20416, 4 April 1916, CO 417/575 (PRO).

41 Jacottet, *Études*, vol. III, p. 150 has a parallel description of the *limbwata*. Coillard never witnessed a royal burial, but the information he gave in 'Quelques remarques sur le travail de M. le Professeur Allier', two drafts, DEFAP, Paris, and 'Notes pour conférence à la Faculté de Théologie', DEFAP, Paris, 16 *déc* 1896 match my observations at the interment of Mbikusita Lewanika at Lishekandinde in 1977. This paragraph draws on both sources.

42 One informant named Ilinangana *ñomboti* of Nakaywe as senior of all *liñomboti* (Ilinangana: one born at the time of the short drought (*'linanga'*)); another said it was Akashambatwa of Imwambo accompanied by certain other *liñomboti*.

43 Gluckman found the institutions to be impenetrable, *ECBP*, p. 35; M. Mainga experienced great difficulty in gathering information about them, *Bulozi under the Luyana kings* (London, 1973), p. 31, n. 32. As part of my work to collect formal tradition, I was given permission to visit several of the most important *litino* during the dry season of 1977 but in one case gave an undertaking, which I honoured, not to ask direct questions about the details of rites. The art of fieldwork is often as much knowing what not to do as what to do.

44 Mainga, *Bulozi under the Luyana kings* and *idem*, 'A history of Lozi religion to the end of the nineteenth century', in T. O. Ranger and I. N. Kimambo (eds.), *The historical study of African religion* (London, (1972), pp. 95–107.

45 Mainga, *Bulozi under the Luyana kings*, pp. 68–9 on Lozi/Mbunda 'system' contrasts; e.g. her account of Lewanika's attack on Mbunda diviners in 1892, *ibid.*, pp. 145–7.

46 The device of blaming unpalatable things onto other people which might have affected the field data and so given rise to the distinctions which Dr Mainga made is venerable. Nalubutu and Lewanika did it for Coillard, ascribing polygamy to the influence of the Kololo and superstition to the Mbunda ('Remarques sur Professeur Allier', p. 11). It was standard practice in the colonial era.

47 Coillard, *Sur le Haut Zambèze*, pp. 535–6; my visit in September 1977.

48 Coillard, *Journal intime*, 6 *av*. 1886. The names of several other kings and *litino* are also curiously spelt in this list. Jalla was still unsure in the 1890s, noting Imwambo as 'tomb. de Mboo?', *Notes privées*, p. 98.

49 Livingstone, *Private journals*, pp. 224–5, 28 Aug. 1853. The editor (p. 225, n. 2) was unable to make sense of 'the Cow of God'. On the basis of my knowledge of *sitino* rites, I suggest this means Liombekalala. Also *idem*, *Missionary travels and researches in South Africa* (London, 1857), p. 219.

50 Coillard, *Sur le Haut Zambèze*, pl. xxxvi, p. 509.

51 Jalla, *Notes privées*, p. 95.

52 *Luwa nembo kwa mangunuunga, mbali u siya mindi kale, u ka wana ni ni ishangangela*. There are two levels of interpretation. 'Things added' superficially apply to the trees planted there, more deeply to its power as a *sitino*.

53 A retrospective description: Coillard, *Journal intime*, Senanga, 23 *août* 1899.

54 First text, collected by A. Jalla during the first half of the twentieth century, exact date unknown (privately held). I am deeply indebted to Rev. J-P. Burger for providing me with this piece. Second text, Jacottet, *Études*, vol. iii, p. 188, no. 4.

55 Coillard, *Journal intime*, 2 *janv*. 1885.

56 F. C. Selous stopped at the grave of 'Nonombing' in 1889, *Travel and adventure in South East Africa* (London, 1893), p. 257; A. Bertrand in 1895, *The kingdom of the Barotsi of Upper Zambezia*, trans. A. B. Miall (London, 1899), p. 164.

57 A. Baldwin, *Journal*, MMS, 22 Feb. 1892, p. 191.

58 Written in original Senanga DNB in 1910, now lost, transcribed in Tour report 6/51 by I. M. Wethey, 'Itufa-Liangati Silalo file', Senanga Boma.

59 Information from Mrs Sutherland, Soekmekaar, N. Transvaal, 1975; Mainga, *Bulozi under the Luyana kings*, p. 29, n. 26.

60 Jalla, *Litaba za Sichaba*, pp. 18, 23.

61 *Ndoana kaso ubika; a Ñundu k'a munine a Nakaywe we mikukuku* (Nakaywe is smaller than Ñundu). Also a slight variation of the first clause: *A ndo na ndo k'a ku yomana*, (etc.): 'Two houses cannot be put together' (etc.).

62 Gluckman, *ELLRP*, p. 93. I did not notice this reference until after I had left Bulozi.

63 Coillard, *Journal intime*, Sesheke, 5 nov. 1884.

64 Coillard, 'Remarques sur Professeur Allier'.

65 *Balimu* – spirits of the ancestors, either royal or not. In this section I use the word with the royal meaning.

66 Coillard, *Journal intime*, 5 *juin* 1889. There are many variations on the theme of the last sentence which I give here simply to illustrate how Nalabutu made the 'seamless whole'.

67 *Ibid*., 1 *fév*. 1885.

68 *Ibid*., 10 *av*. 1886; Coillard à Boegner, 26 *janv*. 1888, *Lettres à la direction*, DEFAP, Paris.

69 E. Holub, *Seven years in South Africa* (London, 1881), vol. ii, p. 302; *idem*,

A cultural survey of the Lozi–Mbunda kingdom in south central Africa (Vienna, 1879), trans. Dr L. Holy (typescr.), p. 9.

70 G. Westbeech, *Trade and travel in early Barotseland*, ed. E. C. Tabler (London, 1963), p. 44.

71 Coillard, *Journal intime*, 31 *janv.* 1890.

72 Jacottet, *Études*, vol. III, pp. 139–40. The translation of the last phrase is on trust, as I cannot follow the transcribed Luyana. Liondo is the *sitino* of another of Mboo's brothers, that of his successor as *Litunga*, Inyambo. It is also (by extension) a general name for the plain. The modern version of this *liloko* collected in 1974 used the wider sense and interpreted the last phrase 'has no mercy, not even to a child'. Since I can see that the following section of the *liloko (ameyi bebi; la mulilo kule)* is correct in Jacottet's translation ('The water is near, the fire is far') and not in my modern informant's, I follow Jacottet above. This is a painful example of my ignorance of Luyana. The modern version was interestingly close to the Jacottet text (*liondo lie iñuwa lya silila ñeke; lya mei bebi, lya mulilo kule*), as have been all those *liloko* in his texts for which I collected modern versions.

73 Livingstone, *Private journals*, 12 Oct. 1853, p. 240.

74 Mainga, 'Lozi religion', p. 98; information near Libonda, 15 Sept. 1977.

75 The symbolic sacredness of whiteness is a common motif in central Africa. It occurs in modern healing cult uniforms; it was present in Kuba society represented in white kaolin (Vansina, *The children of Woot*, Ch. 11). Indeed it is common in other types of non-industrial societies (see C. G. Jung (ed.), *Man and his symbols* (New York, 1964), p. 117).

76 Jacottet, *Études*, vol. III, pp. 150–1; Coillard, 'Remarques sur Professeur Allier'; *idem*, 'Conférence à la Faculté de Théologie', 16 déc. 1896. We must presume that Coillard had had opportunity to see Jacottet's material at one stage, either in Lesotho or Paris. The verbs used are *ku kana* (Luyana: to refuse) and *ku pumena (ku pumenena:* to receive, to acknowledge the royal salute); Jalla noted that blood from the sacrificial animal was also used, the blood being the only part of the animal carried into the enclosure. *Notes privées*, p. 129; information after the burial of Mbikusita Lewanika at Lishekandinde, Feb. 1977.

77 Coillard, *Journal intime*, 9 *nov.* 1890.

78 F. S. Arnot, *Garenganze or seven years pioneer missionary work in central Africa* (London 1889; repr. 1969), p. 78.

79 Coillard, *Journal intime*, 3 *av.* 1886.

80 Holub, *Seven years*, pp. 171–2, 329; Jacottet, *Études*, vol. II, p. 160.

81 Information in Cambridge, 1 and 2 Oct. 1976. Two proven informants in Bulozi also gave me accounts of this.

82 Gluckman, 'Les rites de passage', p. 46; *idem*, 'Civil war and theories of power in Barotseland: African and medieval analogies', *Yale Law Journal* LXXII (July 1963), 1515–46, p. 1542; *idem, Custom and conflict in Africa* (Oxford, 1965), p. 45.

83 Feierman, *The Shambaa kingdom*, p. 167.

84 M. Gluckman, *Order and rebellion in tribal Africa* (London, 1963), p. 20 (quotation); the Yale lectures were published as 'Civil war and theories of power in Barotseland' and later in *IBJ*.

85 M. Gluckman, 'The utility of the equilibrium model in the study of social change', *American Anthropologist* LXX (1968), 219–35 (originally delivered as an address to the American Anthropological Association in 1966). All otherwise unattributed references to Gluckman in the next two paragraphs come from this article.

86 *Ibid*, p. 223.

87 Mainga, *Bulozi under the Luyana kings*, p. 122 supports this general line. She was puzzled that Lewanika did not crush Mataa's disaffection in the bud.

88 F. Coillard, *On the threshold of Central Africa: a record of twenty years pioneering among the Barotsi of the Upper Zambezi* (London, 1897; repr. 1971), pp. 148–9.

89 Gluckman, 'Civil war and theories of power in Barotseland'; introduction to 1971 reprint of Coillard's *On the threshold of Central Africa*, pp. 16–17. Cf. J. R. Lander, 'Attainder and forfeiture 1453–1509', *Historical Journal* IV (1961), 119–51; W. H. Dunham, 'Lord Hastings' indentured retainers 1461–83', *Transactions of the Connecticut Academy of Arts and Sciences* XXXIX (Sept. 1955), 1–175. I am indebted to Dr M. Bowker for these references.

90 Coillard, *Journal intime*, 11 *janv*. 1885.

91 Arnot, *Garenganze*, pp. 94–5.

92 Westbeech, *Trade and travel* (reporting Lewanika), Feb. 1886, p. 45.

93 Coillard, *Journal intime*, 8 *janv*. 1885. Reports of the sinking of *Nalikwanda* at funerals: Mulambwa: Livingstone, *Private journals*, 9 Aug. 1853, p. 203; Lewanika: see above, Section 2, p. 120.

94 Coillard, *Journal intime*, 9, 11, 12, 13 *janv*. 1885.

95 *Ibid*., 1 *sept*. 1884; Waddell, *Diary*, 23 Aug. 1885, 13 Dec. 1885.

96 Coillard, *Journal intime*, 2 *sept*. 1884.

97 Livingstone, *Private journals*, 2 Aug. 1853, p. 196; spelt 'Mokwala'.

98 Coillard, *Journal intime*, 1, 2, 3 *fév*. 1885; 24 *mars* 1886.

99 *Ibid*., 27 *janv*. 1885.

100 Coillard à La Direction, Leshoma, 5 *mars* 1885, *Lettres à la direction*. The sentence about the Commune omitted in *idem, Sur le Haut Zambèze*, p. 153.

101 Coillard, *Journal intime*, 6 *janv*. 1885; Jalla, *Notes privées*, p. 99.

102 Coillard à La Direction, Sesheke, 19 *av*. 1886, *Lettres à la direction*.

103 Waddell, *Diary*, after conversation with MacDonald, 16 Nov. 1886.

104 Westbeech, *Trade and travel*, Feb. 1886, by report from Lewanika, pp. 46–7; Coillard, *Journal intime*, 8 *janv*. 1885; reference to Mambari in Coillard's first report of events, *ibid*., 4 *déc*. 1885.

105 Westbeech, *Trade and travel*, pp. 33–4; Coillard à L'Association Missionaire du Pra-du-Tour, Sesheke, 21 *oct*. 1885, *Lettres à la direction*.

106 Coillard, *Journal intime*, 2 *déc*. 1885. No mention of this appears in Westbeech's journal, *Trade and travel*.

107 Westbeech, *Trade and travel*, pp. 39–40; Coillard *à* L'Association Missionaire du Pra-du-Tour, Sesheke, *Lettres à la direction*.

108 Westbeech, *Trade and travel*, p. 47; Mainga, *Bulozi under the Luyana kings*, p. 137.

109 Westbeech, *Trade and travel*, p. 48.

110 Thus: the execution of the *Mulanziane* of Sesheke, Coillard, *Journal intime*, 3 *janv.* 1886; the selective execution of enemies, Westbeech, *Trade and travel*, p. 47.

111 Coillard, *Sur le Haut Zambèze*, p. 303.

112 Coillard, *Journal intime*, 5 *sept.* 1891.

113 A. Jalla, 'Léwanika, roi des Ba-Rotsi: esquisse biographique', *Nouvelles du Zambèze* Supplement 2 (June 1902), *idem, Litaba za Sichaba*, pp. 13–15.

114 Jalla, 'Léwanika, roi des Ba–Rotsi', p. 12.

7 Cosmology: public rituals and beliefs

1 E. Evans-Pritchard, *Theories of primitive religion* (Oxford, 1965), pp. 6–7.

2 *Journal des Missions Evangéliques* (1921), pp. 98–9. I am indebted to Mlle J-M. Léonard for this reference; E. Jacottet, *Études sur les langues du Haut Zambèze*, 3 vols. (Paris, 1896–1901), Préface (*août* 1895), vol. I, pp. i–iii.

3 Re Seajika and Kalumba: Mme C. Coillard to niece Kate, Paris, 30 April 1880, *Letters to her family*, DEFAP, Paris; M. Goy, *Dans les solitudes de l'Afrique* (Geneva, 1901), pp. 67–8.

4 I spent a great deal of time fruitlessly trying to discover more than Jacottet tells us about these men. Then, as a result of correspondence, in January 1979 I went to Switzerland to see Rev. J-P. Burger. The outcome of this meeting was that from his minute knowledge of the Zambezi Mission's personnel, he assembled what biographical knowledge we have of Jacottet's informants, which is given here. I am profoundly indebted to him for this help. He was also able to confirm from his personal experience in Bulozi from 1927 up until the 1960s that Jacottet's collection of texts was unknown in Bulozi, with the exception of one or two Mission workers at Sefula with whom he had on occasion checked details in the texts. I wish to record my gratitude to the Cambridge Historical Society and to the Managers of the Political Science Fund for entering into the spirit of the chase, being prepared to accept the *fait accompli* of my journey and making grants which, between them, paid for this flying visit.

5 Jacottet, *Études*, Préface, vol. I, p. i; Introduction, vol. III, pp. v–vi. Cf. J. Goody, *The domestication of the savage mind* (Cambridge, 1978), pp. 90–3. Upon reading this section in my manuscript Rev. Burger remarked to me that he had always been puzzled by the evident freedom with which Jacottet's informants had spoken and that the explanation which he had independently reached many years ago was essentially the one I propose here.

6 W. H. I. Bleek, *A brief account of Bushman folklore and other texts (second report)* (Cape Town, 1895), p. 5.

7 Paraphrased from E. Evans-Pritchard, *Nuer religion* (Oxford, 1956), pp. 315–18.

8 This is Horton's criticism of Turner's Thomist quest to 'say the unsayable' about pure being from his Ndembu materials ('Ritual man in Africa', *Africa* xxxiv, 2 (April 1964), 85–103, esp. pp. 91–7), and is my worry with works like C. G. Jung (ed.), *Man and his symbols* (New York, 1964).

9 D. Livingstone, *Private journals*, ed. I Schapera (London, 1960), Sunday 17 July 1853, p. 190.

10 E. Holub, *A cultural survey of the Lozi–Mbunda kingdom in south central Africa* (Vienna, 1879), trans. Dr L. Holy (typescr.), p. 8 (*idem, Seven years in South Africa* (London, 1881), vol. II, p. 301).

11 Jacottet, *Études*, vol. II, pp. 105–7.

12 *Ibid.*, vol. III, p. 118.

13 *Ibid.*, vol. III, p. 116 and p. 152.

14 *Ibid.*, vol. III, p. 118, vol. II, pp. 102–4.

15 *Ibid.*, vol. III, p. 118.

16 Testimony of Mwauluka Mukwala at Sioma, F. Coillard, *Journal intime*, DEFAP, Paris, 3 *fév.* 1885; *idem*, 'Notes pour conférence à la Faculté de Théologie', 16 *déc.* 1896, DEFAP, Paris. A better, fuller version is in A. Jalla, *Notes privées*, pp. 67–70, printed in *idem, Pionniers parmi les Marotse* (Florence, 1903), as Appendix A, pp. 319–22. Yet another version appears in *idem, Litaba za Sichaba sa Malozi* (Oxford, 1959; 5th edn 1969), p. 2.

17 Wells' or Cape Wagtail (*Motacilla capensis*). J. G. Williams, *A field guide to the birds of East and Central Africa* (London, 1972), p. 183; illustr. p. 177. Coillard found a 'Narungoana' bird which he described as 'grey black with a long tail' lying dead in the path. He was told that it was Nyambe's messenger and never eaten, *Journal intime*, 8 *sept.* 1893.

18 Coillard, *Journal intime*, 12 *fév.* 1888. He asked if people changed colour in *Litooma*. Lewanika and Nalubutu replied that they did not really know, but thought not.

19 Jacottet, *Études*, vol. II, p. 109.

20 *Ibid.*, vol. III, p. 116. Livingstone heard the same myth. *Private journals*, p. 190.

21 Witnessed in the case of a sick woman at Lealui, Coillard, *Journal intime*, 13 *janv.* 1894; described by Jalla, *Notes privées*, p. 128.

22 Jalla, *Notes privées*, p. 128.

23 Coillard, *Journal intime*, 2 *sept.* 1884 *à* Sesheke; Jacottet, *Études*, vol. III, p. 140. Cf. the invocation of Mwanambinyi given above p. 126.

24 Coillard, *Journal intime*, 5 *juin* 1889.

25 It was believed that any form of contact with a menstruating woman, even with utensils used by her, resulted in chest pains. This remains a common diagnosis of tuberculosis. Information at Senanga, May 1975.

Even today when artificial substitutes are widely marketed, Lozi children are breast-fed for around two years. Old women assert that formerly (meaning earlier this century) weaning occurred later, so it is reasonable to see Lozi society in terms of the immensely interesting emerging theory of population balance as controlled by lactational amenorrhoea (R. V. Short, 'The evolution of human reproduction', *Proceedings of the Royal Society of London* B, 195 (1976), 3–24). This being so, we must think of women menstruating fewer, possibly many fewer times during their careers than is our cultural assumption (see *ibid.*, Fig. 5, p. 16, reproduced in *Nature* CCLXXII (6 April 1978), 495). This makes it easier for us to understand the tolerance of intrusive rituals associated with each period.

26 Jacottet, *Études*, vol. III, p. 138 and p. 173 (describes 'death' of moon).

27 As does Nalubutu's testimony, Coillard, *Journal intime*, 5 *juin* 1889.

28 Jacottet, *Études*, vol. III, pp. 134–5.

29 *Ibid.*, vol. III, pp. 165–6.

30 W. De Craemer, J. Vansina and R. Fox, 'Religious movements in Central Africa', *Comparative Studies in Society and History* XVIII, 4 (Oct. 1976), 458–75.

31 Jacottet, *Études*, vol. II, p. 144; vol. III, p. 136.

32 Livingstone, *Private journals*, 12 Oct. 1853, p. 240.

33 Jacottet, *Études*, vol. III, p. 168. He translated *mukulu wa mbula* as 'Master of the rain'. It is correct that *mukulu* associates mastery and age; *mbula* was used for both rain and thunder (cf. vol. III, p. 126).

34 *Ibid.*, vol. III, p. 140; rainmakers also use the techniques described to Livingstone. During the 1977 dry season, a colleague visiting me in Bulozi inadvertently uncovered a small pot at the edge of a village in the Kataba Valley. It contained rainmaking medicine and the people were upset. The next night there was an unseasonal downpour in that area.

35 *Ibid.*, vol. III, pp. 49, 125, 141, 142.

36 *Ibid.*, vol. III, pp. 169, 170.

37 Jalla, *Notes privées*, p. 126.

38 Jacottet, *Études*, vol. II, pp. 163–5; vol. III, pp. 157, 109–11.

39 *Ibid.*, vol. III, pp. 86–7.

40 *Ibid.*, vol. III, pp. 153–4. A common modern variant I have heard is that the *muloi* takes the initiate into the bush, gives him a small ritual axe and directs him to sever a root of the *mukwa* tree (which has a red sap that oozes like blood), telling him that at the moment of the act, a certain close relative will die in proof of *buloi* entering the new witch. For 1910s, D. W. Stirke, *Barotseland: eight years among the Barotse* (London, 1922), p. 118.

41 The Luyana word for ghost persists in Lozi; fear of the influence of a dead relative's spirit: A. Baldwin, *Journal*, MMS, 4 May 1893, p. 191.

42 Jacottet, *Études*, vol. III, pp. 107, 109–13.

43 *Ibid.*, vol. III, pp. 86–7. Cannibalism was a prominent feature in the 1956–8 witch trials. The reported technique was to revive the corpse and to 'kill it a second time' (details from notes taken during the proceedings, in private possession, photocopies in my possession). Witches operated in lodges and flesh was distributed around the membership as a ritual bond.

44 Jalla, *Notes privées*, p. 127.

45 It seems that a *silumba* (spirit) is active in its home area. Today, anyone seeking specialist help will search for past patients of the *ñaka* before consult-

285

ing him. Reputation for success – and freedom from risk – account for the dominance of two *liñaka* in this market today, one living near Libonda and one at Machili, each catering for the clientele from the other's area.

46 Holub, *Seven years*, p. 236; F. Worthington, 'Memorandum' (describing 1897), pp. 78–9, G19, HMC/LM.

47 Jacottet, *Études*, vol. III, p. 142 mentions two particular witch familiars: the *lisikita* (Verreaux's Eagle Owl, *Bubo lacteus*, Williams, *Field guide*, p. 155, illustr. p. 160) and the *lundio* (Water Dikkop, *Burhinus vermiculatus*, a sort of stone curlew. Williams, *Field guide*, p. 90).

48 W. Waddell, *Diary*, WA/1/1/1–5(NAZim), 3 April 1887 on power of snake medicines; lion medicine, Stirke, *Barotseland*, p. 118 refers to 1910s; information at Nangweshi, October 1973; Jacottet, *Études*, vol. II, pp. 169–71.

49 Information at Ushaa, May 1977; Coillard, *Journal intime*, 6 *déc.* 1892.

50 Livingstone, *Private journals*, 6 Aug. 1851, p. 48; Jacottet, *Études*, vol. III, p. 165; C. M. N. White, 'Witchcraft, divination and magic among the Balovale tribes', *Africa* XVIII, 2(1948), 81–104, p. 88; observed at Lukulu, Sept. 1974.

51 Jacottet, *Études*, vol. III, p. 162.

52 Jacottet, *Études*, vol. III, p. 161 described divination with an antelope horn. *Likuyeti* were seen and photographed at Luandui May, 1975.

53 Oracle witnessed at Sesheke, Coillard, *Journal intime*, 9 *fév.* 1885; Waddell, *Diary*, 3 April 1887.

54 Jacottet, *Études*, vol. III, pp. 157–9; Jalla, *Notes privées*, p. 126.

55 Jacottet, *Études*, vol. III, p. 155; F. S. Arnot, *Garenganze or seven years pioneer missionary work in central Africa* (London, 1889; repr. 1969), 19 Dec. 1882, p. 66; 19 April 1884, p. 95.

56 Baldwin to his mother, 5 April 1893, *Letters*, Box 1, Central Africa, MMS.

57 Coillard *aux* Diaconesses de la rue de Reuilly, Leshoma, 15 *av.* 1885, *Lettres à la direction*, DEFAP, Paris.

58 C. Coillard, *Journal*, DEFAP, Paris, Tues. 2 Nov. 1886.

59 Holub, *Cultural survey*, p. 8; *Seven years*, p. 322; also Jalla, *Notes privées*, pp. 108, 126.

60 Most work addressing these problems has not had a strong historical dimension (cf. contributions to J. B. Loudon (ed.), *Social anthropology and medicine*, ASA Monograph 13 (London, 1976). Some has now shown awareness of the need for this dimension, but methodological difficulties have been encountered in its pursuit (cf. R. P. Werbner, *Regional cults*, ASA Monograph 16 (London, 1977) and review in *African Social Research* XXVI (Dec. 1978), 506–9); a pioneering attempt to resolve these problems is by J. M. Janzen, *The quest for therapy in lower Zaire* (California, 1978). Elaboration of the argument for the Lozi case is to be found in my paper, 'Disease at the crossroads: towards a history of therapeutics in Bulozi since 1876', *Social Science and Medicine* (Spring 1980).

An erudite example of the potential explanatory forces of the historical study of medicine was given in a lecture on Chinese pharmaceutics by J. Needham (March 1978), the substance of which will appear in vol. VI, Part 4, of *Science and civilisation in China* (Cambridge, forthcoming) (reference from vol. I (1954), pp. xxxvi-ii and pers. comm., July 1978).

61 Coillard, *Journal intime*, 24 *av*. 1890.

62 *Ibid*., 24 *av*. 1890; 27 *déc*. 1884, seen at Sioma. Knotted grass is the commonest type of *sifunda* that I have seen.

63 A prominent motif in modern healing cults. First described to me at Senanga, May 1975.

64 Coillard, *Journal intime*, 31 *juill*. 1887, Matomé village.

65 E. B. Tylor, *Primitive culture*, vol. I (London, 1871; 2nd edn 1873), p. x, pp. 133–6; J. Skorupski, *Symbol and theory: a philosophical study of theories of religion in social anthropology* (Cambridge, 1976), p. 5. I owe the Tylor reference to Skorupski as also the idea of blocks to falsifiability; however, I have extracted a slightly different emphasis from Tylor.

66 Tylor, *Primitive culture*, pp. 134–5; Skorupski, *Symbol and theory*, systematises Tylor's view more.

67 Jalla, *Notes privées*, p. 127.

68 The full argument from analysis of healing cult texts and details of specific treatments is given in Prins, 'Disease at the crossroads'.

69 E.g. G. L. Chavunduka, 'Interaction of folk and scientific beliefs in Shona medical practices', PhD thesis, University of London (1972); information at various hospitals in Bulozi – see Prins, 'Disease at the crossroads'.

70 Field notes 1977; a vernacular Ms collection, *circa* 1935, in my possession; for Kaoma, notes by Symons in O. Coates-Palgrave, *The trees of Central Africa* (Salisbury, 1956); for Balovale, V. Gilges, *Some African poison plants and medicines of Northern Rhodesia*, Rhodes-Livingstone Occasional Paper 11 (Manchester, 1955); map in G. G. Trapnell and J. N. Clothier, *The soils, vegetation and agricultural systems of North Western Rhodesia* (Lusaka, 1937); western Zambia is dominated by *Brachystegia-Isoberlinia* woodlands.

71 I owe this point to Dr A. de Vente.

72 Jacottet, *Études*, vol. III, pp. 158–9; detailed modern description in Prins, 'Disease at the crossroads'.

73 At Ushaa, night of 29–30 April 1977. For fuller sequences, see Appendix to Prins, 'Disease at the crossroads'.

74 Informants all over Bulozi, 1974 and 1975; Jacottet, *Études*, Subiya version vol. II, pp. 138–9 ('Sikulobuzuka'); vol. III, pp. 120–1 ('Muenda ndjongola'); pp. 133–5, ('Njangwa-muloti'). The idiom of a half-man appears elsewhere in central Africa, e.g. J. Cocklin to J. Mullens, Matabele Mission, LMS Archives (1879), p. 3 described the goddess Salugazani – 'The people say she has only one eye, one ear, one nostril, one arm, one leg.'

75 Jacottet, *Études*, vol. III, pp. 133–5.

What next?

1 A. V. Chayanov, most concisely in 'On the theory of non-capitalist economic systems', especially pp. 4–6 in D. Thorner, B. Kerblay and R. E. F. Smith, (eds.), *The theory of peasant economy*, American Economic Association

Translations series (Homewood, Illinois, 1966); J. C. Scott, *The moral economy of the peasant* (New Haven, 1976).

2 M. Hesse, 'Theory and value in the social sciences' in C. Hookway and P. Pettit (eds.), *Action and interpretation: studies in the philosophy of the social sciences* (Cambridge, 1978).

8 The meaning of contact

1 W. Soyinka, *Death and the king's horseman* (London, 1975), p. 53. I owe this reference to Dr Iliffe.

2 F. Coillard to K. Mackintosh, 26 May 1900, Coillard Mss, HMC (NAZim).

3 This literature is admirably discussed in A. D. Roberts, *A history of Zambia* (London, 1976), esp. Chs. 7 and 8.

4 F. Coillard, 'Autobiographie' (Mss), DEFAP, Paris, reproduced in E. Favre, *La vie d'un missionaire français: François Coillard, 1834–1904*, 3 vols. (Paris, 1908–13) (early years unabridged from Mss), vol. I, *Enfance et jeunesse*, pp. 20, 42.

5 *Ibid.*, pp. 20–31; C. W. Mackintosh, *Coillard of the Zambezi* (London, 1907), pp. 3–6.

6 Mackintosh, *Coillard of the Zambezi*, pp. 339–40.

7 Information in Paris, April 1978, one informant removed from the Coillards.

8 F. Coillard à C. Coillard, *nov.* 1876 (the conference was the 28th), DEFAP, Paris.

9 *Ibid.*; C. Coillard to her family, 17 Dec. 1876, Leribe, *Letters to her family*, 1876–91, DEFAP, Paris.

10 F. Coillard to his brother-in-law, 17 Dec. 1876, Leribe, DEFAP, Paris.

11 Numerous references to illness in her *Journal* and in his *Journal intime*, both at DEFAP, Paris, esp. *janv.* 1886; *juin* 1891. The enormous psychological stresses she was under are vividly apparent in her journal for the months that Coillard was visiting Lewanika in 1886. By November her handwriting was deteriorating and her entries revealed deep depression.

12 F. Coillard to his brother-in-law, 31 March 1877, DEFAP, Paris.

13 Coillard, *Journal intime,* 14 *fév.* 1878, cited by Favre, *La vie d'un missionaire français*, p. 158.

14 C. Coillard to family, 5 March 1878, *Letters to her family*; in 1873, Chief Langalebalele, who was supposed to have registered the firearms purchased by Zulu who had gone to the diamond fields but had not done so, was suspected of plotting rebellion. He fled to Basutoland but was there captured ('betrayed') and returned to Pietermaritzberg in chains. The conduct of his trial ended the friendship of Bishop Colenso for Administrator Shepstone. D. Welsh, *The roots of segregation: native policy in colonial Natal, 1845–1910* (Oxford, 1971), pp. 132–7.

15 Coillard, *Journal intime*, 5 *mai* 1878, cited by E. Favre, *La vie d'un missionaire français: François Coillard, 1834–1904*, abridged edn (Paris, 1922), pp. 160–1.

16 G. Westbeech, *Trade and travel in early Barotseland*, ed. E. C. Tabler (London, 1963), Nov. 1885, p. 38.

17 Coillard, *Journal intime*, 1 *nov*. 1878, cited by Favre, *La vie d'un missionaire français*, abridged edn, p. 168.

18 C. Coillard to family, Valdezia, Transvaal, 31 March 1879, *Letters to her family*.

19 Favre, *La vie d'un missionaire français*, abridged edn, p. 172.

20 *Journal Suisse*, 12 *av*. 1897 (loose cutting), DEFAP, Paris.

21 Coillard, *Journal intime*, 27 *oct*. 1884; Les Missionaires du Zambèze [Coillard and Jeanmairet] *aux* Amis des Missions, 1885 n.d., *Lettres à la direction*, DEFAP, Paris.

22 Information at Sefula, 17 Feb. 1977.

23 W. Waddell, *Diary*, WA/1/1/1–5, HMC (NAZim), 19 May 1884. The letter referred to was written for Lewanika by Arnot, presumably just before he left Lealui, who also claimed to have advised the king to seek alliance with Khama rather than with Lobengula. E. Baker, *The life and explorations of F. S. Arnot* (London, 1921), p. 97.

24 D. Jeanmairet *à* Boegner, 27 *sept*. 1884, *Lettres à la direction*.

25 D. Jeanmairet *à* Boegner, Leshoma, 16 *déc*. 1884, *Lettres à la direction*. The letter is dated 1885, but from the contents it is clear that this was a mistake. Coillard *à* Boegner, 15 *déc*. 1884, *Lettres à la direction*, states a meeting with Makuatsa, returning from the Valley.

26 Coillard, *Journal intime*, 1 *sept*. 1884.

27 Coillard, *Journal intime*, 9 *nov*. 1884.

28 The best biographical sketch is R. Sampson, *The man with a toothbrush in his hat* (Lusaka, 1972).

29 Westbeech, *Trade and travel*, Jan.–Feb. 1888 (retrospective), p. 95. Cf. 'Mr Westbeech shook my hand, saying that I could count on him and that he would render all the services that it was in his power to do. . .' H. Depelchin and C. Croonenberghs, *Trois ans dans l'Afrique australe* (Brussels, 1883), p. 157.

30 Westbeech, *Trade and travel*, Nov. 1885, p. 38; Feb. 1886, pp. 47–8.

31 *Ibid*., Sept. 1886, p. 82.

32 *Ibid*., Nov. 1885, pp. 35, 38.

33 *Ibid*.; Westbeech found his judgment vindicated in January 1888 when Coillard ordered his drivers not to help him if he were bogged down on the road: 'Such is a sample of missionary gratitude as a rule, and C has certainly not proved any exception to that rule', *ibid*., Jan.–Feb. 1888, p. 95.

34 Coillard, *Journal intime*, 19 *janv*. 1886.

35 *Ibid*., 4 *juin* 1885.

36 Selous, the hunter and explorer ('a fanatical Darwinist' and unrepentant atheist), *Journal intime*, 8 *sept*., 14 *sept*. 1888; Ware the concession hunter (an advocate of free love), *ibid*., 18 *juill*., 23 *juill*. 1889; Lochner, the Company representative ('an atheist who scorns everything'), *ibid*., 19 *av*. 1890; the Administrator Worthington (licentious), *ibid*., 16 *mai* 1904, even the confessing Christian Col. Harding (who disagreed with Coillard's tactics), *ibid*., 15 *janv*. 1904.

37 Coillard à La Direction, 29 *juill*. 1886, *Lettres à la direction*, passage subsequently excised from the version in F. Coillard, *Sur le Haut Zambèze: voyages et travaux de Mission* (Paris, 1898), p. 205.

38 A. Baldwin, *Journal*, MMS, 2 May 1892, vol. v, p. 4; 3 July 1892, p. 64. Waddell's emotional instability also described in C. Coillard, *Journal*, 14 July 1889.

39 C. Coillard, *Journal*, 12 Sept. 1886.

40 Coillard, *Journal intime*, 19, 23 *janv*. 1886; Westbeech, *Trade and travel*, 25 Jan. 1886, p. 41.

41 Coillard, *Journal intime*, 9 *fév*. 1886.

42 Westbeech, *Trade and travel*, Feb. 1886, p. 44.

43 *Ibid*., p. 48.

44 Coillard à Boegner, Sesheke, 19 *av*. 1886, *Lettres à la direction*, reproduced accurately in Coillard, *Sur le Haut Zambèze*, pp. 184–99.

45 Westbeech had found the river very full and fast (e.g. *Trade and travel*, comment on 3 Feb., p. 43), as did Coillard in March. Therefore the messenger would have also experienced a river like this. From Coillard's writings we can calculate a downstream passage of 100 miles a day (see below for details). Thus Lealui to Sesheke, 259 miles following main course of the river, would take approximately two and a half days.

46 Coillard, *Sur le Haut Zambèze*, Letter, 19 *av*. 1886, p. 185.

47 Coillard, *Journal intime*, 17 *av*. 1886; 6 *janv*. 1885.

48 Coillard, *Journal intime*, 3 *janv*. 1886; *idem, Sur le Haut Zambèze*, Letter, 1 *janv*. 1886, pp. 182–3; Waddell, *Diary*, 27 Dec. 1885.

49 Westbeech, *Trade and travel*, Oct.–Dec. 1885, pp. 33–40: *the Mulanziane* had requested protection from Westbeech should he need it and in late November had already evacuated some of his cattle to the Victoria Falls area. Coillard, *Journal intime*, 23 *janv*. 1886.

50 Coillard, *Journal intime, vendredi soir*, 12 *mars* 1886.

51 Waddell, *Diary*, 7 March 1886 confirms the departure which must have been determined by counting, not by observation. The astronomical time of new moon was 10.04 pm GMT on 5 March (about 12.34 local time). Thus dusk of 6th, when the new moon was eighteen hours old, was the first time that it might conceivably have been seen; in fact dusk of 7th with the moon forty-two hours old was a much more likely possibility. (But cf. the next month: astronomical time of the new moon: 4 April at 2.31 pm GMT. Coillard wrote on 6 April: 'It is the new moon! I don't know when the people saw it but it has been seen'; likely at dusk on 5th (age twenty-five hours).) However, in March the rains were still continuing – we know of a thunderstorm on 11 March – and such rains late in the season tend to be in the evening, so cloudiness might have prevented observation then. *Whitaker's almanack* (London, 1886), p. 19.

52 Coillard, *Sur le Haut Zambèze*, pp. 185, 187.

53 *Ibid*., p. 185.

54 Coillard, *Journal intime, vendredi soir*, 12 *mars* 1886. They had covered 96 miles from Sesheke in 5½ days paddling – an average of 17.46 miles a day of

probably 10 hours paddling, thus 1¾ mph over the ground. But this was fast compared with the much less well equipped Jesuit expedition which in August 1881 had taken six and a half days to complete the same distance. Depelchin and Croonenberghs, *Trois ans dans l'Afrique australe*, pp. 325–43.

55 Coillard, *Journal intime*, 12 *mars* 1886.

56 The paddlers were obviously going at it with a will. Westbeech, who had been piloted through by Matome himself in February, took two days to reach Sioma. Westbeech, *Trade and travel*, Jan.–Feb. 1886, p. 43.

57 Coillard, *Sur le Haut Zambèze*, pp. 187–8.

58 *Ibid.*, p. 188.

59 Coillard, *Journal intime*, 20 *mars*, 22 *mars* 1886. Coillard has jumped a date; in fact Sunday was 21st. His next entries are one day out. He follows the corrected chronology in his report (Coillard *à* Boegner, 19 *av*. 1886, *Lettres à la direction*). I use the corrected chronology here.

60 On the logic that 18th was the previous date in Westbeech, *Trade and travel*, and that Coillard arrived in Lealui on 22nd.

61 Westbeech, *Trade and travel*, March–April 1886, p. 50.

62 Lewanika subsequently made him *Amba*, in charge of much of the royal household. 'Mokano' is Mukanwa in modern Lozi.

63 Named as Felisberto Guedes Sousa by Westbeech, *Trade and travel*, p. 49. The 19 *av*. report states arrival at Lealui at 5 pm. Therefore I assume sometime, not long, after 4 pm but before 5 pm.

64 Coillard, *Journal intime*, given as 'Lealuyi Mercr. 24 mars 1886', pp. 262–5, actually Tuesday 23rd referring to Monday 22nd.

65 Waddell, *Diary*, 18 Apri (*sic*) 1886, spelling and punctuation preserved.

66 Coillard, *Sur le Haut Zambèze*, Letter, 19 *av*. 1886, p. 191. The rather free English translation in F. Coillard, *On the threshold of central Africa: a record of twenty years pioneering among the Barotsi of the Upper Zambezi* (London, 1897; repr. 1971), by Coillard's niece, Kate Mackintosh, further emphasises this view of making light of the affair. However, she appended an editorial footnote citing Mary Kingsley: 'White cloth is anathema to the missions, for it is used for Ju-Ju offerings, and a rule has to be made against it being given to the unconverted, or the missionary becomes an accessory before the fact to pagan practices', p. 218n.

67 Favre, *La vie d'un missionaire francais*, abridged edn, p. 187. M. Mainga, *Bulozi under the Luyana kings* (London, 1973), mentions the event, citing Coillard, *On the threshold of central Africa*, in a footnote and without further comment (p. 144, n. 48). G. L. Caplan, who apparently read the *Journal intime*, does not mention it in *The elites of Barotseland, 1878–1969* (London, 1970).

68 Coillard's hand is spiky and difficult to read. Masheke? Mashitu? It is hard to tell. The two 'Masheka' villages gazetted are near Kaoma, far into the eastern bush. Reluctantly, we must relinquish this scrap of information as being too mutilated to use.

69 Coillard, *Journal intime, vendredi* 12 *mars* 1886: 'I had the joy of sending a

letter to my beloved. She will receive it tomorrow.' Thus ninety-six miles, about fifty-five hours paddling upstream gives a speed around 1¾ mph; ten to twelve hours downstream: 8 to 9½ mph minus 1¾ mph gives a difference of between 6 and 8 mph.

70 I assert this from the experience of my own canoe trips.

71 Mokano made five shuttle trips. If we speculate that Coillard lay off the shore about half a mile, he could do each round trip in ten minutes at 6 mph each way; then we add ten minutes or so for the brief exchange of greetings with Lewanika and we have about an hour.

72 A. Jalla, *Tableau synchronique*, retyped and revised by J.-P. Burger (privately held), p. 7; *idem, Litaba za Sichaba sa Malozi* (Oxford, 1909; 5th edn 1969), p. 70. Clearly it is rather important to locate Ñundu as precisely as possible. I have never visited Nakaywe/Ñundu; it is an infuriating example of the familiar problem of field research that one does not realise until afterwards that one should have done something which, at the time, would have been quite simple to do. Therefore here I give the *Gazetteer* reference for Nakaywe, marked with a circle of probability for Ñundu. I have three reasons for being prepared to trust this reference. The first is simply that it looks right. It places the two villages in that part of the floodplain where most of the other most important of the early grave-sites are also to be found. Secondly, the *Gazetteer's* source was the 1954 1:250,000 District map which was plotted by compass traverse made during routine tours on foot by colonial officers in the 1950s. My knowledge of the nature of the Provincial Administration after the Second World War and my own extensive experience of using District maps in the field suggest to me that they were meticulously made and are not usually far wrong in the positions which they give. Thirdly, when the coordinates given in the *Gazetteer* and District map are translated into compass bearings upon the two villages from Lealui and other fixed topographical features, two adjacent villages fitting the description of Ñundu and Nakaywe given in their praise-saying can be clearly seen on Print 87 of the 1970 1:30,000 Air Survey, *Contract 70/5*, Mongu District, GRZ.

However, to seek further confirmation, early in 1979 enquiries were made on my behalf in Bulozi, in particular to try and obtain the opinion of an expert in Lozi traditional religion. Unfortunately, logistic and postal failures vitiated this. The only finally sure solution – for me to return to Bulozi and travel to the villages – was not possible; however, for the reasons given above, I feel enough confidence to use the *Gazetteer* coordinates. Northern Rhodesia Government, *Gazetteer of geographical names in the Barotseland Protectorate* (Lusaka, 1959).

73 From my experience, I know that they have a range of about twelve miles with the wind carrying them. The photograph of Lewanika's drums in Coillard *Photograph album*, HMC/LM, show them to be basically the same as those which I have heard, so we may reasonably take Coillard's word on this.

74 'All the morning' (*toute la matinée*) in Coillard, *Sur le Haut Zambèze*, p. 190.

75 On the map I have indicated that assuming the best downwind conditions, at

4 mph on course B, it is unlikely that the drums could have been heard from Ñundu much before 11 am, from Lealui slightly earlier.

76 In which case Coillard might have heard the drums first at about 9.30 am on course B at 4 mph, at about 10 am on course A at 3 mph.

77 Again, this would be normal; it would be unusual for the drums to be audible but consistently faint throughout the morning and therefore perhaps worthy of comment, particularly if there were other reasons for suspicion, like an odd course. The journal entry does not display those qualities.

78 Westbeech, *Trade and travel*, p. 48.

79 Remember that the river was in spate. Lewanika of course knew this, and how it would affect passage times so that Coillard might need every day of the waxing moon. This would be a good further reason to support the idea that the departure from Sesheke was regulated by counting in order to make use of the actual day of the new moon's appearance.

80 Full moon was technically just at dawn at 6.00 am on 20th (4.37 am GMT), *Whitaker's almanack 1886*, p. 19.

81 M. Gelfand (ed.), *Gubulawayo and beyond* (London, 1968), p. 407 doubts the giving of this money; Depelchin and Croonenberghs, *Trois ans dans l'Afrique australe*, pp. 311–76; Berghegge to Weld, 1 Nov. 1883, Gelfand, pp. 415–21; *Whitaker's almanack 1881*, pp. 37–9; *ibid. 1883*, pp. 29–45; Booms to Weld, 10 Aug. 1884, Gelfand, pp. 421–6 details Westbeech's hostility. 1883 visit: full moon 22 April; depart Sesheke 23rd; death at Lusu 29th; Kaale rapids 3 May; Sioma falls 5th; new moon 6th Lealui 16th.

82 Coillard, *Journal intime, mardi 23 mars* (entered as *mercr. 24 mars*) 1886; Westbeech, *Trade and travel*, 23 March 1886, p. 50.

83 Coillard, *Journal intime*, 28 *mars* 1886.

84 Westbeech, *Trade and travel*, p. 51.

85 All the detail from the relevant entries of Coillard, *Journal intime*.

86 Westbeech, *Trade and travel*, June 1886, p. 56.

87 Coillard, *Journal intime*, '24 *mars*' 1886.

88 Coillard, *Journal intime*, 5 *août* 1886

89 C. Coillard, *Journal*, 23 Aug. 1886.

90 An important methodological point must be borne in mind in assessing the data upon which this section is based. All missionaries had an image of how the people perceived them; some thought that they were perceived as magicians. We are compelled to rely largely on missionary data for our assessment. Therefore, the only way to penetrate the missionaries' own ideas is rigorously to distinguish *opinions* from *observations* of concrete events or specific conversations and only to use the latter. This I have attempted to do.

91 E. Holub, *Seven years in South Africa*, vol. II (London, 1881), pp. 282, 329.

92 Coillard to K. Mackintosh, (?) 13 Aug. 1878, cited by Mackintosh, *Coillard of the Zambezi*, p. 272.

93 Baker, *The life and explorations of F. S. Arnot*, pp. 100–1.

94 Coillard, *Journal intime*, 20 *sept*. 1884; Baldwin, *Journal*, 9 Aug. 1896, vol. XII, pp. 261–2. Distinguish the nature of chiefship described here very clearly from that perceived in the history of the London Missionary Society else-

where in Northern Rhodesia by R. I. Rotberg, 'Missionaries as chiefs and entrepreneurs: Northern Rhodesia, 1887–1924', in J. Butler (ed.), *Boston University Papers in African History*, vol. I (Boston, 1964), pp. 197–215, esp. pp. 201–5.

95 F. S. Arnot, *Garenganze or seven years pioneer missionary work in central Africa* (London 1889; repr. 1969), April 1883, p. 76; April 1884, p. 94 respectively.

96 Coillard, *Sur le Haut Zambèze*, 19 déc. 1888, p. 302; Waddell, *Diary* 18 Dec. 1888.

97 Waddell, *Diary*, 26 Nov. 1883.

98 *Ibid.*, 20 Aug. 1883; Sept. 1883 respectively.

99 Arnot, *Garenganze*, April 1883, p. 75.

100 Baldwin to his mother, 22 Oct. 1893, *Letters*, Box 1, Central Africa, MMS.

101 Coillard, *Sur le Haut Zambèze*, Sesheke, 15 déc. 1884, p. 145.

102 Waddell, *Diary*, Dec. 1885, Sesheke.

103 Westbeech, *Trade and travel*, April 1886, p. 51.

104 Cf. J. Goody (ed.), *Literacy in traditional societies* (Cambridge, 1968), pp. 2–5; E. Gellner, *Saints of the atlas* (London, 1969).

105 Coillard, *Journal intime*, 1 fév. 1887.

106 Coillard, *Sur le Haut Zambèze*, 24 déc. 1889, p. 335.

107 Waddell, *Diary*, Dec. 1884.

108 Coillard à Boegner, 19 av. 1886, *Lettres à la direction*.

109 Waddell, *Diary*, 5 Jan. 1890.

110 *Ibid.*, 20 Dec. 1885.

111 *Ibid.*, 26 Feb. 1886.

112 Jeanmairet à Boegner, 27 sept. 1884, *Lettres à la direction*.

113 Westbeech, *Trade and travel*, 14 Oct. 1886, p. 88.

114 Waddell, *Diary*, 5 Dec. 1886; 25 July 1887.

115 *Whitaker's almanack, 1886*, p. 67; Waddell, *Diary*, 17 Oct. 1886, report on the journey; Coillard, *Journal intime*, 30 août 1886.

116 Waddell, *Diary*, Sefula, 6 Nov. 1886, spellings preserved. The incident was not forgotten, see below, February 1887.

117 Related by the late Muhau Zaza of Mulé village, Sefula, an old member of the Sefula congregation, Jan. 1974. The event described is clearly the first service held at Lwatile, 30 October 1892: during the service, 'the first rain of the year began to fall. It fell so hard that I had to cut short', Coillard *Journal intime*. The incident was not published in English or French. It had a precedent: at Sioma in December 1884, the people needed rain, Coillard prayed and a storm broke (*Journal intime*, 27 déc. 1884). When Coillard reached Lealui on 8 Jan. 1885, Mataa, the rebel leader, greeted him thus: 'You bring us rain and sleep, peace and abundance', Coillard à La Direction, 5 mars. 1885, *Lettres à la direction*. *Mungole* means literally 'the long rain'. Coillard's nickname derived from this proverb: *Mungole wa cikotomeko ba ngendi banyali mbo lyaula ku coto* (The long rain does not cease, travellers suffer, villagers eat near the fireplace) i.e. when Coillard preached or taught, he was like a rain that did not stop!

118 Baldwin to his mother, 6 June 1891, *Letters; idem, Journal*, 22 April 1891, vol. ɪᴠ, p. 51.
119 Baldwin, *Journal*, 25 April 1891, vol. ɪᴠ, p. 52. Ward's action was being interpreted as drawing a *sifunda* (setting a line which would give misfortune).
120 Baldwin to his mother, 6 June 1891, *Letters*, p. 5.
121 *Ibid.*, pp. 7–10. Goy's version of events, which corroborates the main details of Baldwin's letters and journal, is found at second-hand in Mme Goy's book, *Dans les solitudes de l'Afrique* (Geneva, 1901), Ch. 1, pp. 9–17.
122 Baldwin, *Journal*, 22 Feb. 1892, vol. ɪᴠ, p. 191; see above, Chapter 6, Section 3.
123 *Ibid.*, 26 May 1896, vol. xɪɪ, p. 192.
124 Waddell, *Diary*, 27 July 1884. Could be equally well translated the Great Magician or Wizard.
125 *Ibid.*, 23 Aug. 1885. This could have been Westbeech.
126 Coillard, *Journal intime*, 20 *sept.* 1884.
127 Waddell, *Diary*, Dec. 1884.
128 Coillard, *Journal intime*, 24 *déc.* 1884; 4 *janv.* 1885.
129 Waddell, *Diary*, 18 April 1886.
130 Coillard, *Journal intime*, 6 *nov.* 1885.
131 Waddell, *Diary*, 21 Feb. 1886.
132 Coillard, *Sur le Haut Zambèze*, Sesheke, 8 *août* 1886, pp. 208–9.
133 Waddell, *Diary*, Jan. 1891.
134 *Ibid.*, 7 June 1890.
135 *Ibid.*, 5 Jan. 1890. Cf. J. Johnston, *Reality versus romance in south central Africa* (London, 1893; repr. 1969), p. 170; Waddell, *Diary*, 20 March 1887.
136 Waddell, *Diary*, 16 Oct. 1886; Westbeech, *Trade and travel*, p. 47.
137 Arnot, *Garenganze*, p. 72.
138 Waddell, *Diary*, 21 Feb. 1886.
139 Cf. Gluckman, *ELLRP*, pp. 75–6, 94.
140 C. Coillard to J. Mackintosh, 15 July 1885, cited by Mackintosh, *Coillard of the Zambezi*, p. 323; an identical incident described by Waddell, *Diary*, 21 Feb. 1886.
141 Waddell, *Diary*, July 1889.
142 Johnston, *Reality versus romance*, p. 200.

9 The consequences of contact

1 *Manchester Guardian*, 24 June 1902, reprinted in a leaflet of press cuttings about Lewanika for the occasion of his visit to Bethany House School, Goudhurst, Kent on 8 July 1902.
2 F. Coillard, *Journal intime*, DEFAP, Paris, 11, 12 *oct.* 1886; W. Waddell, *Diary*, WA/1/1/1–5, HMC (NAZim), 17 Oct. 1886.
3 Coillard, *Journal intime*, 8 *nov.* 1886; confirmed Waddell, *Diary*, 14 Nov. 1886.
4 Waddell, *Diary*, 14 Nov. 1886.
5 Coillard to C. Coillard at Lusuma, date illegible, fol. 638, Coillard Mss, HMC, NAZim; Waddell, *Diary*, 14 Nov. 1886.

6 Coillard, *Journal intime*, 23 *déc.* 1886.

7 *Ibid.*, 1 *fév.* 1887.

8 Waddell, *Diary*, 6 Feb. 1887. G. L. Caplan, *The elites of Barotseland, 1878–1969* (London, 1970), pp. 42–3, gives further quotations upon which his analysis of this incident substantially rests. However, they simply do not exist in this source to which he attributes them (n. 21).

9 Coillard *à* Boegner (*Privée*), Sefula, 24 *av.* 1888, *Lettres à la direction*, DEFAP, Paris.

10 Coillard, *Journal intime*, 10 *av.* 1889.

11 A. Goy *au* Pasteur Ch. Schroeder, Mabolela, OFS (en route to collect fiancée) 12 *août* 1889, *Lettres à la direction*.

12 Coillard, *Journal intime*, 22 *sept.* 1889.

13 *Ibid., sept.* 1889. 'Seajika' is rendered as Sacika in modern Silozi; however, I follow Coillard's usage in the text here.

14 *Ibid.*, 23 *nov.* 1889.

15 Coillard *à* Boegner, 24 *déc.* 1889, *Lettres à la direction* (F. Coillard, *Sur le Haut Zambèze: voyages et travaux de Mission* (Paris, 1898), p. 334).

16 A. Baldwin, *Journal*, MMS, 6 Sept. 1892, vol. v, p. 140.

17 Waddell, *Diary*, 5 Dec. 1886.

18 *Nalikwanda*: Chapter 6, Section 2 above; Coillard, *Journal intime*, 17 *fév.* 1889.

19 Waddell, *Diary*, 4 Dec. 1892.

20 *Ibid.*, 8 Jan. 1893; 30 July 1893 (quotation).

21 *Ibid.*, May 1892.

22 Coillard, *Journal intime*, 22 *mai* 1890; Baldwin, *Journal*, 10 Jan. 1893, vol. VI, p. 21; Coillard, *Journal intime*, 3 *fév.* 1893.

23 Waddell, *Diary*, 25 Sept. 1887.

24 *Ibid.*, May 1891.

25 Baldwin to his mother, 31 May 1892, *Letters*, Box 1, Central Africa, MMS; Coillard, *Journal intime*, *mai* 1892.

26 Waddell, *Diary*, 27 Nov. 1892; Coillard, *Journal intime*, 24 *nov.* 1892 (ends 26th).

27 Coillard, *Journal intime*, 26 *juin* 1890.

28 *Ibid.*, 24 *av.* 1887.

29 Waddell, *Diary*, 21 Feb. 1886 reporting Coillard; Coillard to K. Mackintosh, 6 Aug. 1900, Coillard Mss, HMC (NAZim).

30 Coillard, *Journal intime*, 6 *janv.* 1890.

31 Coillard, *Journal intime*, 6 *mai* 1893; Coillard to K. Mackintosh, n.d. fol. 1864, Coillard Mss, HMC (NAZim).

32 Coillard to English friends, 1892, fol. 1175, Coillard Mss, HMC (NAZim).

33 Coillard, *Journal intime*, 9 *nov.* 1884; *idem, Sur le Haut Zambèze*, Sefula, 16 *juin* 1891, p. 376; 2 Timothy, Ch. 4, v. 14, New English Bible, p. 992; Coillard, *Journal intime*, 24 *août* 1893; Baldwin, *Journal*, 5 March 1893, vol. VI, pp. 110–11.

34 Coillard, 27 *oct.* 1884.

35 C. Coillard to J. Mackintosh, 15 July 1885, cited by C. W. Mackintosh, *Coillard of the Zambezi* (London, 1907), p. 323.

36 C. Coillard, *Journal*, DEFAP, Paris, 23 Aug. 1886; 7 Nov. 1886.

37 Coillard, *Journal intime*, 10 *juill*. 1889; C. Coillard, *Journal*, 14 July 1889.

38 Baldwin, *Journal*, 5 March 1893, vol. vi, p. 112.

39 *Ibid.*, 7 Aug. 1892, vol. v, p. 115.

40 Coillard, *Journal intime*, 25 *nov*, 1885.

41 Illustrated in later years by his rebuttal of the accusation of being pro-Boer: 'I am a negrophile . . . How can it be forgotten that the two republics, the Transvaal specially, crushed the natives to establish themselves . . .?' Coillard to K. Mackintosh, 6 Aug. 1900, Coillard Mss, HMC (NAZim).

42 Jeanmairet *à* Boegner, Kazungula, 25 *août* 1885, *Lettres à la direction*.

43 Jeanmairet *à* Boegner, Leshoma, 16 *déc*. 1885, *Lettres à la direction*.

44 C. Coillard, *Journal*, 16 Oct. 1886; 7 Nov. 1886.

45 *Ibid.*, 23 Nov. 1886. Brackets indicate my guesses at parts of words chewed away by white ants.

46 H. Dardier *à sa famille*, Kazungula, 23 *août* 1887; Dardier *à* Boegner, Sefula, 27 *oct*. 1887, *Lettres à la direction*.

47 Coillard to 'brother Hunter', Nov. 1887, Sefula, DEFAP. The sawmill requested in this letter did eventually arrive in 1891. Scottish funds eased the financial straits of the Mission in 1894. F. Coillard, '*Rapport de la Station de Lealuyi*', 1894, DEFAP, Paris.

48 Coillard *à* Boegner (*Privée*), 22 *mars* 1888, *Lettres à la direction*.

49 *Ibid.*

50 Goy *à* Boegner, 10 *fév*. 1888, *Lettres à la direction*.

51 Coillard, *Journal intime*, 7 *juin* 1887; 8 *déc*. 1887.

52 Coillard, *Sur le Haut Zambèze*, p. 260.

53 Coillard *à* Boegner (*Privée*), 22 *mars* 1888, *Lettres à la direction*.

54 G. Westbeech, *Trade and travel in early Barotseland*, ed. E. C. Tabler (London, 1963), Jan.–Feb. 1888, pp. 93–6.

55 Coillard, *Journal intime*, 7 *av*. 1888.

56 Coillard *à* Boegner (*Privée*), Sefula, 24 *av*. 1888, *Lettres à la direction*.

57 Goy *à* Boegner, 10 fév. 1888, *Lettres à la direction*.

58 Goy *à* Coillard, Sesheke, 17 *janv*. 1889 (a letter stating numbered objections to his treatment at Sefula), *Lettres à la direction*.

59 Coillard, *Journal intime*, 16 *mai* 1888: (quotation); Coillard *à* Boegner, (*Privée*), Sefula, 24 *av*. 1888, *Lettres à la direction*.

60 Coillard to Rev. J. Smith of Yarmouth, Sefula, 20 Aug. 1888, DEFAP, Paris.

61 Coillard *à* Boegner (*Privée*), Sefula, 26 *août* 1888, *Lettres à la direction*.

62 Goy *à* Boegner, Sesheke, 13 *août* 1888, *Lettres à la direction*. This passage scored out in the original.

63 Coillard *à* L. Jalla *et* D. Jeanmairet, Sefula, 24 *août* 1888, *Lettres à la direction*, his emphases. Their letter to him is lost; I reconstruct it from Coillard's reply and from their subsequent repetitions of these complaints.

64 Coillard *à* L. Jalla *et* D. Jeanmairet, Sefula, 2 *nov*. 1888, *Lettres à la direction*.

65 *Ibid.*, postscript 3 *déc*. 1888.

66 Goy *à* Boegner, 11 *fév*. 1889, Sesheke, *Lettres à la direction*.
67 D. Jeanmairet *et* L. Jalla *au* Comité de la Mission, 31 *déc*. 1888, *Lettres à la direction*.
68 Coillard *au* Comité de la Mission, 23 *av*. 1889, *Lettres à la direction*.
69 Coillard *à* Boegner (*Privée*), Sefula, 20 *juin* 1889, *Lettres à la direction*; Coillard, *Journal intime*, 9 *juin* 1889.
70 Coillard, *Journal intime*, 25 *juillet*, 8 *août* 1889.
71 *Ibid*., 18 *août*; Coillard, Jeanmairet *et* Jalla *au* Comité, 26 *août* 1889, *Lettres à la direction*.
72 Goy *à* Coillard, 10 *oct*. 1889, Mabolela, *Lettres à la direction*.
73 On Buckenham and Baldwin's personal differences, Baldwin to his mother, 15 Jan. 1892, *Letters*, Box 1, Central Africa, MMS; 'They don't know a word of the language. . .they complain bitterly about the natives and the natives complain no less bitterly about them and detest them cordially.' Coillard *à* Boegner, 16 *juin* 1891, *Lettres à la direction*.
74 Coillard, *Journal intime*, 23 *nov*. 1889.
75 Coillard *à* Boegner (*Privée*), Sefula, 8 *av*. 1890, *Lettres à la direction*.
76 Coillard *à* Boegner (*Privée*), 2 *juin* 1890, *Lettres à la direction*; Coillard, *Journal intime*, 2 *juin* 1890.
77 Coillard *à* Boegner, 13 *juill*. 1890 and 27 *nov*. 1890, *Lettres à la direction*.
78 FO to CO, 13 Sept. 1888, No. 54 of CO 879/29/358, p. 62; CO to FO, 24 Sept. 1888, No. 58 of *ibid*., p. 65 (PRO).
79 Coillard, *Sur le Haut Zambèze, sept*. 1888, p. 291; *idem, Journal intime*, 20 *sept*. 1888.
80 Coillard, *Sur le Haut Zambèze, sept*. 1888, pp. 292–4; Caplan, *The elites of Barotseland*, p. 45.
81 Editor's introduction to Westbeech, *Trade and travel*, p. 9.
82 Coillard, *Journal des Missions*, 65 (1890), 24, DEFAP, Paris.
83 Coillard to Harris, 5 June 1891, cited by J. Johnston, *Reality versus romance in south central Africa* (London, 1893; repr. 1969), pp. 146–8, and M. Mainga, *Bulozi under the Luyana kings* (London, 1973), p. 179 with marginal difference of wording; copy in Mackintosh transcripts of BSA Co. files (originals destroyed in the Second World War), Mss 52, RCS.
84 Enclosure 2 in No. 17, FO/403/6968, Précis of Barotseland Correspondence, p. 30. (PRO). Not 18 January as Caplan states (*The elites of Barotseland*, p. 46).
85 Coillard, *Journal intime*, 9 *juin* 1889.
86 Westbeech, *Trade and travel*, 27 June 1885, when Ware was brought in, injured, by his client, p. 29.
87 Coillard *à* Boegner (*Privée*), Sefula, 20 *juin* 1889, *Lettres à la direction*.
88 Coillard, *Journal intime*, 28 *juin* 1889; Waddell, *Diary*, July 1889.
89 C. Rhodes to A. Beit, 11 Nov. 1889, fols. 171–4, Mss. Afr. t. 14 (Rhodes House, Oxford).
90 Khama to Coillard and Lewanika, 17 July 1889, fols. 14–17, Mackintosh Mss. HMC (NAZim). There are two problems. One is that the letter is jointly addressed so we cannot be sure whether it went straight to Lewanika, or

whether Coillard saw it en route at Sesheke, or whether he brought it with him. If it did go directly, Sesheke– Lealui on foot was twelve days (Waddell, *Diary*, 17 Oct. 1886), so adding the Kalahari, perhaps a transit time of a month?

91 Shippard to Coillard, 1 Sept. 1889, fols. 13–15, Coillard Mss, HMC (NAZim). Lord Knutsford replied for the metropolitan government on 14 September telling Lewanika that 'Her Majesty's Government regarded him with friendly feelings, and would use what influence they had to prevent the Matabele from raiding his country' FO/403/6968 (PRO). However, this letter was unlikely to have reached Bulozi before Christmas. The logic is that we know that instructions were written in London on 25 August 1891 to Loch in the Cape to write to Coillard. The dispatch sent in accordance with these instructions reached Bulozi with the first scheduled Company mail delivery on 7 November – a *minimum* of two and a half months, England to Sefula, which was likely to have been longer in 1889–90 before the postal service began.

92 Coillard, *Journal intime*, 23 *nov.* 1889.

93 Coillard, *Journal intime*, 24, 27 *déc.* 1884, 9, 26 *janv.* 1885, 4 *juin* 1885 (Middleton goes to Pandamatenga with Westbeech); Waddell, *Diary*, July 1886; Coillard à Boegner, 29 *juillet* 1886, *Lettres à la direction* (omitted from published version in Coillard, *Sur le Haut Zambèze*, p. 205).

94 Waddell, *Diary*, 5 Dec. 1886.

95 Coillard, *Journal intime*, 7 *juin* 1887.

96 *Ibid.*, 18 *août* 1889.

97 Not as agent of 'a business firm in Mafeking' (Caplan, *The elites of Barotse-land*, p. 49, n. 44 citing Baldwin's journal). This mistake also appears in R. Hall, *Zambia* (London, 1965), p. 67 who in turn takes it from *Northern Rhodesia Journal* I, 3 (1951), 43.

98 Waddell, *Diary*, 26 Dec. 1889, Sefula; F. C. Selous, *Travel and adventure in South East Africa* (London, 1893), pp. 252–4.

99 Coillard, *Journal intime*, 26 *déc.* 1889.

100 *Ibid.*, 6 *janv.* 1890.

101 Coillard à Boegner (*Privée*), Sefula, 8 *av.* 1890, *Lettres à la direction*.

102 Coillard, *Journal intime*, 15 *mars* 1890. The chronology of Middleton's movements is of considerable importance for the interpretation of his role. Caplan, *The elites of Barotseland*, pp. 49–50, gives the impression that he arrived at Sesheke 'at the beginning of 1890' and remained there until June 1890, so that information about Ware and Lochner came to the capital by messenger alone. The source used is Waddell, *Diary*, 7 June 1890 and the passage is ambiguous. In full it reads 'messenger after messenger has been sent *from the same quarter* to upset the mind of Lewanika and his ministers'. Caplan interprets 'from the same quarter' as 'was hurrying from Sesheke to Lealui'. Whilst this was true for a limited period of March to June, we have seen that Middleton was himself in the capital from late December to late February at least. This being so, it indicates vividly the extent to which Lewanika depended upon and preferred Coillard's advice. Furthermore,

Waddell usually referred to Middleton after his 'fall' with a circumlocution and so the phrase may equally well be interpreted to refer to Middleton, the man, as well as Sesheke, the place. To avoid further confusion, here is the chronology of Middleton's movements as best I can reconstruct it:

June 1887	Expresses desire to leave Sefula.
Dec. 1887	Departs with Dardier, the sick doctor.
Jan. 1888	Nurses Westbeech, goes south with his and the Mission's wagons.
Dec. 1889	Returns to Lealui as Musson's agent.
March 1890	Is recorded passing south through Sesheke.
May 1890	Present in Sesheke.
July 1890	Coillard meets him returning to Lealui.
Aug. 1890	Sick in Lealui, trading.
Oct. 1890	Writes letter (for Lewanika to the Foreign Office) protesting the Lochner Concession of June.
Jan. 1891	Goes south with a load of ivory. Sick at Sesheke.
March 1891	Returns to Lealui.
May/June 1891	Attempts and eventually succeeds in confronting Coillard before Lewanika.
Aug. 1891	Recalled to Mangwato by Musson.
Nov. 1891	Returns to Lealui.
Feb. 1892	Still there, departs soon after (?).
Aug./Sept. 1892	Makes a brief return visit to Lealui and then disappears.

103 Coillard, *Journal intime*, 25 janv. 1890. The intercepted letter must have been in response to that sent to Coillard which reached Lealui in November 1889. Coillard first heard of the Company within weeks of the Commons' vote, from Shippard.

104 Cf. Caplan, *The elites of Barotseland*, p. 51.

105 'This relief of Imperial expenditure has been among the principal reasons for granting the Charter', Baron H. de Worms, 18 March 1890, *Hansard*, Col. 1142 (PRO).

106 Cl. 8 gave FO power of intervention; that is all. *Blue Book* C5918, pp. 227–32 (vol. pagination 635–40) (PRO).

107 24 Aug. 1889, *Hansard*, Cols. 375–6; 26 Aug. 1889, *Hansard*, Cols. 485–7.

108 P. Stanhope, 26 July 1897, *Hansard*, Col. 1097.

109 Charter Cl. 19, 'The Company may hoist and use on its buildings and elsewhere in the territories aforesaid, and on its vessels, such distinctive flag indicating the British character of the Company as our Secretary of State. . .shall. . .approve.' *Blue Book.*

110 *J. S. Galbraith, Crown and charter* (California, 1974), Ch. 10, esp. p. 339; *idem*, 'Engine without a governor: the early years of the British South Africa Company', *Rhodesian History* I (1970), 9–16, pp. 10–11.

111 Hall, *Zambia*, p. 83; C. P. Youé, 'The British South Africa Company and Barotseland, 1890–1907', Dalhousie University Seminar Paper (1977).

112 C. H. Wealtherley to F. Rutherfoord Harris, n. d. (1889), cable confirmation, Letter 27, Mackintosh transcripts; Shippard to Coillard, 1 Sept. 1889,

Coillard Mss, HMC (NAZim); F. Rutherfoord Harris (Kimberley Sec. of BSA Co.) to Lochner, 5 July 1890, Fol. I, p. 8, Mackintosh transcripts.

113 Rhodes to Beit, 11 Nov. 1889, fols. 172–4, Mss Afr. t. 14 (Rhodes House).
114 Coillard to Rhodes, 8 April 1890, Letter 56, Mackintosh transcripts.
115 Rutherfoord Harris to Lochner, 5 July 1890, Mackintosh transcripts.
116 Westbeech, *Trade and travel*, pp. 59, 62, 65, 72; Coillard, *Journal intime*, 26 *mars* 1890.
117 Coillard, *Journal intime*, 26 *mars* 1890.
118 *Ibid.*, 9 *av.* 1890; 19 *av.* 1890.
119 Coillard *à* Boegner (*Privée*), 1 *juin* 1890, *Lettres à la direction*.
120 Jalla *à* Boegner, 5 *mai* 1890, *Lettres à la direction*.
121 Coillard, *Journal intime*, 1–2 *mai* 1890.
122 Coillard *à* Boegner, 30 *oct.* 1890, *Lettres à la direction*. Passage cut in published version, following immediately at the end of Coillard, *Sur le Haut Zambèze*, p. 362.
123 Coillard, *Journal intime*, 8 *mai* 1890.
124 *Ibid.*, 12 *mai* 1890.
125 *Ibid.*, 2 *juin* 1890.
126 *Ibid.*, 2 *juin*, 6 *juin* (party is that day); Waddell, *Diary*, 7 June 1890.
127 Lochner to Rutherfoord Harris, 10 June 1890, Letter 73, Mackintosh transcripts.
128 Not 22nd (Caplan, *The elites of Barotseland*, p. 53). That was Sunday. Missionaries did not transact lay business on Sundays.
129 A. Jalla, *Journal quotidien* (privately held), 24 *juin* 1890; Lochner to Rhodes, Letter 85, Mackintosh transcripts; Makuatsa died at Nalolo in October 1891 whilst bringing Lewanika's eldest son Litia home after a visit to stay with Khama in Mangwato. Waddell, *Diary*, 11 Oct. 1891.
130 Jalla, *Journal quotidien*, 24 *juin* 1890.
131 Coillard, *Journal intime*, 27 *juin* 1890; Jalla, *Journal quotidien*, 25 *juin* 1890.
132 Coillard, *Journal intime*, 27 *juin* 1890; Lochner to Rutherfoord Harris, n.d., Letter 69, Mackintosh transcripts.
133 Coillard, *Journal intime*, 27 *juin* 1890, confirmed Jalla, *Journal quotidien*, 26 *juin* 1890.
134 In fact there were differences between the London and Lealui copies of the Concession; Mainga, *Bulozi under the Luyana kings*, p. 181 explains them. In the medium and long term, and from the Lozi point of view, they were immaterial.
135 Enc. 9, Fol. I, Mackintosh transcripts; Coillard, *Journal intime*, 27 *juin*. 1890. Coillard stated that the tusks were for the Dukes of Fife and Abercorn, but Lewanika's subsequent reactions indicate that he thought they were for Victoria; Jalla, *Journal quotidien* 27 *juin* 1890. Waddell, *Diary*, 29 June 1890, said that they were for the queen via the Duke of Fife.
136 Jalla, *Journal quotidien*, 5–8 *juill.* 1890; Coillard, *Journal intime*, 10 *juill.* 1890.
137 Jalla *à* Boegner, 5 *juillet* 1890, *Lettres à la direction*; Lochner to BSA Co, 30 July 1890, Letter 86, Mackintosh transcripts.

138 Coillard, *Journal intime*, 14 *juill.* 1890.

139 *Ibid.*, 8 *août* 1890.

140 Jalla *à* Boegner, 5 *juill.* 1890, *Lettres à la direction*.

141 Jalla *à* Boegner, 2 *juin* 1890, *Lettres à la direction*; Baldwin to his mother, at 'Tabakies', 20 Aug. 1890, *Letters*.

142 They appeared at Pandamatenga in January 1891, Coillard, *Journal intime*, 29 *janv.*

143 *Ibid.*, 21 *juill.* 1890.

144 Jalla, *Journal quotidien*, 5 *août* 1890; 17 *août* (*à* Lealui).

145 Coillard, *Journal intime*, 5 *oct.* 1890.

146 Jalla, *Journal quotidien*, visit to Lealui, 23–4 *oct.* 1890; Coillard, *Journal intime*, 26 *oct.* 1890.

147 G. W. Middleton to the Marquis of Salisbury, Lealui, 27 Oct. 1890. No. 158 in FO Con. Print 403/6178, pp. 146–8 (PRO).

148 Coillard, *Journal intime*, 26 *oct.* 1890; Jalla, *Journal quotidien*, 31 *oct.*, 1 *nov.* 1890.

149 Jalla, *Journal quotidien*, 3, 5 *nov.* 1890; re letter, FO Con. Print 403/6968, p. 31 (PRO).

150 Coillard, *Journal intime*, 16 *nov.* 1890; 9 *déc.* 1890.

151 Jalla, *Journal quotidien*, 2, 5, 31 *janv.* 1891; Baldwin to his mother, 14 January 1891, *Letters*.

152 Coillard, *Journal intime*, 29 *janv.* 1891.

153 FO Con. Print 403/6968, p. 31 (PRO). Letter of 10 April 1891.

154 Coillard, *Journal intime*, 22 *mai* 1891.

155 *Ibid.*, *jeudi* 4 *juin* 1891, Sefula.

156 Coillard to High Commissioner, (?) 30 May 1891, Letter 121, Mackintosh transcripts.

157 Waddell, *Diary*, 17 June 1890, reporting Coillard. Punctuation preserved.

158 Coillard to BSA Co, Letter 122, Mackintosh transcripts.

159 Coillard *à* Boegner, 16 *juin* 1891, *Lettres à la direction*. Bracketed clause omitted in published version, Coillard, *Sur le Haut Zambèze*, p. 376.

160 Coillard *à* Boegner, 16 *juin* 1891, *Lettres à la direction*.

161 Coillard *à* Boegner, 27 *juill.* 1891, *Lettres à la direction*. Passage omitted from Coillard, *Sur le Haut Zambèze*, pp. 379–80.

162 Coillard, *Journal intime*, 22–4 *août* 1891.

163 FO Con. Print, 403/6968, p. 31 (PRO).

164 *Ibid.*

165 Coillard, *Journal intime*, 18, 23, 28 *oct.* 1891.

166 *Ibid.*, 8 *nov.* 1891.

167 *Ibid.*, 9, 16, 18 *nov.* 1891.

168 Coillard *à* Boegner, 11 *nov.* 1891 (Sefula), *Lettres à la direction*.

169 Coillard, *Journal intime*, 23 *nov.* 1891.

170 Johnston, *Reality versus romance*, pp. 145–6.

171 Coillard, *Journal intime* 17 *déc.* 1891. In fact as a result of being polluted by Middleton, Vollet was sent back to France. Coillard *au* Comité, 12 *av.* 1892, *Lettres à la direction*.

172 Coillard, *Journal intime*, 20 déc. 1891.

173 Comparing Johnston, *Reality versus romance*, with the lower levels of documentation, it appears that it is not correct to interpret his polemical colouring to mean that 'Middleton still held the King's ear' (Caplan, *The elites of Barotseland*, p. 58).

174 Waddell, *Diary*, 24 April 1892.

175 Coillard, *Journal intime*, 9 août 1892; Baldwin, *Journal*, 16 Aug. 1892, vol. v, p. 125; Frost at Kazungula: Coillard, *Journal intime*, 15 mars 1892.

176 F. Coillard, 'Rapport sur la Station de Sefula, 1891', DEFAP, Paris.

177 Coillard, *Journal intime*, 26 juin, 1888, 30 juill. 1888.

178 *Ibid.*, 12 janv. 1890.

179 *Ibid.*, 25 mai 1890; *idem, Sur le Haut Zambèze*, pp. 348–9.

180 Coillard, *Journal intime*, 2 juill. 1890.

181 *Ibid.*, 1 av. 1891.

182 The incident is recorded widely. This is Waddell, *Diary*, 31 Oct. 1890.

183 Coillard, *Journal intime*, 1, 5, 6, 9, déc. 1891.

184 *Ibid.*, 14, 19, 21, 22, 25, 27 janv. 1892.

185 *Ibid.*, 23 déc. 1892, 17 janv. 1893, 3 fév. 1893.

186 *Ibid., janv.* 1893; (quotation), Baldwin, *Journal*, 9 March 1893, vol. vi, p. 130.

187 Baldwin, *Journal*, 10 March 1893, vol. vi, pp. 133–6; cf. T. O. Ranger, 'The "Ethiopian" episode in Barotse history, 1900–1905', *Rhodes-Livingstone Journal*, xxxvii (1965), 26–41.

188 Coillard to Baldwin, Lealui, 29 Oct. 1895, *Letters* (MMS).

189 *Ibid.*; Baldwin, *Journal*, 10 March 1893, vol. vi, pp. 133–6.

190 Coillard to Baldwin, Feb. 1894, *Letters* (MMS); also Coillard *Journal intime*, 24 sept. 1894.

191 Coillard to Baldwin, 22 Jan. 1895, *Letters* (MMS); cf. Caplan, *The elites of Barotseland*, p. 62

192 Coillard to Baldwin, 8 April 1895, *Letters* (MMS); *Jalla, Journal quotidien*, 27 mai 1895.

193 Jalla, *Journal quotidien*, 21 juill. 1895 (the day that she declared her faith in public); Coillard to Baldwin, 8 Aug. 1895, *Letters* (MMS); Coillard, *Sur le Haut Zambèze*, p. 507; A. Jalla, *Pionniers parmi les Marotse* (Florence, 1903), pp. 121, 143, 146.

194 Jalla, *Pionniers*, p. 153.

195 A. Jalla, *Litaba za Sichaba sa Malozi* (Oxford, 1909; 5th edn 1969), p. 23.

196 Coillard, *Journal intime*, 8 juin 1891.

197 Letter, Rev. J-P. Burger to the author, 28 oct. 1977 citing information received from an ex-*Ngambela*, 14 June 1974: *'isibi mwendi a ka swana a loya Mulena, kuli ba kutise bulena bwa bona'*.

198 Muyambana's evidence, verbatim transcript of case record, 'Rex v. Mboo, alias Fwabi, Ikasia and others', 16 March 1911, p. 6 in Dispatch 309, SAHCNWR, 18222, CO 417/497 (PRO).

199 'Review of evidence', F. Worthington, appended to case record, both in Administrator Wallace's report, 21 April 1911, *ibid.*

200 But cf. Caplan, *The elites of Barotseland*, pp. 103–4.

201 Formalised in Article X, 'Draft agreement for the Administration of British territories North of the Zambesi', Enc. 1 in No. 146, FO 403/6482, p. 193 (PRO).

202 H. H. Johnston to Rosebery, 19 Aug. 1893, No. 225 in FO 403/6482, p. 252 (PRO).

203 Rutherfoord Harris to J. W. Colenbrander, 9 Feb. 1892, CO/4/1/1 (NAZim), cited by D. N. Beach, 'Ndebele raiders and Shona power', *Journal of African History* xv, 4 (1974), 633–51, p. 633, n. 2.

204 W. Ellerton Fry, 'State of affairs in Barotseland – Smallpox and incipient revolt', extract from the *Cape Times*, reproduced as Enclosure 8 in No. 26*, FO 403/6482, p. 24B (PRO); telegram, Assistant Resident Commissioner Palapye to Loch, 20 Dec. 1892, Enc. 6, *ibid*. These raids are meticulously documented in Mainga, *Bulozi under the Luyana kings*, pp. 156–7.

205 Coillard to Loch, 7 Feb. 1893, Enc. 2 in No. 91, FO 403/6537, pp. 96–7 (PRO).

206 Primitive Methodist Connexion to Foreign Office, 30 Dec. 1893, Enc. in No. 16, FO 403/6537, p. 9 (PRO); Aborigines Protection Society (acting upon James Johnston's allegations), to Colonial Office, forwarded to Foreign Office, 25 Jan. 1894, Enc. in No. 89 in FO 403/6537, p. 93 (PRO).

207 Coillard, *Journal intime*, 31 *juill*., 4 *août* 1893; Lewanika to Rev. J. Moffat, 24 Nov. 1893, Enc. 5 in No. 91, FO 403/6537, p. 98 (PRO) (a different reading from that in Caplan, *The elites of Barotseland*, p. 60, n. 106); Lewanika to Loch, 27 Nov. 1892, Enc. 6 in No. 91, FO 403/6537, p. 98 (PRO); Mainga, *Bulozi under the Luyana kings*, p. 157.

208 Coillard, *Journal intime*, 20 *sept*. 1893.

209 Loch to Lewanika, 18 Jan. 1894, Enc. 7 in No. 91, FO 403/6537, p. 99 (PRO).

210 FO to BSA Co, 14 April 1894, No. 117 FO 403/6537, p. 125 (PRO).

211 CO to FO, 13 May 1895, No. 183, FO 403/6688, pp. 236–7 (PRO). The *modus vivendi* was extended to 1898 and eventually to 1905.

212 Admitted in FO to Mr Cawston (Private), 28 March 1893: 'All the treaties use the Queen's name without authorisation.' No. 55 in FO 403/6482, pp. 54–5 (PRO).

213 CO to FO, 8 July 1895, No. 4 in FO 403/6784, p. 2 (PRO); FO to BSA Co, 1 Nov. 1895, No. 139, *ibid*., p. 136.

214 Jalla, *Journal quotidien*, 11 *mai*, 30 *sept*., 5, 7, 8 *oct*. 1896; Goold Adams to Lord Rosmead, 21 Oct. 1896, Enc. 2 in No. 38, FO 403/6968, p. 55 (PRO).

215 Lewanika to Dr Jameson, n.d., Enc. 1 to No. 128, FO 403/6784, p. 128 (PRO); (Jameson's reply, Enc. 2); Lewanika to Jameson, 3 July 1895, Enc. 3, p. 129; Coillard to Jameson, 4 July 1895, Enc. 4, p. 130 (Jameson's replies, Encs. 5 and 6), *ibid*.

216 Coillard to Loch, 4 July 1895, Enc. 2 at No. 176, *ibid*., p. 187.

217 CO to FO, 26 Nov. 1896, No. 107, FO 403/6911, pp. 118–19; FO to CO, 16 June 1897, No. 14 in CO 879/52/552, p. 17 (PRO).

218 In Angola, not to be confused with Kakenge in southeast Senanga.

219 Goold Adams to FO, 28 Nov. 1896, No. 65, FO 403/6968, pp. 82–3 (PRO). Documented at greater length in his formal report of 24 Aug. 1897, printed as No. 150 in CO 879/52/552, pp. 146–64 and supported in his letter to the Foreign Office of 10 Oct. 1897 (No. 163, *ibid.*, p. 177): 'I think Lewanika has an excellent case to support his claim to the entire area mentioned by him as "his country".'

220 CO to FO, 16 Jan. 1897, No. 17, FO 403/6968, p. 29 (PRO).

221 CO to FO, 2 April 1897, A and B. Nos. 95 and 96, *ibid.*, p. 101.

222 Youé, 'The British South Africa Company and Barotseland'; BSA Co. to FO, 9 March 1897, No. 73, FO 403/6968, p. 88 (PRO).

223 Milner to Lewanika, 18 May 1897, Enc. 2 in No. 5*, FO 403/7010, p. 16B (PRO).

10 Conclusion

1 A. Jalla, *Journal quotidien* (privately held), 15 *oct.* 1897, 19 *oct.* 1897 respectively.

2 *Ibid.*, 20, 21, 22, 23 oct. 1897; Coryndon to FO, 25 Nov. 1897, No. 12 in FO 403/7074, pp. 10–11 (PRO).

3 Coryndon to FO, 25 Nov. 1897, No. 12 in FO 403/7074, pp. 10–11 (PRO).

4 Jalla, *Journal quotidien*, vol. xvi (1944).

Appendix

1 It is based upon my article, 'Grist for the mill: on researching the history of Bulozi', *History in Africa* v (1978), 311–25.

2 Cf. D. C. Dorward, 'Ethnography and administration: a study of Anglo-Tiv "working misunderstanding"', *Journal of African History* xv, 3 (1974), 457–77.

List of principal primary source documents

Archival and privately held sources

Baldwin, A. *Journal*, Methodist Missionary Society, London
– *Letters*, Box 1, Central Africa, Methodist Missionary Society, London
Burger, J-P. 'Notes on the Sefula canal' (cyclo). Privately held
– *Notes privées*, circa 1930. Privately held
Cocklin, J. to Mullens, J. Matabele Mission, LMS Archives, Doc. 69 (1879). Library of the School of Oriental and African Studies, London
Coillard, C. *Journal*, two segments: 1877–9 and parts of 1886; parts of 1889. Bibliothèque du DEFAP, Paris
– *Letters to her family*, 1876-1891. Bibliothèque du DEFAP, Paris
Coillard, F. *Journal intime*, in numerous notebooks and exercise books, kept throughout the period with which this work is concerned. Bibliothèque du DEFAP, Paris
– Lecture to an unidentified audience, draft notes, 23 *fév*. 1898. Bibliothèque du DEFAP, Paris
– 'Quelques remarques sur le travail de M. le Professeur Allier', two drafts. Bibliothèque du DEFAP, Paris
– 'Notes pour conférence à la Faculté de Théologie', 16 *déc*. 1896. Bibliothèque du DEFAP, Paris
– Letter to Mssrs. Jamieson and Co., 10 Nov. 1886. Bibliothèque du DEFAP, Paris
– 'Rapport de la station de Lealuyi, 1894'. Bibliothèque du DEFAP, Paris
– 'Autobiographie' (Mss), reproduced in E. Favre, *La vie d'un missionaire français: François Coillard, 1834–1904*, 3 vols. (Paris, 1908–13), vol. I
– *Photograph album* HMC/LM
Coillard Mss., CO5/1/1 (transcripts and some original letters). HMC/NAZim
Coryndon, R. T. *Reports on the administration of Rhodesia for the information of shareholders* (1898). Rhodes House, Oxford
Eijkelhof, N. 'Living conditions in Lui Namabunga area, Zambia' (typescr.). Privately held
Goold Adams, H. 'Report on Barotseland' (1897), G40. HMC/LM
Hazell, D. C. 'Notes on native diet', G31/4. HMC/LM

Jalla, A., 'Rapport de station de Lealui, 1905', 9265, M/73/25. HMC/LM
– 'Memorandum concerning the Award of King Victor Emmanuel III, 1905'.
  Privately held
– *Notes privées* (covering 1890s). Privately held
– *Journal quotidien* (1890, 1892 onwards). Privately held
– *Tableau synchronique*, retyped and revised by J-P. Burger. Privately held
– *English–Lozi dictionary* (typescr.) 1936–9
– *Silozi dictionary*, 3rd edn, revised by Rev. E. Berger (typescr.), 1970
Lawrence, J. G., 'Miscellaneous notes', Mss. Afr. s. 1180. Rhodes House, Oxford
Lettres à la direction. Folders of letters received from the Mission in Bulozi,
  collected in annual sleeves, one for each individual, 1884 onwards. Bibliothè-
  que du DEFAP, Paris
Livingstone, D. *Vocabularies of eight East African languages*, XIII, L255, Acc. No.
  34105. Library of the School of Oriental and African Studies, London
Mackintosh Mss., MA/18. HMC/NAZim
Mackintosh transcripts. Transcripts by C. W. Mackintosh of BSA Co. files (origi-
  nals destroyed in Second World War), Mss. 52. Royal Commonwealth Society,
  London
Mongu District Notebook, vol. II, KDE 10/1/1², NAZ
Mwene Kandala. 'The beginning of Mwene Kandala's chiefship' (typescr.).
  Privately held
Ngonda, P. M. 'The system of cattle ownership and the cattle industry in Barotse-
  land' (typescr.). Privately held
Rhodes, C. to Beit, A., Mss. Afr. t. 14. Rhodes House, Oxford
Sesheke District Notebook (1903 onwards). Privately held
Soane-Cambell, J. 'I knew Lewanika' (typescr.), NAZ (subsequently published in
  Northern Rhodesia Journal I, 1 (1950), 18–23)
Suu, F. *et al.* 'The Barotse form of government' (typescr.). Privately held
Venning, J. H. 'Notes on native diets', Lealui (1908), G31/4. HMC/LM
Waddell, W. *Diary*, WA/1/1/1–5. HMC/NAZim
Wethey, I. M. 'Itufa-Liangati Silalo file', Senanga Boma
Worthington, F. 'Memorandum' (describing 1897) G19. HMC/LM
– 'Memorandum on slavery', 26 March 1913, BS3/166. NAZ
Worthington, F. *et al.* 'Notes and documents, 1900–1936', KDE, 2/44. NAZ

Published sources

Arnot, F. S. *Garenganze or seven years pioneer missionary work in central Africa.*
  London, 1889, repr. 1969
Baker, E. *The life and explorations of F. S. Arnot.* London, 1921
Bertrand, A. 'From the Machili to Lialui', *Geographical Journal* IX (Feb. 1897),
  145–9
– *The kingdom of the Barotsi of Upper Zambezia.* Trans. A. B. Miall. London,
  1899
Bryan, M. A. (ed.) *The Bantu languages of Africa.* Oxford, 1959
Chapman, J. *Travels in the interior of South Africa, 1849–1863.* Cape Town, 1971

List of principal primary sources

Christol, F. *L'art dans l'Afrique australe*. Paris, 1911
Clarence-Smith, W. G. 'The Lozi social formation, 1875–1906', University of Zambia seminar paper (1977)
– 'Climatic variations and natural disasters in Barotseland, 1847–1907', University of Zambia seminar paper (1977)
Coates-Palgrave, O. *The trees of Central Africa*, Salisbury, Rhodesia, 1956
Coillard, F. *On the threshold of central Africa: a record of twenty years pioneering among the Barotsi of the Upper Zambezi*, London, 1897, repr. 1971
– *Sur le Haut Zambèze: voyages et travaux de Mission*. Paris 1898
Depelchin, H. and Croonenberghs, C. *Trois ans dans l'Afrique australe*. Brussels, 1883
Faulkner, D. E. and Epstein, H. *The indigenous cattle of the British dependent territories in Africa*. London, 1957
Favre, E. *La vie d'un missionaire français: François Coillard, 1834–1904*. 3 vols., Paris 1908–13; abridged edition, Paris, 1922
Gelfand, M. (ed.) *Gubulawayo and beyond: Letters and journals of the early Jesuit missionaries to Zambesia (1879–1887)*. London, 1968
Gibbons, A. St H. 'A journey into the Marotse and Mashikolumbwe countries', *Geographical Journal* IX (Feb. 1897), 121–45
Gilges, V. *Some African poison plants and medicines of Northern Rhodesia*. Rhodes-Livingstone Occasional Paper 11. Manchester, 1955
Givón, T. *The Siluyana language*. University of Zambia, Communication 6 (mimeo). Lusaka, 1970
Gluckman, M. *The economy of the central Barotse plain*. Rhodes-Livingstone Institute Paper 7. Manchester, 1941
– *Essays on Lozi land and royal property*. Rhodes-Livingstone Institute Paper No. 10. Manchester, 1943
– *The administrative organisation of the Barotse native authorities with a plan for reforming them*. Rhodes-Livingstone Institute Communication 1. Livingstone (cyclo), 1943
– 'Zambezi river kingdom', *Libertas* (1945), 20–39
– *The judicial process among the Barotse of Northern Rhodesia*. Manchester, 1955, 2nd edn 1967, repr. 1973
– *The ideas of Barotse jurisprudence*. New Haven, 1965, repr. Manchester, 1972
Goy, M. *Dans les solitudes de l'Afrique*. Geneva, 1901
Harding, C. *In remotest Barotseland*. London, 1905
– *Far Bugles*. London, 1933
Holub, E. *A cultural survey of the Lozi-Mbunda Kingdom in South Central Africa*. Vienna, 1879, trans. by Dr L. Holy (typescr.)
– 'A journey through central South Africa from the diamond fields to the Upper Zambezi', *Proceedings of the Royal Geographical Society* III (1880), 166–82
– *Seven years in South Africa*. Vol. II, London, 1881
Ikachana, N. S. *Litaba za Makwangwa*. Lusaka, 1952
Jacottet, E. *Études sur les langues du Haut Zambèze*, Paris, vol. I (1896), vol. II (1899), vol. III (1901)

Jalla, A. 'Léwanika, roi des Ba-Rotsi: esquisse biographique', *Nouvelles du Zambèze*, Supplement 2 (June 1902)
- *Pionniers parmi les Marotse*. Florence, 1903
- *Litaba za Sichaba sa Malozi*. Oxford, 1909, 5th edn. 1969
- *Silozi dictionary*. 2nd edn, London, 1936
Johnston, J. *Reality versus romance in South Central Africa*. London, 1893, repr. 1969
Liénard, J-L. *Notre voyage au Zambèze*. Paris, 1900
Livingstone, D. *Missionary travels and researches in South Africa*. London, 1857
- *Private journals*. Ed. I. Schapera. London, 1960
Luck, R. *A visit to Lewanika, King of the Barotse (one of His Majesty's coronation guests)*. London, 1902
Lutke-Entrup, J. *Limitations and possibilities of increasing market production of peasant African cattle holders in Western Province, Zambia*. IAS Communication 7. Lusaka, 1971
Mackintosh, C. W. *Coillard of the Zambezi*. London, 1907
Mupatu, Y. W. *Mulambwa Santulu u amuhela bo Mwene*. London, 1958
- *Bulozi sapili*. Oxford, 1959
- *Y. W. Mupatu: an autobiography*. Ed. G. Prins, Zambia Past and Present Series 4. Lusaka, forthcoming
Northern Rhodesia Government, Ministry of Land and Natural Resources. *Gazetteer of geographical names in the Barotseland Protectorate*. Lusaka, 1959
Parsons Corporation. *Final report, the water resources of Barotse Province, Zambia*. Job No. 4229, New York and Los Angeles, August 1968
Peters, D. U. *Land usage in Barotseland*. Ed. N. Smyth, Rhodes-Livingstone Institute Communication 19. Livingstone, 1960
Ribeiro, M. F. *Homenagem aos Heroes que precederam*. Lisbon, 1885
Selous, F. C. *Travel and adventure in South East Africa*. London, 1893
Serpa Pinto, A. de *How I crossed Africa from the Atlantic to the Indian Ocean*. Trans. A. Elwes. 2 vols., London, 1881
Société des Missions Évangéliques de Paris. *Journal des Missions Évangéliques*. Paris 1921
- *Nouvelles du Zambéze* (published edited letters from the mission field)
Stevenson-Hamilton, J. *The Barotseland journal*. Ed. J. P. R. Wallis, Oppenheimer Series 7. London 1953
Stirke, D. W. *Barotseland: eight years among the Barotse*. London, 1922
Trapnell, G. G. and Clothier, J. N. *The soils, vegetation and agricultural systems of North Western Rhodesia*. Lusaka, 1937
Verboom, W. C. *An ecological survey of Western Province, Zambia*, vol. I, *The environment*. Land Resources Study No. 8, Directorate of Overseas Surveys. Tolworth, 1968
Westbeech, G. *Trade and Travel in early Barotseland*. Ed. E. C. Tabler. London, 1963
Whitaker's almanack. London, 1881, 1883, 1886
Williams, J. G. *A field guide to the birds of East and Central Africa*. London, 5th impr. 1972

Index

Index